THE BEST IN THE WORLD

THE BEST
IN THE WORLD

AT WHAT I HAVE NO IDEA

CHRIS JERICHO
WITH PETER THOMAS FORNATALE

GOTHAM BOOKS

GOTHAM BOOKS
Published by the Penguin Group
Penguin Group (USA) LLC
375 Hudson Street
New York, New York 10014

USA | Canada | UK | Ireland | Australia | New Zealand | India | South Africa | China
penguin.com
A Penguin Random House Company

Library of Congress Cataloging-in-Publication Data
has been applied for.

ISBN 978-1-592-40752-1

Printed in the United States of America
10   9   8   7   6   5   4   3   2

Set in Adobe Garamond Pro
Designed by Alissa Rose Theodor

For Jessica, Ash, Cheyenne, and Sierra. You make me a better man and my world a better place. Thank you for being here for me when I need you and waiting for me when I am gone. I love you with all of my heart and am honored to be one of the Irvine 5!

For my father, Ted Irvine. Thank you for your support, humor, and inspiration. I'm proud to be your son—love and respect forever!

For my auntie Joan Irvine, one of the most interesting and intelligent people I've ever met. Thank you for helping me discover my creativity and imagination. I love you!

CONTENTS

FOREWORD

Hi There!!!

My name is ZAKK WYLDE. I'm in a ROCK BAND called BLACK LABEL SOCIETY, where I play guitar, piano, and sing in a style that many say is a cross between HELEN REDDY and the "Velvet Fog" himself, MR. MEL TORME. I'm married to the girl I've had a crush on since sixth grade, who I lovingly refer to as my "Sexual Pinata." I've been blessed with four awesome kids and yes, LIKE YOU, I too am a JERICHOHOLIC!! And now that you've bought this book you will instantly be FONZARELLI cool in your school, workplace, or even when receiving an hour-and-a-half PROSTATE exam. Plus just by reading FATHER CHRIS'S AWESOME book, everything in your life will get better . . . even if your PROSTATE doctor's hands are the size of ANDRE THE GIANT'S!

There are many things I thank THE GOOD LORD for every day. My LED ZEPPELIN and BLACK SABBATH record collection, my ULTIMATE WARRIOR doll collection, AND for allowing me to become a JERICHOHOLIC! Having FATHER CHRIS in my life as a BROTHER has brought me nothing but joy, happiness, and several visits to the INTENSIVE CARE UNIT. This is because by just being a "Known Associate" of Y2J, whenever I drop off my eleven-year-old son at school, I am attacked and receive mammoth-size beatdowns from his little friends with their little fists of FURY.

But regardless of how many months or years I have to spend in the hospital and the fact that I now have broken more bones than EVEL KNIEVEL, I refuse to stop being a JERICHOHOLIC!

So, sit back and enjoy The TECHNICOLOR DREAMCOAT ADVENTURES of MY BROTHER: The ONE and ONLY LIFE-ENHANCING BESTOWER of ALL THINGS FONZARELLI . . . FATHER CHRIS JERICHO!!!

LOVE YOU, MY BROTHER O' DOOM!

—ZAKK WYLDE xoxo

BONUS FOREWORD

I always say that my Jerichoholics are the Best Fans in the World, and I mean it. It's for that reason that I decided to put my money where my mouth is, and I posted a message on my Facebook and Twitter pages to announce that I was inviting all of YOU to write the foreword for this book. A few weeks later, after reading through literally hundreds of submissions, I chose my favorite. But I enjoyed looking at all of them, and I thank you if you took the time to write something for me. So if you submitted a piece and see me on the street, come and tell me so I can shake your hand!!

I mentioned in my original post that I wouldn't announce the winner until this book was published. So . . . here's your winner!

—CJ

Who is the real Chris Jericho?

WWE Superstar? Rock Star? *New York Times* bestselling author? Inventor? Dancer? TV host? Podcaster?

The answer is ALL OF THE ABOVE, but there's so much more. If there is one thing that Chris has proven throughout his life, it's that you can be anything you want to be.

I've read Chris's other books, and he really is a great storyteller who remembers every detail, every feeling, every emotion. The awkward moments and total disasters he's experienced will have you roaring with laughter, because he manages to turn even the most bizarre situations into funny moments. This is one of Chris's most endearing qualities; his hunger for living every moment to the fullest, never having a dull minute and creating positivity wherever he goes. So when I heard that he was looking for someone to write his foreword, I knew that I had to sit down and write. It would truly be an honor to be a part of his legacy.

Fellow Jerichoholics will stand proud with me when I say that Chris is a truly inspirational person. He has a certain charisma that so few carry, and the hairs on the back of my neck literally stand up when I hear the first few seconds of "Break the Walls Down" and know he's about to enter the WWE arena.

His amazing work with Fozzy has shown me his passion for music and entertainment. Influenced by Iron Maiden, the Beatles, and the Rolling Stones, Fozzy's music is pure heart-pumping adrenaline, and Chris always pours his heart into his thought-provoking lyrics. (My personal favorite is "Broken Soul.")

His show business résumé continues to grow, and I have gleamed with delight at his awe-inspiring performances on *Dancing with the Stars,* belly laughed at his hilarious Web series "But I'm Chris Jericho," and listened in awe to his riveting "Talk Is Jericho" podcast.

Now some might say that he's a crazy wildman, but for me he is genuinely one of the nicest guys I've met. He doesn't judge, he has time for anyone, and he has great hair and tattoos! I met him after a Fozzy concert in 2008 and e-mailed his manager to ask if he could help me grant a wish for a sick child in Manchester, whose dream was to meet John Cena. Before I knew it, Y2J arranged it with the WWE and the little boy's dream came true. Chris has a heart under that tough exterior; he is a kind, warm, and generous person, a good friend and family man.

Following the antics of *A Lion's Tale* and *Undisputed*, I can't wait to read the next wild ride that is the life of Chris Jericho. I'm sure it's going to be another unforgettable adventure! But I just have one question.

When does he sleep?

—Claire Curran, Jerichoholic
Manchester, UK

THE BEST IN THE WORLD

INTRODUCTION

Hiding in the Bowels of the Arena . . .

● ● ● I couldn't believe I'd gotten away with it.

I felt like I'd just pulled off the crime of the century as I hid in the back lounge of the tour bus in the parking garage of the US Airways Center in Phoenix.

I felt that way because there were 18,000 hard-core wrestling fans in the arena above me, watching the 2013 Royal Rumble, and not a single one of them knew I was there. It blew my mind that in this age of social media, when everybody and their blog had Twitter accounts and Facebook pages, my secret hadn't been exposed. I'd re-signed with World Wrestling Entertainment over a month earlier and had looked online every day since, expecting to see my cover blown and my surprise return to the Royal Rumble spoiled.

Thankfully, it hadn't been and I was ready to go out there and try to tear the damn house down like I always did. It was the first time I'd entered the WWE with no warning, no sign, no series of cryptic vignettes to signal my appearance, and I felt the crowd was going to blow a gasket when they saw me. I'd only been out of the company for a few months, but my passion for the WWE burned brighter than ever because over the last few years, I felt I was on a career high. I'd left the company in 2005 a bitter man and it had been a long and winding road that had led to my return in 2007, but in the five-plus years since, I felt I'd done the best work of my career and wanted to keep the Y2J ball rolling. I'd learned so much as a character and as a wrestler in the past half decade that I'd become a completely different performer. My work had gone to a different level and I'd helped create and deliver the two best angles of my career as a result.

As I took cover in the back of the production bus waiting for the cue to head to the ring, I closed my eyes and began reflecting back on the past five years. I thought back to November 2007, when I was standing in the Gorilla Position ready to hit the stage in Fort Lauderdale as my countdown clock ticked down from 10. . . .

CHAPTER 1

Wha' Happen?

9...8...7...

It had been twenty-seven months since I'd stood in the darkened area of the Gorilla position, and it was a kind of homecoming. Despite all the places I'd been and all the projects I'd done since I'd left the WWE, there was nothing quite like hearing the roar of the crowd when my countdown hit zero. And I fully expected tonight's roar to be one of the biggest of my career.

7...6...5...

With the Save Us vignettes, the wrestling world was abuzz with the anticipation of who would be revealing himself on *Raw* that night in Fort Lauderdale. After the incredible response I received for my surprise WWE debut back in 1999, I was ready for another monstrous reaction that would make this feel like the first time, and I ain't talking about Lou Gramm.

4...3...2...1...

Randy Orton paced in the ring intensely like an apex predator as the clock ticked away to the moment where I would make my entrance and once again accept my crown as the hottest star in the WWE.

0.

The moment had arrived. The iconic battle cry of "BREAK THE WAAAALLLLLS DOWWWWWWNNN!!" echoed throughout the arena as I walked out through the curtain and embraced my people, the precious and adoring public who were about to give me the response of a lifetime.

Except they didn't.

Something had happened in the split second it took for me to walk from behind the curtain onto the stage, as if a group of aliens had beamed my raucous crowd up to their flying saucer and replaced them with an arena full of dazed drones. When I started into my promo, they didn't react to my catchphrases like they once had, and the response to the insults I was throwing at Orton seemed forced and hesitant at best.

Now, it's not like the crowd didn't react at all, but it certainly wasn't what I'd expected and was a fraction of the explosion I'd received eight years earlier during my '99 WWE debut. Wha' happen?

The next day, after some serious reflection, I came up with the patented "Chris Jericho List of Excuses™" as to why the crowd had gone from hotter than hell to lukewarm like leche in the span of eight years.

1. My 1999 debut was in Chicago, which has the reputation of being the best crowd in the United States. The previous night's *Raw* had been in Fort Lauderdale, and even though that city has some great fans, they didn't have the same reputation as the rowdies in the Windy City. So it's obvious my reaction wouldn't be as loud . . . right?

2. I had been off WWE TV for twenty-seven months, and in that time John Cena had become the face of the company. He'd brought a legion of new fans into the fold, kids who probably hadn't heard of Y2J before . . . right??

3. For the fans who did remember Chris Jericho, I had appeared on WWE TV for the first time ever with SHORT HAIR. I'd

sported a few awkward hairstyles before I left the WWE in 2005 (Why didn't anybody tell me the "too long to be short, too short to be long" hairdo was a hair-don't?), but my weeds were still at least longish back then. Now my hair was cut over the ears and closely cropped to the back of my neck, with a peacocklike spike at the front. I'm not sure how I settled on that style, but it has inspired many imitators. I might even venture a guess that "The Jericho" has become more popular than "The Rachel" in several Eastern Bloc countries. But as suave and debonair as my new haircut was, it created a disconnect for some of my fans, who were used to me having a certain look. The Y2J character was associated with long flowing hair, and my new look was akin to seeing The Ultimate Warrior with a crew cut. Now, I could totally relate to this as I was totally turned off by Metallica when they all cut their hair (especially James Hetfield) in 1996, or when Bruce Dickinson returned to Iron Maiden with a businessman's coif in 2000. They were still the same great singers, making the same great music ("Mama Said" and "The Nomad" notwithstanding), but it took me a while to get used to it even though in the big picture it made no difference . . . right?

4. My Save Us vignettes had gone on for about four weeks too long. The anticipation had been huge up to a point, but after week six, there was a collective sense of "Let's just get this on and get it over with already!" In a way, the 2007 return of Y2J had been overhyped. A month before I came back, at a PPV in Chicago a mystery opponent was going to fill in for an injured Cena. There was a big "Y2J" chant from the crowd, and Vince told them on live TV that it wasn't going to happen. After that, the anticipation deflated as we had kept the fans waiting just a little too long, so when I walked out onstage in Lauderdale,

the vibe was almost like "OK, we knew it was gonna be him. So he's back. What else ya got?" Makes perfect sense . . . right?

Now, six years later in hindsight, I know the real reason why my return wasn't the grand slam I was expecting.

My act was stale.

The Y2J character who had gotten over in the Attitude Era was known for mispronouncing names, frat boy insults, and gimmick sight gags, which worked every time. But in the words of S. E. Hinton, that was then, this is now. When I walked onto the stage in Lauderdale dressed in tight black jeans, white wifebeater, and sparkly purple tuxedo vest (Vince hated that ensemble) spouting off jabs about Randy Orton having childbearing hips, a nose that looked like it had been flattened by a frying pan, and that he'd once appeared on the cover of *Blue Ball* monthly, it didn't come off cutting-edge; it came off behind the times. When I announced that my mission statement for returning to the WWE was to win Randy's world title, it sounded forced. I didn't even buy it and I was the one trying to sell it. In all fairness, it's not like my Second Coming bombed like The Situation on a Donald Trump roast, but it wasn't what I was expecting.

Even though the initial reappearance hadn't gone the way I wanted it to, I planned to make up the lost ground the next week on *Raw*. No matter what I was asked to do, I was going to make it GREAT. I wanted the Jerichoholics to walk away from my performance thinking, "Wow, I forgot how good this guy is." But when I found out I was scheduled for a match with Santino Marella, I realized that goal might not be so easily achieved.

Santino had gone from independent journeyman, to Russian shooter in the WWE minor leagues, to Italy's favorite son when he defeated Umaga for the Intercontinental Champion in his first match on *Raw* in Milan. But with his bland character, the fans felt he was being shoved down their throats and soon turned on him so badly that he was in danger of getting let go. Then Santino changed his whole persona and became a slightly confused buffoon with an exaggerated Mario Brothers Italian accent, who innocently butchered the English language as well as the names of the entire WWE roster. He was one of those rare (but necessary) performers who got a great reaction by making people laugh with his ridiculous character. But for me to have a memorable match with anyone in seven minutes, especially someone I'd never worked with before, was going to be a challenge. Not to mention Santino wasn't exactly known for in-ring prowess (Cena and I gave him the nickname Worst to First due to his cringeworthy ring performances that suddenly became comedically amazing with his gimmick change).

I thought the best thing we could do together would be a face-to-face promo, where I was just as confused about his name as he was about everybody else's. The idea was I'd mispronounce his handle multiple times and he would keep correcting me until I finally got it right, which would cause Santino to mispronounce his own name.

Vince liked the idea but nixed the end part where Santino would say his own name wrong, saying it "wasn't believable." Believable? Nothing about Santino's character, or this entire bit for that matter, was believable, but that's Vince.

I started the segment by saying, because I had just returned to the WWE, I wasn't familiar with all the new talent and wasn't sure what his name was. He answered with great pride, "My name is Santino!"

"Santito?"

"No, Santino!"

"Santana?"

"Santino!"

"Sandusky? Santico? Santoco? Santokyo? Santadista? Santamaria? San Luis Obispo? Tuxedo? Suxedo?" (I'm disappointed in myself for not getting a Sussudio reference in there.)

"It's Santino, Santino, Santino, SANTINO!!!" he said stomping his feet like a petulant pansy.

I calmly replied, "Well duh, everyone knows your name is Santino."

It was completely ridiculous and got over great specifically for that reason.

Then we had our match and it was . . . meh.

Now, those of you who have read my previous books (the madly entertaining *A Lion's Tale* and the brilliant sequel, *Undisputed*) might be thinking the match was JERICHO CURSE worthy. Well, just hold on to your britches, bitches. It wasn't a bad match, it was just kinda there. It started, some stuff happened, and then it ended when I gave him my new finisher, the Boomstick . . . umm I mean the Codebreaker (thanks to Lance Storm). The fans cheered, but they didn't roar. I was rusty and I knew I would get better with a little more ring time. At least I hoped so, especially since I had a shot at the World Championship in only a few short weeks.

My first PPV match after my return was against Orton for the world title. To build up the match I went back into my old bag of tricks and pulled out one of my favorites . . . the funny picture promo. That was where I would find dumb images of my opponent, Photoshop them into comical situations, and flash them on the Tron to accentuate my points. They were designed to get cheap laffs (I ain't talkin' about Martin Short) and they usually did. Brian Gewirtz, my old writing partner in crime, and I came up with the idea that Orton wasn't very smart (not true, although Randy once told me he "wasn't the sharpest bulb in the shed") and therefore I needed to relay my request for a title match in a way that even a Neanderthal could understand. I told him very slowly, "ME.

WANT. TITLE. MATCH," while a helpful picture popped up on the Tron illustrating each word: a picture of Jericho for *ME*, a picture of the Cookie Monster for *WANT*, a picture of the WWE Championship for *TITLE*, and a picture of a lit match for *MATCH*. Fairly obvious, but people laughed and I was slowly regaining some of my old magic. But I started wondering how far I could go as a babyface in this new Cena-dominated kid-friendly climate.

I had initially wanted to come back as a heel, but Stephanie McMahon was convinced that since I hadn't been around for a while, people would want to cheer for me. For a few weeks she was right, but the bloom was fading fast off the babyface rose and I knew I'd have to make a change quickly if I had any chance of staying relevant.

For now, I was still waving the good-guy flag and in Randy Orton I had a great heel to work with at Armageddon in Pittsburgh. He's an amazing worker and his timing, selling, aura, and believability are all off the charts, plus with the RKO, he has one of the best finishers in the biz. He helped me knock the rest of the ring rust off pretty quickly that day and we had a good match. Despite a dead Pittsburgh crowd, I was starting to feel comfortable in the ring again and hit all of my patented moves with crispness: crossbody to the floor, second rope dropkick to the apron, enziguri, and my brand-new Codebreaker. Toward the end, he threw me over the announce desk into commentator John Bradshaw Layfield, the former World Champion who had decided to make an in-ring comeback. A few minutes later, when I had Randy locked in the Walls of Jericho in the middle of the ring, JBL ran in and gave me his wicked Clothesline from Hell. Orton was disqualified and I got the win, but more important, this was the start of the Y2J vs. JBL program that was going to take us to WrestleMania.

But something funny happened on the way to the forum . . . or in this case the Mania stadium.

I'm not sure why our program didn't click. In John and me, you had two excellent talkers who knew how to build a match and had good chemistry in the ring, but for whatever reason, our feud never took off. Maybe it was because we both had just returned or the lack of a real issue between us, but the bottom line was we only had enough steam to last through one PPV, the Royal Rumble in Madison Square Garden. It was a largely forgettable match, with the only two highlights being me getting majorly busted open (ahhh, the days of blood) and missing JBL completely on a bulldog attempt. He bumped anyway, leading to a huge "You fucked up" chant from the crowd (still THE most embarrassing chant to endure as a performer). Afterward I asked Vince what he thought, and he said, "Well, you lost the crowd on that bulldog, didn't you? That was pretty rotten."

Ouch! After that, I stopped asking Vince what he thought of my matches for a while.

It was déjà vu all over again. When I first arrived in the WWE in 1999, I had a massive buildup and a legendary verbal duel with The Rock, but a scant few months later, I was feuding with Chyna and losing to Gangrel on *Sunday Night Heat*. This time I returned with another massive buildup, a top-of-the-mountain big-money contract, and a verbal duel with the World Champion, but a scant few months later I was getting "You fucked up!" chants in Madison Square Garden against a recently returned former commentator.

As a wise man once said, enough was enough and it was time for a change.

CHAPTER 2

Team Cock 'n' Ballz

When the WWE went to Iraq for the first Tribute to the Troops special in 2003, I had no interest in going. I had nothing against the soldiers or their efforts, but I didn't feel comfortable heading into a war zone. Plus, I never had to worry about turning the offer down because I was never asked to go.

But during my sabbatical from the WWE, my band Fozzy was invited to Fort Benning in Georgia for a signing, and the soldiers were so thankful and happy to see us that I reevaluated my feelings. When I saw how much these men and women were sacrificing for their country, I decided I really wanted to do whatever I could to support them. So when Vince personally asked me to be a part of the next Tribute to the Troops tour a few weeks after my return, I answered yes without hesitation.

After my second *RAW* back and my match with Santino, we went straight from the arena in Charleston, South Carolina, to a nearby army base where we boarded a giant military transport plane. There was a sense of adventure and nervousness as we filed on; after all, we were going to war. The army had outfitted the inside of the massive fuselage with rows of economy class seats crammed tightly together to accommodate as many of us as possible. Between the boys, office personnel, and production people, there weren't enough seats for everybody, so the remaining unlucky few sat on benches bolted onto the side of the plane. The back of the massive vehicle was packed with towering pallets of camera equipment, the ring, and our personal baggage, all held together with huge sheets of Saran Wrap. After we were all seated (I snagged a decent seat next to Cena), we received a briefing from our army liaison, who informed us that while we would be headed to Iraq, the exact destination was being kept a secret to cut down on the chances of us being bombed by insurgents.

Bombed by insurgents?? Yes, kids, this was the real deal.

Once we received our briefing, we embarked on our sixteen-hour secret journey and the tale of two flights. The first flight was a veritable rock 'n' roll party. Everybody was milling around the cabin vocalizin' and socializin', guitar screechin' and hair bleachin', telling jokes, laughing, listening to music, and having a few cocktails to get their sticks, tricks, and lipstick fix. Jeff Hardy was learning how to play acoustic guitar and was so impressed when I showed him the opening riff to "Crazy Train" that he proclaimed me the best guitar player on the plane. (He was probably right, although I hear Funaki plays a mean "Eruption.") As the flight progressed, everyone broke up into little groups; some slept, some watched movies, and others hung out on top of the pallets eight feet in the air. But no matter where you went, the plane was brutally cold and incredibly loud. We were all required to bring a sleeping bag for the tour, so I went to the back of the plane and wedged myself between a column of pallets and the side wall of the hull, trying to catch some sleep. I failed miserably since even though I was fully clothed and inside a down-filled sleeping bag, it was still freezing; not to mention, lying on the metal floor was completely uncomfortable with all of the rivets sticking into my various body parts.

So I went back to the cramped row of seats and tried to fall asleep there, but it was too confining (and Cena snores) which made me 0 for 2 in my battle with the sandman. So I climbed up on top of the pallets and found it to be the only comfortable place on the plane. Not exactly FAA approved, but a good place to crash for a few hours until it was time to gas up in Germany.

We landed at Ramstein (so that's where that band got their name) Air Base and everybody shuffled off the plane. While most of the crew headed to the officers' lounge to have some food and more drinks, Vince, Cena, MVP, and I went to the base hospital where the wounded U.S. soldiers were recovering. Any time you visit a hospital, it's always a touching and gratifying experience, but it can also be mentally grueling. You never know who you're going to meet and what condition they're going to be in, and considering we were going to an army hospital treating casualties from the Iraq war, I was expecting the worst.

The first soldier we visited half smiled as we came in the room. When I asked him with grave concern how he was doing, he answered nonchalantly that he was fine. I inquired why he was in the hospital, and he said, "Ah, I fell off a ladder outside of the barracks and sprained my ankle. Who are you again?"

We moved down the hallway to another room, this one occupied by a female solider. After another sensitive inquiry as to why she was in the infirmary, she replied, "Because I had to have my appendix removed."

"Ouch," I said. "Did that happen in combat? "

"Huh? No, my stomach was bugging me and the doctor told me I needed the operation."

We visited another half dozen wounded soldiers who had suffered from such war atrocities as pneumonia, strep throat, and an ingrown toenail. Turns out the Ramstein hospital was mostly used for household injuries suffered on the base, not during the call of duty.

We took off again and for a few hours the party continued. I was having a conversation on top of the pallets with Ron Simmons and Carlito, when suddenly all of the bright lights in the plane turned off and were replaced by dim red-colored bulbs as an announcement was made throughout the cabin.

"Everybody take your seats and put on your seat belts for the rest of the flight. We are now entering a war zone."

Welcome to the second flight.

My stomach rose into my gullet (fun word) and I realized while we weren't in Kansas anymore, Karbala was right next door. I felt like I was in a video game, except this was real and it was serious. Deadly serious.

I was in a WAR ZONE. People die in WAR ZONES. And there was no turning back now.

The cabin lights were turned off to make it harder for the enemy (or the insurgents, as the army called them) to target the plane. And the fact that I was part of said target made me feel sick to my stomach.

I sat in the confinement of my tiny seat prison, not able to move and too nervous to sleep, hoping for the best and waiting to land. We finally did and I was never so happy to get off a plane in my life.

But when I did, there was nothing there.

Well, nothing except for a desert that I could see for miles and miles in every direction. No buildings, no trees, no roads, no power lines, nothing. I surveyed the great divide of emptiness as I boarded an old school bus that shuttled us to our accommodations. These digs weren't barracks or tents like I was expecting, but a palace . . . Saddam Hussein's palace, to be exact.

After the fall of Saddam, the U.S. Army had transformed a number of his exquisite palaces into de facto hotels for their guests and troops to stay. This particular one was on the banks of a toxic lake (which didn't deter Jeff Hardy from jumping in for a dip) and featured a driving range where you hit the golf balls straight into the water. To do something so American from the balcony of Saddam's former home felt like poetic justice to me.

Team Cock 'n' Ballz: Me, Morrison, Punk, and MVP decked out in our battle gear. That rifle is one of the only guns I've ever shot in my life.

But there wasn't much time to enjoy the fruits of Saddam's evil labor, as a few hours after landing, we were divided into groups and escorted on to our individual assignments. My team included CM Punk, MVP, John Morrison, Eve, and Alicia Fox. We were issued heavy flak jackets and helmets (WAR ZONE), and taken to the mess hall for a quick lunch. I was expecting a big green tent, like in *M*A*S*H*, with a chef named Cookie wearing a greasy wifebeater and a ciggie hanging out of his mouth, doling out ladles of hash and gruel. Horse hockey, was I ever wrong.

This place was like a mall food court with more choices than Polo Park. (Winnipeg represent.) They had everything: stir fry, pasta station, roast chicken, burgers, pizza, salad bars, fresh cookies, you name it. It was like a Golden Corral for gold-star colonels. It made me think how much money we were spending on this war, as the cost of food for the troops alone must've been in the millions on a weekly basis.

After a fine lunch of roasted chicken and salad, it was off to the helicopters to fly to the outposts to greet the soldiers. What makes WWE tours to Iraq different from the average USO visit is that USO tours generally stayed within the bigger base areas, whereas our tours went everywhere. Vince's motto was that no outpost was too big or too small and if there were soldiers there, we would visit them.

My group flew across the desert to a tiny post in the middle of nowhere. We were greeted by a four-star general, who took us around the base so the troops could give us demonstrations of their various jobs and responsibilities. Then we had an autograph-signing meet-and-greet with whoever wanted to say hi. The best part was the legitimate joy and excitement that the troops had about us being there. Over and over again I was thanked for coming all the way to Iraq to see them, and over and over again I thanked them right back for being there and protecting our country. It was the least I could do to come to Iraq for four days, when these men and women were there, away from their families, for upwards of eighteen months.

I realized there was a lot of propaganda on the news in the States about the war. While I'm sure not everybody was thrilled to be there, the majority of the soldiers I met were there to do their job and weren't interested in leaving until that job was done. I didn't hear any complaints from any of them about why they were still in Iraq.

Another thing I felt was a true sense of pride that the soliders had for their jobs. Each one took the time to meticulously point out and explain every detail of what their duties were, whether it was cleaning a missile launcher, repairing a Jeep motor, or disarming an Iraqi land mine.

We were taken "outside the wire" (beyond the protected perimeters of the base) and were taught how to fire machine guns. We rode in tanks across the desert, and when I asked the driver what his favorite music to shoot missles to was, he answered Metallica and Fozzy. (Shameless pandering that I'll accept every time!) We stood on top of choppers and swung from a Tarzan rope that hung from the rafters of a massive airplane hangar. We had a blast, and Punk, Morrrison, MVP, and I even christened our group Team Cock 'n' Ballz, after a cartoon drawing someone had scribbled on the back of one of the bus seats, of a set of male genitalia with a face and little arms (his testicles were his feet).

Mr. Cock 'n' Ballz, our illustrious Iraqi mascot. Look how the testicle feet even have pubes.

We flew across the desert to another outpost and shot machine guns into the salt flats of Iraq as I sat in the open cabin of the chopper, with the wind blasting in my face and the captain relaying information into our headsets. I felt like I was in every Vietnam movie ever made and all it needed was "All Along the Watchtower" playing in the background. It was Full Metal Jericho and I was Private Y2Joker.

Except this was no joke.

We were flying over a Third World country that had been ravaged by war, rubble surrounding the small clusters of clay huts scattered about the countryside, each one of them curiously boasting a satellite dish. Apparently, after the fall of Saddam, the people of Iraq were allowed to have them for the first time. I could see random men and women staring up at us from the ground and wondered whose side they were on. Our gunner had his finger on his trigger at all times, watching out for anything unusual, and if anybody on the ground held up anything resembling a gun or a missile launcher, his orders were to shoot them on sight.

This was war. No rules, no judge, and no jury . . . only executioners.

At the next base, I met a huge Y2J fan who was so excited to meet me that he showed me around his barracks and invited me to be his roomie. We formed a makeshift improv comedy team called Coffee and Cream, since he is black and I am white (you are blind as a bat and I have sight), performing bits and spewing punch lines in front of the ever-present WWE cameras.

The next day, Team Cock 'n' Ballz split up and my new group was made up of Dean Malenko, Carlito, JBL, Ron Simmons, and Mickie James. We flew into a town called Taji and once again were greeted by a friendly commander with a firm handshake, who told us how happy he was to have us there. He took us over to our meet-and-greet, where the majority of the guys (there were hardly ever any women this far outside the wire) were most excited to meet and greet Mickie. She was the star of the show, signing autographs and taking pictures for every soldier whether they knew who she was or not.

After another lively visit, we split up into two choppers and were whisked off toward Tarmiyah, the farthest city outside the wire that anybody in the WWE (or any entertainer, for that matter) had been to. Tarmiyah was a war-torn former Al-Qaeda stronghold that the U.S. Army had overtaken. We were told that even though it was under control, it was still classified as an "unsecured WAR ZONE," which meant that they thought they had forced all of the terrorists out of the city but didn't know for sure. It looked like something out of *Platoon*: half-standing bombed-out buildings with smoke drifting over the rooftops and wafting through the open windows of the burned-out husks of cars that sat unoccupied in the deserted streets.

We hovered over a dusty parking lot as the surrounding trees bent back from the force of the wind created by the chopper blades. Then just as we started to descend, I heard a loud bang, and smoke began to plume up from the ground.

This is it, I thought, *we are being attacked!* My heart raced like Jeff Gordon as we landed quickly in the lot, with smoke and dust rising all around us. We were still in one piece as we weren't being attacked; rather, smoke bombs had been set off to camouflage our arrival and make it harder for any insurgents to target us as we landed. That was the second time in a day I'd been considered a target and I wasn't down with that clown at all.

We hopped out of the chopper and this time, there was no smiling official waiting to shake our hands and tell us how great we were. Instead, there was a fully armored soldier waving his arms, shouting, "Go! This way! This way!" Dean and I started jogging confusedly in the direction the soldier was pointing and as we headed toward a dingy orange-colored building, I took stock of my surroundings. The smoke was dissipating and the dust was settling, which made it easier to make out the random fires burning and the dead dogs lying all around. I wasn't sure what was going on, but I was scared, and felt my heart fluttering like a spastic butterfly in my chest. They hustled us down the dusty path flanked by barbed wire fencing, as soldiers hid in the trees with machine guns held up to their faces, scouring the area for danger. I got the impression that if someone . . . anyone . . . off our beaten path moved too fast, they would be shot. We were all in a dead run at this point and as I was rounding a corner, a bigger bang (and I ain't talking about Charlie Watts) went off beside me. I screamed, convinced my arm had been blown off and I'd have to carry it around with me for the rest of the tour like that guy in the opening scene in *Saving Private Ryan*. Thankfully, it was just another camouflaging smoke bomb, and even though we were all still in one piece, it had shaken us up pretty badly. Especially Ron Simmons, who growled, "All this for a meet-and-greet? I would have just mailed them a fuckin' autograph."

We finally made it to the command post, which was essentially a converted youth center, and were quickly ushered inside. We knew we were in uncharted waters when the first thing the commander said was, "What the hell are you guys doing here? Nobody comes out this far!"

It really hit home just how far into the danger zone we were, when even the soldiers thought we were crazy for being there.

We gathered in a communications center, which wasn't the high-tech army installation I was expecting, but a total shithole. The dilapidated walls were streaked with rusty water stains, and cobwebs festooned (awesome word) every corner. The tiny control room was equipped with the type of old-school radio equipment you would see Radar O'Reilly using (I know it's the second *M*A*S*H* reference of this book, but I loved that show when I was a kid, ya dig?) and might as well have been controlled by a crank. It was strange to me that while I could still text my wife, Jessica, in Florida with my smartphone, these guys seemed to be using equipment that came out when Pong was all the rage.

Once again, we were briefed on our situation, this time by the base leader who explained that Tarmiyah had been overrun by insurgents until our troops came in and secured it sector by sector over a six-month period with a total of seventy-five sectors. They had all the roads blocked in and out of the city, and the Al-Qaeda operatives were gone, or so they thought. They weren't completely sure that there still weren't a few renegades hiding within the ruins of the city, which is why they still classified it as an unsecured WAR ZONE.

The soldiers stayed for eighteen-day periods inside the control center, and since there was no running water or showers, they brushed their teeth with bottled water and stayed dirty. All they had to eat were MREs (meals ready to eat), which were nonperishable foods that came in thin silver tubes and were available in two flavors: tuna fish or chipped beef. I'd never tried an MRE before and decided to indulge, in spite of the warnings from soldiers who told me, "You're not gonna like it!"

They were right.

The tuna fish and the chipped beef tasted exactly the same, like cowshit-flavored cardboard. I gagged and forced down the swill with some lukewarm water, desperately trying to cleanse my pallet. I grabbed a piece of chocolate, which tasted like sweetened cowshit-flavored cardboard, and promptly spit it out as a handful of soldiers stood around giggling. The only things they had that tasted normal were Pringles and orange Gatorade, the cornerstone of any balanced breakfast.

The sleeping area was a large open room with army-issue cots side by side, wall-to-wall. Each one had a personal item stashed underneath to distinguish it from the rest: a book, a picture frame, a guitar (I should've strummed a few chords since I was the best guitar player in the WWE). There was a small, primitive gym set up on the side, like the kind I had in my high school (Westwood Collegiate represent, yo): sand-filled plastic plates, a bench where the resting arms were too close together to get a proper pressing grip, larger weights made of poured concrete, whatever they could piece together to use for some kind of workout.

In the middle of the compound was a small concourse where the guys hung out, shooting baskets, smoking, talking about home, smoking, playing cards, and smoking. They gathered around a small campfire, sitting on lopsided cushioned backseats they'd ripped out of the deserted cars throughout the city.

We signed autographs and took pictures, and while some of the guys didn't know who we were, all of them were very appreciative of our presence, excitedly telling us all about their home lives. When one corporal told us he was going home in a few days to get married, Simmons cracked me up again by saying, "Married? Damn, you're going from one war zone to another, aren't you?"

Luckily, my home life was the farthest thing from a WAR ZONE and since the moment I landed in Iraq, I'd constantly checked my pocket to make sure I had my phone. It was my security blanket, my lifeline back to the sanity of a peaceful world and my beautiful wife and family. And the fact I could still communicate with them via text made me feel a little better about my situation.

After ninety minutes of hanging out with the soldiers, we were getting ready to leave, when we were told that there was a problem. One of the choppers we had flown in on had landed on a steel girder that had punctured through its floor, and since combat helicopters travel in pairs for safety, we had to wait until another one could arrive before we could go. To make matters worse, a serious dust storm was brewing, which was delaying the second chopper's arrival. In other words, we were stranded in an "unsecured WAR ZONE" indefinitely, and for the first time since I got to Iraq, I wasn't completely sure that I was gonna leave.

Left to die with only friend, alone I clenched my phone. . . .

CHAPTER 3

Unsecured War Zone

With the uncertainty of when we were going to be able to leave the base setting in, we started getting restless. Some of us sat outside, trading war stories (literally) with the soldiers, some lifted weights, and others hung out in the control center trying to chart the second chopper's progress. Lilian Garcia (who sings the best "Star-Spangled Banner" I've ever heard) got scolded after ignoring the warnings not to feed the scrawny mongrels that were wandering around outside the command center. It was a big no-no because the dogs carried parasites and fleas, and many of them were dangerously rabid, so feeding them caused them to hang around expecting more, which made them a safety and health risk to the soldiers. The dogs were promptly shot and Lilian (she wasn't the only one) was devastated.

I didn't kill any dogs, but I did kill some time by working out in the makeshift gym, curling tomato tins that had been filled with cement and had a metal handle embedded in the middle. I watched a couple soldiers jumping skateboards over a row of plastic gas cans and they were pretty damn good. Then again, if I was stuck in that hovel for eighteen days, I woulda been Jason Ellis too.

I started wondering what exactly it was that the soldiers were doing there. I mean, were there times when they came under fire or was their presence just a preventive measure at that point? I asked a few of them that question and one of them beckoned me over, pulling out his phone.

"Check this out," he said.

He showed me an image of a weird soupy, sludgy mass, like someone had spilled a bowl of oatmeal and then drawn a face on it. It took me a few seconds to figure out that it really was a face belonging to a head that had been caved in by bullets.

Let me ask you this: Have you ever seen an actual dead person before? I hadn't. I mean I'd seen them in the movies and on TV, but looking at this photo of a distorted head was making me feel queasy.

The soldier explained that the disfigured head belonged to an insurgent sniper who'd stationed himself on a rooftop three hundred yards away from the compound. He'd picked off a number of the soldiers around the command center, some of them dying in the arms of their friends. Finally they decided to eliminate the problem and stormed the apartment block where the sniper was holed up.

They busted through the front door of the barricaded building and the terrorist dashed up the stairs to escape, with the soldiers giving chase directly behind him. The insurgent ran through a rooftop door at the top of the stairs and tackled the first soldier who followed behind him, pinning him to the ground and trying to stab him with a hunting knife. The soldier threw his arm up and luckily was able to block the knife from plunging into his chest. The two of them were locked in a battle to the death, rolling back and forth, trying to gain control of the knife. Finally the other troops wrestled the terrorist off and shot him in the head, killing him instantly.

I was introduced to the soldier who had narrowly survived the attack, and the kid couldn't have been more than nineteen years old. He described his brush with death and explained he was certain he was going to die, screaming for somebody to help him and expecting the knife to penetrate his chest any second. I looked into his oddly placed eyes (they were almost on the sides of his head) and realized he would be carrying the horror of that moment with him for the rest of his life. I'm sure he's still having nightmares about it to this day.

Afterward, I was taken to the medical center, which was really nothing more than a few tables pushed together with some field dressing kits stacked in the corners. I noticed a chart on the wall with *Wins, Losses, Ties* written in black marker at the top. Under each column were four lines with a fifth crossing through, like the markings a prisoner would write on his wall to count down the number of days until his release. The wins had three full sets of lines plus two, the losses had one full set plus one, and the ties had two full sets plus two. *Wins* stood for the soldiers on the base who had been shot over the last year and had lived. *Losses* stood for the soldiers who had been shot on base and had died. And *Ties* stood for guys who had been shot on base, survived, and died elsewhere after being restationed.

As I was counting the number of losses, a private approached me, saying he was a big fan and wanted to say hi. I noticed he had a small angel tattooed on his trigger finger and asked him why. He explained that when he was in high school, he and his best friend decided to join the army. They enlisted together in Seattle, trained together, shipped out together, and ended up in the same company in Iraq. Two weeks after they arrived, the same sniper that had almost stabbed Wide Eyes shot his best friend in the head and killed him. The private got the angel tattoo as a tribute to his friend, who he felt would always be looking out for him from heaven, keeping his trigger finger true.

After hearing rumors that the dust storm was going to force us to spend the night in Tarmiyah, we were informed that a chopper was coming for us in ten minutes and we HAD to be ready. The window of time for us to take off and beat the storm was slim, so we threw on our flak jackets and helmets in preparation. Ten minutes later, the smoke bombs went off and our chopper landed in a giant cloud of dust. We scrambled aboard as the chopper's blades sliced through the air, pelting us with rough sand.

With all of us onboard ready to take off to safety, a soldier came running across the open field, waving his arms in a *Stop, Stop, Stop* motion.

Don't stop! I thought to myself. *Lift off and let's get the fuck out of here before it's too late!*

The guy continued to make a beeline toward us, and the pilot motioned he was going to have to wait to see what he wanted. I was freaking out at this point, yelling above the whirring blades to anybody who could hear (which was nobody), "SCREW THIS GUY! We have to get out of here now!"

He ran up to the open side of the chopper and yelled as loud as he could, "WHOSE PHONE IS THIS??"

Phone? You mean we weren't taking off from this hellhole because some idiot forgot his cell phone? Which one of these morons forgot his phone? Simmons? JBL? Funaki?

It was mine.

I'd taken it out of my pocket while working out and this soldier found it in the nick of time. I thanked him sheepishly while nine sets of eyes bored holes in me as we lifted off the ground.

My bad.

Standing in front of a giant statue of Saddam Hussein in Iraq. The detail is immaculate, even down to the war medals hanging around his neck and the crease of his tie.

The next day, the show at Camp Liberty was a huge success, as the troops packed the parking lot area and the makeshift bleachers set up around the ring. All of them were in full uniform, holding up signs proclaiming where they were from, their wives' and kids' names, and the names of their favorite wrestlers. It was the ultimate feel-good show, with all the good guys winning, highlighted by the surprise return of John Cena, who had suffered a shoulder injury a month before and was still in a sling. He came to the ring disguised as Santa and attacked a cranky Vince McMahon for being such a Scrooge. Santa's voice was this horribly high-pitched, over-the-top campy whine, similar to the one Chris Farley used in the *SNL* skit when the waiters asked him if he would like some fresh ground pepper on his salad.

"Why, YES! I'd LOVE some fresh ground pepperrrrrr!" Farley replied, cracking up the cast and the audience.

Cena's delivery was much more ridiculous and whammo . . . Fresh Ground Pepper Santa was born. To this day, any reference to that spicy St. Nick still makes the two of us laugh.

At the end of the show, the entire crew came out to the ring (save a recently Attitude Adjusted Vince McScrooge), and did a massive curtain call. We threw presents to the crowd, shook hands, took pictures, and signed more autographs. I even found the other half of the world-renowned wacky duo "Coffee and Cream" and got him some well-deserved screen time by giving him a huge high five and a hug.

The experience was honestly one of the best and most gratifying of my entire career. Despite my initial reservations about going, I was ecstatic that I went. So much so that I went straight to Vince after the curtain call and requested to return the following year. He obliged and I was booked on the tour the next year and the year after that too.

So I'd like to say thank you to every member of the United States Armed Forces who is reading this book right now. If I had the pleasure of meeting you in Iraq during my tours there in 2007–09, I hope I made your life a little brighter the same way you did mine.

CHAPTER 4

Ask Him!

When I first started getting a push in World Championship Wrestling in early 1998, I figured out I needed a catchphrase if I wanted to stand out from the pack. Something that would instantly identify my fans the same way *Hulkamaniacs* defined Hulk Hogan's. I came up with *Jerichoholics* (if you want to get the rundown on exactly how it was created, read the modern-day classic *A Lion's Tale*, now available on Kindle) and since then, I've created many other catchphrases, some of them classic, some of them crappsic. So I thought it would be fun to go through them and explain their origins and if you don't agree, then skip to the next chapter, ya Sourpuss!

Hmmmm, maybe *Sourpuss* should be my next catchphrase?

AYATOLLAH OF ROCK 'N' ROLLAH: Many of my catchphrases were lifted from movies or TV shows, and this one is probably the most popular of those. I nicked this from The Humungus in the movie *The Road Warrior.* People still ask me to sign this below my autograph and I always say I don't know how to spell it (I kind of do, but I'm just too lazy to write the whole thing). This one is also noteworthy for pissing off The Iron Sheik, who said he was going to "break my fuckin' back and fuck me in the ass" because I'm not a real ayatollah. Guilty as charged . . . but the last time I checked, he's not a real sheik either.

SHUT THE HELL UP: This one was taken from the movie *Happy Gilmore*, when Adam Sandler's sweet grandma asks for a warm glass of milk, and Ben Stiller's evil character tells her she's gonna get "a warm glass of SHUT THE HELL UP" instead. One of my most effective catchphrases because it's the perfect way to interrupt somebody and always gets a great reaction from the crowd.

PARAGON OF VIRTUE: This one started when I turned heel in WCW and the band Savatage had just released the record *The Wake of Magellan*, which featured the song "Paragons of Innocence." I thought *paragon* was an interesting word, so I looked it up in the dictionary (remember those?), found out it meant "a model of excellence," and incorporated it into my act. I used the old reverse-psychology bit, claiming to be everyone's favorite wrestler, their role model, their paragon of virtue. This of course prompted everybody to boo me because I was the exact opposite.

MONDAY NIGHT JERICHO: WCW's main show was *Monday Nitro* and I claimed to be its biggest star, so I changed the title accordingly.

***RAW* IS JERICHO:** When I came over to WWE from WCW, I brought a few of my bits with me. I wanted Monday Night Jericho to be one of them, but in August of 1999, the WWE changed the name of its flagship show from *Monday Night Raw* to *RAW IS WAR*. JERICHO IS WAR didn't have the same ring to it and made no sense, so I tried *RAW IS JERICHO* instead and it worked—despite being grammatically awkward.

GO JERICHO GO: I only ever used this once, during my debut promo with the WWE. I said something along the lines of "all of you people are going to get off your chairs, put your fat little filthy hands together, and chant, Go, Jericho, Go." Even though that was over fourteen years ago, it still pops up from time to time on signs in the crowd and chants from die-hard Jerichoholics during matches and autograph signings. Guess I should've put it on a T-shirt.

COME ON, BABY!: In 1995 when I was working with *WAR* in Japan, the leader of my heel group, Team No Respect, was Hiromichi Fuyuki. During a match, he would bump a guy, put his foot on his chest, strike a crab pose, and scream. I always loved the audacity of his actions and started doing it when I turned heel in WCW. But instead of screaming, I decided I wanted to say something that matched the sheer cockiness I was displaying (as if you could ever pin somebody that way). It started as "Yeah, Baby!" then morphed into "Come On, Babayyyy," and I liked it so much I started saying it during my ring entrance.

ASK HIM!: During my time in New Japan, Jushin Liger would always say "Ask him!" in his matches at the oddest times, like when he had somebody in a headlock or some other move that he had no chance of winning with. When I started doing the Lion Tamer as my finish in WCW, I said it the same way as Liger because I liked the intensity. Fans started picking up on it, and it became an inadvertent catchphrase. I should've put that on a T-shirt too.

ARMBAR: When I did the famous 1004 Holds promo in WCW in 1998, the majority of the moves I listed were armbars of some sort. I just never know what you fine fans are going to pick up on and this is the perfect example, for it's still quoted to me all the time. As a matter of fact, I'll bet when I retire, I'll forever be known as the armbar guy. Some company did put this on a T-shirt, but I don't get any royalties from it and it doesn't count. So don't buy it.

SEXY BEAST: This was the name of a movie starring Ben Kingsley that came out in 2000. I thought Ben Kingsley was the most unsexy beast on the planet and that I could do so much better with the name, so I stole it. Christian claims he came up with both this one and Vitamin C but he's wrong, I did. And while I was never allowed to put Vitamin C on a T-shirt because it was trademarked, it did become the unofficial name of the Jericho/Christian tag team.

ASS CLOWN: What came first . . . the Jericho or the *Office Space*? The first time I said this was during a promo with Kurt Angle at a house show in Bakersfield. Not sure if I made it up on the spot or if I subconsciously had heard it was used in the movie *Office Space*, which I hadn't seen at that point. My friend and visual timekeeper Ed Aborn told me it had been used already, but I'm taking credit for it until Mike Judge contacts me and fights me for it.

NEVER EEEVVVEEERRR BE THE SAME AGAIN: One of my biggest hits, this is another one that started in WCW when I was obnoxious Jericho. I had been tearing off the tuxedo jacket of ring announcer Dave Penzer regularly after my matches but was in the ring apologizing and promising to never do it again and decided to stutter the *ever* just to be an idiot. The pronunciation "agayn" is just how we say the word in Canada (and in England too). Want proof? Listen to how Bruce Dickinson sings it at the end of Iron Maiden's "Infinite Dreams."

HIGHLIGHT OF THE NIGHT: I was looking for a nickname similar to Shawn Michaels's The Showstopper and thought it was genius when I came up with Highlight of the Night. I was certain it was going to be huge and make me millions, but it didn't really get over and the T-shirt bombed. It did, however, provide the inspiration for the name of my in-ring talk show "The Highlight Reel."

WANNABE: Another one I thought was going to be a tremendous heat magnet but fizzled out quickly. I figured if I accused people of spending their whole lives trying to be like me, they would go banana (Pat Patterson TM) and try to kill me. It didn't work. But the offshoot of WANNABE, where I suggested all of the ideas I created were being ripped off by the entire WWE roster, was the genesis of the whole "Jericho Invented Everything" shtick that I still see online multiple times every day. ("Jericho invented Mr. T's mom.")

GELATINOUS PARASITES: This was born during my 2008 "Jericho Uses Big Words" phase. I was looking for an alternative word for *hypocrites* and came up with this. Surprisingly, it got major heat, as did BULBOUS MANATEES, if you can believe that!

KING OF THE WORLD/KING OF BLING BLING: "King of the world" was taken from the iconic Leonardo DiCaprio line in *Titanic,* and I said it in the same context when I became the undisputed champion. It eventually morphed into THE KING OF BLING BLING, but my attempts to put that on a shirt were roadblocked because somebody owned the trademark to the term *bling bling.* My question is WHO? (Just found out it's Lil Wayne . . . that bastard!)

BAD MAMA JAMA: I called myself this because I thought it sounded funny. Later on I found out the term is normally used to describe a hot chick. Gotta brush up on my gender-specific street slang next time.

BEST IN THE WORLD AT WHAT I DO: I first started saying this during the 2008 HBK feud, because I wanted to let people know that nobody in the business came close to my skills. And in reality at that time, I felt (on certain nights) I really was the best. When I had the idea, there was a little hesitation from the WWE writers about me using it because Triple H had recently claimed to be the best in the business. So I modified it to being the Best in the World at What I Do. When I left the WWE in 2010, CM Punk started using a paraphrased version of it, which eventually worked out to be huge for both of us. (That's called foreshadowing, kids.)

MONKEYS IN THE TRUCK: This one started when I was about to show a clip on the Obscenely Expensive JeriTron 5000 during an early edition of "The Highlight Reel." I wanted to give our hardworking techs a little shout-out but didn't want to be too respectful, so I called them Monkeys. The guys loved it and still scratch themselves and make gorilla noises whenever I go into the production truck.

GET IT, GOT IT, GOOD; RAZZLE DAZZLE; APROPOS: Not every catchphrase I used was a success; in fact, a few of them were only used once or twice before disappearing into obscurity. GET IT, GOT IT, GOOD was designed for crowd participation. I would say "Get it" (pause so the crowd could repeat it), then "Got it" (which the crowd would again repeat after me), and finish up with a resounding "Good." It didn't get over because I didn't use it enough times for the fans to learn their lines. Had I said it on *Raw* ten times, maybe it would've done something. *Razzle Dazzle* sounded froot, but I kind of gave up on that one pretty quickly too. Teddy Long used this a few times afterward. *Apropos* is another froot-sounding word that I said a bunch of times, but there really wasn't anywhere to go with it. It's not like I could sell APRO-POS foam fingers.

CHAPTER 5

The George Harrison of the WWE

After the less than classic MSG match, the program with JBL was scrapped, leaving me directionless. I pinned him quickly the next month in an Elimination Chamber match (before being eliminated myself) and then at WrestleMania 24, I was one of eight guys in the Money in the Bank match. Now, don't get me wrong. MITB matches are always fun (hell, I cocreated the damn thing), but to be in one at WrestleMania means you have no relevant angle to speak of. It was almost busywork, a way to just get you on the show. To make things worse, the last Mania match I had before I left the WWE in 2005 was a MITB, so even after all the buildup for my return, I was in the exact same position that I'd been in three years earlier. I was just another (baby) face in the crowd and I was slipping fast. Something had to be done quickly.

I had to turn heel.

Over the course of my career, I had the most success as a bad guy, especially in the WWE. It's not like I wasn't over as a babyface, because I was, but when I was at my peak as a good guy in the Attitude era, I was like the George Harrison of the WWE. George was one of the most talented and popular musicians of all time, but his only problem was he was in The Beatles with Paul McCartney and John Lennon, the two most talented and popular musicians EVER. As a babyface in the WWE with The Rock and Stone Cold Steve Austin at their peak, I was in the same yellow submarine as George. It didn't matter how good or popular I was, there was nothing I could do to become bigger or more over than those two juggernauts. I was always going to be number three. But I found my true niche in the company working AGAINST Rock and Austin, so playing the heel was still where I felt most comfortable.

My plan was not only to revert back to my villainous ways but to completely overhaul my character in the process. I wanted the stale Y2J persona to metamorphose into something completely different (the larch) and fresh. I was Kiss in 1982 and it was time to take off the Y2J makeup. I wanted to dump all of the things people liked about me . . . the countdown clock, the jokes, the nicknames, "The Highlight Reel," even my ring gear. I'd worn long tights for seventeen years, but now it was time to switch to the short trunks that I'd only worn briefly (pun intended) in 1992 when I was working for Carlos Elizondo in Monterrey (as documented in the hilariously entertaining *A Lion's Tale* available at a garage sale near you). Otherwise, it had always been tights and it was a nerve-racking experience to think about making the switch, to say the least.

With long tights, you at least have some form of pants on. Tight formfitting spandex pants that let people know what religion you are, but pants all the same. But to change to trunks, which were nothing more than spandex underwear, was an intimidating proposition. What would I look like in them? Did I have the right legs to pull it off? What if there was a wardrobe malfunction and my frank and beans suddenly fell out for all the world to see?

If you think I'm joking about that, I'm not. . . . I saw it, I saw it, with my own two eyes.

At a *SmackDown* taping in Rockford, Illinois, an enhancement guy named Rapid Delivery Rory Fox was working a match with Zack Ryder. Ryder pulled him into the turnbuckle by his waistband and suddenly, for no apparent reason, Rory's tights exploded.

Yeah, that's right . . . they literally disintegrated into a thousand threads of spandex. And he wasn't wearing any undertights.

The poor guy, not realizing that his ball bag had just made a rapid delivery into the open air, continued the match and took a nude sling-shot into the ropes. He made his way to the corner and covered his junk with both hands, as the camera got a close-up of him mouthing *Oh GOD!* with a pathetic look of shock on his face.

Zack pulled him out of the corner and bent the naked Fox over for his swinging neck breaker finish, giving the crowd a bird's-eye view of the always appealing beanbag/asshole combo. It was by far one of the funniest things I've ever seen in my life, but I have to give the Rapid One credit. After the match, he was walking around backstage laughing about the whole thing, whereas I would've run straight out of the arena and never looked back. Rory showed a lot of balls that day . . . both figuratively and literally.

Poor Rory Fox covers his junk after his tights explode mid-match. Look on the bright side: At least he was now the owner of a pretty rad spandex belt.

Even with the threat of exposure looming over both of my heads, I was still certain I wanted to make the costume change. So I e-mailed Vince to tell him I was thinking of making the switch and he retorted by telling me to start tanning my legs. But I had a hunch Vince preferred trunks to tights, being that the majority of his World Champions wore them. Obviously, there were some exceptions, like Bret Hart, Shawn Michaels, and Undertaker, but the bulk of his top guys wrestled in trunks, and the reason I was creating a new character was to become a legit top guy.

After I got WWE costume seamstress Julie Youngberg to make me a pair of trunks, I sat in the dressing room in Knoxville, Tennessee, nervously staring at my new duds, wondering if I was really ready to make the change. I brought a pair of my old tights with me in case I was too chicken to go through with it, but I decided it was now or never and put the damn things on.

It was weird at first to see so much skin exposed, but after a few minutes I started getting used to the look and liked it. But the big question was, would anybody else? There was only one way to find out, so I left the safety of the locker room for the wilds of the arena hallway and ran straight into producer Bruce Prichard.

Now he looks me up and he looks me down and says, "Hey, man, what be this and what be that and why you gotta look like that . . . because you look great! I can't believe you've been hiding those legs for that long! You should've switched to trunks years ago."

I'd never been told by a man that I had nice legs. Normally, it would have been awkward . . . and a little naughty . . . but at that moment, I felt pretty damn good about my gams (I wear short shorts). I thanked Bruce and bopped down the hallway with an extra pep in my trunk-clad step. It lasted for about five seconds, until I bumped into Dean Malenko, who asked, "Are you going to wear those out there? You look ridiculous."

Wahh wahhhh wahhhhhhhh!

If Dean had been the first person I saw in the hallway, I would've run back into the locker room, changed back into my tights, and that would have been the end of it. But because I heard Bruce's words first, I had the confidence to stick with the new look and run with it. Plus, it was another step toward distancing myself from Y2J and another discernible change from good guy to bad guy.

Between my haircut and my new outfit, I'd taken a big step toward changing my outer character. But how could I update my inner character into something new and unique?

That answer came from two different sources.

The first was when I was sitting in a hotel room in Phoenix, watching the newest Coen brothers movie, *No Country for Old Men*. I'm a huge fan of the Coens (*The Big Lebowski* and *Fargo* are two of my all-time favorites) and I'd been looking forward to seeing *No Country* since it had won the 2007 Academy Award for Best Picture. It was an amazing movie, but the most brilliant part was the performance of Javier Bardem (who also won an Oscar) as Anton Chigurh, the epitome of evil and a complete psycho who goes on a killing spree in a completely calm manner without a hint of remorse. Never raised his voice. Never made threats. He just spoke what he felt was the truth to his victims in a matter-of-fact way and struck swiftly.

Chigurh was a new type of villain and I thought this character would be perfect for me. At the time, most of the guys in the WWE were yelling during their promos, making threats, more the typical pro wrestling way of doing things. I thought if I spoke quietly during my promos and drew people into what I was saying and made them really listen, it would come off more realistic. More importantly, it was a direct contrast to the loud and boisterous Y2J way of doing things and therefore was exactly what I needed to make my character fresh again.

Another thing I liked about Chigurh was that in his mind, the evil deeds he was committing were warranted. He had conviction in his beliefs. I've always found that the best heels are the ones who have an element of truth to their boasts and claims. When Ric Flair bragged about flying in private planes, wearing the best clothes, and having lots of money, he said it with total convinction because he really had all of those things, and that pissed the fans off even more. They were sick of hearing what they knew was the truth and wanted him to just shut up about it already.

The second part of my new character came from the legendary Nick Bockwinkel. The WWE had recently released an AWA retrospective DVD, and while watching it, I remembered how great a heel Bockwinkle was. He wore suits for all his interviews and used ten-dollar words that went over the average fans' heads, pissing them off markedly. Here was this pompous blowhard using the fancy talk and wearing the fancy suits, claiming to be the best because he was the World Champion, which was the truth. Nobody was doing this seventies-throwback-type heel in 2008 and I knew I could make it work. If you listen to what the man says, what's old is new, and I was going to push that ancient adage to the max.

It wouldn't be an easy character to play, but with the tricks I had learned from my time studying in Los Angeles with acting coach Kirk Baltz and working with The Groundlings (both described in the Emmy-winning novel *Undisputed*, available at dollar stores worldwide), I knew I could drop into this part and pull it off. The most important lesson I learned was, in order to make any character come alive, I had to commit one hundred percent and play it to the max.

Whenever I was in the vicinity of a WWE arena, I would *never* break character. If I pulled into the arena parking lot, I wouldn't look at the fans or acknowledge them and would never sign an autograph, no matter how hard it was for me. Once I was heading over to Madison Square Garden from the adjoining underground parking lot, when a father with his young son about the same age as my son, Ash, happened to get on the elevator at the same time as I did. I stared straight ahead at at the floor numbers for the entire ride, as Dad continuously asked me to sign an autograph.

"Hey, Jericho, can you sign something for my kid?"

I didn't say a word.

"Hey, no need to be rude. My kid's a big fan and he'd like an autograph."

I continued staring intently at the flashing numbers, further incensing Dad as a tear welled up in little junior's eye.

"You're not even gonna look at me, you son of a bitch?!?" Dad practically screamed as I escaped off the elevator the moment the doors opened.

It didn't make me feel great to be such a jerk, but I didn't need the two of them going into the arena and smiling to each other as I made my ring entrance and telling the people sitting around them that I was actually a "nice guy in real life." I wanted them to boo the shit out of me and tell anybody who would listen how much of a total asshole I'd been to them.

I also wouldn't allow the WWE to make any more Jericho merchandise. I didn't want one person wearing my T-shirt and cheering for me because it was the froot (Jericho-ese for "cool," as described in my street slang guide, *Undisputed*, available in comic book shops everywhere) thing to do. I vowed to myself I would never be the way the nWo was in WCW, the cool heels who everybody cheered for because they didn't give a shit about anything, which ate babyfaces like me alive in the process. I wanted to be the ultimate heel with no redeeming qualities. I wanted to be Anton Chigurh, a bastard with an edge who was totally convinced what he was doing was the right thing and who people would be a little scared of as a result . . . and with good reason.

Now that I had a new character and a battle plan all fleshed out, I needed the right babyface foil to help get it off the ground. And fatefully, I was matched up with the perfect heroic yin to my villainous yang.

The Heartbreak Kid, Shawn Michaels.

CHAPTER 6

Shawn the Liar
(Thanks to Ryan Frye of the *Bleacher Report* for Time Line Assistance)

Anybody who knows me (or has read my second book, *Undisputed*, available at a pawnshop near you) knows that Shawn Michaels is one of my biggest inspirations to get into wrestling, and in my opinion, the greatest sports entertainer of all time. We'd had a classic match at WrestleMania 19 in Seattle (some say we stole the whole effin' show, and I have to agree), but hadn't really worked with each other since. That's why I was happy to hear that I was going to be the guest referee for an HBK-Batista match at the Backlash PPV in Baltimore in April of 2008. I would officiate the match without bias and then turn heel on Shawn at the end, causing him to lose. Then we would have a match at the PPV the next month, when Shawn would exact his revenge on me and that would be it. Not the most well-thought-out plan, but it was a start. At the very least, I'd end up a heel and get another match with HBK.

Little did I know that the planned one-off between Michaels and Jericho would last seven months and end up as one of the greatest feuds in WWE history.

When we showed up in Baltimore the day of the show, the finish for the HBK/Batista match hadn't yet been decided. We asked Vince what he wanted, and he said, "I've got no idea; I just book the stuff. You guys figure it out."

Shawn and I agreed that there was no reason to rush my betrayal and subsequent heel turn, so we sat down to think of a different scenario. After a few hours of throwing various thoughts back and forth, Shawn came up with the idea that he would "injure" his knee on a powerbomb reversal, which would lull Batistsa into a false sense of security, allowing Shawn to superkick him and get the win. The twist was nobody would know whether he had really hurt himself, and that would get under my skin. If he truly did fake the injury in order to win, why were the fans still rewarding him with their undying devotion?

We were both babyfaces, but I became more convinced week by week that he had feigned the whole injury to win the match and had been lying about it ever since. I held a mock Academy Awards ceremony on *Raw* and awarded him an Oscar for best acting job of the year. As the result of my suspicions, the people were slowly turning on me for accusing their beloved HBK of deception. He eventually convinced me he had really hurt himself and I did an in-ring promo apologizing for doubting him. After suckering me in even further, he admitted he was lying and wasn't actually hurt. Then he superkicked me in the face and he obnoxiously danced out of the ring like one of Chippendales' finest as the people cheered the hell out of him the whole time. And he was supposed to be the babyface!

It was the perfect situation for my new heel persona. How could the fans cheer and admire a man who had lied to their face?

What a bunch of hypocrites!

In that moment, not only was a new catchphrase born, but my whole modus operandi for turning heel was hatched along with it. The brilliant part was it all happened so organically. It wasn't a meticulously planned story line that had been mapped out for months beforehand; it was a story we booked on the fly that caught fire because it felt real. I had every reason to be mad. If someone you considered to be a friend lied to you for months until you felt legitimately bad for him, then admitted he was kidding and kicked you in the face, wouldn't that piss you off?

What made my case even stronger was that when the fans were forced to make a choice between Jericho and Michaels, they chose Shawn the Liar. He was such a heroic legend to the WWE Universe that even this blatant display of bullshit wasn't enough to turn the WWE Universe on him and there was nothing the lowly Chris Jericho could do to change it. The whole situation couldn't have been plotted better if we tried. Then we started trying.

Week by week we met in the writers' room with Michael Hayes, Brian Gewirtz, and Vince himself to plot out the upcoming twists and turns. We had stumbled onto the rarest of things—a hot moneymaking angle—and we wanted to fire it up as much as we possibly could.

The next step was a babyface vs. babyface match at Judgment Day, where Shawn got the victory with a quick roll-up. After five years, it was great to be back in the ring with my favorite opponent of all time, and our in-ring chemistry was as good as ever. Physically, psychologically, mentally, and attitudinally, we were the perfect rivals. It was an excellent technical wrestling match and yet it was the last one we would ever have like it, because a few weeks after the Judgment Day PPV, I made my own judgment on Shawn Michaels.

He had to be destroyed.

We decided I would make my official heel turn on Shawn the next month after the One Night Stand PPV, where he had a stretcher match with Batista. I suggested to Brian that I could have Shawn as my guest on "The Highlight Reel" the next night on *Raw* and throw him through the obscenely expensive JeriTron 5000.

One of the most famous moments in *Raw* history was in 1992, when Shawn turned on his partner, Marty Jannetty, and threw him through the plate-glass window of Brutus Beefcake's Barber Shop. I thought it would be a froot homage and a bit of poetic justice to smash Shawn's head through my own pane of glass. On June 9, 2008, in Oakland, I went on *Raw* and told the audience my next guest was my inspiration, my mentor and, most important, my friend. Shawn came to the ring, and while he was soaking in the adulation of the fans, I reminded them how he had deceived them about his knee injury. He cut me off and reminded me that he'd said from the start he would do whatever it took to beat Batista and that's what he'd done. So he never lied to anybody . . . except me.

I could hear the swell of boos rising up from the audience as I continued defending myself, claiming to be the only honest man in the whole scenario and calling Shawn out for his deception. Then I asked him, "How does Shawn Michaels, HBK, one of the greatest performers of all time and one of the most highly decorated superstars in the history of this business, turn into such a lying, cheating, pathetic little worm of a human being?"

With that, I clotheslined him to the mat and began pounding on him as the crowd looked on in horror. The turn had been such a long time coming, I think the fans were wondering if I was ever going to actually do it. But they reacted huge when I finally did, especially when as he rallied back I cut him off with a swift kick to the plums.

He crumpled to the ground like a sack of dirty potatoes (just as he did when I nutted him at the end of our 2003 Mania match) and the crowd went silent. I towered over him, staring into his eyes and his eyes only. In my mind at that moment, there wasn't another living soul on the planet. There was only Shawn and me.

I told him quietly, so that only the camera mics could hear, that he had caused all of this by lying to me. Then I dragged him to his feet and cradled his face in my hands.

"The worst is yet to come," I said, and threw him face-first into the JeriTron 5000.

Earlier in the day, the WWE prop team had gutted the TV and removed the flat screen, replacing it with sugar glass. Now, I already didn't trust sugar glass because it never worked properly the times I'd used it in the past. It cut the shit out of me when Kane threw me through a sugar-glass picture window back in '02 and then again months later when X-Pac broke a sugar-glass wine bottle over my head.

But despite my reservations, the gimmicked JeriTron looked perfect as it hung above the ring like an overgrown ugly square spider and nobody suspected what was going to happen (even though there were some concerns from Vince that the "Highlight Reel" graphic wouldn't be displayed on the screen because it wasn't a working television). We'd rehearsed earlier in the day to see if Shawn could break through the glass quickly and realistically and if the ensuing shard explosion would be visual enough. We filmed the dry run and it looked amazing—but it didn't even come close to the real thing.

When I grabbed Shawn by the back of his head and ran him toward the screen, I let go just before impact so he could take his own bump. He put his hand in front of his face and used his momentum to head-butt the JeriTron as hard as he could. And the results were spectacular.

The sugar glass disintingrated and thousands of minute shards sprayed over the ring, as the Tron swung wildly askew over the crowd's heads. Shawn writhed in pain, holding his eye with both hands, as the audience gasped and the announcers stopped talking to enhance the severity of what I'd done.

The heel Jericho of old would've been doing a war dance or the electric slide in the center of the ring to rile up the fans even further, but this was a new man. Everyone was waiting for me to say something clever or deliver some kind of witty quip, but instead I walked straight to the back without a second glance, leaving the announcers to speculate about how badly Shawn was injured.

The segment wasn't just a home run, it was a mafakkin' grand slam in the bottom of the ninth in the final game of the WWE World Series. Jericho vs. Michaels was now the hottest angle in the company. But in the words of Karen Carpenter, we'd only just begun.

The WWE announced the next day that due to my vicious onslaught, Shawn had suffered a detatched retina and his career was in jeopardy. It was pure coincidence that Shawn does have a bit of a wandering eye, but that added to our angle the same way Jim Carrey's real chipped tooth added to the Lloyd Christmas character. People still ask me if I'm the reason for that wonky eye, and as much as I'd like to take credit, that was all God's doing.

The next step was a grudge match at the next PPV, The Great American Bash. We heated up the angle even more a few weeks earlier when I gave HBK a drop toehold into the corner of the announce table, further "injuring" his eye. This was an Arn Anderson idea that sounded good in concept but ended up great with Shawn's execution. There was a dangerous margin for error with him driving his eye toward the corner of the table at high speed and then pulling back at the last second to protect himself. But as usual, Shawn's selling was masterful and it looked totally real.

On the night of the Bash, Shawn stormed to the ring intensely, ever so subtly selling his eye. Our match was a war for the ages that was as good as our "technical wrestling match" a few months earlier, but in a totally different way. This one was a brutal bloodbath. We beat the unholy hell out of each other until I busted Shawn open and he bled so profusely that a few days later, Vince banned blood forever from all further WWE shows. He's stuck to that verdict ever since, with dire penalities for anyone who dared to challenge him on it. Believe me, I know. (That's more foreshadowing, kids.)

I won the match by ref stoppage when I kept visciously pounding his wounded eye until he couldn't defend himself any longer. The new Jericho character had arrived and was a huge success. My combination of Bockwinkle suits and big words, Chigurh slow-paced, intense speech patterns, a more intense in-ring style, and Shawn's incredible performances had made me the most hated man in the company. The kernel of truth that I continued to use as the crux of my motivation to act the way I did was still a thorn in the fans' sides as well. They were the hypocrites, and whenever I reminded them of that, the "Jericho Sucks" chants were deafening. My character had no catchphrases, merch, or redeeming qualities whatsoever and that was exactly the way I wanted it.

CHAPTER 7

Public Enemy Number One

As a result of the reactions I was getting, Vince decided he wanted to put me with a "heater," a big guy who would help me cheat to win and be an intimidating presence I could hide behind whenever things got bad. Gewirtz mentioned that they were considering a new recruit named Ricky Ortiz, who was standing out in the WWE developmental system and had a personality similar to mine. Ricky did have great charisma, but he was playing a goofy over-the-top character that would have meshed great with the old Y2J, but not with the new me. We were also pretty much the same height, and if I was going to have a heater, I wanted somebody a lot bigger.

So I went to the Florida Championship Wrestling (FCW) training center, where the WWE prospects worked out, to scout for a better fit. When I saw this massive, jacked-up, good-looking dude with a similar haircut to mine I thought, *I want that guy*. His name was Rob Terry, but it turned out his days in the WWE were numbered. As much of an amazing physical presence as he was, he was let go shortly afterward (he eventually made it to TNA) and I was left empty-handed. A few days later, the name Lance Cade was brought up and I thought he would be perfect.

Lance was a handsome six-foot, six-inch muscular kid, who'd originally been trained by Shawn, so story line–wise he was perfect. He became my protégé after he attacked Michaels on *Raw*, with the explanation he wasn't going to wait around for Shawn to attack him first like he had with all of his other friends at one time or another. It was the truth. Shawn's track record with tag-team partners was pretty awful, which substantiated my claim that HBK was the true villain in all of this.

I really enjoyed working with Cade, for his presence gave me a completely different set of options for my matches. He could be my excuse for winning or losing a match and help me get heat on my opponent. He was still a little green but was on his way to becoming a well-rounded performer and a real asset.

Then he passed out on a plane and got fired.

When I heard the news, I called John Laurinaitis (the head of Talent Relations) to see if he would give Cade another chance, but the plane incident was another in a long line of incidents for Lance, and that was his last straw. I was really mad at him for blowing his big chance and affecting our angle at the same time. I never heard from him again after his firing, until a few years later when he dropped by a live event to apoligize to me. He eventually got hired back by the WWE but was let go again soon after, and died of heart failure in 2010. It was a damn shame because I really liked Lance, and if he were alive today, I think he'd be a big star.

After The Great American Bash, Shawn was off *Raw* for a few weeks selling his eye injury, with his career seemingly in jeopardy. Behind the scenes, the plan was for us to have our last match at SummerSlam, but Shawn had a real issue with that. The PPV was being built around the double main event of John Cena vs. Batista and Undertaker vs. Edge in a Hell in a Cell and Shawn felt that our story line would be lost in the shuffle. Vince argued that he needed the attraction of the Michaels-Jericho blow-off match to solidify the SummerSlam lineup.

But Shawn had an idea for an even bigger attraction. He'd advertise that he was going to be making a major announcement at the PPV, with every indication pointing toward him retiring. Vince loved it, and thought people would pay to hear what Shawn would say, especially if they thought he was announcing the end of his legendary career. So it was agreed that our story would continue through SummerSlam and finish up at the September PPV.

The plan for the PPV was for me to interrupt Shawn's announcement and beat him down, which would lead to him putting everything on the line to face me in one more match. But I was driving in my car one afternoon, when he called me to say he'd been toying with the idea of having his wife, Rebecca, and their two kids come to the ring with him. When I came down for the interrupt, I'd go to sucker-punch him, but he'd move out of the way and I'd hit his WIFE instead.

I couldn't believe what he was suggesting, but I loved it. Vince agreed it was a great idea (but nixed the kids) and gave it the go-ahead. I knew it was so controversial that it would put me even deeper in the doghouse with fans all over the world, but I never expected it to work as well as it did. It ended up being the final catalyst that made Jericho-Michaels one of the classic WWE feuds of all time . . . but it came at a steep price.

Shawn stood in the ring at SummerSlam with his wife by his side, giving one of the best promos of his career. He talked about all of the amazing things he had done in the WWE and how many obstacles he'd overcome to be the man he was today. The fans held on to his every word, hoping against hope he wasn't going to deliver the news they were dreading. He gave another outstanding performance, as he reflectively, regretfully, and tearfully explained that after consulting with his doctors and his wife, due to all the injuries he had suffered during his career, he was going to have to retire from the WWE. The crowd gave him a huge standing ovation and an even bigger "HBK" chant, as the cameras zoomed on people actually crying. Just as the chants reached their crescendo, my music cut them off and the cheers turned to boos. The fans knew something was coming, but nobody knew just how heavy it was going to be.

I told Shawn I wasn't going to allow him to end his career without admitting the real reason he was retiring was me. He was being forced to quit the WWE because of the eye injury I had given him, and he would forever have to remember that Chris Jericho was the one who drove the final stake through the heart of the legendary HBK. Shawn responded that I was a "vile and selfish human being," who would have to go home and tell my family that no matter what, "I would never ever be Shawn Michaels." The crowd erupted and I sold the indignation with a vacant glare.

As Shawn and Rebecca turned their backs to walk away, I spun him around and threw a punch at his head. He ducked out of the way, leaving his wife directly in the line of fire, and I smacked her full force in the mouth.

For real.

Earlier in the day, we had gone over the whole scenario and I timed my punch to stop right before it made any contact with her. I've thrown thousands of "working punches," as we call them, but this one was a little more important because it wasn't another trained worker I was swinging at; it was Shawn's wife we were talking about. In order to time it right, I told her not to move so I could judge the distance and throw the punch accordingly.

Even though Rebecca had been in WCW for a short time working as Nitro Girl Whisper, she had never wrestled or taken a bump as far as

I knew. But that didn't matter because if I executed the punch perfectly, it was going to look vicious.

But I didn't execute it properly.

When Shawn ducked, I leaned slightly forward and so did Rebecca. Neither of us meant to shift our positions, but we did, and in a total fluke, my fist smashed her right in the mouth. It wasn't a glancing blow either. I nailed her hard. I felt her lip mash against my knuckles like I'd popped a grape.

She went down fast as the crowd gasped in horror. Shawn dropped to his knees beside her crying and I stood there helpless in disbelief. Before the show, Vince told me to act concerned about what I did, but not exaggeratedly. He didn't want me to show remorse, but he also didn't want me to laugh or act cocky. The look on my face said it all, as I was the kid at the birthday party who'd tried to get attention by pushing the cake on the floor but now knew he'd gone too far.

But the look on my face wasn't an act. I felt like the biggest piece of shit on the planet and I knew I was in trouble. I could only imagine what Shawn was going to do to me when he got back through the curtain. After I had just knocked his wife out, if he wanted to knock me out in return, I was going to let him.

I also didn't know just how badly she was hurt. Had I knocked her teeth out? Cut her open? Would she need stitches? It was the worst feeling ever, walking through Gorilla as everyone looked over at me in silence, nervously waiting to see what kind of damage I'd caused. The paramedics were in the ring now, surrounding them, and when I saw the blood on her mouth, it made me want to fucking puke.

They carted her out on a stretcher and when they got backstage, I kept repeating over and over again, "I am so sorry, man. I am so sorry." The doctors tended to Rebecca as Shawn stared at me blankly like he wanted to kill me.

He finally broke the silence. "I never should've allowed this to happen. This never should've happened. I can't believe I brought my family into this." If it was possible to feel worse than me, he did. We were both staring at our feet in silence, waiting to see if Rebecca was okay, when she suddenly sat up off the stretcher and looked me in the eye.

"Is that the best you got, Jericho?" she said with a crooked smile. Shawn and I looked at each other and started laughing as he gave his wife a hug.

Thankfully, Rebecca was all right. Her teeth were fine, and even though I'd given her quite the fat lip, no stitches were necessary. She didn't make either of us feel any guiltier about what had happened, but I still felt horrible and sent her flowers later in the week to apologize.

But once we knew for sure that she was okay, Shawn and I realized that the accidental punch in the mush was the best thing that could've happened to our angle. The story had now ceased to be fiction; it had just crossed over into reality. Wrestling fans have seen everything and experienced everything these days, and when people watch the show, they know deep down inside that it isn't real. But as Nick Bockwinkle himself once told me, "I could stand in the ring and tell the crowd that wrestling isn't real for thirty minutes, then have my match and have those same people call me a damn liar afterward." And he was right. The best workers in the business can make people forget it's a show with a great match, even though the audience still knows that what they are viewing is entertainment. But this angle was different. There wasn't one person watching who didn't feel the impact of that punch, and every one of them had the same reaction.

"I don't care if it's a show or not. If that motherfucker punched my wife (or husband, girlfriend, dad, mom, Auntie Elsie, or anybody important in their lives) in the mouth like that, I would kill him." No *ifs*, *ands*, or *buts* about it: The WWE Universe REALLY wanted to see Shawn kick my ass now.

As a result of my heinous crimes, I was now officially Public Enemy Number One in the WWE, and people wanted to get their hands on me. Literally.

CHAPTER 8

Attack of the Fans

After I assaulted Shawn's wife, the crowd reactions I was getting rocketed to another level of hatred. The chants of "Jericho Sucks" had a whole different tone, almost barbaric in nature. The kind I imagined you might hear at a lynching. People were legitimately furious and wanted my head on a stick, and they weren't going to wait for Shawn to put it there.

I was working a live event at the Cow Palace in San Francisco, and before the match, I grabbed the mic and stared angrily at the crowd, not saying a word. I was in mid-silence when a fan threw a beer at me. It exploded across my chest and I shrugged it off as the amber liquid streamed down my torso, but the dam had burst and suddenly I was being pelted with a wave of beer cups, popcorn boxes, and various pieces of trash. But I was lovin' every minute of it like Mike Reno, because in my world this was a standing ovation.

I was pacing the ring waiting for the barrage to stop, when suddenly I felt a sharp pain at the base of my skull. Stars fanned out in front of my eyes and an intense agony exploded inside my head. I looked down and saw a Duracell D battery (the big ones you put inside a flashlight) rolling across the mat. I searched the crowd furiously wondering who had thrown the battery and, even more important, how did they get it into the arena? I mean, who brings a fucking D battery to a wrestling show? Did they smuggle it into the building inside a talking Teddy Ruxpin doll? Any way you slice it (and I ain't talking 'bout Gene Simmons), I decided I'd had enough of that shit and stormed to the back, pissed off that I'd been battered with a battery and that our security had done nothing about it.

I saw our head of security, Jimmy Tillis, backstage and gave him a major bollocking.

"Where the fuck were you? Did you see what happened out there? I got hit with a battery!! I'm not going back out there, you got that?? Nothing you can say is gonna make me go back out there, do you understand? You can't make me, you can't make me, you can't make me!!"

Then I saw The Undertaker standing behind me.

"You're not going back out there, huh?" he asked with a bemused look on his face.

"No!" I said, even though Taker was the locker room leader of the WWE and not someone you wanted to talk back to.

The big man intensified his glare. "You sure that's the best idea?" he said, like a colossal Clint Eastwood.

"Yes! . . . No! . . . Maybe! . . ." I pouted, as Taker stared at me with an *are you done yet?* look on his face, glancing at his watch with his arms crossed.

"Ummm . . . I'm just gonna go back out there now," I said softly.

Taker nodded wisely and patted me on the back, guiding me on my not so merry way. I think he found my tantrum funny and was curious to see how far I'd take it. I was ready to take it pretty damn far, as I was so pissed off, I would've told Vince McMahon himself I wasn't going back to the ring. But The Undertaker? Nah . . . I'll take the zero.

I swallowed my pride, ignored the pulsing goose egg on the back of my noggin, and did the walk of shame back to the ring, getting pelted with junk every step of the way.

The next time I got pelted in the ring was in England, but it wasn't with trash. I guess the English are more dignified, so they threw something a little more posh. . . . Glow sticks.

We were in the O2 Arena in London and I was against Cena in the main event. (Why does a wrestler always feel the need to specify when he's in the main event? It's not like I would ever say, "I had a match against Funaki in the third match on the card.")

DX were having problems getting approval to sell their trademark neon-green glow sticks at the show because the O2 brass were afraid fans would throw them and hurt somebody. Eventually they got it worked out and the sticks were selling quicker than molly at a rave.

I was in the middle of a prematch promo explaining how all Londoners were hypocritical, gelatinous parasites with bad teeth, when someone threw a glow stick and hit me right in the eye. (What was with the aim of these Jericho haters? They should all be trying out for the Yankees!)

I was surprised and my eye was pounding, so I angrily surveyed the crowd, looking for the culprit.

"You wanna throw stuff? I'd love to find the son of a bitch who threw that glow stick! You wanna throw stuff? Go for it! Come on, throw some stuff!" I yelled into the mic.

The crowd obliged and showered me with a hailstorm of neon-green glow sticks. If you think I'm exaggerating, go look it up on YouTube now. Go ahead, I'll wait.

Go on, then! I don't have all day.

. . .

See, I told you!

It started like most storms do, with just a few drops here and there, but when it kicked in, it was a gargantuan green glow stick gale. I saw the first few flying through the air and batted them away easily like Obi-Wan Kenobi during his Jedi Trials, but as the bombardment built, I stood my ground and took it like a boss. I was the most hated man in Great Britain and it felt jolly good!

Fearing a riot, producer Johnny Laurinaitis hit Cena's music to bring him to the ring and we went on to have a really good match (as we always did). When I walked through the curtain afterward, instead of receiving salutations and congratulations, everyone seemed to be avoiding me. Apparently, a little boy had been hit by an errant glow stick and had been brought backstage to calm him down and pacify the situation. DX had taken photos with the kid and given him some merch, so all was now well, except DX were not happy with me. Hunter made a point of walking into the dressing room to let me know that he and Shawn had "saved my ass" by taking care of the little guy. I felt bad the kid got hit, but I didn't understand what HHH was so mad about. It was an amazing heel moment, the best reaction any villain worth his handful of salt could hope for.

I took a shower and was on the bus, waiting to travel to the next city, when I got a call from Laurinaitis telling me that Stephanie wanted to fine me ten thousand dollars for provoking the incident. I couldn't believe it. I was going to be punished for getting heat? Let's not forget that I was the one who got hit with the damn glow stick in the first place and had the black eye to prove it! I took a picture of it with my phone as evidence that I'd almost lost an eye, yet nobody seemed to care (cue the playing of the world's smallest violin). I was so irate that I called Vince directly.

"Listen, Vince, if I'm going to get fined for this glow stick incident, I'm letting you know that I think it's total bullshit! It was one of the most amazing things I've ever experienced in my career and I'll tell you this, Vince McMahon the corporate boss might not like it, but Mr. McMahon the heel character would've loved it! And if you're gonna fine me for doing my job and getting a reaction like that, well, then we are gonna have a problem!"

I hung up with authority and waited for the shit storm that was sure to follow. There was no way I was going to accept being fined for this. I was mad as hell and I wasn't gonna take it anymore! I couldn't wait to hear Vince's response to my challenge and if I didn't like what he had to say, I was ready to quit the damn WWE!

My phone buzzed as I received a text from the boss.

"Take two aspirin and call me in the morning :) You get heat naturally!"

I wasn't sure exactly what he was saying, but I assumed that any text that included a smiley face meant I was off the hook. It turned out I was. Despite what Hunter and Stephanie thought, Vince obviously loved what I'd done and I never heard another word about it.

But as far as I'm concerned, when it comes to DX glow sticks, I've got two words for ya. . . .

As much of a pain in the ass as it was to get pelted with beer cups, boxes of popcorn, batteries, and rave party favors, it was nothing compared to being physically assaulted. Now, granted it took some audacity to throw inanimate objects at the ring, but to actually have someone lay their hands on me showed a true commitment. I'd heard of guys back in the days of territorial wrestling who'd been stabbed by old ladies' hat pins, been sucker-punched in bars, and had their cars set on fire by irate fans, but those types of incidents were few and far between in the new and improved PG WWE. But my character was now a different animal as the assault on Shawn's wife had changed the rules, and people wanted to get their hands on me in any way possible.

I was in Greenville, South Carolina, cutting another promo before my match and threatening to "fight every single member of this audience, man, woman, or child, right here, right now. Do you understand what I'm saying?"

One rogue in particular did understand and decided to do something about it. I saw him climb over the rail into the aisleway about twenty rows back and start running toward the ring. I continued talking shit, following the dude in my periphery as he made his way down the aisle. I calmly waited for him to slide into the ring, because when he did, I was going to kick him in the side of the head . . . hard.

Just a note for any idiots out there who are considering jumping into a WWE ring for a joke or a sneak attack: The ring is our world and once you enter it uninvited, there are no rules. We have the right to kick your ass as much as we wish. It's like entering our house at three A.M.: As soon as you come through the front door, we can hit you in the face with a baseball bat and there will be no legal consequences whatsoever. And this clown running toward me was about to get curb-stomped for breaking and entering.

Bozo slid into the ring, and I prepared to kick a field goal with the guy's melon, but he never made it all the way in. As soon as he got halfway under the ropes, our ringside physician, Dr. Chris Amann, and referee, Charles (Little Naitch) Robinson, grabbed his legs and pulled him right back out again. It looked like *Jaws*, when the hapless victim breaks through the surface of the water and scrambles up onto the deck of the boat, only to be pulled back down to the depths by the hungry shark seconds later.

My boys held the dummy down until security dragged him back into the bowels of the arena, as I stood in the ring laughing with my arms crossed.

"Take him away! I want that man arrested for trying to assault me! Put him away for the rest of his life. . . . I demand it!! You see what happens when you try to put your hands on Chris Jericho?" I goaded.

This got tons of heat as I didn't even have to get my hands dirty by touching the solipsistic blowhard (I actually used the word *solipsistic* on *Raw* once even though I had no idea what it meant), but was taking all the credit for his arrest.

Unfortunately for me, my next attacker . . . or attackers . . . wouldn't be stopped before getting to me.

We had just finished a show on a Sunday afternoon in Victoria, British Columbia, one of the most beautiful cities in the world but a real pain in the ass to get to, due to the two-hour ferry ride from mainland Vancouver. I'd just worked in the main event (there I go again) against CM Punk and was under a time crunch to make it back to the boat on time.

Problem was there was a huge group of fans waiting outside to catch a glimpse of us getting in our cars. Nothing new, but the difference this time was the crowd was practically on top of us because there were no barriers or fences to separate them. They stood on the sidewalk a few feet from the cars and as soon as I slowly pulled onto the street, the mob converged on me like a herd of zombies. Now, if I was their hero, it wouldn't be so bad, but as the guy who had just been antagonizing them incessantly only minutes before, I was in a little bit of a quandary (great word).

I slowly made my way through the pack and rolled to a stop at a red light a few feet away from the parking lot. Suddenly, there was a loud noise to my left and I saw some jack-off kicking in the driver's-side door of my car. I didn't have the insurance option on the rental, so I knew he'd just cost me the amount of the repair and he was now standing in a fighting pose bouncing back and forth on his legs like a scrawny Brock Lesnar. Ever since my bud Dimebag Darrell had been shot and killed onstage at a Damageplan concert by a disgruntled, psychopathic fan, I'd taken fan attacks a little more seriously. What if this asshole had a gun? Was I just going to sit there and find out? Fuck that. I got out of the car and yelled at him to back away.

I figured as soon as I got out of the vehicle, security would intervene and eliminate my problem, but I figured wrong. Nobody came to my rescue and in the interim, another mob of fans converged on me and knocked the door shut behind me. Now I really did feel like Rick Grimes surrounded by shambling, mindless, drooling drones, and considering how drunk some of these zombies were, I wasn't too far off. Unfortunately, I didn't have a gun and I could smell the booze on the breath of Mr. Car Kicker as he circled around toward me. I could tell he was spoiling for a fight by the look in his eyes, the booze on his breath, and his nonsensical accusations of "You screwed Shawn Michaels. You're a disgrace to Canada!"

Good Lord, dude, it's a fucking show! When Anthony Hopkins walks down the street, he's not wearing a straitjacket, ready to eat a human liver with some fava beans and a nice Chianti! Hannibal Lecter is a character, the same way that Chris Jericho is a character. Not that this guy understood that as he was ready to go to war with his nemesis, the Jericho he knew from TV.

I had spent the afternoon doing my job by giving the fans an evil villain to hate, and now those same fans were allowed to just waltz right over and attack me? I never should've been put in this situation in the first place. Where was the security?

My question was answered when a dopey-looking rent-a-cop wearing a yellow SECURITY shirt came wandering over to assist me. Or so I thought, but all he did was stand in there with his back to the crowd and tell me to get back in my car. Meanwhile the attack of the fans continued as the gathering crowd blocked my way and Eddie Drunk advanced on me quickly.

"Turn around, this guy is going to swing at me!" I yelled, but the security slow had no idea what I was talking about, so I pushed him aside. Dory Drunk Jr. swung at me and I took a step backward to avoid his blow, grabbed his shoulders, and shoved him straight to the ground, scattering the crowd.

"DO YOUR FUCKIN' JOB!!" I screamed at nobody in particular, as the fans continued asking me for autographs and filming the proceedings on their cell phones.

I took stock of the situation and decided it was too far out of control, with the potential to get a lot worse VERY quickly. It was time to bail. I was wading through the crowd back to my car, when I felt someone weakly punching me in the ass and trying to grab my package. I spun around and saw a chick with glasses and a bad blond dye job screaming in my face, "You hit my boyfriend!"

Car Kicker's more inebriated worser half was now trying to take me out as well. I wriggled out of the way and managed to open the car door, slipping into the front seat. Before I could shut it, Bad Dye Blonde followed me inside. I have no idea what she was planning to do and I'll bet she didn't either, but I knew what I was going to do . . . and spit a big greener into her face.

It was the quickest thing I could think of to get her out of the car without actually touching her. My saliva salvo caused her to recoil, but she bounced right back and tried to force her way in again. I pushed her in the chest as hard as I could to get her away from me. She disappeared into the crowd and I started the ignition, just as another dipshit jumped on the hood of the car and held on to the windshield wipers like a bad guy in a James Bond movie.

I did a hard swerve to throw Odd Job off the car and drove away as fast as I could, glancing in the rearview mirror as I sped down the downtown street. The mob was waving their arms and hurling profanities at me like villagers out to kill the monster. All they needed were pitchforks and torches.

I was on my way back to the ferry, when I got a call from Jimmy Tillis (the same head of WWE security who wasn't around when I got hit with the battery in Frisco a few months earlier) saying that the cops (where the hell had they been when I was getting attacked?) wanted me to come back to the arena to discuss what happened. I told them both to go fuck themselves, as I was fuming and had a ferry to catch.

I texted Vince to tell him what happened so he would hear the news from me first. It was a lesson I learned when I got into the fight with Goldberg years earlier (as told in the self-help classic *Undisputed,* available at a flea market near you) and Vince was mad he heard about it from everybody other than me. I explained there had been an altercation with some fans in the parking lot of the Victoria arena and it was a good thing I told him when I did because when I woke up, the word that a WWE wrestler had gotten into a fight with a bunch of fans (one of them a woman) was all over the news.

This was a big story to the mainstream press, and I was deluged with requests asking for my comments. Soon afterward, I got a call from the head of WWE PR telling me that the networks had gotten ahold of some footage that made me look really bad and now wanted my head on a platter.

A clip of the fight filmed on somebody's cell phone had been released and it appeared to show me punching Bad Dye Blonde in the face. Of course I hadn't punched her in the face or anywhere else, for that matter, but the clip sure made it look that way. It had been filmed from a close-up side angle and when I thrust my arm forward to push her away from the car, my hand disappeared offscreen. The last you saw of my fist, it was heading toward her face, so the natural assumption was I had punched her in the mouth (even though I'd only pushed her in the chest), and that's all the gossip news channels needed to see. They were like a school of piranhas frenzied over a drop of blood in the water and ready to rip me apart, with the worst of them all being Nancy Grace.

She had treated me with respect when I'd chosen her show to offer my thoughts about the Chris Benoit tragedy a few years earlier, but now it was like we had never met. She ran the clip multiple times, demanding my immediate firing by the WWE and subsequent arrest by the Canadian police. "This hooligan thinks he can do whatever he wants by strik-ing a female fan and getting away with it? Not on my watch! I demand Chris Jericho be punished for his actions to the full extent of the law."

It was typical sensationalist bullshit, but I wasn't worried in the least, because I knew the truth. The clip didn't do much for my reputa-tion, though. When I was told the two idiots who had attacked me were pressing charges, I was advised by WWE legal to press my own set of charges as part of their strategy to protect me. I spoke to the Victoria Police Department, who gave me the good news that they'd arrested Car Kicker and BDB and had found witnesses willing to testify that I was in the right for defending myself. The only drawback was I would have to fly back to Victoria (one of the farthest places to travel to in North America from Tampa) to appear in court in a few months.

It was a brutal situation that could get a lot worse depending on Vince's reaction. I'd already heard that some of the higher-ups in the company were angry with me and wanted to release a statement vilifying me for what had gone down, but that didn't matter. They weren't my boss . . . Vince was.

I went into his office in the arena in Oakland the next day at *Raw* and explained what happened. He listened intently and said something that meant the world to me. "You did the right thing and we will sup-port and defend you as a company." To hear he was behind me washed away the stress I was feeling about the whole situation—even though I knew I was in the right, I worried on some level that I had overreacted. Vince agreed that I never should've been left alone in the parking lot and put in that position in the first place. Not only was he not mad at me, he promised it would never happen to me again.

I know that he was secretly proud of me for the work I had been doing and the reactions I was getting. I had struck gold with this char-acter, and because it was so believable, sometimes I had to face the con-sequences. If the odd fan tried to kill me once in a while, then so be it.

Vince told me a story of how he was once on a private runway waiting to board the company jet years earlier, when an unidentified man raced toward him on the tarmac. The intruder was tackled by security and was found with a gun in the waistband of his jeans. So Vince completely understood my motivation for defending myself.

A few days later, I got another call from the Victoria police saying that all charges against me had been dropped due to the lack of evidence. That also meant that the charges against Drunk and Drunker had been dropped as well, but I didn't give a shit as it saved me having to take the twelve-hour journey to Victoria. The most important thing was I was innocent and my good name had been cleared, even though the story that "Chris Jericho was cleared of all wrongdoing in the Victoria incident" didn't have quite the same ring as "Maniacal WWE wrestler goes on woman-beating rampage," and the news of my innocence wasn't mentioned on *Nancy Grace* or anywhere else.

I'm still waiting for my apology, Nancy. You know where to find me.

CHAPTER 9

Six Years and Five Months Later

As hated as I was and as many times as I was attacked by random fans, there was one person who despised me more than anbody else on the planet: Shawn Michaels.

But that was only within the confines of a WWE ring, because in reality, Shawn and I were the closest we'd ever been. We'd created something special and as veteran performers in the wrestling business, we knew that didn't happen every day. But it was time to once again up the ante.

On *Raw* the night after SummerSlam, HBK came to the ring wearing his heart on his sleeve and made a shocking announcement. He told the crowd that after looking his injured wife in the eye, there was no way he was going to retire no matter what the doctors said. Against their orders, he challenged me to a match at the next PPV Unforgiven, but since WWE officials wouldn't sanction the match, it would only be allowed to happen if Shawn signed a waiver stating that if he was seriously injured, nobody at the company would be held responsible.

At a *Raw* in Indianapolis, Vince told me I would be working twice at Unforgiven. First off I would do the unsanctioned match with Shawn with the finish being him kicking the ever-living shit out of me to get his revenge for all of the horrible atrocities I had committed on him and his family. Then I would come back and work again in the main event (and there it is again) in the Championship Scramble, a slightly confusing concept where five superstars would come to the ring in five-minute intervals until everyone was fighting each other at once. Then, whoever got the last pin before the time ran out would end up as the World Champion.

I wasn't supposed to be officially in the match, but I'd replace CM Punk, who would be deemed unable to compete after being attacked backstage earlier in the night. Got all that? I was confused too, but what Vince said afterward didn't confuse me in the least.

"You will go over in the match and become the new WWE Champion."

Chris Jericho was going to be the new WWE Champion? I had been waiting to hear him say those words since I dropped the Undisputed Championship to HHH at WrestleMania 18 back in 2002.

Finally, six years and five months later, I was getting another shot at the ultimate prize in my business. Even though I was technically a three-time World Champion (WCW title from The Rock 11/2001, WCW title from The Rock 12/2001, WWE title from Steve Austin 12/2001), it had been a long time since I'd held the gold. And the first three times, I wasn't really a top guy anyway, but this time was different. I was the most hated heel in the company embroiled in the hottest feud in years (veteran Blackjack Lanza told me it was the best feud in WWE history), and on certain nights I believed I was the best sports entertainer in the world. It was my time, and now (after almost getting a pay cut before I left the WWE in 2005), I was going to be THE MAN.

The best part was I knew I deserved it.

My getting this ipso facto promotion to World Champion was also a testament to the work Shawn and I had done. When we started our story line, I was the Intercontinental Champion, scheduled to do a quick turn on Shawn with a one-match blow-off. But Shawn had done everything in his power to put me over and now I was embroiled in the angle of my career.

The unsanctioned match was made official during an in-ring contract signing on *Raw* that was one of my favorite performances ever. I sat at the table that had been set up in the ring across from HBK and never looked him in the face once. I totally avoided eye contact and it came off so slimy, such a cowardly reaction after all I had done to him. I showed no remorse, no repentance for punching his wife, offered no apology for messing up his eye, and made no excuses for anything that had happened.

Shawn stewed silently as I signed the contract, but the moment I did, he attacked, throwing me out of the ring and flying out after me. But he landed awkwardly on the floor and immediately grabbed his elbow, leaving me to scuttle to the safety of the backstage door.

I thought nothing of it until I found him in the trainer's room afterward, grimacing in pain as Doc Amann twisted and turned his arm in a multide of directions, deducing that he may have suffered a torn tricep.

A torn tricep sounded pretty serious . . . and it was.

If Shawn had torn his tricep, it meant immediate surgery and a four-to-six-month recovery period. It meant our angle was over. And it meant I wouldn't be ending up as the World Champion.

My cell phone rang and when I saw the name SHAWN MICHAELS on the screen, I answered with bated breath. I'd been waiting all week to find out if his tricep injury was real or prognosis negative (or was it *Rochelle Rochelle*). Thankfully, it was prognosis positive (the sequel) and I proceeded to do the Future World Champ Dance around my living room.

If you want to know what it is, just ask me about it the next time we meet. And trust me, it's much better than the Nitro Dance.

It turned out that Shawn had only suffered a partial tricep tear and would be totally fine for our match on Sunday. The Lord had come through and answered both of our prayers, although if I'd known then what Shawn was going to do to me, I might've had a different prayer request.

The unsanctioned match was barbarically brutal and one of the best I've ever had. During my prematch promo, I again showed no remorse and proceeded to blame everything that had gone down on Shawn and his fans, declaring that I was proud of what I'd done to him and his family.

That was enough to send him completely over the edge and he totally dominated me—or maybe *massacred* might be a better word. He was beastly in his battery (awesome alliteration), never letting up as he relentlessly pounded me from the mount like he was a UFC fighter.

I eventually stopped him and climbed up the top rope, but he bashed me in the head with a chair and sent me crashing through a table that had been set up earlier. I'd never bumped backward through a table before and I was a little nervous, but it was postioned perfectly, allowing me to land directly in the middle and break it completely in two. The crowd roared its approval as I sold the effects of the fall, with the outer band that encircled the edge of the table wrapped around my forehead like a plastic crown of thorns.

Shawn was wearing street-fighting clothes (I thought it would be cheeky if I wore my wrestling trunks, as if I was underestimating the viciousness of the match), so he took off his belt and whipped me like a redheaded mule. He was relentless with his strikes and must have lashed me a dozen times. Have you ever been whipped with a leather belt? It hurts! The crowd could feel (and hear) every blow, due to the loud crack that emanated off my poor back every time Shawn punished my exposed flesh. The massive welts that were rising on my back added to the effect and there was nothing "sports entertainment" about them.

As he annihilated me with pure rage, in classic HBK fashion, he added an extra element of emotion that took things to yet another level.

He started crying.

It was pure genius. Even though he was getting the revenge that he and the audience wanted him to get, in the end, it accomplished nothing. Just like when Maximus kills Commodus at the end of *Gladiator* and gets revenge on the man who murdered his family, it still didn't bring them back. Shawn would have to live with what I'd done to his wife for the rest of his life, and the emotion and facial expressions that he displayed during that match were nothing short of masterful. It was one of his finest hours and the perfect example of why I've always felt that if Shawn chose to pursue acting, he would be very succcesful in Hollywood.

He continued to pound me, with tears streaming down his face, until the referee stopped the match in a turnaround of our finish from a few months earlier. Despite the victory, Shawn was a defeated man battling with his own conscience over what had happened. Meanwhile, I was beaten, bruised, and scarred as blood dripped out of my nose. But the night wasn't over.

HBK beats the hell out of me during the unsanctioned match. Notice his heavily taped-up elbow due to the feared torn tricep. Jess took this picture from the front row.

I went to the dressing room and waited for my turn to enter the Scramble, with the blood still drying on my face. I decided not to wash it off, change my wrist tape, or fix my hair, because I wanted to come back to the ring the exact same mess I was when I'd left it. Nobody was going to forget the beating Shawn had given me.

The scramble match was supposed to include Rey Mysterio, Batista, Kane, JBL, and World Champion CM Punk, but Punk was taken out of the match by a Randy Orton attack earlier in the show and nobody knew who was going to replace him. Every five minutes a new competitor came into the fray, until I eventually staggered out last. I was only in the match for a few minutes but was able to pin Kane for the three-count after he was powerbombed by Batista just as the clock ran out. That was enough to earn me the World Championship for the fourth time.

I clutched the title to my chest as I walked out of the ring with a gloating smirk on my bloody face. The crowd was agog (froot word) over what had happened and silently watched me celebrate my victory, aghast (another froot word) that the most hated man in the company was now the WWE champion.

It was kind of a tradition that when someone was going to become the champion, they would have their family there to celebrate. One of my biggest regrets about winning the Undisputed Championship in 2001 is that none of mine were with me, because I wasn't completely sure I was going to win the title. I wasn't told for sure until the day of the show that I was going over (as described in my riveting second book, *Undisputed*, available now via the barter system), so I didn't have the chance to fly Jessica or my dad in to witness it. But I wasn't going to make the same mistake twice and it was special to have them in the front row to watch me capture the championship the fourth time. It was even more special to celebrate my victory in the Championship Scramble at the PPV with a Heartland Scramble at Denny's, which was a hell of a lot better than the cold Domino's pizza I had eaten after I won the title in 2001.

CHAPTER 10

Broken Teeth

Vince wanted Shawn and me to blow off our feud in a ladder match in the main event of the No Mercy PPV in Portland, Oregon. Neither of us were thrilled when we heard his idea, even though it was a no-brainer as an attraction since Shawn was known as the King of the Ladder match, and I was no slouch in that department either. After all, my ladder match with Chris Benoit for the Intercontinental Championship in the 2001 Royal Rumble is considered a classic as well.

We were hesitant at first because we knew how much of a toll those matches can take on your body, yet we also knew how important it was to main-event a PPV in a world title match. It was the ultimate testament to our work that this angle was going to culminate in a battle for the championship. How much frooter could it get? (It got a little better when "All Nightmare Long" by Metallica was added as the theme song for No Mercy. The thought that one of my lifelong favorite bands was providing the sound track for my main-event championship PPV match was surreal on many counts.)

We had another outstanding thirty-minute match (that's four in a row for those of you keeping track) that was meticulously constructed to not feature a bunch of crazy bumps. Just like Benoit and I had in 2001,

Shawn and I used the ladder mostly as a weapon to focus on the brutality of the match. However, it worked a little too well when my teeth got knocked out.

I forgot just how dangerous a ladder can be, how it can bite you quickly and harshly at any time, and I paid the price for it. When I pulled the ladder over the second rope with the intention of Shawn slingshotting it into my face, I didn't get my hand up to protect myself quick enough and it hit me square in the mouth. My knees went weak as I spit out large chunks of broken teeth, probing the newly uneven edges with my tongue to gauge how badly they had been damaged.

I looked at myself in the Tron and saw that one tooth had almost completely disappeared and another was broken in two. Even scarier was that with the missing tooth and the intense look on my face, I looked exactly like Chris Benoit. It was if the ghost of his image had morphed directly onto mine, like I'd been possessed. It was an eerie feeling, to say the least.

The legimate loss of my teeth added even more fervor to the match and drew the crowd in even further. This wasn't two guys "playing" wrestling . . . we had a serious score to settle, and blood had been shed, Jerry.

The match was spectacular as we pulled out all the stops in a unique, inventive way: Shawn pushed me backward off the top rope as I held the ladder and then dropped an elbow onto both; turned my belly-to-back suplex off the top of a ladder into a crossbody, causing both of us to crash through the announce desk. I hit him in the face with a ladder as he was about to superkick me and Lionsaulted onto one that was draped over his prone body.

But the finish was the crème de la crème of creativity, as the two of us stood on top of the ladder, clutching each end of the title in a midair tug-of-war, fifteen feet in the air. I held on to my end of the title with one hand, arching my body backward as the crowd screamed, willing me to lose my grip and fall. Finally, I pulled myself back up and bashed Shawn in the face with the plate of the belt. He held on for a few more seconds before toppling off the ladder, leaving me clear to unhook the title. With that win, the best story line of my career was over.

Doing my best Lloyd Christmas impersonation after having my teeth broken in half by an errant ladder shot. Both Ash and Andy Summers aren't too happy about it.

I wasn't the only one who felt that way, as Jericho vs. Michaels won the feud of the year in the *Wrestling Observer*, *Pro Wrestling Illustrated*, and WWE.com year-end awards (I think we won an Emmy in Luxembourg as well). The ladder match also won the 2008 Match of the Year in the *Observer* and *PWI* awards (I consider it to be one of the best ladder matches of all time), and I was voted the 2008 Wrestler of the Year in the *Observer* by the fans and my peers, which was one of the most prestigious accolades you can receive in the business.

It had taken me eighteen years, but I'd finally become the Chris Jericho that I had always wanted to be. My work rate, understanding of the business, ring psychology, character, promos, image, attitude—everything had peaked. I had shown flashes of it in the past but truly understood what being a main-event superstar was.

Vince knew it too, for his whole demeanor toward me changed and our relationship strengthened almost instantly. There was no more intimidation, no more insults, no more dismissing my ideas. I had become one of his most valuable players.

Over my fourteen years of working for the WWE, I've forgotten more matches than I can remember, but I'll never forget that angle with Shawn. Yet it was only when I started writing this book and revisiting the details that I realized how damn special it really was. We created and executed a money-drawing feud that organically grew and built for SEVEN months before culminating in a main-event PPV match for the world title. When does that ever happen in this day and age?? It doesn't. And that's why I think WWE should assemble all of the matches and promos from our angle and produce a special on it for their network or release it on a DVD.

I'd buy it. Wouldn't you?

CHAPTER 11

Seven Million Dollars

When I heard WWE head lawyer Jerry McDevitt's voice on the other end of the phone, I knew something serious was up. McDevitt only dealt with the heavy-hitter legal issues within the company.

"Hi, Chris. Just wanted to inform you that we have recived a deposition from a lawyer in California saying that you're being sued."

Sued? Hmmm, that was interesting but it wasn't the first time. "Really? How much am I getting sued for?"

"Seven million dollars."

Stop. Hold On. Stay In Control.

SEVEN MILLION DOLLARS!!?? Was this some kind of rib?

McDevitt wasn't joking as he explained that I had done a "Highlight Reel" back in 2005 with Cena as my guest. During the ensuing brawl, John threw me over the top rope and I landed on a cable runner, who was paying no attention to what was going on and didn't even try to get out of the way. Luckily, I didn't hurt myself, but I lost my temper and supposedly dragged the guy across the floor, cursing him out the whole time.

I remembered nothing about the incident and I had to find the segment on YouTube to see just what I'd done. It made me laugh because, besides using my impressive Manitoban strength to move the guy a scant fifteen inches (at the most skinning his wittle kneesie), I hadn't done much assaulting at all.

The guy had filed his lawsuit claiming that he wasn't able to work anymore due to the effects of my "vicious attack" and was asking for seven million clams in quittance. Might I remind you he was a cable runner, so even if I had hung, drawn, and quartered him, there is no way this guy, his mother, his brother, his entire high school graduating class, and the Six Million Dollar Man would've made seven million dollars combined in their entire lifetimes. So where did he come up with that figure in the first place?!

Not to mention the guy had hired a dodgy Saul Goodman–type lawyer who had already been disbarred for shady lawsuits. McDevitt assured me the case would get thrown out and I would be free and clear, but there was still that sliver of doubt in the back of my head. What if I lost the case and was legally bound to give this guy seven million dollars? That type of verdict would leave me and my family totally broke.

I would lose everything!

The prospect of bankruptcy horrified me, and I spent the next few days preparing for my imminent financial fleecing. I had visions of my family and me living in the ghetto, wearing barrels around our waists with a pair of rope suspenders holding them up. I'd have to busk in front of the bus station, playing "Kumbaya" for spare change just to be able to afford ramen noodles for dinner. I'd have to teach my kids how to hip-hop dance so they could do street performances as I passed the hat. I'd have to travel in the dead of night in an empty freight train car with a kerchief containing all of my worldly possessions tied to the end of a stick slung over my shoulder! I'd have to . . .

The phone rang and I was told the case had been dropped and wouldn't resurface again. I was ecstatic, but I wondered how the WWE was able to resolve the lawsuit so quickly. I asked Vince about it a few days later and he explained he had a "no tolerance" policy toward lawsuits.

"Most of these guys file bullshit suits, hoping that we will pay them twenty grand or whatever for them to go away. But if I did that with every lawsuit we got, it would cost a fortune. So we never pay out anything. I would rather spend hundreds of thousands of dollars on lawyer and court fees than voluntarily pay any of these assholes one dime."

I was glad his policy worked, but if I had known how much stress the little bastard was going to cause me, I would've done things differently. Instead of dragging him across the floor, I would've given him a hard kick to the stone.

CHAPTER 12

All Sold Out

Winning the world title six years and five months after I had it last was a real monkey off my back. Within my first two years of being in the WWE, I had beaten The Rock and Stone Cold Steve Austin in the same night to become the first ever Undisputed Champion in history (if I had a dollar for every time I've said that . . .), but since then, I hadn't done anything close to that level.

Sure, I won a bunch of secondary titles but I hadn't reclaimed the big prize, and quite honestly, I wasn't happy with my Undisputed title reign either. Cleaning up Lucy the Dog's shit and being Stephanie McMahon's lackey really wasn't my idea of how a world champ should be portrayed. If winning that title was my legacy in the WWE, I would've been the "Gangnam Style" one-hit wonder of wrestling.

Not to trivialize it, but as much of an honor as it is, anybody could win the world title one time. Look at David Arquette. But winning it a second time, well, that showed that Vince really had faith in you. The first time was almost an experiment to see if a performer could handle it, what they would do with it, and how the crowd would respond to it. But the second time you were made champion was the proof that you really deserved it and could make the company money by holding it. Therefore, by winning the title again, my legacy was now going to be spelled Y2J, not PSY.

But just because I'd regained my world title status, it didn't mean I was always going to be living in palaces with kings and queens. Sometimes I was still going to be sleeping in the gutter, eating pork and beans (Dusty Rhodes TM) . . . or sleeping on a hotel lobby floor, if you weel.

I had just finished my match in Springfield, Missouri, and had a five-hour drive to Cape Girardeau for a show at five P.M. the next day. There weren't a lot of places to stay along the journey, so I decided I would just drive all the way that night. But it was a dismal drive along a miserable two-lane back road that twisted and turned through rural areas. It actually creeped me out to think what might happen if I ran out of gas or slid into the ditch in this *Albino Farm*–esque (cheap plug) terrain, with the trailer parks and weird shacklike houses flanking the road.

Even worse, it was snowing hard and the roads were icy, which forced me to plod along the long and winding road at a snail's pace. So it was almost five A.M. when I pulled into the Cape Girardeau Holiday Inn as the snow sentries towered over me, watching my every move.

I trudged into the lobby and asked for a room.

"Sorry, sir, we're all sold out."

That's the worst thing you can be told at five A.M. and I'll tell you why. If ONE hotel is sold out, that usually means that ALL the hotels in the area are sold out. Sure enough, I went into three other places and all of them were booked—a result of the huge snowstorm that had knocked out the power in most of the homes in the area. This was bad news for me, as I was cold and tired with nowhere to go, and even the arena was closed at this hour. I got out the phone book and called the rest of the five hotels listed, only to hear the same answer.

After hearing that yet another hotel was sold out, I asked the lady at the front desk of the Drury Inn I was in if there were any other options in town and she said, "Well I know the YMCA has set up a shelter with cots and blankets. You can always go down there?"

Stay in a YMCA on cots and blankets? I was the damn WWE World Champion and I was going to do no such thing! So I did the only thing left a champion could do. . . . I begged.

"Madame, can you please help me? I'm with the WWE and I'm actually in the main event here tomorrow at the Enormodome and I need a place to stay. Are you sure you don't have any room at all for me?" I batted my eyelashes and squeezed my tits together, hoping to seduce her with my boyish charm.

It worked and it turned out she did have some extra room for me— in the conference area.

She offered to let me sleep under the big desk they used for meetings in the boardroom, but only until seven thirty A.M. That was when her boss started her shift and apparently wouldn't be happy if she found out I was crashing in there. I didn't care what time the boss arrived. She was going to have to pick me up over her shoulder and carry me out herself if she wanted me out of there that early in the morning. Once I crashed, I intended to stay that way until whatever time I damn well decided to wake up.

I followed her into the boardroom, where she grabbed a pillow and blanket and graciously helped me assemble my makeshift bed under the desk. She wished me good night, turned off the lights, and closed the door.

I lay on the hard floor, staring up at the underside of the table, smelling stale cigarette smoke and coffee that had probably been spilled on the carpet during the Nixon administration. In the light of the moon shining through the window, I could see wadded-up pieces of gum stuck there in all colors of the rainbow. What kind of meetings had taken place in this boardroom and why had there been so much gum chewing?!

It wasn't the most comfortable of accommodations, but it was better than the backseat of a frozen Taurus, and eventually I fell asleep.

When I was shaken awake seemingly minutes later, the sun was shining through the windows.

"Excuse me, sir, you can't sleep here anymore."

Apparently, this was the dreaded BOSS and, as promised, she wanted me out. I glanced at my phone and saw it was seven thirty A.M. (BOSS sure was punctual), so there was no way I was ready to get up off the floor. I was tired, sore, stiff, cranky, and not interested in what BOSS had to say.

"Lady, with all due respect, after the night I've had, you're gonna have to call the cops to come drag me out of here if you want me to leave." I closed my eyes, rolled over, and went back to sleep, not caring if BOSS called the cops or not. At least I'd have a heated cell to sleep in if she did.

But she must've decided I wasn't worth the trouble, so I was able to get a few more hours' sleep after all. When I finally got up off the floor, stiffer than ever, I caught a glance of myself in a mirror on the wall. My hair stood up in corkscrews, there were bags under my eyes big enough to pack my wrestling boots in, and the whites of my eyes were now bright red.

I opened the door and walked out into the lobby, which had transformed into the breakfast area. It was a packed house that morning and every table was occupied with people eating their Cheerios and pressed-egg patties. Every one of them paused in mid-chew to take a glance at the crazy homeless man who had just staggered into the room. If there had been music playing, it would've stopped with a screech as the needle was dragged off the record.

I made my way through the packed tables and a little boy about ten years old tugged his dad's shirt excitedly. "Dad. . . . DAD!! That's Chris Jericho!! He's the WWE Champion!!"

I grabbed a bagel off the counter and stared at him with crimson eyes.

"Yes, I am, kid . . . yes, I am," I said and walked the fuck out of the Cape Girardeau Drury Inn forever.

CHAPTER 13

Angel of Vince

The original plan was for me to hold on to the title until November, when I would drop it to Cena at Survivor Series. But Vince was trying to build the brand name of Cyber Sunday, a show in which the fans could vote for who they wanted to see wrestle. The "fans decide the matches" concept originally started with the Taboo Tuesday PPV in 2004, where I was the Intercontinental Champion, and fans decided on my opponent out of a possible twenty candidates. Shelton Benjamin won and I was forced to call the whole match in the ring (for the full story, check out my classic home improvement manual, *Undisputed*, available on Craigslist), which ended up being really good. This time I knew Batista was my opponent, but it was the special guest referee who was to be voted on. The choices were Randy Orton, Shawn Michaels, and Steve Austin. Vince was pretty sure that Austin would get the vote (over Shawn) and wanted to reward the fans for their participation. So he made the decision that Big Dave would go over on me at Cyber Sunday and I'd win the title back a week later on *Raw*. This type of title flip-flopping was in vogue in the late 2000s and even though it seemed like the wrong decision to cut off my momentum solely for a PPV gimmick, it technically meant that I was going to become the World Champion for the fifth time. That was OK by me.

Our Cyber Sunday match ended with a myriad of interference and run-ins from the other ref candidates and JBL (who, along with Shawn and Randy, were the only three guys I'd had angles with since my return a year earlier), with the end result of Austin making the three-count after a Batista powerbomb. The match was good and the dips and doodles were fun, but all I could think of was getting the title back and continuing my roll.

The following Monday, true to his word, Vince booked our rematch in a steel cage on the 800th episode of *Raw* from Tampa. It was a smart way for the two of us to have an exciting match and allow me to regain without Batista having to get pinned. Dave seemed happy with the plan originally but came to me later saying he didn't feel comfortable with the way we had mapped things out.

"It feels weird for us to have a cage match with no blood."

There would be no blood in this (or any other) match by decree of Vince, who, in order to attract high-dollar sponsors, had banned bleeding of any kind from the WWE months earlier (after HBK bled a gusher in our PPV match).

"Vince is dead set against blood, Dave. Do what you have to do, just don't tell me anything more about it." That was the last we spoke of it.

We had an excellent match and probably the best cage match I've ever had, made even better by the fact that it was for the title and that Jess and my family were once again sitting in the front row. Cage matches are quite a simple story to tell in theory: All you have to do is attempt to climb the cage as much as possible and tease the audience as to who will be able to get out first.

We had built the match perfectly and the crowd was on the edge of their seats as I climbed up the ten-foot-tall fence and put one leg over the scaffoldlike top. Batista caught me and pulled me on his shoulders as if he were going to powerbomb me from the top rope all the way down to the mat. I held on desperately and, with a last-ditch effort, pulled a steel ring off the cage rigging (I'd hidden it there earlier in the day) and used it like a pair of brass knuckles.

I nailed Dave in the forehead a few times, and as he fell to the ground, I pulled myself over the top of the cage and hung there dramatically like I was too scared to let go. The Animal scrambled up the side and stuck his hand through the top of the cage and bottom of the scaffold, grabbing me by the throat. He grimaced like a gargoyle as a thick line of blood streamed down his forehead. I thought, *Wow, he's actually bleeding.*

He tried to pull me back over the top by my hair, but I swung off the side and drove my feet into his knee. He loosened his grip and I dropped ten feet to the floor and won the match, much to the dismay of the fans. Jericho had done it again. . . . I was the new World Heavyweight Champion for the fifth time!

I was on a natural high, but the moment I walked through the curtain, I could tell by everyone's demeanor that something heavy was going down. The match producer, Dean Malenko, approached me like he'd just seen a ghost.

"Vince is furious that Batista got color. He's blaming me. Did you know?"

I guess the answer to that is . . . kind of?

I knew Dave was thinking about it from our earlier conversation but hadn't heard anything since, and I remembered noticing the stream of blood traveling down his face and having no idea when or how it happened. But even though I didn't know much about Dave's plan, I can say with total certainty that neither Dean nor referee Mike Chioda knew anything about it at all.

"Vince got up and stormed off," Dean continued wanly. "Said he won't talk to any of us about this until next week. He was really pissed off."

Talk about putting the damper on a great night. This reminded me of the night when Benoit and I beat HHH and Austin to become the tag-team champions back in 2001 (in what some say was the best match in

Raw history). The joyous moment had been ruined by the extenuating circumstances of Triple H tearing his quad and writhing in pain on the dressing room floor afterward.

Between Vince's reaction and the thought of waiting a whole week to find out what our penance would be, I was a nervous wreck. I couldn't wait that long with such a dark cloud hanging over my head, so I decided to call him.

"Hey, Vince," I said when he answered the phone. "I didn't know what Dave was going to do, but I take responsibility as the veteran in the match."

"Bullshit!!" Vince barked at me. "I'm so fucking angry with you right now! I don't want to talk to you. We'll deal with this next Monday. Don't call me again." His words hung in the air like drying laundry as the phone went dead. I looked at the screen and saw the call had lasted eighteen seconds.

Over the next seven days, I awaited my sentence from the billionaire judge and jury like a prisoner on death row awaiting my inevitable execution. In the meantime we traveled to the UK for a tour, and the following Monday, *Raw* was in Manchester, England. After the show was over, the four guilty parties were summoned into Vince's office, where a row of chairs was set up in a semicircle around a big-screen television. John Laurinaitis was waiting for us, and I sat down in silence between Dean and Dave, while Chioda took a seat on the end. It was a nerve-racking few minutes, sitting there waiting for Vince and wondering what was about to happen.

Finally he walked in and addressed Laurinaitis, completely ignoring the rest of us.

"John, play the footage."

Johnny walked over to the DVD player and pressed a few buttons, but nothing happened. He bent down over the machine and tried to start it again, with the same results. The mood in the room lightened when Vince walked over and tried to figure out the problem with no luck either. They were like Moe and Curly trying to figure out how to turn on a light switch.

Finally, Chioda got up and started the machine in one-two-three seconds (which was like a guy throwing the switch on his own electric chair). The footage started and it was one of the weirdest things I've ever experienced. It was an edited montage of Batista's crime from a multitude of angles; hard camera, side camera, overhead camera, and one from a camera in the high corner of the arena that I never even knew existed. WTF?

Batista and I battle for the world title in Tampa, as the mysterious hidden UFO camera films the entire thing. Another Jess front-row capture.

Was this secret camera filming at all times? If it was, I suddenly regretted the time in Fresno when I picked my nose in the empty stands. . . . Had that been filmed too?

We watched the footage of us struggling on the top of the cage and Dave pulling me onto his shoulders to give me the top rope powerbomb. I grabbed the steel ring and bashed him on the forehead and then tossed it over the cage onto the ground. Right at that moment, Dave made himself bleed. I had no idea when he did it while we were working the match, but now I saw it plain as day from a number of various angles. What made the montage even more bizarre was the bright circle that had been added around Dave's head to highlight his actions. It was like the type of graphic you see on a UFO show, when they pinpoint the flying saucer in the sky and show you exactly where you are supposed to be looking.

How much time had Vince's editing team spent on this? I mean, it was a cage match, not the Zapruder film! It was as if he wanted to shove what had happened down our throats and prove that he had gotten to the bottom of the mystery. But there wasn't much of a mystery to get to the bottom of, because Dave never denied what he'd done. Not that he could have anyway, as the cut was right in the middle of his forehead and stood out like a sore thumb on his bald dome.

Before we went into the office, Dave told me he was prepared to take full responsibility for his actions, and I appreciated his gesture, but I was ready to take my share of the blame as well. However, I did feel bad for Dean and Chioda, who were only guilty by association.

After the Batista Blades/Ancient Aliens highlight reel ended, Vince addressed us sternly.

"As you all know, there is a strict ban on bleeding in the WWE and you have broken this rule. I could fire all of you for this, but I'm not going to. Instead, I'm gonna hit you where it hurts."

Dave broke the silence and told Vince that the rest of us had no knowledge of what he did.

"Bullshit." Vince spat out angrily. "Enough of this 'sticking together with the boys' mentality. As far as I'm concerned, you're all guilty. Dean, if you didn't know about this, you should've guessed it was going to happen! It was your match!"

Dean looked on helplessly, even though Vince's statement made no sense. But Mr. McMahon had gone past the point of no return. He was furious and was ready to dole out some serious punishment.

"The worst thing is none of you even called me to talk to me about what happened. None of you had the balls to own up to this!"

I put my hand in the air even though I wasn't in school, as it still felt like the politest way to get Vince's attention.

"Um, Vince, I called you last Monday night to talk and you hung up on me."

His eyes burned a hole through me for cutting him off, but he acquiesced.

"OK, nobody called me BUT Jericho. Doesn't change the fact that you directly ignored my rules and could've cost me millions of dollars from sponsors. I spent the week thinking what I was going to do about this and I decided I will be fining all of you."

A fine? I spent all week worrying about what was going to happen to me and all he was going to do was fine us? Ha-ha, bring it on, Vincenzo!

"Dave, I'm going to fine you one hundred thousand dollars."

The smile dripped down my face like ice cream on a warm summer's afternoon. One hundred thousand dollars? I could barely compute the figure as my mind calculated how many bumps Dave would have to take to make up that amount. I never in my wildest dreams thought he would get fined that much. . . . Could Vince even do that?

"I can fine you however much I want," Vince said, seemingly reading my mind. Dave remained stoic, saying nothing.

Then Vince's gaze shifted over to me. My body was numb and my throat was dry as I waited for his next verdict. Surely he wouldn't fine me a hundred grand too . . . or would he?

Vince stared at me with his steely, beady eyes and said, "Chris, I'm going to fine you . . ."

This was it. I watched his mouth and waited for him to put his pinky to his lip and form the words *ONE HUNDRED THOUSAND DOLLARS*.

The tension filled the air like toxic smoke and I felt as nervous as a contestant on *Dancing with the Stars* waiting to hear if I would be advancing to the next round. (Clever Editor's Note: This is even more foreshadowing, kids.)

"I'm going to fine you . . . five thousand dollars."

Five thousand dollars! Five thousand doll hairs? Ha-ha, I felt like I'd received a pardon from the governer and wanted to jump into Vince's arms so he could swing me to and fro like a baby.

I broke into a huge smile and I was about to say, *Five grand? I'll give you ten!* until I noticed Vince's stern look hadn't changed.

"Something funny, Chris?"

"No, sir," I said, shaking my head feverishly, realizing he could easily change his mind. I decided to shut my trap until the Angel of Vince took his attention elsewhere. He did and told Dean and Chioda that they were going to be fined five thousand bones as well. Then he said a pretty damn froot thing.

"Once I leave this room, I'm totally going to forget about this whole incident. I don't want to hear or talk about this again. Understand?"

We all nodded, and Vince and Johnny walked out of the room. The four of us stared at our feet and I noticed I was the only one of us who felt relieved about our punishment. Five grand was a lot of money, but it was a small price to pay, considering a few moments earlier I'd been convinced I was going to be hammered with the same one-hundred-large punishment as Dave. (I'm convinced I would've been if I hadn't called Vince after *Raw* that night.) While Dean and Mike were down in the dumps about the five grand, Dave's expression hadn't changed the whole time. When he finally spoke, he told us he was going to pay all of our fines and there would be no debate about it.

It was a surprising decree, but it showed Batista's integrity. He was taking full responsibility for his actions and it was costing him 115 grand. I walked out of that room with a whole lot of respect for Dave Batista. He's a stand-up guy and that's the bottom line 'cause Jeri-Cold said so.

A few minutes later I saw Vince in the parking lot of the arena, waiting for his limo, and he motioned me over.

"Give me a hugski, kid," he said with a smile. I did, and as I was walking away he yelled out, "Don't cause me any more trouble in the future!"

"I'll try not to, boss!" I laughed.

I would fail miserably at that request soon enough.

CHAPTER 14

On Your Knees!

The Batista debacle aside, my relationship with Vince continued to strengthen. He started putting me in more elaborate scenarios, where I got to show off not only my wrestling skills but my acting skills as well.

Vince had written a story line in which he left Stephanie in charge of *Raw* alone. She and I always had great chemistry when we worked together in the past, but the dynamic had changed with her as the baby-face and me as the hard-core heel. We had a few confrontations leading to a final showdown on *Raw* in Sioux City, Iowa. I had found out that Vince was returning the next week, so I was cajoling (amazing word) and antagonizing her, criticizing all of her decisions past, present, and future. She took all the abuse she could handle and ended up firing me on national TV. I stood in shock as she walked out of the ring and left the crowd to serenade me with a rousing rendition of "Na Na Hey Hey Kiss Him Goodbye." (Any idea who sang that song?)

One week later, in Chicago, Vince returned and I kissed his ass, trying to convince him to rehire me. Vince was unimpressed and said that since he and Steph were now running *Raw* together, all of her decisions were final, but if she would consider giving me a second chance, I could be reinstated. Steph then suggested that if I gave her a heartfelt apology, she would consider it. (The answer is Steam, by the way.)

It was such a great position for me to be in as a performer, especially since the character I was playing had shown no regret for anything he'd done over the last six months. Yet there I was, having to eat some serious crow and humble myself by apologizing to my bosses. I made a pathetic first attempt as I pulled a Fonz and acted like I couldn't say the word *sorry*.

"Stephanie, I am truly suuuu . . . suuuu . . . suuu . . ."

The crowd ate it up with a spoon.

I finally delivered a half-assed apology, but neither Steph nor the fans were buying it. She told me to try it again with feeling, but before I could continue, the always amazing Chicago crowd took over. They started in with a huge chant of "ON YOUR KNEES!" and I couldn't believe my good fortune in having this hot crowd chanting orders at me whilst my boss stood in the ring. We were scheduled to end the segment at this point, but I took control and stared at Steph. She knew exactly what I was thinking and asked me, "What are they saying, Chris?"

The chant got louder as I protested, insisting that bowing down to her wasn't necessary. Of course, the fans disagreed and I took full advantage of their on-the-spot audience participation. I glanced nervously from side to side and grimaced with annoyance as I slowly bent down and took a knee like a football player on a punt return. Then I stood back up again, milking it for all that it was worth.

"ON YOUR KNEES! ON YOUR KNEES!"

Finally I crouched down on both knees, and the crowd roared its approval as Vince and Stephanie looked on with amusement. I delivered an even less sincere apology when I explained, "I have a certain gift and when someone like me has this gift that makes them the best at what they do, sometimes it makes them come across a little arrogant even though it's warranted. If I have said or done anything to offend anyone, well, then I apologize." Such a smarmy smart-ass way to weasel out a message of repentance. But the McMahons (and the fans) had gotten what they wanted and I was hired back into the WWE.

Backstage, Vince complimented me on my acting prowess and told me he was impressed with my ability to adapt to any situation. I'm sure my performance that night helped him decide I was the right guy for his next very important mission.

CHAPTER 15

Premature Announceulation

I had just been eliminated by The Undertaker from the 2009 Royal Rumble in Detroit and was changing in the locker room. I got a text from my wise cousin Chad, who informed me that Mickey Rourke had just challenged me to a match at WrestleMania. Huh? Why would Mickey Rourke do that? Sure, he was in wrestling mode after just delivering the performance of his career as Randy "The Ram" in Darren Aronofsky's masterpiece *The Wrestler*, but why was he challenging me? I gave Chad a call and he wisely told me Rourke had been on the red carpet at the Screen Actors Guild Awards and had dropped the bomb that he was "going to kick Chris Jericho's ass" at WrestleMania. I had no idea what he was talking about, but it was froot that Mickey had dropped my name instead of mentioning Austin or Cena.

The plot thickened when Vince told me after the show what was going down. He had brokered a deal between the WWE and Mickey Rourke's agents for Mickey to have a match at Mania . . . against me. Rourke had just been nominated for an Academy Award for Best Actor and was the hottest thing in Hollywood. Vince felt I was the perfect guy workwise, promotional-wise, and acting-wise to wrestle him and get the angle over but was annoyed that Rourke had announced the match already since he wasn't planning on starting the story line until after the Oscars in February.

It was a lot to process during one sitting, but when I had a moment to think, I knew how huge an opportunity this was going to be for me. As Rourke's opponent, I was about to be thrust into the Hollywood mainstream as well as having a guaranteed main-event spot for the biggest show of the year. I was ecstatic, until I heard the next day that Rourke's people were furious about Mickey's premature announceulation and wanted him to pull out of WrestleMania. They were concerned that if the Academy knew that Mickey was about to get involved with the low-life denizens of the WWE, it would affect his Oscar chances. I did some digging and found out that their concerns were legit. Apparently, a few years earlier, when Eddie Murphy was up for Best Actor for his performance in the movie *Dreamgirls*, he was considered a shoo-in to win. Then *Norbit* was released and the Hollywood cognescenti balked at giving the prestigious Best Supporting Actor award to a guy who was currently starring as an overweight racial sterotype in a shitty movie, no matter how amazing his performance was in *Dreamgirls*. Maybe that's the actual reason why Murphy ended up losing to Alan Arkin in 2006, but either way, Rourke's people didn't want to take the chance of having the same fate befall their client.

With Rourke's involvement in Mania now in jeopardy before it had even begun, the WWE went into survival mode. The next night on *Raw*, Vince had me do a promo about how everybody was talking about the movie *The Wrestler* and how all of the washed-up wrestlers hanging around the fringes of the WWE loved it, including Ric Flair. I commented on how Flair had given the film a rave review to get over with Rourke, since even though he'd retired a year earlier, he still craved the spotlight. Then I claimed Flair had gotten what he wished for because he'd become friends with Mickey (which was true), but now he needed to teach his buddy to shut his mouth. I rolled the clip of Mickey's comments from the SAG Awards the night before and said, "Your comments have offended me, Rourke. And the last thing you want to do is offend Chris Jericho."

The promo was part damage control, part preventive medicine, as Vince figured since the Rourke was already out of the bag, it was a good idea to tie in Flair and start the angle on our own without Rourke's physical involvement. This way if Mickey (or more accurately, his people) agreed to the match, we would have the jump-start, and if they pulled out, I would already have something going with Flair. But I had no idea what that something would be, since he had been retired by HBK the year before in an incredible match at WrestleMania 24. Vince was adamant that Flair would never wrestle in the WWE again, so how would he fit in if Rourke pulled out?

Mickey still hadn't made his final decision because he still wanted to do the match even though his managers were insisting he cancel, but we moved forward as if he was going to do it. I went and saw *The Wrestler* as research and thought it was excellent. Mickey's performance was mesmerizing, the script well written, but the sad thing was I knew many guys in the business who were like Randy the Ram. Guys whose glory days were long gone but who were still waiting for that last big break. It reminded me of my time in ECW when the roster included up-and-comers like me and RVD, main-eventers like Taz and Sandman, and former major stars whose time had come and gone, like Terry Gordy and Bam Bam Bigelow. The only difference was I wasn't breaking lightbulbs over my head or stapling dollar bills to my face in ECW. (Although I did have a barbed wire death match in Calgary in 1993, so I shouldn't throw stones. Or fireballs in this case.)

What made the movie so special was Rourke's acting, which brought life to such a horribly flawed character. Randy the Ram's eventual fate was a stern warning for me to make sure I never ended up at the bottom of the barrel. However, Mickey already knew what it was like to be there both professionally and personally. At the beginning of his career he had been christened the next Marlon Brando, but after a great start he had made some bad choices with both his roles and his lifestyle and had been banished from leading-man status. He had bounced around for years in B movies and had even gone into professional boxing, but *The Wrestler* gave him a new life and was deemed his big comeback. As a result he had changed his rebellious fuck-you ways and decided he was going to listen to his managers and agents for the first time in his career. It was for that reason that he finally called Vince and told him he wasn't going to do the match.

I was really disappointed; over the last few weeks I'd set my heart on working with him. After watching him actually wrestling in the movie, I knew we could put together a decent five-to-eight-minute match and have some fun. I wished he had just kept his mouth shut and stayed the course with Vince's original plan, but what was done was done. However, all wasn't completely lost, for there was still one last chance to try to talk him into doing the match.

Weeks earlier, Mickey and I had been booked on *Larry King Live* to discuss WrestleMania. Even though Rourke had pulled out, Larry still wanted us on the show. I thought it would be fun to do, as I always enjoyed being Larry's guest and he liked having me on. He even referred to me as "my boy Chris Jericho" when promoting the episode.

Vince wanted me to fly to L.A. to do the show live in the studio, but I had already made plans to see Metallica on the World Magnetic Tour in Chicago. So he arranged for me to do the interview backstage in the Allstate Arena via satellite. And gave me one simple mission:

"I want you to try to goad him into accepting the match. See if you can use his bravado against him and bait him into doing WrestleMania."

That was a challenge I could sink my teeth into and I decided to play it to the fullest extent of my heelness. There would be no kowtowing or ass kissing for Mr. Hollywood. No friendly ribbing or niceties. I was going for the throat and would use all of the dirty tactics I had learned over the years to try and get him to snap.

I got to the Allstate Arena early with my best friend and partner in crime, Speewee, and was escorted to the exact room in the backstage area that we used for catering when we did WWE shows there. It was empty except for the cameras and the equipment that was set up to beam me across the country onto Larry's show. I was able to watch it live on the monitor as I anxiously awaited my turn, which was scheduled near the end of the show.

Mickey was introduced and came across great in answering questions about his start/stop career and his subsequent storied comeback. He was personable and humble, everything he should've been, considering this was the first in-depth interview he'd done since he seemingly fell off the face of the planet years earlier. After a good twenty minutes of banter, Larry brought up that Rourke had been in negotitations with the WWE to actually work a match at WrestleMania, and then introduced me to the show.

I started by saying that I respected what Rourke had done in *The Wrestler* but that he was out of line in challenging me to a match. Mickey was in great spirits and politely admitted immediately that he was a visitor in my world and he had indeed put his foot in his mouth when he challenged me. I'm sure he was coached to say those lines, but I wasn't letting him off that easily and I told him flat-out that if he stepped in my world for real, I would teach him a lesson. Larry, ever the journalist, asked him if he was going to wrestle me. Mickey almost let it slip that he still wanted the match and replied, "If it was up to me . . . ," then paused as his better judgment took control.

King, always a pro, picked up on where this was going. "If it was up to you, Mickey, you'd wrestle him?"

But that bird had flown as Mickey changed his course and smiled. "Like I said, I'm a visitor in his world. Wrestling isn't my thing, but I *was* a professional fighter. Would I box him in a boxing match or a bare-knuckle match? Yeah."

Jackpot! He had taken my bait, hook, line, and sinker, and it was better than I could've imagined. Jericho vs. Rourke in a bare-knuckle brawl at WrestleMania . . . Now, that was money!

Grasping my opportunity, I replied instantly, "Hmmm, a boxing match, huh?"

King muttered, "Ah, here he goes!" but Rourke backtracked and tried to end the segment by calling me brother and wishing me luck at Mania. I didn't have much time as the segment was ending, so I made one more last-ditch effort.

"Like I said, Mr. Rourke [was I on *Fantasy Island* now?], you may respect me and what I do, but I don't have respect for you. I really don't."

Rourke's demeanor changed slightly and I knew I'd gotten him. He was pissed off. I'd barged in during his interview and completely ignored his apology and his attempts to play nice. I'd punked him out and disrespected him to his face on live national TV and there was nothing he could do about it.

"I'm going to take the high road, brother, and wish you luck. You go do your thing."

But I'd drawn blood, so I stayed on him, reminding him of his boxing match or bare-knuckle fight challenge.

"I'll be here, Mr. Rourke . . . waiting. You know where to find me. But be careful what you wish for, because it may come true."

Rourke was over being nice and was stewing as Larry told me to have a good night and enjoy Metallica. Just as we went off the air, Rourke threw out a thinly veiled insult with a straight-faced glare. "You're looking sharp tonight, Chris," something you would say when you're about to take the first swing and start a barroom blitz. When I reminded him I was waiting, his retort was simple and direct.

"Have a good night . . . son."

Aha! He called me son, which was one step away from calling me boy, the ultimate manly cutdown. Had I been sitting next to him in Larry's studio, I think Mickey would've taken a swing at me and that was good enough for me, even though I hadn't been able to get him to agree to a match. Mission accomplished!

The next day, I asked Vince what he thought and he said both he and WWE executive producer Kevin Dunn thought I'd been a little too stiff on Mickey.

"Once you knew he wasn't going to take the match, you should've smiled and let him off the hook." I disagreed and was very satisfied with how I'd stayed in character and hadn't let him off the hook. But I still wanted to thank Mickey for the segment and asked Flair for his number. Flair texted me back and said that I could send all messages to Rourke through him. I found it kind of strange that he wouldn't give me his digits himself, but I wrote a text thanking him and forwarded it over to Ric anyway. I never heard back from him, but I later found out that was because the last thing Mickey wanted from me was a thank-you.

What he wanted was my head on a platter.

After the Rourke confrontation, I took Larry's advice and enjoyed Metallica. They put on an amazing show as always, and afterward I was escorted back to the dressing room area for the VIP after-party. I was a little nervous as they were one of my top three all-time favorite bands (Do you know the other two? Answer at the end of this chapter) and I'd never really met any of them before. Would they be in a bad mood? Or would it be the greatest moment of my life? They always say you should never meet your idols because they may disappoint you, but I was ready to take the chance.

The room was crowded with fans, friends, and dignitaries (where's your crown, King Jericho?), all waiting to say a few words to the band. I noticed guitarist Kirk Hammett, who I'd kind of met once before in 1994 in Atlanta. I had asked him to sign the cast on my broken arm (I'd broken it trying a shooting star press in Knoxville) and he said he would if "I could use his boner as a speed bump." I'm still not sure what he was getting at, and he wasn't either when I asked him about it fourteen years later in Chicago. He said, laughing, "I was really drunk on Frangelico that night." I could relate, considering I had crashed my car and split open my forehead whilst under the influence of said spirit in Calgary back in 1995. (Full versions of both of these stories are available in my book of medieval poetry entitled *A Lion's Tale,* available at a Renaissance fair near you.) Then I saw Lars Ulrich and he was even friendlier. The thing I love about Lars is, when you talk to him, he seems really interested and engaged in the conversation. He'll stand there, head cocked like a cocker spaniel, eyes locked on yours, paying attention to every word you're saying. It also seems that he has a story to tell about every city in the world.

"You're from Winnipeg? River City, right? Cool, that's the home of the Golden Boy. I checked it out once back in '89."

I went into total fanboy mode and told him how much I'd loved them since I was a teenager as he looked on and nodded with a smile. I asked him if he was sick of hearing people say such things and he replied, "In the nineties I was, but now I realize how much of an honor it is to mean so much to people and have such a special place in their lives." It was a really interesting thing to hear, because I feel the same way.

Whenever somebody recognizes me and tells me how big a fan they are or says thanks for all the years of entertainment, I never take that for granted. It really makes me happy to know that I have made somebody's life a little better and means the world to me to hear it. As a matter of fact, if you ever see me on the street and want to say hi, please do!! Tell me Chris sent ya. . . .

I shot the shit with Lars about our favorite heavy metal bands for a few minutes, until I saw the man I'd been waiting to meet for twenty-five years walk into the room.

The mighty Hetfield had arrived.

Ever since I started listening to Metallica in 1984, I'd been enamored of one James Alan Hetfield, the leader, the singer, the main song writer, and the frootest-looking guy I'd ever seen (especially after Cliff Burton died in 1986). I had always related to James's lyrics and knew he'd grown up in a broken home with a sick mother the same way I did. I felt the same pain and in turn was able to harness all the emotions I felt after my parents' divorce and my mom's crippling accident by finding solace in their music. I'd been a die-hard fan since the day I first heard them and my commitment to the band had never wavered through any of the band's phases. I remember going into Records on Wheels (there used to be these things called record stores, kids) in 1984 and looking at the back of the *Kill 'Em All* album, at the picture of the four scruffy-looking bums with zits and teenage mustaches, and liking them instantly. Because they looked just like me. Since that day, Metallica were my indisposable heroes, my gods that never failed, my phantom lords . . . and James was their leader.

And now he was standing only a few feet away from me. I'd been in this position before, when I met Wayne Gretzky in 2002, scared and nervous to approach him but dead set on doing so. However, Hetfield was different, he was . . . well, he was JAMES HETFIELD! I didn't want to come off like a blathering fanboy, but how could I not? I was going to have to play this one frootly.

I approached him slowly and quietly, like Steve Irwin advancing toward a rare poisonous snake.

Crikey, here is the elusive Hetfieldus maximus, *only seen in the catacombs of arenas worldwide. Approach slowly or he will growl in your face and disappear back into hiding, crikey, crikey!*

He glanced at me as I got closer and I knew I'd reached the point of no return.

"Hey, James," I said calmly. "I'm Chris Jericho. Nice to meet you, man."

"Hey. I know who you are," he said with a smile.

Wow . . . James knew who I was? That was an unexpected plus; this was going to be easy!

Then my mind went blank. I felt like I should say something, but I had no idea what. I couldn't wipe the stupid grin off my face or stop shaking his hand. It was awkward and uncomfortable and after being in the public eye for twenty years with millions of fans of my own, I was now totally starstruck.

James knew it too and, thankfully, broke the silence. "Did you have a good time tonight?"

That was all it took to break the floodgates open. I told him that I'd had a blast and proceeded to say everything I'd wanted to tell him since I was thirteen years old. How much Metallica's music had meant to me, how much I related to his lyrics and his story. How he and his band had helped me through so many hard times. How much I admired him as a person for turning his life around in a positive way. After a five-minute soliloquy, I finally got around to saying what I really wanted to say.

"I just want to thank you for all you've done for me."

James continued to smile as he nodded his head and thanked me right back. My confession finished, I put my arm around him and Speewee snapped a picture. I said thanks again and took my leave. Trying to stay froot, I headed toward an empty corner of the room on trembling legs. When I was sure no one could see me, I put my hands on the wall to brace myself and took a deep breath. My heart was pounding and I felt like I was going to cry, because no matter how much I've done or how many places I've been, I'm still a fan. That's why meeting James for the first time was one of the best moments of my life and the memory remains.

CHAPTER 16

Rookie "The Dagger" Sweatboat

After my appearance on *Larry King* as a straight-up heel, Mickey Rourke never responded to my text Flair had forwarded to him. Plus, Vince and Kevin were annoyed at me, and I received tons of backlash from fans via e-mails and social media posts. Due to the deluge of insults and disrespect I showed him, people felt sorry for poor old Mickey and felt I had gone too far.

I disagreed and thought I deserved an Emmy for my acting performance, even though nobody seemed to understand or appreciate my dedication to the craft.

Nobody, that is, except the William Morris Agency, only the biggest talent agency in Hollywood. A few of their top guys had seen me on *King* and wanted to take a meeting with me immediately. I'd had a few agents during my flirtations with acting, but none of them came close to the size or prestige of William Morris. This was my big break! Wait until Hollywood got a load of me. I was ready for my close-up. I was . . .

. . . completely wrong and my delusions of grandeur were shattered like The Rolling Stones when I went for my big meeting, to find out that William Morris had no intention of bringing me in as a client. The agents just wanted to meet me and get a few pictures for their kids because they were big fans of my work in the WWE. Ugh. In the words of Ron Simmons, I could've just mailed them a fuckin' autograph.

When the whole Rourke match fell through, Vince switched over to Plan B. One of his favorite mottos was "Always turn a negative into a positive," and that's exactly what he planned to do. He pitched a scenario where I would continue comparing Flair's career with that of Randy the Ram. Except now I wouldn't just be insulting Flair but all of the other aging legendary WWE superstars who were still a part of the company. Vince's criteria for the legends I'd be antagonizing were:

a) They had to be in the WWE Hall of Fame

and

b) They had to have competed at the first WrestleMania.

Using those guidelines, his idea was I would end up in a 3-on-1 handicap match at WrestleMania 25 against Roddy Piper, Jimmy Snuka, and Greg Valentine.

It seemed like an interesting plan, not as much of a main-event spot as the Rourke scenario, but still an attraction all the same. As a matter of fact, to the fans in the WWE Universe, the handicap match would probably mean more than the Rourke match anyway. The only problem I could see was the quality of the bout. While Piper, Snuka, and Valentine were all good workers in their prime, none of the three moved all that well in 2009. I knew that while the buildup would be great, the match itself had the potential to be rotten.

When I told Vince the match might not be good, his response was classic.

"The match isn't supposed to be good."

Maybe so, but this was WrestleMania we were talking about and I wanted to have the best match possible. So I suggested we use Jerry Law-ler instead of Valentine. Lawler had been lobbying for a Mania match for years and this would be perfect because not only could he still work, he was one of the best talkers of all time.

But Vince shot it down instantly, because Lawler hadn't wrestled in the first WrestleMania. Now, keep in mind these were McMahon's self-imposed rules. We'd never mentioned them in any way on *Raw*, so it's not like there were any real restrictions in place. Vince could put who-ever he wanted in the match, but in his mind they had to fit that exact criteria. So then I thought about suggesting Tito Santana, but after some brainstorming I had an even better idea.

Ricky Steamboat.

Ricky was the perfect third man. He'd just returned to the WWE as a producer, had wrestled in the first WrestleMania, was about to be inducted into the WWE Hall of Fame that year, was one of the greatest workers in the history of the business, and was one of my biggest influ-ences. I mentioned his name and I could see by the look on Vince's face that he thought the idea might work. But there was one major problem.

"Does he own his name?"

I'm not sure of the specifics, but apparently when Ricky got divorced, his ex-wife somehow ended up with the rights to the name Ricky Steamboat and kept it. Ricky hadn't wrestled in years, but if he ever decided to get back in the ring, it seems he'd have to change his name to Rookie "The Dagger" Sweatboat or Rocky "The Draggin'" Streamfloat. So even though Vince liked the idea, we had to obtain further nomenclature knowledge about Ricky before he would sign off on it.

After a few days of waiting, word came back that Ricky had indeed reacquired the rights to his name and was Steamboat once again. So at WrestleMania 25 it was going to be Chris Jericho vs. Roddy Piper, Jimmy Snuka, and Ricky Steamboat with Ric Flair in their corner—a pretty great group of guys to build a story line with. Plus, I was getting the chance to work with one of my all-time heroes and I knew that Steamboat in his fifties was still going to be better than a lot of the current roster.

The plan was I would confront one of the legends every week and bury them to where they would have no choice but to accept my challenge for the handicap match. I was so sure of my abilities as the Best in the World that I felt I could beat all three has-beens at the same time. Another character might have gotten cheers with these boasts, but not me. I was such a piece of shit at this point that the fans wanted to see the old-timers take me down and shut me up.

The first confrontation was with Roddy Piper on *Raw* in Spokane, Washington. I was going to tell him how his time had come and now it was time for him to disappear forever. But before the show when we were going over the promo, I gave him one request.

"Roddy, when we do this tonight, I want you to forget about the Roddy Piper who tells jokes and talks in funny voices. I want the Roddy Piper who made the first WrestleMania such a success. The rat bastard who made Hulk Hogan a superstar and who gets no credit for making that show what it was." I really believed that. If it wasn't for Piper being such a strong heel, Hogan would've had nobody to go after, nobody for the fans to rally behind him to beat. Piper took my advice and later that night delivered one of the best promos I've ever heard from him. No jokes, no comedy, just a straight-from-the-heart kick-ass dissertation from one of the best ever.

He dressed me down by saying that I had once reminded him of himself, but now I had become insufferable and boorish. He stood up for Flair and Rourke, explaining that Mickey's performance in *The Wrestler* wasn't about an old-timer trying to get one last run, it was about doing what you love to do and enjoying the thrill of performing. He explained that guys like him, Flair, and all of the legends had respect and love for the fans, while I had neither. Then, with a tear in his eye, he explained how people came up to him and reminisced about watching his matches with their families, their parents and grandparents who had passed away, and how I was trying to bury those moments instead of celebrating them. Roddy never raised his voice or pandered to the crowd; as far as he was concerned, it was just him and me in that arena. He delivered a riveting performance and absolutely nailed it (he had crib notes on his wrist tape, but I let that slide), finishing up with a serious delivery of his new catchphrase, "Old-school's cool."

He went to shake my hand as the crowd chanted, "HOT ROD, HOT ROD," and I looked remorsefully at the ground. Then I kicked him in the knee and proceeded to beat the shit out of him. The silent crowd that had been sucked in by Roddy's performance now erupted in a tidal wave of boos.

"You want respect?" I yelled at him as he rolled around on the mat in pain. "Roll around, Piper! Roll around!" I kept shouting as the fans continued yelling their disproval. I walked up the ramp to the top of the stage, relaxed my face, adjusted my suit and tie, and smirked. It was such a smarmy way to end the segment and the perfect demonstration of the dickery (is that a word?) of Jericho.

Next up was Jimmy "Superfly" Snuka. Snuka was almost a mythical figure in the WWE, a dynamic performer who had captivated fans for years with his high-flying moves. He was even directly responsible for Mick Foley (did you know Mick has never beaten me in an officially sanctioned match?) wanting to be a pro wrestler. But Superfly had deteriorated quite a bit from his glory days and, while he still wrestled on the indy circuit, was now a shell of his former self. However, he was still a beloved character in the WWE Universe and the perfect target for evil Jericho.

One of Snuka's most famous moments was when he was beaten down with a coconut by Roddy on the set of "Piper's Pit" twenty-five years earlier and to play off that historic moment, the WWE was promoting a rare "Piper's Pit" on *Raw* with Superfly as the guest.

The famous "Pit" set had been assembled on the stage, and the crowd cheered vociferously (big word alert) when Piper's famed bagpipe intro hit. Those cheers turned to jeers when I strolled out to the stage instead. I had hijacked the segment to inform Snuka that he was just as washed up as the rest of the so-called legends in the WWE.

Jimmy was never much of a talker and as his age progressed, he became harder to understand. At this point the majority of his communication skills consisted mostly of him flashing the *I love you* sign (aka the Dio horns) while vacantly smiling and saying, "It's all about the love, bruddah." The segment was designed for me to do most of the talking, so I taunted him about being washed up and threatened to hit him with some fruit (not froot) of my own. I pulled out a bunch of bananas and two coconuts and waved them in his face, taunting and punking him out until he batted them from my hands and got in my grille. I slowly backed down and skulked away, tail between my legs, leaving Jimmy to bask in the glory of his fans. He went down on his knees and hit his signature pose, arms extended with both hands holding up the horns. Meanwhile I had circled around behind the "Pit" set, waiting for my cue. When Snuka stood up, I was going to push the set down on him and attack. So I waited . . . and waited . . . but Jimmy never stood up. He continued posing on his knees, and the camera stayed on him far too long. This was known as an angle alert, a situation where it becomes way too obvious to the fans that something is going to happen. I'm not sure if he went blank, zoned out, or just decided he didn't feel like standing up again, but I couldn't wait around for him any longer. I pushed the balsa wood set onto to his back and he went down like a ton of bricks (and I ain't talkin' about Metal Church). It looked really lame, since hitting him with that flimsy wall was about as dangerous as being hit with a toilet paper roll. But it did the trick and the crowd gasped incredulously, not believing that I would stoop so low as to attack Jimmy Snuka from behind.

But I was about to stoop a lot lower, as I bashed him with pieces of the lethal balsa wood. I slowly took off my jacket and unbuttoned my shirtsleeves to illustrate that I wasn't screwing around (it was one of my favorite tricks as a suit-wearing villain). Then I booted him in the stomach and started screaming like Walter Sobchak.

"You see what happens? Do you see what happens? Do you see what happens, Jimmy, when you fuck a stranger in the ass?!"

Well, I didn't actually say that last line, but you know what I mean. The beatdown was drawing serious heat and at that point I had the Midas touch of heelism . . . everything I did made people boo. I then delivered the ultimate insult (according to Vince) when I grabbed a banana off the floor and shoved it in Snuka's mouth. Once again, after the cowardly sneak attack, I calmly straightened my tie, fixed my hair, and sauntered off the stage, leaving Superfly down and the crowd steaming.

The next chapter in the story came on *Raw* the night after Mickey Rourke lost the Best Actor Oscar to Sean Penn. I don't know if the Academy voted against him after his red carpet WrestleMania challenge, but I felt that he should've won. In my opinion, his portrayal of Randy "The Ram" Robinson kicked Sean Penn's portrayal of Harvey "Spoiled" Milk's ass all over the silver screen. But regardless of what I thought in real life, my character took great joy in Rourke's defeat and I expressed this live on *Raw*.

My foil that week was the returning Ricky "The Dragon" Steamboat, who received a hero's welcome from the WWE Universe, as they hadn't seen him in over fifteen years. My idea to add him to the match appeared to be a smart one, for the fans were genuinely happy to see him—until I came into the picture. I waltzed on the stage like my name was Len Goodman and I owned the damn place. I was in the promo zone at this point and cut an intense (albeit a little long-winded) speech about how Steamboat had sold out to the WWE when he became The Dragon in the '80s and how he had now sold out for the second time by accepting an office job with the company.

"Now the loyal dog gets his bone by getting inducted into the WWE Hall of Fame. You, Steamboat, are the ultimate hypocrite."

Steamboat's face told a million tales as he raised the mic to his mouth. Ricky had never been known for his promos, but on this night he delivered like he was The Rock. He started by telling the story from my wildly successful roman à clef, *A Lion's Tale*, about how I waited in line to get his autograph over twenty years ago at a World of Wheels show because he was my hero. Then he fast-forwarded to today and addressed what I'd become, how I'd embraced and then turned on the fans so many times, how I'd become the ultimate hypocrite. Then he finished with a killer-go-home line.

"I am not a hypocrite, Jericho. But I am something you may never be: a WWE Hall of Famer."

I'd been served and the crowd loved it. Of course they didn't love it when I popped Steamer in the head with the mic and threw him into the LED screen on the stage. I continued my onslaught, berating him incessantly and calling him Mr. Hall of Fame over and over. Then of course I straightened my tie and strutted off the stage to a litany of boos.

The angle had gotten over better than we expected and a big reason for that was the passion projected by Piper, Snuka, and Steamboat. These were main-event players for the majority of their careers who had been reduced to bit players in the WWE for the last decade or so. But now that old fighting spirit to be the best had returned. We worked our asses off to make the match a true attraction for WrestleMania and it became one. Then a few weeks before Mania, I heard that since the Oscar race was over, Mickey Rourke was going to appear after all. He was going to sit in the front row and be involved in the finish of the match, which meant my Hollywood coverage was back, baby! The match also had a major cherry on top, with the inclusion of Flair in the legends corner, his first appearance at Mania since his retirement match a year earlier. Everything was going my way!

Everything, that is, until I had a confrontation with Flair on *Raw* that ended up getting me more heat than Miami . . . with Vince McMahon.

Flair started the promo on *Raw* by accepting my challenge on behalf of his friends to a 3-on-1 match at Mania, guaranteeing he would be in their corner and that Mickey would be in the front row. I interrupted him from the production truck, where I was standing in front of TV screens showing highlights of Snuka, Steamboat, and Piper. I left the truck and walked down the halls of the backstage area, through the Gorilla position and into the ring, all the while vilifying the legends with my diatribe. I boasted that I was going to beat them all at once, and there was nothing he could do about it. He told me I was wrong and then cut a classic Flair promo, describing how at the end of the match, all five of my opponents would be standing over my broken body, while 70,000 people shouted "WHOOOOOO!"

That's when I sucker-punched him in the forehead.

Earlier in the day, Ric implored me to hit him as hard as I could, so I nailed him with all I had and he went down fast. I was surprised when he rolled over and blood was streaming down his face, but I went with it. There's an old trick in wrestling when someone is bleeding and you want to open the cut further, you keep striking it repeatedly. So I kept punching that cut as hard as I could, in the ring, out of the ring, on the announce table, anywhere I could get ahold of him. I ripped his suit jacket off (after slowly removing my own of course), pulled his tie over his head, and threw his shoes into the crowd (Flair's idea). The blood-stains bloomed on his dress shirt while I grabbed the camera off of a nearby cameraman's shoulder and lined him up. He pulled himself to his feet as I ran across the floor and slammed it into the top of his head. To add blood insult to blood injury, the camera split him wide open as well and a crimson sheet cascaded down his face.

He looked like he'd just stepped out of an abattoir. But I wasn't fin-ished.

I stood over his prone body, staring at the Rolex on his wrist, given to him by HBK after their classic Mania match. Earlier in the day, I'd pitched the idea to Vince of destroying that watch, but he balked as he felt nobody knew about the watch or cared. I argued that they would care if we brought it to their attention and made it into a big deal. Strangely, he agreed to let me smash the watch though he didn't want to mention where it came from or the legit sentimental value it held for Ric. So when I pulled the fake Rolex off Ric's wrist (the real one was safely in the locker room), the crowd didn't respond as much as they would've if we had explained its significance beforehand. Even so, it was still Flair's Rolex and there was a good reaction when I placed it on top of the steel stairs and slowly walked to the top step. I raised my foot over his biscuit like a guillotine, then dropped the blade of my heel into the glass face-plate and shattered it instantly. I stomped on it a few more times for good measure and the Midas touch of heelism struck again. Huge chants of "You suck!" rang throughout the arena as I made my way back through Gorilla, satisfied with a job well done.

Until I saw Vince's face. I could tell he was furious again.

He started yelling about Flair getting color and bleeding all over the place, but this time I truly had nothing to do with it and didn't want to deal with him. So I walked out of Gorilla and headed to the trainers' room to wait for Ric.

He was covered in so much blood that he looked like he'd been in the front row of a Gwar concert as he sat down on the trainer's table to be examined. While the camera shot had busted open (LaGreca) his head for fifteen stitches, the punch I'd thrown that caused him to bleed in the first place had only left a small cut in the middle of his forehead. You could barely notice it. Word was getting back that Vince was freaking out about all the blood that had been shed, but since I was completely innocent this time my attitude was "My name's Paul and this is between y'all." Unlike the Batista incident, this was an honest mistake, and if Vince felt differently he could take it up with Flair. So I left the arena without saying a word and figured that was the end of it.

But later that week I got a message that Vince wanted me to call him. That was never a good thing. If he wanted to talk to me about something good, he would've called me himself.

Now that I knew I was in some sort of trouble, there was something that had been bothering me all week that I needed to investigate: Why had Flair bled so much from one punch? I'd been cut open from punches many times before, and most of the time they would quickly swell up and close on their own. It might leave a mouse or a welt, but whatever minor blood flow there was would usually stop fairly quickly. So it didn't make sense to me that Ric bled enough to stain his shirt after only one punch.

The other thing that was really irking me was the small cut in the middle of Flair's forehead. It wasn't the type of cut you'd get from a punch, which would be more of a lump with an uneven abrasion running through it. This one was straight and neat . . . like it had been done surgically. Like with a razor blade.

Had Flair done this to himself without telling me?

I called Doc Amann and asked him what he thought.

"Chris, I've been working in the WWE long enough to know that cut wasn't caused by a punch."

That was all I needed to hear. All evidence pointed to the fact that Flair had done this voluntarily without telling me. The crazy thing was I watched the segment a dozen times, and never once did I see his hand touch his forehead. But Flair was a wizard, and if he did do this to himself, he did it with such precision that it was impossible to pinpoint the exact moment when.

Any way you slice it (no pun intended), I owed Vince a call and it was time to face the McMusic. He answered after the first ring, and I could tell by the tone of his voice that he wasn't happy.

"Chris, we need to discuss what happened last Monday and decide what the punishment is going to be. Ric was bleeding so bad that I almost pulled the plug on the segment and went to commercial early. You know how I feel about blood on the show, Chris! I'm going to have to fine you."

Are you effin' kidding me? I was going to be fined again for somebody ELSE getting busted open (Mortman)? Talk about blood money!! I asked him why I was getting punished for hitting Flair with a stiff shot, something that happened every day in the line of duty.

"Come on, Chris, that's bullshit and you know it. Flair got busted open [Riker] and in the old 'rasslin' tradition, you kept punching him in the head trying to get him to bleed more [well, Vince was right about that]. Dammit, Chris, do you know how many sponsors we might lose because of this? It was old-school shit and I don't allow it anymore! And the worst thing is, you didn't even stop in Gorilla to talk to me about it. Did you think if you just ignored it that it would go away?"

I should've learned my lesson to call him after doing so saved my ass in the Batista incident, but I hadn't and now the tide was turning completely against me. I went to my last resort.

"Have you considered the fact that Ric might've done this to himself?"

"Yes, I've considered it, and you know what? I don't care. I can't fire him because he's not under contract (Flair had cut a deal to work up to Mania only), I can't fine him 'cause he'll probably just go home, and I can't yell at him 'cause it will just make him upset. Whether you knew about it or not, you went along with it and tried to punch the cut open further. So you're going to have to take the heat on this one." Then he spouted out another classic Vince-ism. "Sometimes you have to eat shit and like it, Chris."

Oh, brother. Vince felt he had to set another example that to bleed on purpose was the ultimate sin in this new PG world and I was the sacrificial lamb. There was no way out this time, but what would my fine be? Would he bring out the big guns like he had with Dave and drop the hundred-thousand-dollar hammer on me? Or would he just Eugene Levy the laughable five-grand fine on me again?

"I'm going to fine you fifteen thousand dollars, Chris. And this can't happen again."

It hadn't even happened once, as far as I was concerned! But I weighed the amount of the fine on the scales of justice inside my head and realized I had come out OK. Vince could've easily decided that, as a second-time offender, I had crossed over into Batista territory and slip me the big one. If I was playing "Fine or No Fine" and the banker offered me fifteen grand, I would've told Howie Mandel I was taking that briefcase right then and there.

I hung up and resigned myself to the fact I had been fined a total of twenty thousand bucks for bleeding, even though I hadn't lost a drop of my own blood. I guess I was eating a big mouthful of Vince's shit, but like Bill Murray found out while chewing on a log at the bottom of the pool in *Caddyshack*, it didn't taste too bad.

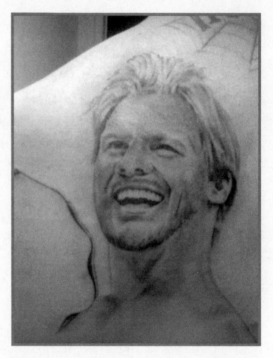

As hated as I was after what I'd done to Flair and the legends, there were still a few fanatics who idolized me. Overall, I think this is a pretty damn good tattoo, but, hopefully, in a few years the owner won't feel the same way I do about my Screech ink.

CHAPTER 17

Rourke's Dorks

The night before WrestleMania 25, the legends and I were scheduled to have a rehearsal to discuss what we wanted to do in the match. The layout was pretty simple: I would beat Snuka in a minute, Piper in two minutes, and then Steamboat in about five. Afterward I'd then beat up Flair and challenge Rourke, who would enter the ring and hit me with a knockout punch. Mickey's spot was easy, but a rehearsal was necessary since it was his first time in the WWE. I was looking forward to finally meeting him after our Larry King confrontation and the subsequent weeks of buildup I'd done on *Raw* without him.

I got to Reliant Stadium in Houston at midnight and walked out onto the massive set that had been constructed at one end of the field. I could see Rourke in the ring with his entourage and they appeared to be the size of ants, and I started walking the one hundred yards down the ramp, when I ran into a WWE publicist.

"Hey, I just talked to Mickey and he's mad at you," she said. "He thinks you have a real problem with him."

That surprised me. "Well, did you tell him I don't?"

"No. Should I have?"

Uh, yeah . . . I mean, what did she think the letters *PR* stood for in the first place? I was part of the Public and it was her job to Relate to Mickey that I was a good guy.

As I got closer to the ring, I could see Rourke staring at me and noticed that his entourage looked less like Turtle and Drama and more like the Delta Force. Three shredded bodybuilders glared at me with their heavily tattooed arms crossed in front of them. . . . One was even wearing army fatigues, for Pete Fornatale's sake! I knew my work was cut out for me as I climbed into the ring and greeted Mickey with a warm smile.

"Hey, man, nice to finally meet you!" I said cheerily and gave him the kind of hug you see two dudes in da club do when they don't really know each other. I could sense the last thing he wanted to do was embrace me and he couldn't pull away fast enough.

He was about the same height as I and looked like he'd been through the ringer a time or two, with the wear and tear on his face to show it. His hair was braided with blue and green extensions and held up in a topknot à la Jericho circa 1999. His face was oddly puffy, and with his dyed-black goatee, gold front tooth, and slight hint of BO, he reminded me of an older Jack Sparrow, you savvy?

He also looked tough as shit and ready to snap, not the kind of guy I wanted on my bad side. Especially since I was supposed to be taking a punch from him the next day.

We exchanged some small talk as Rourke's Dorks kept staring at me, seemingly ready to pounce at any given moment. To make matters even worse, I recognized the one on the left as Frank Shamrock, and even though he was the shortest of the three, he was one of the toughest UFC fighters ever. What were these guys even doing here?

I decided that the direct approach was in order. "Hey, man, I hear you're a little pissed off at me for the Larry King thing, but I want you to know that I was just putting on a show, ya dig?"

Rourke's face hardened as if he'd been waiting to get to the heart of the matter from the moment I got into the ring.

"No, brother," he said with his distinct New York accent. "You don't say the things you said to me and not mean it. In my world, in the boxing world, when you say that shit, it's because you're looking for a fight."

Wow. That explained why he'd never replied after I'd sent the text through Flair. He was legitimately pissed with me.

"No, it's not like that, man. I was trying to get people interested in seeing us wrestle each other. I was just playing a character. Same thing you do when you do a movie."

Here I was explaining acting and the inner workings of pro wrestling to a man who had just won a Golden Globe for Best Actor for his portrayal of a pro wrestler. After a few more minutes, I was finally able to convince him that I'd had been playing a role on the King show. His face softened as he realized I was telling the truth.

"So you're telling me that even though I'm the one who got nominated for an Oscar, you outacted me?!" He burst out with a *you son of a bitch* laugh and gave me a bear hug for real this time. All the tension floated away and the entire vibe in the ring changed. He went on saying how he was so mad after the show that he'd called his agents and demanded them to allow him to fight me. They of course said no, so he had planned another form of revenge.

He pointed to the bruisers standing beside him and said, "I flew these guys into Houston on my own dime to make sure everything went smoothly. If you tried anything funny, I told them to kick the shit out of you."

I was flattered but told him that maybe he had overestimated me a little.

"Mickey, to be honest, you didn't need to bring three guys. I'm sure just one of them would've sufficed."

All of us laughed except the guy wearing army fatigues, an Israeli bounty hunter who didn't find any of this funny and continued to stare me down for the rest of the night.

Vince made his way down to the ring, unaware of the confrontation Rourke and I had narrowly avoided and went through his ideas for the match. As a wrestler, I would listen to what Vince wanted, think about the logistics of it, run through it once or twice, and move along. But as an actor, Mickey was much more concerned with camera angles and minor movements. He wanted to rehearse his punch over and over again, discussing his motivation, his positioning, everything. There would be no improv for this guy.

Then we discussed how he was going to hit me. I told him not worry about pulling the punch and just swing like he would in a boxing match. He shook his head and warned me, "I don't know about that. I'm Golden Gloves, brother. If I hit you with this right hand, you're going to feel it." I convinced him that it was OK and told him he could hit me as hard as he wanted as long as it looked good. After being walloped in the forehead for real by the seven-foot-tall Big Show, I thought I could take a punch from a 160-pound actor. After about a half hour of going over the punch spot a dozen times, Mickey was happy and he left ringside with his posse in tow.

I went over to Vince and told him what had almost happened.

"You know, Rourke hired those guys to kick my ass if I tried to double-cross him."

Vince stared down the rampway at Rourke's gang. "Are you kidding me? Those guys?!" He laughed. He motioned at Dean Malenko and Fit Finlay, who were talking at ringside. "You, me, Finlay, and Malenko would've beat the shit out of them. I mean look at that one guy. . . . He's a midget!"

The "midget" Vince was referring to was Shamrock, the multiple-time UFC champion. I smiled at Vince and said, "Well, if anything goes down, I'll take Rourke and you take the midget."

"Damn right I will," he murmured and swaggered out of the ring.

The next day when I showed up at the stadium, Mickey called me into his dressing room still raving over my performance on Larry King. He told me I had what it took to make it as an actor and gave me a list of method books he wanted me to read. It was pretty froot to get that kind of feedback from an Oscar-nominated thespian (even if the hint of BO remained), but the adulation didn't end there. He told me over and over that we should do a movie together, said I could stay at his house whenever I was in Hollywood, sent me a giant autographed poster of *The Wrestler*, invited me to visit him on the set of *Iron Man 2*, and asked me to call him before my next audition so he could help me run through my lines.

The footage of him "knocking me out" after the match (even though his feared right hand barely grazed the back of my head) made it onto all the Hollywood gossip shows, but I didn't quite get the mainstream exposure I'd expected; the majority of the media never even mentioned me by name. It was always the host saying something as simple as "Mickey Rourke gets the knockout punch at WrestleMania!" while the footage ran of him KO'ing some unnamed fall guy. (But I'm Chris Jericho!) In the grand scheme of things, it doesn't matter what my name is (The Rock TM), because the angle was a success and that was all I cared about.

Plus, I made a friend out of the deal as Mickey and I exchanged numbers and kept in touch for months afterward, until we eventually lost contact.

So, Mickey, if you're reading this, gimme a call and we'll do lunch, babe.

While the angle had been built up great, the match itself went even better than I could've expected. It started off fairly slow since Snuka couldn't move much and Piper did the best he could. I beat them both quickly, but business was about to pick up (Jim Ross TM) when Steamboat got in the ring. Our styles meshed together perfectly and he was the big surprise of the show, even though it wasn't much of a shock to see him steal it away from the rest of us. He was one of the absolute best performers in the history of the business, and it was a blast to work with him, both on a professional and a personal level. Steamboat was the second of my three major pro wrestling heroes that I got to work with (the first being HBK and the third being Owen Hart, who passed away before I had the chance to grapple with him), and it was a childhood dream come true to be in the ring with him at WrestleMania.

It wasn't like Ricky's performance was good just for "an old-timer." He exceeded everyone's expectations with his fluid, acrobatic style and it seemed like he hadn't lost a step in the ten years since he'd last wrestled. The crowd was going wild for him, erupting into a gigantic 70,000-strong chant of "You Still Got It!" as he nailed all of his signature moves: the double chop, the high armdrags, and, of course, the majestic crossbody from the top rope, which provided the biggest false finish of the match. But it wasn't enough to beat me, so the fans groaned in disappointment when I kicked out at 2.9 and hit him with a quick Codebreaker for my third win of the night.

Even though Ricky lost, the crowd was buzzing over his performance, and Vince was so impressed that he booked him as a wrestler/ coach for months afterward to work with the young guys at live events.

We wrestled each other another half dozen times, including single matches at the next PPV and in Tokyo, Honolulu, and Greenville, South Carolina, which is where we had the best match of them all.

I was scheduled to win, but South Carolina was one of Ricky's old NWA stomping crowds and the crowd was going bonkers when he came to the ring. (This was also the night the guy charged the ring from twenty rows out.) Eventually, Ricky hit me with the high crossbody and the fans were certain he was going to beat me, but just like at Mania, I kicked out in the nick of time and hit him with the Codebreaker for the planned finish. But as I covered him, I told him, "Kick out, you got it? No matter what, KICK OUT." Then I whispered sternly to referee (and fellow Stryper/Evil Dead fan) Charles Robinson, "Ricky is going to kick out. Do NOT count to three!"

Ricky waited until the last microsecond and kicked out of my pin. Charles motioned that I had only scored a two-count, and I went berserk. I had the crowd freaking out and right where I wanted them, so I kicked the rope and got in Charles's face as I came up with the new finish in my head. I wanted to pick Steamboat up for a body slam and have him roll me up for the pin, the exact finish of his famous WrestleMania 3 match vs. Randy Savage, which is one of my all-time favorites.

But my mind had gone completely blank and I couldn't remember the term *roll up*. I was flipping through my mental moves Rolodex, but the harder I thought, the less I remembered. The crowd was exactly where I wanted them and I didn't have much time to waste, so I grabbed Steamboat by the hair and said under my breath, "WrestleMania 3 finish." Of course The Dragon knew exactly what I meant and rolled me up tightly.

Charles counted to three and the crowd erupted, ecstatic that their hero had vanquished the evil Jericho in their hometown. When I got to the back, Arn Anderson (who was running the show) was laughing.

"Dammit, Jericho, you dumb motherfucker!" he said, clapping me on the back. "Even when we want to give you a win, you still won't take it! I wish you were around when I was working . . . I coulda got a victory too!"

I joined in with Arn's laughter because he was right. But it was all worth it when Ricky came back through the curtain and shook my hand.

"Chris, I just want to tell you that it's a joy to work with you and it's so damn easy. Thank you for helping me get back in the groove. I'll wrestle you anytime." He gave me a hug and walked away.

I stood there in that hallway with an ear-to-ear grin for a long time. Having one of my childhood heroes thank me for helping him get back in the groove and telling me I was a joy to work with?

Yeah, I'd have to say that even though I lost the match, I still won pretty damn big that night.

CHAPTER 18

Santino Gump

I was happy with my performance at Mania and proud that all of our hard work had culminated in an entertaining twenty minutes that the fans enjoyed. Now it was time to relax . . . for twenty-four hours. You see, we always say that WrestleMania is the Super Bowl of the WWE, and it is. But the big difference between our crown jewel and the NFL's is that when the Super Bowl is finished, their players get to take some time to relax and go to Disneyland or whatever. But when WrestleMania is finished, we all get to go back to work the next day.

Before we do, though, there's always a huge private party for all of us that starts as soon as Mania ends. It's always first-class, with gourmet food, full open bar, amazing decorations, and a killer live band to set the tone. Some bands were better than others, with Los Lonely Boys at one end of the spectrum, The Hillbilly Jim band at the other, and the band that played one set dressed as AC/DC (Vince's favorite band) and the other dressed as The Rolling Stones (Vince's second favorite band) ending up somewhere in the middle.

But this year the entertainment was going to a whole new level. This year it was all about . . . MUSCLEMANIA. This was a bodybuilding contest between Cody Rhodes and Santino Marella that was going to be held during the biggest (and sole) company party of the year. Only in the WWE, right?

The seeds for the contest had been sown on an overseas tour when Cody told Santino that he had gotten fat and needed to shape up. Cody was instantly ambushed by catcalls and snide remarks from the rest of the crew, who felt he was out of line; or more likely, we were just bored and thought it was funny to gang up on him. Santino, of course, took great umbrage (try using that one on Words With Friends, kids) to this and bet he could get in better shape than Cody in time for Mania. Within minutes the contest was booked for the post-show party, the judges were picked (Taker, Regal, JBL), the rules were set, and the T-shirts were printed featuring a knockoff of the famous Mega Powers Explode poster from Mania 5, with Santino in the Hogan spot and Cody in the Savage position.

Both men dieted and trained as hard as they could, and on the night of the show, it looked like it was going to be a tight contest; even though Santino was on a roll as his "sister," Santina had already won the Divas title earlier in the night. (I'll let Santino tell the story about why he was dressed up as a woman in his own book.)

It was also a pretty hard task having to explain why there was a guy in a dress parading around the ring with the women's title to Kid Rock.

Yeah, that Kid Rock.

I first met Kid years earlier at a joint MTV/WCW event in Cancun (read all about it in my gladiator novel, *A Lion's Tale*, available in armour shops worldwide) and we'd been buds ever since. He had done a mini concert at Mania earlier that night and invited me to come hang in his dressing room after we were both finished. We had a few beers while watching the show with his massive entourage and even though Kid was a big wrestling fan, he was a little weirded out by the "tranny in the ring."

"He ain't no tranny, he's my brother," I said, and sipped my PBR.

Santina winning the Divas title was the silly side of wrestling, but the Shawn Michaels/Undertaker match was the epitome of what the business is all about. As a matter of fact, I'll go on record and say it's the best match I've ever seen in my life, a five-star clinic that was perfect in every way. Kid and I watched it, cheering along like two fourteen-year-olds getting our first taste of the WWE. We gasped at the intensity of the battle, gave each other high fives at the false finishes, and practically hugged each other in fear when Taker did a dive out of the ring and landed directly on his head. Both of us jumped off the couch and waited in silence, praying that he would move his legs, his arms, anything.

"Come on, big man, get up, get up," Kid kept repeating under his breath, until Taker finally rose to his feet. We sank back into the couch with a big sigh of relief.

When Mania finished, Kid and I and his entourage headed to the after-party and set up shop in the corner of the hall. We drank more beers, told jokes, and had a great conversation about everything from our initial meeting in Cancun to our second meeting in Vancouver, when I got trapped under the stage after introducing him on *Raw* (Confused? Get my self-help book, *Undisputed*, for your Kindle now); his dear departed sidekick, Joe C; how AC/DC was the best rock band of all time; and the pros and cons of smoking weed.

Suddenly an announcement was made . . . MUSCLEMANIA was about to begin!! The DJ stopped the music and the live band started laying down some grooves to set the scene. Kid wasn't too sure what was going on, but when the band started rocking, his ears perked up like a Pavlov dog and he hit the stage. He set himself up behind some bongo drums and began jamming along. Suddenly the music stopped as Taker grabbed the mic and called Cody and Santino to the stage. Kid looked on, dejected, wondering why the vibe had been interrupted.

"What's going on, man?" he asked me. "Why did the music stop?"

"Those guys are going to have a bodybuilding contest," I explained.

He looked at me like I was a devil without a cause and watched what was transpiring onstage. Cody and Santino had taken off their clothes and were flexing their muscles, wearing nothing but skimpy posing trunks (well, Santino was, but poor Cody was wearing a pair of cheap Speedos and looking like he was going to puke), while the mostly male audience stood at the front of the stage hooting and hollering. Triple H was the MC calling out traditional poses, which the two performed dutifully, as Vince, Taker, Cena, and Kane cheered from the front row, laughing hysterically.

Kid's face scrunched up in disgust like he had a spider in his mouth as he watched the two oiled-up half-naked men flexing and writhing on the stage. When Santino hit a crab and the audience cheered wildly as if he were Mandy Melons taking off her top at The Cheetah Club on a Friday night, Kid Rock decided he had seen enough.

"That does it, this sucks, I'm outta here," he said, and without another word walked straight out the door, his entourage filing out behind him with no questions asked. I haven't seen or heard from him since.

One of the biggest and most decadent rock stars of all time, a man who had seen and taken part in the kind of sexual debauchery that would've made Caligula blush, had finally reached his decency limit and been completely disgusted by the atrocity known as MUSCLEMANIA.

World Wrestling Entertainment: 1

Early Morning Stoned Pimp: 0

Poor Cody didn't stand a chance at MUSCLEMANIA and was booed out of the building; he was nothing more than the straight man in this comedy duo. Santino, on the other hand, was the star of the show and walked away with the seven-foot-tall JBL-designed trophy adorned with tiny female sports figures (ice-skaters, gymnasts, ballet dancers, etc.). It was no surprise Santino was voted the winner, for he was probably the most popular guy on the entire roster. Everybody loved him because he was so ridiculously goofy in every way.

As a person, he was impossible to dislike—great sense of humor, laid-back vibe, and the best stories ever. He'd seemingly done everything in his life, so I called him Santino Gump. As I was writing this modern-day *Catcher in the Rye*, I couldn't remember all of the jobs he'd told me he had over the years, so I texted him to get the details. This was his response verbatim:

"I've been a dish washer, bus boy, bartender, bouncer, master of cere-monies, scrap metal worker, sub sandwich maker [his autographed picture still hangs in a Mr. Sub in Toronto], retail seller in the mall, male stripper, singing telegram delivering Power Ranger, personal trainer, account man-ager in a telecom company, event marketing coordinator, mechanical installer, customs broker, ad salesman for a magazine, high school teacher, truck refrigeration parts delivery boy, warehouse worker, roadie for a cir-cus, landscaper, pizza shop worker, pro fighter and of course pro wrestler."

He knew everybody and had seen everything, like the WWE's ver-sion of Bob Sakamano, plus he had the strangest of talents. He was a great speed walker . . . for real. He had entered speed-walking contests and won. He was great at rolling and I'm not talking about joints. I'm talking about actually getting on the floor and rolling back and forth. I've seen him roll across the dressing room with perfect speed and preci-sion like a Buzz Droid. Who does that?! And how do you find out you're good at rolling in the first place?

He would go to a club and glide across the dance floor like Danny Zuko, yelling at the top of his lungs, "Here it comes! Here it comes!" then jump in the air and land in a full split. Then he would pop straight back up onto his feet and keep on dancing like Jimmy Hart and The Gentrys.

He also knew exactly how to play his character for maximum laughs at all times. He purposely mispronounced names (calling *Raw* guest host Snoop Dog Snoopy the Dog while dressed in full Charlie Brown regalia was my personal favorite), wore his hair in a goofy mullet/faux hawk combo, and drew a unibrow on his forehead every night for maximum comedic effect. He formed a partnership with The Glamazon Beth Phoenix and christened their team Glamarella. He seemingly tore his ball bag while attempting Melina's splits-on-the-apron ring entrance. He won the IC title and claimed he would beat the Honky Tonk Man's record as the longest-reigning IC champion, then introduced the "Honky Meter" to measure his progress. He only kept the title for like twelve of the sixty-four weeks necessary to beat the record, but was so over that the fans loved him even more when he lost. Actually, they cheered him no matter what: when he won, when he lost, when he broke the record for the quickest elimination in Royal Rumble history (Kane got rid of him in two seconds and Santino protested, "I wasn't ready!" all the way to the back). When he seemingly won the 2010 Royal Rumble or was in the final two of the Elimination Chamber in 2012, he got astonishing ovations from the fans begging him to win the big one. His character was bulletproof in that he could do anything and still stay over, the rarest of rare things in pro wrestling.

Santino ridiculously dressed as Charlie Brown. You can see the lineup for that weekend's live events, taped on the wall behind him.

Then there was his actual in-ring work, which was the most entertaining part of his character, because you never knew when he was trying to be bad or when he was just bad. He would jump toward his corner to make the hot tag and land two feet away from his partner with his hand extended like Charlie Brown sliding into home plate. This was on purpose.

He'd do a flying head butt that looked (as Arn described it) "like a salmon swimming upstream to spawn." There would be no grace whatsoever, no technique at all. He would simply jump in the air straight as a pencil and drop straight down like a brick. That was not on purpose.

He'd do an elbow drop where he would mime to the audience that he was sharpening his elbow like a pencil before he dropped it. That was on purpose.

Then he would give a totally awkward stiff-legged hip toss that looked ridiculous and made Cena and me laugh every time. That was not on purpose.

Then there were his famous finishing maneuvers. The Cobra was a ridiculous move where he would turn his hand into a snake with a series of taps to various parts of his arm and then "bite" his hapless victim. He upgraded the move a few months later when he began reaching down his pants to pull out a full-length spandex glove painted to look like a cobra. That's when you knew shit was getting real. In typical Santino fashion, the move got over huge in spite of looking completely stupid. Heel after heel was vanquished after being struck in the throat by the dreaded snake sock puppet.

When Santino got bored with the Cobra, he began working on his new finish, the Maserati Clutch, which was a "high-risk running top rope submission maneuver." He got the mic at live events to warn his opponents that when he made the sign of a giant *M* with his arms, "that stands for Maserati," and then locked his hands into a clutch, "that stands for Clutch," the end was near. During the course of the match, he would signal for the devastating move, and get cut off every time. We never did see Santino unleash the Maserati Clutch, which is probably best for the survival of mankind.

Half of the stuff he did was comedic genius and the other half was rotten, but it still made people laugh, so his matches were always entertaining.

Unfortunately, not everyone felt that way. He was in a tag-team match against Cody Rhodes and Bob Holly in Vienna that didn't turn out the way it had been planned. According to Bob, Santino made a few mistakes during his comeback that caused some timing issues and screwed up the match.

Bob was quite high-strung, with a hair-trigger temper, and was fed up with Santino's perceived incompetence, so he went off on him in the dressing room afterward.

"Santino, you are the absolute shits! You are the worst performer I've ever been in the ring with! The absolute worst!"

Bob Holly had been around for a long time, so for him to say Santino was the WORST opponent he'd ever faced covered a lot of territory and was a huge insult. But Santino didn't think so, and looked at Bob completely unfazed.

"Come on. Really? The worst? Are you sure? You must've worked with SOMEONE worse than me."

The best part was he wasn't trying to be sarcastic; he just honestly couldn't believe he was the worst guy Holly had wrestled.

Santino's logical tone made Bob backtrack a step and reconsider his hostile statement.

"OK, you're not the worst . . . but you are ONE of the worst!"

Santino nodded his head, satisfied with the upgrade.

After that tour, we went straight to South America and did a string of shows in Chile, Costa Rica, and finally Panama (jump back, what's that sound). Whenever we toured internationally, accommodations were paid for and we always stayed in nice places. After the show, we went back to our hotel, which was also a huge casino. We were enjoying a few cocktails, when we were told the bar area was about to be converted into a karaoke bar. I kicked things off with a rousing rendition of "Enter Sandman," followed by Punk, Mickey James, and me doing a kick-ass version of "Summer Lovin'" from the *Grease* sound track (it's on YouTube if you want check it out). Then Santino got up and made his way to the stage. He cracked his knuckles and hopped up and down like Royce Gracie before a fight as he prepared to sing his tune, "The Summer of '69" by Bryan Adams.

He sang it right on time and completely in the pocket, each word of Adams's iconic lyrics delivered perfectly in tune. "I got my first real six-string . . ."

He had the scattered crowd in the palm of his hand . . . then he started changing the words for no apparent reason.

"It was the summer of motherfuckin' '69 . . . not '68 . . . oooh yeah!" he screamed, like Adam Sandler singing about the lunch lady. The crowd, which only moments earlier had been responding to Santino like he was the King of Pop, turned on him like he was the King of Poop.

He continued messing with the chorus, changing the year of that famous summer, from '69 to '68 to '77 to '08, as the audience became increasingly hostile. Then, for no apparent reason during the guitar solo, he started chanting, "Hogan! Hogan! Hogan!" and marched across the stage stiff-legged, like Basil Fawlty confronting the Germans, while the Panamanians wondered what the fuck he was doing.

This was the final straw for the unforgiving crowd; they got up out of their chairs and streamed toward the exit. In the three minutes and thirty-four seconds that it took him to sing "Summer of '69," Santino had cleared out the entire bar, with the exception of his peers.

He was far more effective than "Closing Time" by Semisonic, that's for damn sure.

Afterward, we split back to our hotel bar to keep the party going and met up with Ted DiBiase, Cody Rhodes. and Beth Phoenix. Cena had just done the movie *12 Rounds*, and the Finnish director Renny Harlin had taught him how to make a special drink where you put a certain high-proof liqueur into a glass and light it on fire. Then you place the palm of your hand over the glass, which stifles the oxygen and causes a suction allowing you to lift it off the table. Then you down the shot, pour the last few drops on top of another overturned glass, and snort those drops up your nose.

After a few of these Harlin specials, everybody in the room had either thrown up or was acting a damn fool. Santino speared DiBiase (whose only pair of shoes I stole and didn't give back until the next afternoon) over a set of tables and smashed a Styrofoam cooler lid over his head, breaking it into a hundred pieces and making a huge mess in the lounge. I watched the carnage, all the while greasing the palms of the waiter who was ready to kick us out unless we paid him off.

At the end of the night, only John and I were standing, and we carried the lidless Styrofoam box up to my room so as not to waste any of the unopened beers. When I woke up the next morning, I couldn't figure out why there was an oversize beer cooler sitting in the middle of my floor. So I cracked open a Corona and tried to piece it all together.

CHAPTER 19

Twanging Koto

One of the most integral components of a pro wrestler's ring entrance is his or her accompanying music. It sets the tone of the character, and from the first note, the fans should know exactly what to expect. Whether it's the breaking glass of Stone Cold Steve Austin, the tolling funeral bell of The Undertaker, or the twanging koto of Funaki, ring music is the most important way to alert the fans as to what kind of performer they're about to see.

Being a music fanatic, I've always given a lot of thought to what song was going to herald my arrival in the ring. I perform with a lot of energy and I always want my ring music to reflect that. If I had the right song, I felt like I could kick the world's ass, but if I had the wrong song, it was like trying to bang Asa Akira with a case of the shrinkage. Unfortunately, I wasn't always in control of my ring music and some of the choices made me feel like George Costanza in the Hamptons.

The following is a log of every song I've entered the ring to, some of them classic, some of them OK, and some of them just plain Johnny Rotten.

"UNSKINNY BOP" (POISON): This is the song I used for the first dozen or so matches of my career. About a week after I arrived in

Calgary to start my training, Poison's new album *Flesh & Blood* was released and I loved it. I was always more of a Maiden/Metallica type guy, but I had a soft spot for some of the better hair metal bands and they were one of them. I liked the groove of "Unskinny," especially the drum/bass intro, and thought it would be a good representation of the swagger I was showing at the time. I stopped using it after it inexplicably starting playing backward during my entrance one night in Strathmore, Alberta. Instead of the bass/drum intro, I came down the aisle to the sound of weird echoey loops and a slow voice saying, "I buried Paul."

"TEASE ME PLEASE ME" (SCORPIONS): I'm a big believer that an entrance song needed to have some sort of intro, a few bars of instrumentation that would build the anticipation to the big reveal. This song had that, and I remember on numerous occasions a nervous community center stagehand trying to push me through the curtain saying, "GO! GO!" while I dug in my heels, insisting, "It's not time yet!!"

"OVERNIGHT SENSATION" (FIREHOUSE): Lance Storm and I used this on our first tour of Japan, in 1991, when I decided our team, Sudden Impact, needed something heavy to hit the ring to. I have no idea why I settled on Firehouse, as they weren't exactly Venom, but the song started with a heavy riff that led into a long, high scream, which was our cue to run out from backstage slammin' and jammin' all the way. I accidentally left the Firehouse cassette with the FMW sound guy at the end of the tour and forced the bus driver to go back to the arena to retrieve it. We almost missed our flight home and everyone was pissed at me, but I didn't care. . . . No cassette is left behind, dammit!

"SILENT JEALOUSY" (X JAPAN): When I made my grand return to Japan in 1992 I had these delusions that the fans were going to go crazy to see me. I figured since they'd been waiting for my return for so long (less than a year), Jerichomania would be running wild. I wanted to give them something special to let them know I'd missed them just as much, so I figured if I came to the ring to the biggest Japanese metal band of all time, it would ingratiate me to the culture and I'd be loved even more, right? Wrong. The song played to veritable silence as I ran to the ring before an apathetic crowd. When I jumped on the second rope and screamed, "Watashi Wa Modottekita!!!" ("I'm back!"), nobody gave a shitsu.

"YOU'RE INVITED (BUT YOUR FRIEND CAN'T COME)" (VINCE NEIL): I made my first "Highlight Reel" to this song from the sound track of *Encino Man* (sweet Pauly Shore, where are you now?), by assembling the highest flying moves in my repotoire to the driving beat of the tune. (Should I post it on YouTube? Hit me up on Twitter at @iamjericho and let me know.) The heavy-ass riff, froot singing, and total guitar wizardry from Steve Stevens made this the perfect (albeit slightly out of fashion, thanks to the onslaught of grunge) ring song for me at the time.

"ENTER SANDMAN" (METALLICA): Seems a little too obvious a choice, doesn't it? Well, that's because I didn't choose it. This was used during my time in Mexico and I guess the office figured, since I was the "rocker guy," they would use the biggest "rocker song" they knew for my theme. But it wasn't the best song to come down to the ring to as it builds for about a minute before it kicks in, and it only took me forty-five seconds to get to the ring. But it was a fuck of a lot better than "Gonna Make You Sweat (Everybody Dance Now)" by C+C Music Factory, the song they used for me when I first got there.

"ROCK AMERICA" (DANGER DANGER): Another song that I had no involvement in choosing and my least favorite ring song of all time. Jim Cornette picked this squeaky-clean tune to represent his squeaky-clean new babyface team, The Thrillseekers, and it couldn't have been cheesier if it came in a bag of Cheetos. Super polished with a horrible a cappella early '90s vocal intro followed by a keyboard heavy pop metal hook, it was the exact opposite of what was happening musically at the time and the image I wanted to portray. I felt like a right wanker whenever the song started and wanted to hide when it played, which was the exact opposite of what I needed from an entrance song. But Cornette loved it and wouldn't consider changing it. While I like a lot of other songs by Danger Danger, this one was Shitty Shitty.

"THUNDER KISS '65" (WHITE ZOMBIE): When I started working full-time in Japan, I wanted to change my song to something dirtier and with attitude, something that better represented the evil side of Jericho. I loved this track since the first time I heard it on KLOS in Los Angeles during the summer of '92 (I originally thought it was by Pantera) and started using it when I was working for WAR in '94. It was the quintessential track for me until Paul Heyman nicked it and started using it as the theme for his ECW TV show. Not to be outdone, I moved on to another White Zombie song called . . .

"ELECTRIC HEAD, PT 2" (WHITE ZOMBIE): This tune worked even better as it started with a sample of some BMF proclaiming, "I just said up yours, babay . . ." which was the perfect slogan for my attitude. I wanted to use it when I moved over to WCW, but unless you were Hulk Hogan (apparently the company bought the rights for his "Voodoo Chile" music from Jimi Hendrix's estate for a hundred thousand dollars), I was told they didn't use outside music.

GENERIC JOURNEY RIP-OFF SONG (GENERIC JOURNEY RIP-OFF BAND): The story of this song was told in *A Lion's Tale*, my book of Russian philosophy (available at a university bookstore near you), but as a recap, let's just say that this was an awful tune that fell as flat as Miley Cyrus's ass. I hated it, as it sounded like castrated Journey. Not something rad like "Escape" or "Any Way You Want It" but a song so weak it made "The Girl Can't Help It" sound like Cannibal Corpse.

"BASKETBALL HIGHLIGHTS #12": This song's story was also told in *ALT* and was a huge improvement over its predecessor. But it was still pretty lame. I'd gone from nutless Journey to rip-off Pearl Jam . . . but at least this had some attitude. Years later I found out the name of the song was "One Crazed Anarchist," which was such a froot title that I stole it for a Fozzy tune.

"BREAK THE WALLS DOWN" (JIM JOHNSTON): Not only is this my most famous entrance theme, it's also the best one I've ever had. Perfect vibe and feeling for who I am as a performer, with the classic opening line ("Break the Walls Dowwwwnnnn!!") to let people know exactly what's up. I've used it since my 1999 WWE debut and I can't imagine coming to the ring to anything else, even though I've been forced to use a few different variations since.

"BREAK THE WALLS DOWN" (SEVENDUST): This was a remake of Johnston's original by a pretty damn good band. I thought it was pretty froot and used it a few times, but nothing could match the intensity of the original.

"BREAK THE WALLS DOWN" (ZAKK WYLDE): I asked Zakk to redo my song prior to the 2007 return and he worked hard to create a suitable remake. I really dug his version but, sadly, Vince did not. I still have this on my iPod, but since I listen to music almost exclusively on my iPhone nowadays, I never hear it. Maybe I should put this one up on YouTube as well?

"KING OF MY WORLD" (SALIVA): Nothing against Saliva—they're a good band—but this original song they wrote for me didn't work. I was asked what I thought of it during an on-camera interview and said I didn't like it, which made it back to them. It was nothing personal; it just didn't have the vibe or bite I needed to get into character. I never wanted to ditch "Break the Walls Down" but was asked to use this a few times for business purposes, and I did once or twice before reverting back to the original.

"NIGHTMARE" (AVENGED SEVENFOLD): When I pitched Vince the idea to come back at the beginning of 2012 with the End of the World promos, I wanted to once again change my character and my music. I thought the intro of this song (with some editing) would be perfect for the tone I was setting, with the creepy vignettes and the evil warnings of my arrival. I spoke to their singer M. Shadows about it and he was totally down with my idea.

But Vince wasn't.

He said my original ring song was evergreen and would be my WWE music until the day I left the company. In retrospect, I believe he's right.

Hustling through the ruins of Tarmiyah, Iraq, with Dean Malenko behind me and Ron Simmons in the lead.

Amazing shot of Shawn's head smashing through the obscenely expensive JeriTron 5000. One of my favorite moments, from the best angle of my career.

Mike Chioda raises my hand after I become the World Champion for the fourth time in Cleveland. My arm was sliced open during the previous match against HBK and wouldn't stop bleeding the whole night.

Sierra, Ash, and Cheyenne make war faces with Daddy. Being the cutest kids in the world, they're used to my constant group selfies. I was the one who chopped their bangs so badly, by the way.

Vince and Steph look on bemusedly as I apologize to them after the Chicago crowd demanded I get on my knees. Steph's leather pants rock.

Hanging with James Hetfield backstage in Chicago. My Cheshire cat smile is completely legit. I went tanning earlier in the day, which explains the major difference in our skin tones.

I asked Ozzy Osbourne for a picture after our pretape in Worcester, Massachusetts, and he started throttling me. My face is screaming, but my heart is over the mountain.

This reminds me of the cover of Pantera's *Vulgar Display of Power*. Iron Mike threw the best working punch ever and didn't touch me, but it still scared the crap out of me to have to stand there and take it. One of my favorite pictures EEVVEERR.

Unlike Tyson, Mickey Rourke actually connected with this punch . . . to the back of my head. It still looked good, and Mickey finally got his revenge for my Larry King smear job.

Rybo and I photo bomb Steve and Lars backstage in Los Angeles. If you look closely, you can see Kerry King in the mirror behind us.

Brian Gewirtz took this pic of Jason Sudeikis, Will Forte, and me roaming the streets of Manhattan. I suggested the "Rat Pack" photo, where everybody laughs at something off camera. Will's face is the best.

This picture is pretty self-explanatory, but I'll give you a description anyway: me dressed as Santa, ready to rumble with a posse of little people wearing full camo. By far, the most bizarre picture in this book.

Best picture in the whole book—
Shads and Ash playing Call of
Duty with the exact same zombie
face. My son was so impressed
with Matt that he went and got
tattoos the next day.

Cheryl and I kill the Viennese Waltz
on American Night, which was the
best of our *DWTS* performances, and
earned us the highest scores of the
competition. I was kicked off the show
a week later.

FYI—I'm wearing Sea-Bands under
my jacket to keep from getting
nauseous.

ABC via Getty Images

My gorgeous wife, Jessica,
and I pose after my first *DWTS*
performance. Every week after the
show, there was a massive press
scrum in the ballroom. You can see
the various cameras and interviewers
in the background as a result.

Working the crowd on *The
Tonight Show* as Jay Leno waits
to get a word in edgewise and
Diane Lane wonders who the hell
I am.

Cousin Chad and I share a wise laugh on the eve of my fortieth birthday. My hat rules. PS: This is the third picture of Abbey Road in this book.

In the parking garage underneath the Nokia Theatre, Josh Bernstein and I explain to Joe Perry why I want him to call me a douche, as he stares off into space wondering what the hell we're talking about. But he is wearing a rad scarf.

Slash, fellow Winnipeggers Geoff Loughery and Brent Fitz, and I have a chat about Canadian rock music behind the scenes at the Golden Gods. Slash's shirt says it all.

Here I am in my "Fat Jericho" phase, although standing next to Orton ain't helping me much. Sad thing is, I thought I looked svelte (great word) at the time.

After DDP Yoga and the Hetfield diet, I lost thirty pounds, and I included this picture solely because of how ripped I am. A second later, Kane lifted me up by my head and threw me back into the ring.

CM Punk hits me with a top rope flying clothesline at WrestleMania 28. Such a great picture, as you can see both the intensity in our faces and the expansiveness of the stadium filled with 75,000 fans.

There's a great picture in *A Lion's Tale* of me, Dean, Eddy, Benoit, and Brian Hildebrand (my WCW gang) in 1998. There's another one in *Undisputed* of the surviving four of us after Brian passed away. Now only Dean and I remain. Hopefully there will be another picture of the two of us in my next book.

One of my favorite pictures ever, and the looks on our faces explain the reason why: a triumphant band, an amazing gig, and a massive crowd. Fozzy Is Download!

Sporting white contacts to signify my possession in the "Sandpaper" video. I guess becoming a demon gives you giant bags under your eyes as well.

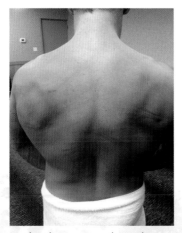

My back, sporting the ugly welts from Punk's kendo stick shots at Extreme Rules. It ain't ballet, baby.

My beautiful rock 'n' roll family backstage at the Uproar Festival in Tampa in 2012. Ash and Chey loved the show, but SiSi was staring at me from the side of the stage the whole time like I was completely insane. I guess I kinda am.

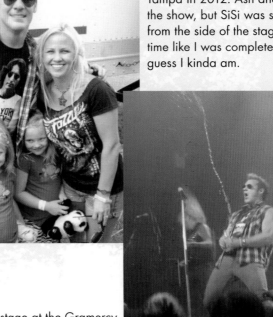

Fozzy explodes onstage at the Gramercy Theatre in New York City. Premature Announce-ulation indeed.

Three generations of Irvines. My dad is holding one of Ash's Animorph books, which my son read in just three hours. All of my kids are avid readers, just like me.

Right before I hit the stage with Stryper in Anaheim. It was such an honor to sing with them after dreaming about it for more than twenty years. I still kick myself for wearing a black and *blue* shirt, though.

The end of a Fozzy show is always chaotic, exciting, and acrobatic. Here, the Duke and I have a contest over who can do the best David Lee Roth jump off the riser. Obviously he wins. Frank's Peter Criss stick pose is awesome too.

CHAPTER 20

I'm the Joker

Meanwhile back at the ranch, when I found out I was going to be starting an angle with Rey Mysterio in May of 2009, I flipped out. Not literally, as that was Rey's job, but we'd been working in the same company together for basically the last fourteen years from WAR to WCW to WWE, and I'd only wrestled him a few times. We'd never done a full-blown program and I was stoked, because due to my time in Mexico and Japan, I really understood what he could do with the right partner.

It wasn't like he hadn't wrestled dozens of amazing matches during his time in the WWE, because he was one of those rare perfomers who could kill it with anybody. But I wanted to do something different that he hadn't been able to do yet. I wanted to tell a story that people could sink their teeth into, like I had done with Shawn Michaels and his wife. Something that went above and beyond the norm. I had an idea to do something involving the most important element of his character . . . his mask.

He'd been in the WWE for years, but during that time, nobody had ever gone after his mask and exploited it fully. It was the crux of his very existence in wrestling, a symbol of courage that he and his family had worn proudly for decades. It was the perfect reason to start a story line . . . but only if Vince agreed.

I met with him in his office before a *Raw* in Pittsburgh and pitched my idea.

"Rey has been in the WWE for seven years and we've never explained why he wears a mask. Why it's so important to his family, his legacy, his dignity. We should make our fans aware of the history of the mask in Mexico and how it means everything to a luchador to hide his true identity. And after we explain it, I want to take that mask away from him."

Vince looked at me and rolled his eyes, "Nobody cares about the mask."

I was surprised by his response and disagreed.

"If nobody cares about his mask, then why do we sell them by the thousands? Kids are wearing those things all over the arena at every show."

Vince was still hesitant. "He wears a mask, so what? What does it really mean? Why would you feel so compelled to take it away from him?"

My response was quick and to the point.

"Because I can."

McMahon looked intrigued and I knew I'd hooked him . . . ever so slightly . . . but this was my chance to reel him in.

"Nobody wants to see Batman without his mask except The Joker—and I'm The Joker. I want to take his mask the same way a bully takes a kid's milk money, whether he likes milk or not. He takes it because he can. What he does with the money afterward is irrelevant. It's the act of taking something from someone that turns the bully on, and taking Mysterio's mask turns me on." Vince was looking at me with a contemplative face and I knew I had him. "I want to take his mask to embarrass him and steal what's his. I'm gonna push him around and laugh at how small he is because for pretty much the first time in my WWE career, I'll be bigger than my opponent. I'm the bully, Vince . . . and I'm gonna take what I want from him."

Vince thought for a few seconds and said, "OK, let's do it."

I suggested we build up the signifigance of the mask by flying to Mexico to do vignettes. Get footage of Arena Mexico and Rey's neighborhood; interview his family and fans; really tell that story. But Vince wasn't interested in the history of Rey's mask. All he cared about was my desire to bully it away from him. That was fine since I'd already gotten his approval to fight for Rey's mask, and that was all I needed. Now the rest was up to us.

Rey was the Intercontinental Champion and I built up our first match by doing a promo questioning why Rey wore a mask in the first place. What was he hiding? Was he scared to show his face? I ranted that the only people who insisted on hiding their faces were criminals and cowards. And if he was a criminal, why was he cheered by the WWE Universe? In my mind, Rey was another complete hypocrite just like HBK, and I vowed to take his mask and reveal his guilty face to the world.

Finally, at the Judgment Day PPV in May 2009, we had our first match, with the title at stake. Much like my initial match with Shawn in our 2008 program, this one was more straightforward in order to set the stage for what was about to come. Rey and I had always had stellar chemistry, and we jam-packed the contest with froot reversals, false finishes, and all of the mask-removal teases that were commonplace in Mexico but had never been seen in the WWE. I pulled his mask half off, exposing the bottom of his face until he was barely able to pull it down. I slammed his head into the turnbuckle and tried to rip his mask off his face, only to have him hold on with the tips of his fingers or his teeth. Then I shot him into the turnbuckle chest-first, and when he hit, he took his mask off for a split second, then adjusted it back into place quickly. Eventually, he won the match with a beautiful 619–top rope splash combination and retained his title, which of course did not sit well with me. I demanded another shot, which Rey refused, and I vowed my revenge.

A few days later I got it.

Every time I worked with Rey, we had amazing matches and did moves that defied gravity. This is a picture of me spiking him on his head from the top rope.

Rey had a great relationship with his fans and every night as he walked down the aisle toward the ring, he lightly head-butted the kids lined up at the guardrail, who were wearing his souvenir masks. Halfway down, he would stop and give one lucky fan the ornamental mask he wore over his ring mask. Kids went nuts for this and it was a big part of his unique appeal.

Years earlier, when I was a nameless, faceless babyface in WCW, the only thing I did that got me any reaction at all was to throw my back against the guardrail on the way to the ring and let the fans slap me on the chest. I was just trying to do something different and while it might've been a little homoerotic to put myself in the position to be caressed by a slew of guys, good or bad it helped me stand out a little. When Masa Chono and I were building up our match for the nWo Souled Out PPV, he hid in the crowd and attacked me during my ritual. Harkening back to that angle, I wanted to do the same thing to Rey, except I'd add the twist of disguising myself in one of his own masks before ambushing him.

We were doing *SmackDown* at the Staples Center in Los Angeles and it was time for Rey to come out. I was waiting behind the massive stage set, wearing a Mysterio mask, large baggy Rey T-shirt, and black baggy sweatpants. His music started and I was led through the crowd to a row of seats about halfway down from the ring. I didn't want it to be obvious and have security clear a path for me, so at this point it was up to me to push my way through the fans and get to the front of the guardrail on my own.

"Excuse me, pardon me," the overgrown kid with the Rey shirt and matching Mysterio mask said as he elbowed his way through the excited glut of kids jockeying for prime pole position to get the nod from their hero.

He walked down the aisle, tapping heads with one young fan, then another. It was obvious they were kids as they were the same height as he was. For the first time ever in my career, I was too tall, so I spread my legs apart to appear shorter and remain inconspicuous. I waited my turn as Rey made his way down the line, until he got to me and we lightly butted noggins. As soon as he walked past me, I grabbed him from behind and smashed his head into the guardrail.

"Hey, what are you doing?" I heard a little kid say as I jumped the rail and further attacked my fallen pRey. I stomped him a few times, then ripped the mask off and continued to beat him down as the crowd screamed in outrage when they recognized me. My attack was a legit surprise, and there was a buzz in the arena as I walked up the ramp. But when I walked through the curtain, Vince motioned me over.

I checked the monitor to make sure Rey wasn't bleeding, wondering what I'd done wrong this time. "You rushed that," Vince said simply. "You should've taken more time for the reveal."

I thought he was just nitpicking but when I watched it back, he was right as usual. Instead of ripping my mask off after a few quick stomps, I should've beaten Mysterio down longer and forced people to guess who it could be. Then I should've faced the camera and slowly revealed my face, like a burlesque stripper peeling off her evening gloves. Vince's comments put me in my place and made me realize that even though I was on a roll, I wasn't doing everything perfectly. Plus, it was a good reminder that the boss was always watching me.

The situation between Rey and me got even crazier at the Extreme Rules PPV, where every match on the card had some sort of gimmick. There were quite a few choices thrown at us, including Falls Count Everywhere and a hard-core match. I wasn't happy with either of those, since I didn't want to throw away the technical aspects of the match that Oscar (Rey's real name) and I could display like no other. We had such good timing that I wanted to do another fairly straight match, and suggested a No-Holds-Barred stip because I knew in that scenario we could do whatever we wanted and not sacrifice the integrity of the bout in the process.

Vince agreed but only if we could think of an interesting finish, something where I would go over for the title but protect Rey so we could have a rematch. I needed to figure out a way to unmask and pin him quickly to take advantage of the distraction. I wondered if it was possible to rip off his mask as he was executing his famous 619 finishing move. As I always do when I need to figure out if an idea can work, I went into a dark corner of the arena by myself and closed my eyes to try and visualize it in my mind. I envisioned lying prone on the second rope as Oscar swung through the ropes and aimed his knees at my head for the 619. I knew if his mask was loose enough and we timed it perfectly, I could pluck it off of his head like a fly's wing just as he rotated.

When I asked him about it, he totally thought we could pull it off (pun intended) and had the perfect prop for the job. He showed me an open-backed mask he had in his bag with crisscrossing straps that would be ideal for me to hook my fingers into. The day of the PPV, we got in the ring to try it out and I draped myself over the second rope as Oscar bounced off the ropes behind me to go for the 619. Just as he swung his legs around, I hooked my fingers in the open area at the back of his mask and pulled it off with perfect timing, moving out of the way of his rotation at the same time. He landed in front of me unmasked and we laughed at how easy it was. We had our finish. Now, as always, we just had to get Vince to approve it.

Ricky Steamboat was the agent for our match, but when I told him what we wanted to do, I could sense that he either didn't like the idea or didn't understand it. He went to run it past Vince, but in my mind this was the finish and I wasn't going to take no for an answer. I had learned years earlier that if I had any chance of getting the boss to approve an idea, I needed to pitch it to him myself. If he heard the passion and belief in my voice, he'd be more apt to trust my instincts and let us do it. But I didn't want to disrespect Steamer and disrupt the chain of command, so I thought I'd see what Rick would come back with first.

Sure enough, he returned and told us Vince had shot down the idea, saying we couldn't do it. I couldn't believe the boss didn't like our genius finish and asked Ricky exactly what he'd said. He explained that Vince was concise in saying we couldn't do it and to think of something else. There was nothing else, so I told Dragon I was going to go ask Vince myself.

I marched into his office . . . again . . . and asked him why he didn't like our finish. He said bluntly, "Because you can't do it."

I wanted him to be more specific.

"You mean we can't do it because you don't want us to do it, or because you don't think it's physically possible?"

"I don't see how it's physically possible."

Aha! I knew it was physically possible because we'd just done it. I asked him to come with me to the ring immediately, before he got wrapped up with something else. He hemmed and hawed, mumbling how "this better be good," or some other similar grumpy-old-man sentiment, before reluctantly following me into the arena. I grabbed Oscar and we got into the ring so I could I drape myself into position. He ran across the ring and swung his knees around toward my face. I waited until the exact right moment, slid my fingers into the webbing of the back of his mask, and slipped the damn thing right off his head.

Vince had a look of true bewilderment like he'd just seen me make an elephant disappear.

"Do that again," he demanded, as if we'd used some sort of Criss Angel sleight of hand to hoax him.

We performed the magic trick flawlessly a second time and Vince nodded his head approvingly with a big smile on his face. "Amazing; it's a home run! There's your finish, guys."

The mysterio of our finish solved, we went on to put together the rest of the match—and what a match it was. Working with Oscar reminded me of working with Ultimo Dragon or The Rock in that we didn't have to go over much because we had so many spectacular moves we could do together almost intuitively.

He set me up for a 619, but I shot up quickly from the second rope, met him in the middle, swung him onto my shoulders, and gave him a spinning fireman's carry into a backbreaker. Then I sat him up on the top rope with his face to the crowd and tried to pull his mask off. He elbowed me off to the mat and followed up with a super Thesz press that knocked me off my feet. Then he came off the ropes with a flying body press, a kick to the head, and a frankensteiner, but I nailed him with a HUGE clothesline and grabbed a chair. I brought it into the ring, but before I could use it, he kicked it in my face, drop toeholded me onto it, and set it up as a platform to jump off. I caught him midair, just as he went to give me another frankensteiner, and turned him quickly into the Walls of Jericho. The crowd pleaded with him to escape as he reached desperately for the chair that was still set up behind my back. He finally grabbed it, squirming over onto his back, with me still holding his legs, and whacked me in the head with it. It was a killer spot and the crowd roared as I fell over onto the second rope, putting me into position for the dreaded 619. It was time for the finish and the fans were going loco as he hit the ropes and ran toward me at full speed, convinced he was going to nail me for the victory.

It was time for the moment of truth. Even though we'd done the unmasking twice in a row in rehearsal, I was nervous. If I messed up, Vince would be pissed and Steamboat would get chewed out royally. Another of the boss's favorite sayings was "Shit rolls downhill," and whenever something went wrong in a match, it was rarely the wrestlers who got yelled at; it was the agent (or producer) of the segment. But it was too late to second-guess myself and when Rey swung through, I burrowed my fingers into the straps and robbed him of his mask for the third straight time.

Oscar swung to his feet and covered his face with his hands as I rolled him up and scored the victory, still holding his flaccid mask. I was the Intercontinental Champion for the record-breaking ninth time, after one of the most surprising finishes ever. If any of you fearless readers claim to have called that ending before it happened, I will respectfully tell you that you're full of frijoles.

The next night, Rey demanded a rematch, which of course I refused, leading to his offering to put up his mask in exchange for one more chance at the title. But if I beat him again, he would be forced to unmask forever.

At the next month's PPV, the two of us put on another clinic of one-of-a-kind reversals and false finishes. When I tried for the spinning fireman's carry, this time he DDT'd me out of it. He tried for the 619, but I caught his legs as he swung through and twisted him over into the Walls of Jericho. He escaped and finally connected with the 619, then springboarded onto my shoulders and swung down for one of his patented frankensteiners. But when he swung between my legs, I switched my grip and suddenly had him locked in the Walls a second time. He squirmed his way out of the hold, so I muscled him into the air, but he slid down my back and pulled me into a sunset flip. I rolled through onto my feet, grabbing his mask as I went and pulling it off yet again. I held it in the air like a trophy, unleashing a triumphant war cry, but unbeknownst to me, Oscar had been wearing a SECOND mask the whole time. It was a classic lucha libre trick that we'd done many times before in Mexico against different opponents, but never in the WWE. I turned around and, to my surprise, he dropkicked me to the second rope. One 619 and West Coast pop later, he had regained the Intercontinental Championship belt and I had another Feud Of The Year under mine.

Gracias, WeeWeeto!

Our program lasted three consecutive PPVs, with a couple more contests on *SmackDown*, all of which were very good to excellent. One of our TV matches had a beat-the-clock scenario, where if Rey could beat me within a 7-minute 19-second time limit, he would advance in a title tournament. We were told to come as close to that time as possible but not to push our luck and cut it too close. So when Mysterio, referee Scotty Armstrong, and I went over the finish, I told Scotty, "Don't tell anybody about this, but we're going to beat the clock by one second."

Scotty was a little nervous, but the three of us had been around a long time and trusted each other wholly, so he agreed with a smile. Rey and I had another sensational match, but time was running out and our producer, Malenko, was screaming at us via Scotty's earpiece "GO HOME!" The clock was ticking; 7 minutes 10 seconds, 7 minutes 11 seconds. Rey rolled me up at 7 minutes 13 seconds, and Scotty started his count and reached three as the clock hit 7 minutes 18 seconds . . . leaving us with one second remaining on the clock.

When we got through the curtain, Dean was shaking his head in disbelief, claiming that we'd almost given him a coronary.

"You motherfuckers, I can't believe you crazy bastards did that! Now don't ever do it again!" he said with a shaky laugh.

But I have to say I would be honored to do it again with Rey Mysterio anytime, anyplace, anywhere.

CHAPTER 21

Hosts with the Most . . . or Least

The Mysterio feud was another big success for me both personally and critically. For the second year in a row I was voted Wrestler of the Year by the *Wrestling Observer* newsletter, a feat accomplished by only a handful of other performers in history, including Ric Flair and Kenta Kobashi. I'd also been named the Superstar of the Year at the 2008 WWE Slammy Awards, an accolade I mentioned on *Raw*, like, 365 times over the course of the next 365 days.

Vince gave me the Slammy because he could count on me in any situation and knew, no matter who he put me in the ring with, wrestlers or non-wrestlers, I could make them look good.

He wanted to increase the mainstream celebrity involvement within the WWE, so he came up with the idea of having a guest "host" on *Raw* every week. Much like *Saturday Night Live*, somebody from the outside world, whether it be an actor, musician, politician, or assorted other public figures, would appear every Monday night and act as the de facto general manager for the night. They'd make the matches, be involved in backstage bits, and sometimes even wrestle.

Some of these stars were superfans who felt that working with the WWE was a massive honor and went the extra mile to make things great. Others could give two shits about the company and were there just to be on TV. Those latter types would put in minimal effort, and their segments would usually bomb, making for a bad show. At first the die-hard WWE audience mostly booed these hosts with the most . . . or least . . . for they weren't kind to outsiders coming into our world. To remedy this, Vince put ME in with them almost every week to ensure I was the one who got booed, not the hosts, and to give their segments a fighting chance to be good. Sometimes I succeeded and sometimes I failed.

There was only so much I could do if the host was uninterested (Bradley Cooper), uninformed (Jeremy Piven, referring to SummerSlam as SummerFest), or unexciting (Jewel and Ty Murray), but when people ask me who the worst hosts in *Raw* history were, five names come to mind.

DENNIS MILLER (Honorable Mention): I consider Dennis to be one of the worst hosts, more on how he was received by the audience rather than anything to do with his actual performance. I thought he did a decent job hosting the 2009 Slammy Awards, but in typical Miller fashion, most of his cerebral, sophisticated material flew right over the heads of the live crowd in Corpus Christi and caused him to suck worse than Edward Cullen. He dug himself a massive hole when he called HHH The Show instead of The Game (to which Hunter replied, "Thanks, Dennis Milburn") and then admitted that if he had known all along that all he had to do to get a reaction from the fans was say "Suck it," things might've gone better.

Before the show, I saw Vince and Dennis talking at length, and later on, Miller was wandering around the arena, hair tousled and eyes tired, so I asked him how he was doing.

"I'm doing great," he said, his voice dripping with sarcasm. "I spent all day getting comedy advice from Vince McMahon. My life is complete."

Classic Vince. He would've told Wayne Gretzky how to score a goal.

JON LOVITZ: After apparently turning down Kiss because they weren't "relevant," the WWE invited Lovitz to host. He hadn't done anything relevant since *The Wedding Singer* back in '98. His backstage bits were awkward and weird because Jon's personality is awkward and weird. I warned John Morrison that I'd met Lovitz before, backstage at a Fozzy concert (another wacky story found in my botany book, *Undisputed*, available at a fine florist near you), and he had spent twenty minutes asking me what the ring ropes were made of. Morrison was convinced Jon couldn't be that bad, but when I saw him a few hours later, he ran over and admitted, "He IS that bad! He cornered me for thirty minutes asking me what ring ropes are made of!" (It's rope, BTW.)

KYLE BUSCH & JOEY LAGANO: For some reason, these two NASCAR drivers were invited to host even though they had the personality of windshield wipers. They seemed to know nothing about the product and had even less interest in learning. When Lagano referred to Double H during a backstage rehearsal, I corrected him that it was Triple H.

"Whatever" was his flippant reply.

Their performance in front of the live crowd was even more whatever. I had no idea who these two clowns were and neither did eighty percent of the people in Buffalo, which wasn't exactly NASCAR country. They delivered their lines like furniture salesmen from a local TV commercial (Come. To. Fast. Eddie's. Furniture. And. Get. A. Great. Deal.) and their horribly timed insults fell flatter than Nicko McBrain's nose. Also, like Ricky Bobby, they weren't quite sure what to do with their hands and fidgeted constantly, like a pair of seven-year-olds in church. I did everything I could to make the segment good, but dammit, Jim, I'm an entertainer, not a miracle worker!

AND THE "WORST GUEST HOST IN *RAW* HISTORY" AWARD GOES TO . . . AL SHARPTON!: Vince is a huge fan of Martin Luther

King Jr, which is why you'll always see an inspirational video package about the good doctor before *Raw* on every MLK day. Sharpton was a young protégé of King, and Vince was ecstatic to have him host the show. But it wasn't without a price.

Sharpton demanded to be flown in on the WWE's private jet, showed up ninety minutes before showtime, and left fifteen minutes after *Raw* started. His role consisted of kicking off the show in-ring and two backstage pretapes, both of which he did in one take with as little effort as possible. As for the opening promo, he pulled a Brando, not bothering to read the script beforehand or have any idea the points he was supposed to get across.

Once again, I drew the shortest straw (witch hunt riding through) and was designated the "general" of the segment, making sure everything went smoothly and that Al hit his cues. Vince handed me a script he'd personally written, full of lines complimenting Sharpton for his bravery and applauding his civil rights accomplishments, all underlined with a black Sharpie. Now, keep in mind I was the most hated heel in the company, who hadn't said anything nice about anybody in over a year, but now I was supposed to kowtow to Al Sharpton and claim he was frooter than Arthur Fonzarelli himself? It didn't make any sense to me, and I told Vince so.

"Chris, this is your promo and you will not change a thing. Do you understand?" he said, staring at me intensely. I understood and went off to learn my verbiage exactly as it was written.

What followed was one of the most boring segments I've ever been involved in. I said some stuff, Sharpton said some stuff, and the crowd in Albany, New York, said nothing. I don't remember anything else other than it was the shits of the drizzling variety. Usually when I'm writing a book, if I can't recall the exact details of the story I'm telling, I'll look it up online and check it out. But I'm not gonna do that now because it's not necessary. I sucked, Sharpton sucked, and the less said about this steaming pile of horseshit, the better. So let us never speak of it again, ya dig?

Fortunately, plenty of the guest hosts were excellent, going above and beyond what was expected in energy (Hugh Jackman), creativity (Seth Green), and comedy (William Shatner, who sang various entrance themes in his deadpan, hamazing style. "He's just . . . a . . . sexy . . . boy." Please Google this now; it's hilarious.)

But when people ask me who the best hosts in *Raw* history were, four names come to mind.

SHAQUILLE O'NEAL: Judging from Shaq's backstage demeanor, I wasn't expecting much out of him at all. He nonchalantly sat in his private dressing room, surrounded by his entourage, and played with his phone the whole time we were going over the plan for that night in Washington, DC. Big Show and I were the unified tag-team champions and I was taking every opportunity possible to hide behind my giant partner. Shaq was going to kick off the show, but halfway through his opening speech, I was going to come out and antagonize him. He seemed OK with it but totally uninterested and practically blew us off, but when showtime arrived, Shaq delivered a three-pointer (#basketballanalogyfail).

A few minutes into his opening promo, I marched to the ring and stared at him face-to-face . . . face to chin . . . face to collarbone. Actually, it was more like face to nipple, as Shaq was a good foot taller than me. But I'm Chris Jericho, and I didn't care.

I stared him down for a good forty-five seconds before telling him forcefully, "When I heard the most dominant player in NBA history was guest hosting *Raw*, I automatically assumed it was Kobe Bryant." Now,

I don't know much about basketball, but even I knew that one was a zinger, as did the crowd, who "oohed" in astonishment at my audacity. I continued on, "Everyone knows the most powerful duo in sports isn't Shaq and LeBron James, its Chris Jericho and the Big Show."

Shaq interrupted me authoritatively and said, "Hold on . . . CHRISTINA."

I had no idea the big man was going to say that, and I could barely keep a straight face as the fans erupted accordingly to the insult. Then at the apex of their cheers, Shaq leaned down and planted a big wet kiss on my forehead.

I also had no idea he was going to kiss me. But he did it with such perfect comedic timing that it brought the house down. Every fan in that arena, no matter how fickle they usually were with the celebrity guests, became a Shaq fan at that moment. Then he cut off his own gigantic pop by asking me quickly what I was doing out there. His kiss ad lib was too good a moment to waste, so I didn't immediately respond and just kept looking at him with the most over-the-top astonished expression. I slowly lifted my hand to my forehead and wiped his spittle away, milking it for all it was worth. As I expected, the crowd came back, buzzing like Aldrin at the ridiculousness they'd just witnessed. Then I corrected Shaq, slowly and deliberately. "It's Chris . . . NOT Christina."

Of course the crowd took the bait and chanted, "CHRISTINA, CHRISTINA," like a pack of horny teenagers at a taping of *The Voice*. I laid into Shaq about how I was the "best in the world at what I do" (at what I have no idea) and was sick of being disrespected by everybody in the WWE, especially the guest hosts. Shaq pushed me around a little until the Big Show finally came out to save me. Show and Shaq had a tension-filled staredown, and even though nothing ever came of it (I think at one point they were supposed to have a match at Mania), it still ended up being a historic WWE moment.

OZZY OSBOURNE: When I heard Ozzy was going to be hosting

Raw, I called Vince and demanded (OK, begged) him to let me do something . . . anything . . . with the Prince of Darkness. I pointed out that I had been his guest host go-to guy for weeks and this could be my reward for all the nerdy NASCAR drivers, weird comedians, and sanctimonious civil rights leaders I'd tried to make watchable. When I arrived at *Raw* in Worcester, Massachusetts, and found out I had a backstage pretape with the madman, I jumped around the room doing the zombie stomp. Even though I'd been close friends with his former guitarist Zakk Wylde for years, I'd never had the chance to meet Ozzy face-to-face and was pretty nervous. To me, Ozzy lived in the same rarefied air as James Hetfield and I didn't want to freak out meeting him like I had with Papa Het.

I showed up in the pretape room and Ozzy and Sharon were already there. She was friendly and chatted my ear off about how much fun they were having. She was so nice that I decided not to bring up our horrendous first meeting backstage at Ozzfest years earlier. Ozzy, however, was disengaged and barely said anything to me.

I was trying to play it froot, but the camera had some technical issues and it was taking forever to get rolling, so I mentioned to Ozzy that I was close friends with Zakk, and that broke the ice. He told me how much he loved Wylde (who had recently departed from Ozzy) and how great a player he was. Eventually the camera was fixed and Vince came in to run through our pretape, a scene where I was going to admonish Ozzy for losing his edge over the years, before Oz shot me down and put me in my place just like every other guest host had.

"I don't need all of these hypocrite fans because I am better than them . . . and I'm better than you, Ozzy."

"I really don't think so," Oz said, stroking his chin wisely.

I warned him if they ever crossed me again, it would be the Ultimate Sin, and walked away. Then Vince's idea for the closing line was Ozzy asking, "Who was that wanker?"

When Ozzy heard his last line, he stared at McMahon and said, "Oh no, man, I can't call him a wanker!"

"Why not, Ozzy?" Vince said in his deep voice.

"Because it's a really bad word, man. I mean you can't say that on national television; do you know what it means, man?"

Vince didn't and asked him for the definition.

"*Wanker* means a tosser. Like a giant cock that you're about to jerk off, you know what I mean, man? It would be the same as calling him a fuckin' jack-off, yeah?"

Vince contemplated Ozzy's revelation and replied, "But does anybody know what it means in the United States?"

Ozzy was exasperated now. "Of course they do! And besides, this show airs in England too, right?"

Vince nodded his head and thanked Ozzy for the sage advice.

Kids, you know there's a problem when Ozzy Osbourne is the voice of reason about what's acceptable language on American television.

After I walked out of the shot, Ozzy instead said, "Who was that joke?" and Sharon added, "That was a crazy guy." It was a totally lame ending on paper but ended up great because of Ozzy's confused delivery.

After our pretape was done, Ozzy pretended to strangle me for a photo op and then told me he liked my character. We were just two guys hanging out at that point and I knew it was my chance to ask him all of the questions I'd been building up for the last thirty years.

"Oz, can I ask you a question? What does S.A.T.O. stand for?"

"S.A.T.O." was a song off Ozzy's second solo album, *Diary of a Madman*, and I'd always thought it stood for Sail Across The Ocean.

"Well, whenever I'm writing lyrics and I can't think of a song title, I just use initials as a placeholder. Some of them stick, some don't. I had just written this song and didn't know what to call it, so after having lunch with me and my ex-wife and Sharon and her ex, I decided to use our initials. So it stands for Sharon, Alan, . . ."

Ozzy paused for a good ten seconds before continuing.

". . . THELMA, and Ozzy."

I didn't know what was frooter, the fact that I'd finally learned the meaning of S.A.T.O. or the fact that it took Ozzy ten seconds to remember his ex-wife's name.

I pressed on. "So what does A.V.H. stand for from the *No More Tears* record?"

"That stands for the Aston Villa Highway, a road that runs past my house in Birmingham."

Another mystery solved! But there was still one more thing I needed to know.

"So what does N.I.B. stand for?"

"N.I.B." is a Black Sabbath classic and its meaning had been debated during late-night drinking sessions for many years. Did it stand for Not In Body? Name In Blood? Nazarine Is Burning? Or my personal favorite, Nativity In Black?

"I don't even know what a nativity IS, man!" Ozzy said with a laugh. "I thought of that one because the drummer in Black Sabbath [Bill Ward] used to have a really long pointy beard that looked like the nib of a pencil. So that's what I called the song . . . NIB."

The riddle had been explained and it wasn't as evil as I'd expected, but neither was Ozzy. He was funny, sharp, witty, and having a great time hosting *Raw*. I ran into him again in the hallway later as Santino was filming a backstage segment dressed like Ozzy from the *Diary of a Madman* cover.

"He looks just like me," Ozzy said, laughing. "I used to look just like that, man!"

Yeah, that's the idea, Oz.

Sharon came over and I told her we'd met before. I told her the story of when she yelled at me and Zakk backstage at Ozzfest for playing baseball in the parking lot (as explained in the classic rock chronicle

Undisputed, available at music stores everywhere). When I hit the punch line of her yelling, "WHO THE FUCK ARE YOU?!" she gasped out loud, seemingly mortified that she'd spoken to me that way. However, Ozzy thought it was great. "Who the fuck are you, man?" he giggled for the rest of the night whenever he saw me.

When *Raw* finished, I thanked them again and bid farewell. Ozzy walked away giggling and mumbling, "Who the fuck are you?" one more time, as Sharon gave me a hug and apologized again. Then she pinched my ass (hard) and gave me a wink as she got in the limo.

In case you're wondering . . . I totally would.

MIKE TYSON: Mike had a huge part in the revitalization of the WWE in 1998 and hadn't appeared with the company since. So it was a huge honor when I found out I'd be working with him during his first live *Raw* appearance in over ten years. Even better, he was going to be my partner in a tag match against DX, which would be his first-ever wrestling match.

When Tyson showed up in Minneapolis, The Baddest Man on the Planet was also one of the friendliest. He, along with his son (who called everyone sir, at Mike's insistence), introduced themselves to everybody they ran into before the show. Not only was Tyson ultrarespectful, he was also an überfan who knew more about wrestling history than I did. He kept talking about how Bruno Sammartino was his favorite WWE champion of all time, and when we went into the ring to discuss the night's activities, he was looking around like a kid in a candy store.

"There's Arn Anderthon! There's Michael P.Sth. Hayeth! There's Ricky Thteamboat!" he squealed, chasing after The Dragon to say hello.

Tyson's famous lisp was more pronounced in person, and combined with his thick New York accent and high voice, it made it difficult for me to have a conversation with him, because all I wanted to do was burst out laughing. It's that bad. But I held my tongue, for I didn't want to pith him off before he was to knock me out later. Yeah, that's what I said . . . Iron Mike Tyson was going to punch me in the face at the end of *Raw*.

The story was I'd been getting fired and rehired on *Raw* for weeks and this was my last chance to stay. If I lost this match against DX, I was going to be banished from *Raw* for good, so I needed a Bad Mama Jama (yeah, yeah, I know what it means) to have my back and called Mike Tyson. He had a history with DX after turning on HBK during the Michaels vs. Austin main event at WrestleMania 15 when he was the guest referee, so story-line–wise, I knew he was the right man for the job.

We spent a few hours going over some simple spots as HHH wanted him to look good at whatever he did. Even though he had retired from boxing, having THE Mike Tyson work a pro wrestling match was a huge deal and the WWE knew his involvement would get major coverage from mainstream sports media.

Then we all discussed the best way for him to punch me. Shawn mentioned when Tyson knocked him out at Mania, he'd thrown the punch by stepping in and swinging upward, driving his elbow into Shawn's stomach, which stopped its momentum just underneath HBK's chin. That seemed a little risky and I suggested Mike throw a "Hollywood punch" like he had when he decked Zach Galifianakis in *The Hangover*. Take a swing across my jaw, but miss by a few inches and have the camera shoot it from behind. I'd turn my head just as his fist passed in front of my face and it would look like he walloped me.

We decided that was the proper way to go and Mike and I went backstage to film a pretape of the two of us sparring in preparation. I put on the special flat-sided gloves but since I'd never sparred with anyone before, I got a little mixed up, causing Mike to start chuckling loudly.

"You put the glovth on the wrong handth!" pointing at me like he was seven years old. "You've got them on the wrong way! Thath hilariouth!"

I sheepishly switched hands and Mike started hammering the pads with his blows. Even though he was forty pounds overweight and twenty years past his prime, his punches were HARD. He was rocking my hands back with such power that my shoulders were hurting and I felt like my rotator cuff was going to tear in half.

He was still very fast too, and I could hardly see his hands as they machine-gunned back and forth into the sparring pads. I could only imagine how hard he must've hit in his glory days and there was no way I would ever agree to box him past, present, or future. Yet I'd agreed to stand there and let him take a free swing at my face on national TV. What was I thinking?! This was no Mickey Rourke I was going to give a free shot to . . . this was Iron Mike Tyson!

The main event (there I go again) began and the arena was awash with anticipation of what Tyson was going to do. He started off with HHH for a few minutes, pushing him into the corner and peppering him with body blows. I tagged in and kicked DX's mascot, Hornswoggle, in the face when he ran in to interfere on behalf of his buddies. Then I stood in the middle of the ring, bragging to Shawn and Hunter that I had the baddest man on the planet on my team as Tyson entered the ring behind me. He slowly took off his baggy black T-shirt to reveal a DX one underneath. The audience roared with approval at his double cross as I turned around to face my fate.

Earlier in the day, I told Mike to take his time before punching me so we could milk the crowd reaction to the max. Before he made his move, I wanted every fan in the arena sitting on the edge of their seats, slapping their friends on the shoulder in anticipation, saying, "This is going to be great! Jericho is gonna get his ass handed to him!!"

Now, I'm not the world's most passionate guy, but when I turned around and looked Mike Tyson in the eye, I was legitimately scared. Here was one of the most feared men on the planet staring at me, ready to attack. I could see every detail—the open pores on his face, the pointed eyebrows, the shiny gold tooth, the tribal tattoo outlining his eye—and at that moment, I felt like the craziest man in the world. I was standing in the ring in front of millions of people, ready to let the baddest man on the planet take a free swing at my face.

I was a sitting Canadian duck (a mallard?) and was putting my health . . . my very life . . . in the hands of a documented lunatic. A nutcase who could be drunk, high, pissed off at life, in a bad mood . . . who the fuck knew? Maybe he harbored some sort of grudge against me or didn't like my hairstyle? How did I know for sure? None of that mattered anyway, because as soon as I gave Mike his cue, the iron hammer was going to fall. I raised my hands, palms forward in a defensive position, and time stood still as he pulled back his fist and launched a right hook directly at my chin.

I couldn't believe how fast he was and the punch flew by me so quickly that I actually felt a breeze. I barely had enough time to turn my chin in tandem with his swing, but when I hit the mat, the crowd gasped as they thought he legitimately tuned me. I'd seen guys get knocked out back in my bouncing days and it was never pretty. Never did the dude take a perfectly flat bump or roll around in pain holding his chin. I wanted everybody to think I was really KO'd so I splayed out on the mat like a dead bug, with my arms bent up in the air and hands askew.

It must have looked pretty damn vicious, because the ref came over and asked me under his breath if I was OK. Kevin Dunn was convinced I was out cold and the replays from multiple camera angles (but not the secret one in the corner of the arena) backed him up. The way Tyson timed his punch, and the way I sold it, left no doubt that he had annihilated me. Except he hadn't even touched me, and I had to suppress a smile as he and the rest of DX celebrated my demise by crotch-chopping over my fallen carcass.

What a way to make a living.

———

AND THE "BEST GUEST HOST IN *RAW* HISTORY" AWARD GOES TO . . . BOB BARKER!: When it was announced Bob was going to be hosting *Raw*, I felt bad for the old guy. I was convinced our fans would boo the shit out of him, chew him up and spit him out like a sunflower seed, especially since we were going to be in Chicago, the home of our rowdiest crowd. But I couldn't have been more wrong. Bob had the crowd in the palm of his hand the whole time, like the fifty-year show-biz veteran that he is, and walked away as the most entertaining guest host ever.

He opened the show by welcoming the crowd as if they were a live studio audience and had them on his side within minutes. Then he introduced what is still one of my all-time favorite segments of my career: "The Price Is Raw."

"The Price Is Raw" was designed to be a knockoff of *The Price Is Right*, where WWE Superstars would guess the prices of various items, and the winner would get a prize. With the TV show's famous cheesetastic theme song playing in the background, Bob stood on the stage with his badass SKINNY MICROPHONE, as Howard Finkel, the greatest ring announcer of all time, introduced the contestants. The lucky winners ran through the crowd screaming and waving their arms with joy as the camera panned back and forth through the sold-out arena, looking for them. The first contestant chosen was Santino Marella, who was yelling so loudly and was so excited that he tripped jumping over the barricade, much to the crowd's delight. Then Howard announced Jillian Hall, Irwin R. Schyster (one of Brian Gewirtz's favorite characters, who was written into the show as much as possible), and finally . . . Chris Jericho.

Keep in mind I hadn't played anything for comedic value (or even smiled) in almost two years and I balked when I first heard I was going to be involved in the segment. I wasn't sure I wanted to open that door and make people laugh like I had in the past. But Brian convinced me that's exactly why I was the perfect candidate for the bit. I could play the whole thing completely straight, which would make things even funnier in the midst of all the inanity. I figured if I was going to go there, I was gonna take it all the way and stuck the giant, bright yellow CHRIS name tag right in the middle of my baby-oil-slathered bare chest. It was a slap-stick visual that Carrot Top would've been proud of, and it still makes me laugh to this day.

Bob called my name a few times ("Where's Chris? Chris, where art thou?"), until I finally strolled onstage like I owned the place, complete with scowling face and a bad attitude. Bob was a big WWE fan and knew exactly who my character was, and had no problem taunting me to get a laugh. All of his insults were improvised and it was all I could do to keep a straight face when he commented right off the bat, "Look at Chris. He's taking his time because he knows he's getting more camera time that way."

Bob announced the first item up for bid was a *SmackDown* DVD and we all bid on it. After asking to buy a vowel, Santino looked at the crowd for encouragement and bid 1,465 American dollars. Jillian guessed 75 bucks, IRS (after asking if the bid included taxes) bid 50. When asked for my bid, I just stood at the podium. Bob was unfazed and asked, "Are you awake, Chris? Hypnotic trance perhaps?"

Annoyed at his sassiness, I sauntered up the stage toward him and got in his grille. The shit was on.

"Your mother would not be proud of how you're behaving," Bob said, his breath smelling of mint gum. The quip took me by surprise and I had to bite my bottom lip.

"First of all—" I growled menacingly, before Bob cut me off with "The man talks! He's actually speaking!" The crowd loved that one and roared as Bob went silent, letting the zinger breathe.

I moved closer into Barker's face and went into my typical "the guest hosts always disrespect me and I deserve to be pandered to because I am The Best in the World at What I Do" tirade. The crowd was pissed when I ended my speech by calling him Old Man, and booed louder. It was hilarious to hear them react that way, as if they were listening to a verbal dual to the death between Rock and Austin and not a battle for the bid between Jericho and Barker.

I stared into his eyes menacingly like I was about to spay and neuter him and informed Bob that I was a pretty big deal in the WWE.

"I am one—" but before I could finish saying I was one-half of the tag-team champions (with Big Show), he cut me off and said that it was official . . . my bid was one dollar.

My demeanor changed and I went from crazy man to crybaby in one beat, like Stuntman Mike in *Death Proof.*

"One? No way . . . one isn't my bid! I wasn't ready, Bob!" I protested as he shooed me off the stage, repeating that one dollar was my bid, end of story. I yelled that he was a liar and threw my name tag to the ground in defiance.

"Pick up your name tag right now and be a good boy, Chris," Bob scolded me, then followed up with the crack-up coup de grâce: "Or I'm gonna have to take you over my knee." And for a split second I lost it. I've never cracked up on camera . . . ever. Nor have I ever cracked up on a movie set or onstage live with The Groundlings, but when Barker hit me with that line, I literally had to squeeze my lips together to keep from breaking up completely. Thankfully, the camera wasn't on me or I would've looked like Jerry Seinfeld trying to keep from smiling in that *Seinfeld* episode where . . . well, in just about every *Seinfeld* episode really.

I went back to the podium realizing that I'd just been schooled by one of the best in show business history. I gained a whole new respect for Bob that night and learned a lot about how to win over a crowd no matter what the demographic.

By the way, I won "The Price Is Raw" and the *Smackdown* DVD with the closest bid of one dollar, but come to think of it, I don't recall ever getting the thing.

Bob and I randomly continued our feud for a few years afterward, and fans still ask me if they'll ever see Bob Barker vs. Chris Jericho at a future WrestleMania. I never say never, but I will say this: Barker, I will take you on anytime, anyplace, anywhere . . . and I want my damn DVD!

Barker and me, getting in each other's faces on *Raw*. Between my name tag and Bob's kick-ass skinny mic, I can barely keep a straight face.

CHAPTER 22

The Flatland Mafia

When I got a call from the WWE magazine editors asking if I'd like to interview Iron Maiden for a story, I said yes before the chance went running free. I'd been a major fan and friend of the band for years, but to actually sit in a room and ask them anything I wanted was a fanboy's dream come true.

They were set to play The Forum in Los Angeles on their Somewhere Back in Time World Tour and I was planning on going anyway with my best friends, Speewee and Rybo, and my cousin Chad, who was very, very wise. The concert was in L.A. on a Tuesday after *Raw* on Monday in Anaheim and a PPV on Sunday in Las Vegas, so we decided to make a rock 'n' roll weekend out of it. The plan was to meet in Vegas and then fly to Anaheim on Monday morning.

So the Flatland Mafia (the name we called ourselves 'cause we're all from the prairies, eh) assembled in Sin City and after the PPV was over, we hit the strip. We were hanging in da club throwing down cocktails, when I saw Wise Chad standing next to a sweet-lookin' mama with a face like a gent and a pair of boobs bigger than his head. He was chatting her up with some of his best lines.

"What type of camera lenses do you like to use?" he asked.

Funbags Flanagan stared at him blankly and changed the subject quickly.

"So where are you from?" she asked, her chin resting on her mammaries.

"Yorkton, Saskatchewan," he replied wisely.

"I used to dance there."

"Oh, really! What kind of dancing? Ukranian?"

Tits McGhee looked perplexed and disappeared into the crowd. Chad, never one to give up easily, decided to jump up on the table to show off HIS dancing skills, which were most definitely of the Ukranian variety. (This was one of the few unwise decisions he ever made in his life.)

He drew quite a crowd with his hybrid moves that combined traditional Ukranian Koloneku with modern-day Krunking. He had just done a leaping Cossack kick straight into a dirty twerk, when a drunken (and apparently jealous) Speewee gave him a two-handed shove to the chest and pushed him off the table. Wise Chad fell hard onto the wooden floor, shattering a tray of shot glasses and yelping out in pain as the broken glass sliced into his back. I was furious at Speewee for messing with my family and knocked him out cold with a pefect jumping crane kick before helping Chad off the ground.

"I think I cut my back," he surmised wisely. He turned around and Rybo and I were repulsed by a giant gash in the middle of his back that looked like a vagina.

"Oh my gosh," Rybo gasped, "he has a BACK PUSSY!"

The ridiculous concept of the back pussy gave us a case of the giggles in spite of poor Chad's predicament. The bouncers took him to a back room to examine the gaping wound and insisted he needed stitches.

"Stitches?" I said with annoyance. "He don't need no stinkin' stitches! Besides, we don't have time to go to the hospital. [There was a party going on after all.] Can't you just butterfly the cut? That'll be good enough."

We were loaded, so this solution seemed perfectly rational. Combine that with the fact that the alcohol acted as an effective anesthesia (pulling teeth), so Chad wasn't feeling any pain, and it wasn't long before he was laughing along with us wisely. The gaping BACK PUSSY was bleeding through his shirt and it was obvious he needed stitches. But the joint was jumpin' and we were having far too much fun to take him to the hospital to get sewed up. Talk about a buzzkill. Besides, it was his fault for jumping up on the table so unwisely in the first place!

Chad had about twelve hours to get stitched up before the cut healed badly on its own, so we decided to take him into the arena when we got to *Raw* in Anaheim the next day and let Doc Amann take care of him. With that problem solved, we were kings as we raised our double Crowns to the sky and drained them in one gulp as the party raged on. . . .

. . . I woke up in our suite in the Planet Hollywood hotel sprawled across the floor with my clothes on, eyes red and head pounding. I gazed at the authentic *Terminator* outfit worn by Arnold Schwarzenegger on display in the middle of our room, and vaguely remembered using a chair to try to break through the bulletproof glass it was encased in so I could wear the leather ensemble myself. Thankfully, I'd failed.

I could tell by the way the sunlight was streaming through the window that we had overslept. We were supposed to take a nine thirty A.M. flight to John Wayne Airport in Santa Ana, but the clock on the dresser said 9:22 A.M. Since we were on the West Coast, *Raw* was going to start at six P.M. sharp, which meant my call time was eleven A.M. I'd inquired about changing my flight the day before and found out all of the later ones were sold out. So in order to make the show that night, I had no choice but to drive the five hours to Anaheim . . . but to get there on time, we were going to have to leave ASAFP!

"Wake up! Wake Up!" I screamed, running from room to room throughout the suite, trying to arouse the corpses strewn about the floor. They looked like extras from Drunk of the Dead as they slowly shambled from their alcoholic graves, hair askew and clothes disheveled. Twenty minutes later, the five of us (including BACK PUSSY, which had swollen to an ugly size) were in the car on the way to Anaheim. We had rushed out of the room so fast that I almost forgot something . . . my hangover. But once we got in the car, it caught up to me with a vengeance and slammed me harder than Big John Studd.

The sun was shining brightly that day, my friends, and it beamed directly into my eyes for the whole trip, driving its warm spikes of brightness straight into my brain. To make it to the arena on time we had to drive straight through with no stops for eating. So we were a tired, hungry, sweaty, motley crew when we arrived at the Honda Center in Anaheim a little after three P.M.

I hustled Chad inside to get stitched up, and after giving a valiant fight, BACK PUSSY was closed up for a thousand years like Satan in the abyss. Then a few minutes later I found out that for the first time in a decade of being employed by the WWE, I wasn't booked on *Raw*. Usually, I would've pitched a fit and demanded to know why, but considering that I felt like prison ass, I considered this to be a gift from the heavens. I wasn't totally free to go into the dressing room and puke on my pants, though, as my boy Larry King was there to film a behind-the-scenes look at the WWE and insisted I be involved. Larry decided he wanted to end the show with a shot of me escorting him out of the arena to his car. Not sure exactly why he chose me specifically, but I was happy to do it despite the fact I was as green as Gumby.

King greeted me with a hug and we filmed a quick segment explaining some of the backstage preparation that was required to make *Raw* happen. Then I walked with him to the parking lot ("I'm surprised you actually have legs, Larry. I thought you were just a talking torso.") and off he went. The whole thing took ten minutes, but I still felt like a shit sandwich and needed some fresh air. I propped myself against the wall of the arena and closed my eyes to clear some of the cobwebs out of my head. When I opened them up, Lindsay Lohan was standing beside me, smoking a cigarette.

With her reddish-blond hair and devil-may-care attitude, she was looking kind of right. She was there for a Make-A-Wish appearance and I hadn't seen her since I was hanging out with Axl Rose in NYC at four A.M. years earlier. (Don't cry if you haven't heard the story; it's all in my travel guide, *Undisputed*, available at service stations everywhere.) We exchanged nods, then she crushed out the smoke with her heel and got into her waiting SUV. As the driver pulled away, she looked out the window and blew me a kiss.

I blew her kiss back, then threw up all over the side of the Honda Center.

Twenty-four hours later I was in a room with Adrian Smith and Dave Murray, asking them every question I'd ever wanted to ask them since I was a teenager.

"Who were your influences as a guitar player?"

"How was it being involved with the Hear 'n Aid project?"

"What are your favorite Maiden songs to play? Your favorite solos you've ever written?"

It was like hanging with Ozzy all over again as they answered everything I wanted to know about the band, their early years, and their memories about wrestling (Mick McManus was their favorite as kids). It was a great experience as a fan and as a writer and I got a killer story out of it to boot.

The interview had been set up by Maiden's manager, Rod Smallwood, who invited us to the band's after-show party later on. After a sweaty and amazing show (I elbowed my way through the crowd to get to the very front of the stage), me, Speewee, Rybo, Wise Chad, Eli Roth (who was wearing an awesome T-shirt with *Fellini* spelled in Maiden lettering across the front), and his brother Gabe went backstage to "Rod's Room" for the party. Being that the show was in L.A, there was a star-studded who's who of heavy metal royalty milling about. Kerry King was talking to Scott Ian, Tom Morello was debating with Phil Campbell, and Paul Gargano was having a Jack Daniel's with Lemmy. I had a short conversation (of course it was) with Ronnie James Dio, who remembered me spilling red wine on him years earlier and checked my hands to make sure I wasn't holding a glass. I didn't have any wine, but there was plenty of vodka poured for me by Maiden guitarist Janick Gers himself.

Then Lars Ulrich walked in, wearing a Saxon T-shirt and holding his leather jacket over his shoulder. We talked for a bit ("How's Winnipeg?" he asked me, apparently thinking I still lived there) before Rybo told him the story of how Lars had rear-ended his girlfriend . . . literally. Before a Metallica show in Winnipeg, Lars had rented a car to check out some local sights and ran through a red light. He rammed right into Rybo's woman from behind (still doesn't sound right) and got her passes to that evening's show as a peace offering (Canadians never sue). With the ice once again broken and the fact I'd had a few more of Jannick's vodkas at that point, I decided to do my patented Lars imitation for him. (You wanna hear it? Ask me next time we meet.) He didn't seem to think it was as funny as I did but gave me a sympathy smirk and said he'd see me in a bit.

A few minutes later I saw him in the corner talking to Steve Harris, Maiden's bassist and one of my all-time heroes. I couldn't believe that the architects of two of my top three favorite bands (alas, no John Lennon) were having a conversation together. What could they possibly be talking about?! It was a great moment in metal history and I had to get a picture with them . . . I HAD TO!! But how? I couldn't very well interrupt them, as this was a private party with no fans allowed and, if I outed myself as one, I could get booted.

But there was another way.

When I was in high school in Winnipeg and hung out at the Polo Park Inn, hoping to meet wrestlers, my friend Wallass and I devised a system to get pictures with the guys we were too afraid to talk to. He would stand next to the wall, and when a wrestler walked into camera frame, I would call his name. The guy would turn and look at the lens, Wallass would smile, and bingo . . . it looked like the two of them had taken a picture together. Since Steve and Lars weren't on the move, I gave up on the idea of having them look at the camera, but I could still stand behind them for a snap, right? They were having a face-to-face conversation, so if I went to the right place, it would look like I was standing between them.

So I grabbed Rybo and gave my phone to Eli, assuming he'd get the right shot since he was a famous film director and all. I was totally nervous walking behind them for I could feel the majestical electrical force field of rock they were creating just by being in the same room together. Their combined metal powers could've messed up the entire time-space continuum had they so desired, but luckily for all of us mere mortals, they had decided to use their powers for good.

We got to the exact spot we needed to be in and looked up at the camera. Eli was cocked and ready to shoot, knowing we might only get one chance, as one glance in either direction by Steve or Lars would kill the moment. If they saw the two of us standing behind them smiling or noticed a guy pointing a phone at their faces, they would be onto us and the jig would be up. Thankfully, they were so ensconced in their metal summit, they didn't notice us. Rybo and I looked at the camera with a goofy grin, and Eli, the master auteur, snapped the perfect picture of the two of them engaged in conversation with the two of us standing perfectly in the middle, grinning like maniacs.

Not only was the groundbreaking metal meeting caught in time forever, Eli's picture also documented the sole gathering of the heaviest supergroup ever: Iron MetalliFozzBo.

Maybe I need to work on that name a bit.

It was great connecting with Eli at the Maiden gig, as we'd been friends for years but hadn't seen each other in a long time. We rekindled our friendship that night and he invited me to the Hollywood premiere of *Inglourious Basterds*, the epic Quentin Tarantino film that Eli had a major part in, a few weeks later. It was fun watching him in the role of the Bear Jew in the Arclight Theater on Sunset, the exact theater where he'd shown me the rough cut of his movie *Hostel* a few years earlier.

After the film ended, he had a big party at his house in the Hollywood Hills to celebrate. I was hobnobbing wih the beautiful people outside by his pool, when I saw a decidedly unbeautiful person hanging in the corner. He had a hook nose, a strange ruffled haircut, and a little bit of a potbelly. He was quiet, he was a little awkward, he was Quentin Tarantino.

The director stood in a crowd of people, looking like he would rather be somewhere else. But he wasn't being rude; he was actually engaging and cordial. So I was working up my courage to go and say hi (he's one of my favorite filmmakers of all time) but I couldn't think of the right opening line, and saying "My name is Chris too" wasn't gonna cut it this time. But before I could get up the nerve, I saw him and Eli making their way through the crowd, as if they were leaving.

Not knowing too many people at the party, I figured if Eli was gonna split, then I would too. I chased him down and asked him what was up.

"Quentin and I are going to go upstairs to my theater room and watch *A Fistful of Dollars*. Wanna join us?"

I wasn't much of a spaghetti Western fan, but getting the chance to watch a movie in an intimate setting with a cinematic genius like Tarantino was a once-in-a-lifetime opportunity. I was looking forward to hearing the insight and thoughts he would have while just checking out the film like a regular Quentin.

Eli's theater room was very froot, exactly the type of place you'd expect to find in an award-winning director's house. He introduced me to QT, who was much more animated inside the house than he was outside. You could tell he was much more comfortable around smaller groups of people.

"I'm going through a huge Sergio Leone phase. He was definitely the front-runner and king of all spaghetti Western directors, don't you agree?" he said with his trademark rapid-fire speech pattern. I agreed with him, even though I couldn't name another spaghetti Western director to save my life.

"Really? You like the spaghettis too, huh? What's your favorite?"

Uh-oh, this was getting uncomfortable. I didn't want to give the obvious answer, *A Fistful of Dollars*, since the DVD case was on the table in front of me. So I searched through my mental Rolodex and found the title of another "spaghetti," *The Good, The Bad and The Ugly*.

"Ahhhh." He nodded his head vociferously. "Another classic. What's your favorite scene?"

Wow, that was a tough question. So many classic scenes to choose from! And since I'd never seen the movie, I didn't know any of them.

I hemmed and hawed, stuttering back and forth about how there were so many amazing Eastwood moments in the film (was Eastwood even in it?), hoping that some cinematic higher power would send me some sort of escape, fast.

The Gods of Movie Trivia didn't appear, but the Goddesses of the Female Bladder (works for me) did, as two starlets slammed open the theater room door at that exact moment, looking for the bathroom.

Quentin may not have been much of a conversationalist in a crowd, but he was a smooth-tongued devil with the ladies and persuaded the two of them to stay and watch the spaghetti with us. I breathed a sigh of relief to be let off the fork as he'd shifted his attention to the girls and forgot what we were talking about.

When Eli started the movie, Tarantino's former shyness was left on the cutting room floor and he became a fountain of information, analyzing and explaining every minute detail of the film. I was excited to hear what observations he would have.

"Those saddles were handmade in Italy to Leoni's exact specifications."

"The flies on that dead body were imported from America. Leoni wanted bigger flies and they weren't available in Italy, so he had them flown in."

"Did you notice how the color balance shifted there? It's obvious the camera was getting slightly overheated."

He was giving us a crash course on spaghetti Westerns, western spaghetti, cinematography, entomology, scatology, leatherworking, mustache grooming, speaking Italian, acting Italian, Technicolor, technology, and technical ecstasy. At first it was an interesting look into the mind of one of the greatest directors of all time, but as he kept talking and excitedly interrupting the dialogue on a constant basis, it wasn't long before it got just plain annoying. He became the guy talking loudly behind you in the movie theater who won't shut up. I wanted to turn around and "shhhh" him. If I had popcorn, I would've thrown it at him. But I was a guest in Eli's house, and Tarantino was his bro, so as he continued talking I excused myself and walked out of the room. I could still hear him yapping as the door closed.

"Eastwood and Leoni left for linguini after this scene!"

CHAPTER 23

Boots

SummerSlam 2009 was in Los Angeles and I thought it would be fun to have Speewee fly out for a few days before the show to hang, and my bro John Howarth, the head of RIOT Records, Fozzy's label at the time, decided to join us. We holed up at the Roosevelt Hotel in Hollywood for three days listening to music and drinking Grey Goose. We christened our gang the GG3 and roamed the halls at five A.M., looking for the ghost of Montgomery Clift (who died in the hotel and has been haunting room 928 ever since), hung at the Rainbow with Ron Jeremy (Speewee regaled him with tales of the boner contests he used to have with the other kids at summer camp), went to see Rush in concert, and then to Ozzfest the next day (I lost my car keys in a field packed with twenty thousand people and two hours later saw a guy holding them up and asking if they belonged to anybody, a half a mile from where I originally dropped them), and ate at The Breakfast Place on Hollywood Boulevard, where we sat next to a Rambo impersonator complaining to a Marilyn Monroe impersonator that the Elvis impersonator down the street was a "fucking diva asshole."

Looking for the ghost of Montgomery Clift, who supposedly haunts room 928 of the Roosevelt Hotel in Hollywood. The GG3 haunted the hallways for the rest of the night.

We were having a total blast, so it was a drag when I had to leave for a Japanese tour the day after SummerSlam. Speewee and Riot didn't miss a beat and were planning on staying in L.A. for a few more days to continue their adventures as the GG2. I knew they'd have a good time without me, but I didn't expect the text I got from Speewee when I arrived in Japan.

"Met George Clooney and Brad Pitt at the Skybar in Hollywood last night and they loved me!"

I was surprised that he'd met them, but wasn't surprised that they liked him since he's charismatic, outrageously funny, and doesn't get starstruck. He could give two shits if somebody was famous and treated everyone the same, which I'm sure was quite refreshing for A-listers like Brad and George. I texted him back and asked what happened.

"I bought them a drink and they thought it was funny, so their bodyguards let me stay. I gave them my best material and had them laughing their asses off. Brad liked my crazy eyes!"

Speewee always bragged about his "crazy eyes" . . . a wild look he achieved by bulging out his eyeballs, making him look like a cross between Simon LeBon and Canadian serial killer Paul Bernardo. I was blown away by his story and, quite honestly, a little jealous that I'd missed out on such a classic night.

"He gave me his agent's card and told me to e-mail her. Wants to put me in a movie."

Wow. That one really annoyed me. I'd been trying to break into Hollywood for years, and while I'd made some headway, I'd never come close to being in a movie with Brad Pitt. But Speewee goes out for one night and gets a part?

A few minutes later I got a text from Riot telling me about their night and how fun it was.

"Pitt loved Speewee! He had him laughing all night. Wants to put him in a movie."

So Speewee wasn't exaggerating? I turned a darker shade of envy even though I was happy for him. Plus, if he booked the part, maybe he would pay for the drinks once in a while.

I texted him congrats and didn't think any more about it until a week later when I got another message from him.

"Just got a call from Pitt's manager, Cynthia! They want to cast me in Brad's next movie. I can't believe it!"

OK, this was getting ridiculous. I'd spent enough time in Hollywood to know things didn't work this way. I don't care how much they were impressed by his Crazy Eyes or how many boner contests Speewee told them about, unknown actors just didn't get cast that quickly. Not to mention, Speewee WASN'T a professional actor! I mean, if there was ever a human being on this planet who should've been on a reality show, it was him. But an actor? He'd done a local car dealership commercial years earlier and was about as good as Wayne Gretzky on *Saturday Night Live*, so I wasn't buying it.

But he was playing it so smoothly. Not overselling it and not texting me back as quickly as he usually did. Most of the time if he was trying to wind me up, he'd bombard me with the same lame joke over and over again until I fired back. Plus, in the back of my mind I kept thinking about Ashton Kutcher, who'd landed *That '70s Show* after his first-ever audition. Was Speewee, with his white teeth and perfect hair, going to be THE new teen heartthrob?

Then there was Riot. He wasn't saying anything and he normally kept a secret about as well as Julian Assange. But he hadn't so much as hinted that Speewee's claim wasn't legit.

I decided to take matters into my own hands and do some research. So Speewee claimed Brad's manager was named Cynthia, huh? OK, smart guy, let's see whatcha got.

I Googled "Brad Pitt's Manager" and to my surprise, her name really WAS Cynthia . . . Cynthia Pett-Dante. But that didn't prove anything; he could've Googled her name the same way I did. I still wasn't buying it, but if my mind was a courtroom, there was a mental hung jury going on in there like a John Grisham novel. Eleven members of this mental tribunal were convinced Speewee was guilty of lying, but the lone Fonz-like member was insisting that Speewee COULD be telling the truth. I still had a sliver of doubt deep inside.

I reached out to Riot and demanded he come clean. This had been going on for a few weeks and if it was indeed a rib, enough was enough.

Once again, John insisted that they had really met the two stars in L.A., and Speewee had made a great impression. I filled him in that Spee was talking to Pitt's manager, and Riot said, "The crazy bastard is pulling it off!"

That's what I was suspicious of.

I got the next text a few days later and that's when I was convinced Spiv was ribbing me.

"Dude! Cynthia just made me an offer for the movie!! They're filming it in L.A. and I've been offered fifty thousand dollars and first-class round-trip travel for two weeks of shooting. I leave next week."

There was no way that could be true. Cynthia was Pitt's manager, not the producer of the movie, so she would have nothing to do with making the actual offer.

"And she signed me to her management company!"

This was getting ridiculous. Now he'd been signed by one of the most powerful people in Hollywood? I asked him which company and after he said Management 360, a quick Google search found that that was indeed Cynthia Pett-Dante's company. But it still didn't prove anything, as once again he could've Googled it the same way I did. He could've pulled these figures from another contract. He could've . . . STOP!!

Whether he was ribbing me or not, he was ribbing me! I was so worked up over the whole stupid story that I was obsessing about it every waking moment. I couldn't stop trying to rationalize what was happening. So I told him he was full of shit and he replied he was over my negativity and wasn't going to bother responding to me anymore. Besides, he was leaving for L.A. in a few days to get to know his fellow cast members before filming, and he needed to focus.

"I need to devote my energy into learning my lines for *Boots*."

Boots? That's what he came up with for a title? Fuckin' *BOOTS*?!

That was a brutal name for a movie. But was it so brutal that it could be true? I mean it was a better title than *Sisterhood of the Traveling Pants*. But as far as Speewee going to the set a few days early to "get to know" his fellow cast members, I'd filmed enough movies to know it didn't work that way. You met everybody on the first day of shooting.

But what if Brad worked differently? What if he liked to have coffee and donuts with the people he was working with for the next six weeks? It could be possible. I mean what the fuck did I know about filming a movie with Brad Pitt, right?

My paranoia about *Boots* was out of control, but I couldn't let it go. I had to get to the bottom of this, so I called my agent, Barry Bloom, and asked him if any of this sounded remotely possible. After hearing all of the "evidence," he agreed with me that it was probably bullshit. But just to make sure, he was going to call the management company and see if there was a David Spivak on their client list.

The next day he called me back and told me that Management 360 in California had never heard of a Dave Spivak. I had caught the lying bastard! But Barry was also told that all new clients were registered through the company's New York branch, so he could be in the system there.

I told Speewee that I was onto him and to admit that he was making the whole thing up. Then he sent me his contract.

I read through the first couple of pages and couldn't believe what I was seeing. I'd signed dozens of contracts in my time and it sure looked legit to me. All of the sections and subsections were in the right places, the compensation wording was perfect, and the facts and figures matched up with what Speewee had told me.

This was war. I needed closure that this stupid *Boots* wasn't real, so I sent the contract over to Barry, who was now as entrenched in the saga as much I was. He came back a few minutes later and said the contract was very amateur . . . not at the level of what you'd expect from a major production such as *Boots*. I called Speewee and demanded to know the truth (or should I should say, begged to know the truth) because at this point I was acting crazier than Howard Hughes shitting in a jar by the nightstand.

"There is NO way this is true! I want the director's number! I want Cynthia's number! I want Angelina Jolie's number!" (Who doesn't?)

In the midst of my rant I got another text: "I'm in a production meeting for *Boots* and can't talk. But read the contract. Section C explains it all."

So he was in a production meeting, huh? He'd gone from Crazy Eyes to decision maker for a blockbuster motion picture? I was over it. None of this shit was true and I was so frickin' annoyed that he would even try to keep selling me this bullshit story.

I went to Section C to find out what other stupid crap he'd come up with and read:

(c) Promotion—In all promotional appearances, your client will be required to relay the story of how absolutely everyone including, but not limited to, Rosie the Dog, was in on the joke to "get" Chris Jericho aka Chris Irvine. In addition, your client will fabricate and embellish the story to have Chris Jericho appear to be beside himself with jealousy at how easy your client made it appear to "break in" to the entertainment industry.

Those SONS OF BITCHES.

It was the greatest rib ever pulled on me, orchestrated by Speewee and Riot during a quiet evening in Los Angeles the night I left. They swore to each other to never tell me the truth under any circumstances and couldn't believe I'd fallen for it this long. They'd Googled Pitt's people's info the same way I had, gotten their idiot savant friend Laun "The Great Panini" Wilby to find a contract online and replace it with Speewee's name. (*BOOTS* was the only title Panini could think of for the film . . . idiot savant indeed.) They came up with a salary they felt was reasonable and then sat back to watch as my own jealousy and paranoia took it the rest of the way. It turns out that Speewee was a damn good actor after all. I mean, he had outacted the guy who had outacted Mickey Rourke, right? Excellent job . . . you bastard.

Oh, and just to clarify, Rosie the Dog is Speewee's.

Buying mix with the GG3 on the Sunset Strip in 2009. Speewee
holds the bag of water as Riot and I embrace lovingly. We asked
a random stranger to take this pic and I'm glad he didn't run away
with my phone.

CHAPTER 24

Giant Heat

As my feud with Mysterio was winding down, I started thinking about what I was going to do at WrestleMania. It was June, which was prime idea time for Mania as the main matches were decided months in advance. After tossing around a few ideas with Brian Gewirtz, it was obvious that the best angle for me had been a long time coming: working with Edge.

Edge and I had flirted with doing a long-term story line a few times in the past, but for various reasons, it never came to fruition. There was an idea for SummerSlam 2002 to have Edge with the Osbournes (Who the fuck are you, man?) in his corner vs. Jericho with Fozzy in my corner, which got derailed when Edge suffered a shoulder injury. Then the original plan for WrestleMania 19 was for me to wrestle Edge, but that got called off after I got involved with HBK and we went on to have our show-stealing classic. But now that Edge and I finally had our chance, we were determined to get it right this time.

Edge, Michael Hayes, Gewirtz, Vince, and I sat down together after a *SmackDown* taping in Bakersfield and mapped out our whole angle. Edge (Adam) and I would win the Unified tag-team titles in a three-way dance with Carlito and Primo and Ted DiBiase and Cody Rhodes. We would hold the titles as heels, wreak havoc on everybody for the next few months, and then start an angle with DX. Then I would turn on Edge, leading to our showdown at Mania with him as the good guy. Vince wanted to build Edge up as a babyface and make him the face of *Smack-Down*, and this was the perfect way to start.

The first step of the plan came together like George Peppard when Adam speared Carlito and we won the tag-team titles. The ironic thing was the match took place right after I lost the IC title to Mysterio. So just like when I lost the unsanctioned match to HBK and won the world title minutes later, winning the tag titles this way put us on the fan's shit list right off the bat.

We had good chemistry since Edge had the same natural ability to piss people off as I did. He also had a tremendous mind for the business and had orchestrated a classic feud with The Undertaker on *SmackDown* at the same time Shawn and I were having ours on *Raw*. Edge and Jericho as a team was a match made in Heel Hell and I knew we'd have great chemistry as opponents as well because we'd worked together countless times before. Therefore, wrestling each other at WrestleMania after a strong nine-month buildup was a surefire recipe for Show-Stealing Soufflé.

But the soufflé was about to fall . . . fast. (Brutal analogy, I know, but it's my book, junior.)

A week later I was putting my boots on at a live event in San Diego, when somebody ran into the dressing room yelling that Edge was hurt. During his match with Jeff Hardy, he'd ducked under an up-and-over and heard a pop in his ankle. He couldn't stand up, so they called off the match and stretchered him to the back.

When I saw him in the training room squirming with pain, it was obvious he'd suffered a serious injury. Doc Amann was certain Edge had torn his Achilles tendon and was going to be out six to eight months.

That was bad. Real bad. Don't get me wrong. I felt terrible for my fallen partner, but I selfishly felt just as bad for myself. In six months it was going to be December and eight months was February, so there was still a slight chance he could make it back in time for Mania. But for now, our carefully laid plans of mice and Edge were out the window.

Adam had indeed torn his Achilles and flew home to get surgery the next day, which left me without a partner or an angle. The good news was we'd already won the tag titles, so it wasn't like Vince could just sweep our burgeoning story under the carpet. As a matter of fact, he decided not to strip the tag titles from us and wanted to get someone to take Edge's place. Then I would berate Edge for the next six to eight months for being injury-prone to build sympathy and get people primed to see him shut me up. Now only one question remained: Who would be my partner?

There were a few newer guys' names bandied about off the bat, but I nixed them pretty quickly. If I was going to end up in a feud with DX for the titles, I needed a lover who wouldn't blow my cover, and a partner who could stand up to them verbally, physically, and historically. DX was very popular and didn't care what they said about their opponents and would eat them alive if given the chance. I couldn't have a rookie by my side, for that reason. The job opening for Jericho's new partner could only be filled by a select few, and much like Vince's WrestleMania 25 selection process, I had my own criteria that had to be met.

The guy had to be an ex–World Champion, be physically imposing, and have the ability to verbally joust with those two. The first guy I thought of that fit those qualifications was Kane. He was massive, so I could hide behind him when things weren't going my way, something I hadn't been able to do since I was with Lance Cade.

I pitched for the Big Red Machine to be my lawfully wedded partner, but Vince shot me down quickly. "Actually, I have somebody else in mind."

Who could it be now . . . Giant Silva? Outback Jack? Funaki?

"Show."

Big Show? I hadn't thought about The Largest Athlete in the World, and I'm not sure why, as he fit all of my criteria. Multiple-time world champ. Physically imposing (he's a GIANT after all). Plus, Show's dry sense of humor was the perfect weapon to combat DX's sarcasm.

But I had a few concerns about teaming with Show that I wanted to address with Vince right then and there.

"I think it's a great idea, but there are some things I'd like to tweak about his character."

If I was going to do this, I wanted Show to update his look the same way that I had when I dropped the Y2J character.

"I'd like to update his gear, get rid of that one-strap Tarzan singlet thingy, and switch to tights."

The single-strap singlet had been the trademark of Andre the Giant and since Show had been brought into the business as Andre's son, I guess he still felt it necessary to wear the same style of clothes as his dad. I'm glad I didn't feel the same way, as a full-length fur coat and cowboy boots would've looked ridiculous.

But I felt if Show switched to trunks, it would both signify a change in attitude and make his physique look even more imposing.

Vince nodded and asked what else I wanted to change.

"I want him to drop all of the comedy he's been doing. He's a legitimate giant and I want us to start promoting him like one again."

The problem with Show was the WWE was taking him for granted. Over the last few years he'd seemingly been booked to take the entire roster's finishing moves. I'd even locked him into the Walls during a Royal Rumble match a few years earlier. He was such a great athlete and moved so well that we almost forgot he was a foot taller than most of the rest of the crew. It wasn't until you saw yourself standing next him in a picture or on TV that you remembered how huge he really was.

On top of that, he had such a great sense of humor and was so laid-back that WWE had a habit of making him the butt of everyone's jokes. Whether it was Goldust as The Crocodile Hunter finding Show napping in the corner and calling out, "It's the sleeping elephant, Crikey!" or Show coming to the ring imitating other superstars (The Showster, who preached about "Showamania running wild, brother")—all of that had to stop. I wanted him to be a badass monster again.

Also, I felt, in order to compete with DX, Show needed to adopt a more serious character. New suits, no bullshit. He was up for it, and once he made the minor changes, we were ready to get over like Rover. And we worked together so well that eventually we got over like Clifford the muthafuckin' Big Red Dog.

Show was fired up about our new partnership, and I wasn't surprised. I'd always found him to be a great performer when he was motivated and this new scenario gave him something to sink his huge bicuspids into. He tried wearing trunks but didn't like the look (he must've run into Malenko first) so he switched to a full-on singlet that worked for him, and he still wears it today. But either way, first step in my plan to rebuild the perfect beast was accomplished.

I wanted to cleanse the fans' Big Show palate and remind people just what an intimidating powerhouse he was. Since we'd known each other for years, I figured the chemistry would be there, but it wasn't quite right at the beginning and we got off to a sluggish start. We debuted at the July PPV against Rhodes and DiBiase and the match was clunky at best, as Show and I tried a few double-team moves that weren't really our style. I hit the ropes so Show could press me onto a prone Cody, but he wasn't really a press slam guy and our timing was off, so it looked like shit. Even though we won the match. I knew we'd have to rethink what kind of team we wanted to be.

The secret to Show and Jericho was that we weren't like most "big guy, little guy" teams. Whereas in the past, Rey had used Show's shoulders as a platform to do splashes off of, and Eddy had Show catapult him in the air straight onto his opponent's shoulders, we weren't that kind of team. As evidenced by our less-than-spectacular debut, we weren't about dynamic flashy moves. We were about being devious and using each other's strengths to win.

We decided to base everything around his knockout punch, called the WMD (Weapon of Mass Destruction), which he'd been using as his finish for a while. As a matter of fact, the first guy he tried it on a few years earlier was me and I told him beforehand to hit me as hard as he could with his ham-hock fist. He nailed me so hard my forehead had knuckle prints in it (no joke). Vince loved it.

"Damn, you're a tough bastard," the boss said in admiration afterward. I smiled bashfully as my forehead swelled up like a tsunami.

So every time we won a match, it was because Show found a way to plaster our opponent behind the ref's back, and I would capitalize by jumping on the guy for the pin.

We got a lot of easy heat because Show was so damn tall he could do things most guys couldn't. He could punch somebody in the ring while he was standing on the ground by simply reaching up from the floor. He could legally tag me from pretty much anywhere on the apron because he could hold the tag rope and stretch out almost three quarters of the way across the ring. He could cut off a babyface by merely holding up his foot or body checking the guy when he hit the ropes close to our corner. Plus, I could bump around for the good guys and, when things got rough, tag Show in and hide behind him with a shit-eating grin.

Our chemistry backstage was great too, although we got along so well, we bickered constantly . . . if that makes any sense at all. Since I had an overall master plan for who and what I wanted us to be, I came up with most of the ideas for the matches and wasn't particularily politically correct in overruling Show's suggestions.

"Hey, what if we did it this way?" Show suggested after I'd laid out some ideas.

"Nope, my way is better, so let's just do it as is."

Show would get all sulky and say, "OK, I'll just shut my mouth and sit here like a big dumb giant."

Then I'd console him and tell him his ideas were good . . . it's just that mine were better.

We got to know each other so well, we started acting like an old married couple.

"When is our match?" Show would ask, squinting at the card taped on the wall.

"Would you put on your glasses? You're driving me crazy!"

"You need to chill out and quit bitching at me! Have a diet soda, for shit's sakes."

Then we'd walk away from each other in a huff, only to get back together a while later and continue talking like nothing had happened.

But it was a lot of fun teaming with Show and I'd have to say he is my favorite tag-team partner ever. We got over great, to the point I had to start protecting our heelish integrity, much to Show's chagrin.

The announcers nicknamed us Jeri-Show, but I refused to refer to ourselves that way and asked Show not to either. I felt that having an official team nickname was too cute and would give the fans a familiarity, like we were their buddies. Every time the writers gave us something with "Jeri-Show" in it, I ignored it and requested that Show do the same (although I think he slipped and said it a few times).

The merch department wanted to design Jeri-Show T-shirts, which I nixed for the same reasons I did when I was on my own. But now I had to answer to my seven-foot partner who wanted the extra royalties. I was able to convince him that the minimal money we'd make from a Jeri-Show coffee mug would be far eclipsed by the money we'd make from being top heels working in the main events against DX.

My favorite tag-team partner and one of the sweetest guys I've ever met. This pic shows just how massive Show really is . . . although he's wearing high heels and standing on a box.

Meanwhile, we were decimating every team on the roster, on our way to the critical mass showdown against Hunter and Shawn. I did the talking while Show did the knocking . . . out, as he'd reclaimed his crown as the biggest, nastiest monster in the WWE. He was a giant and nobody could touch him . . . nobody! Well, nobody, that is, except The Great Khali.

The other giant in the WWE.

Khali and Show had been at odds for years, as they had what the boys called "Giant Heat," which meant they resented each other because they were both Brobdingnagian (best word in this book). They had spent their lives being the biggest person in the room, astonishing specimens that everybody stared at and instantly feared. Now, for the first time, they had to deal with competition for that honor and neither of them liked it. Khali was taller, Show was better in the ring, and each was jealous of the other as a result.

We were in Aricebo, Puerto Rico, having a tag match against Khali and Taker. It was the first time I'd ever wrestled Taker, and experiencing his ring entrance live was surreal. When the lights went out and that Taco Bell gong hit, there was no feeling like it. The crowd hushed in awe, then went batshit when the blue lights pierced the veil of darkness, and Vince McMahon's greatest creation slowly marched to the ring. He stalked his way up the ring stairs and took off his hat to expose the pure whites of his eyes as his tongue rolled out of his mouth. Creepy, classic, and exhilarating, all at the same time.

The match itself was nothing special, highlighted only by Khali stealing one of Show's spots right in front of his face. Show had this trademark move where he took a guy into the corner, shhh'd the crowd with his finger, and delivered a BRUTAL overhand chop that sounded (and felt) like it had caved in his opponent's chest. It hurt like a mutha, but always got a huge reaction, which made it a little more bearable. Khali had stolen it from Show and used it all the time during his matches, even though Show had asked him more than once not to. But who was going to stop him? Khali was seven feet tall and didn't give a shit what anybody thought, especially his nemesis, The Big Show. But even still, he had *huevos El Gigante* to do the chop right in front of Show's face.

"Motherfucker just stole my move," Show mumbled on the apron, and I knew something was gonna go down. He was mad as hell and wasn't going to take it anymore.

We were in the dressing room after the match, and Show was still fuming, steam practically bellowing out of his ears. When Khali came in a few minutes later, the shit was on.

"Hey, motherfucker, why do you keep stealing my spots, huh? That's total bullshit and you need to stop it now!"

Let me say that I really like Khali and respect what he's done, because I know what it's like to be the only foreigner in the locker room who doesn't speak the native language. He still made every effort to fit in, despite the fact that his minimal knowledge of English, deep voice, and heavy accent made it almost impossible to understand him at first. He peppered every sentence with liberal doses of *bro* and *man*, and they were the only words you could understand at times.

"Wha' you talkin' 'bout, bro?" Khali retorted, his accent as thick as his upper torso.

"Don't play that innocent bullshit with me! I've told you before to stop stealing my stuff. You can't do any of it properly anyway, because you're the fuckin' shits!"

Khali stared at him stoically and replied, "You're the shits too, bro."

That made me laugh in spite of the tension; I thought it was great that Khali didn't deny he was shits, but wanted to make it damn clear that he felt the same way about Show . . . bro.

That pushed Show over the edge and he threw Khali's bag in the corner, which was the equivalent of slapping him across the face with a glove and challenging him to a duel. Khali accepted and rose to his feet as quickly as he could (which took about five seconds).

The two biggest men in WWE history stood face-to-face and I'm not sure either of them knew what to do. Show had spent some time training as a boxer, and Khali had been a police officer in India (can you imagine running through a stop sign and seeing that monster walking up to your window?), but I wasn't sure how many actual street fights either one of them had been in. I mean, they were giants; who ever messed with them in the schoolyard? I guessed that, due to the intimidation factor alone, they had avoided fisticuffs for most of their lives.

But this was different. This wasn't just about stealing spots, this was years and years of "Giant Heat" coming to a head. It was the law of the jungle and only the biggest beast would survive. Plus there was going to be a fight no matter what; they had gone too far to back down now and the boys were watching. Taker, Kane, Regal, Punk, everyone was gathered around now, and to pussy out at this stage would be locker-room respect suicide.

A few seconds later, Show threw the first punch, which connected with a loud smack to Khali's overdeveloped jaw. It rocked him backward, but he didn't go down and Khali landed a punch of his own. With the opening shots fired, the floodgates opened and the two titans began swinging like Tiger Williams. I counted at least five more smacks and cracks as the blows connected with each other's faces, shoulders, necks, and chests.

I had a front-row seat for King Kong vs. Godzilla and they were in a fight to the death. Nobody in the locker room was too keen to break them up either, and besides, how could we? Their fists were as big as my head! If I tried to intervene, I was going to get swatted away like a biplane trying to shoot Kong off of the Empire State Building. And I wasn't the only one who felt that way. Cody Rhodes was hanging in the corner as far away from the melee as possible, and even though Kane had the size to intercede, he was wearing only a towel and I'm guessing he didn't want to get involved in case it fell off and exposed his big red machine.

The battle raged on until finally Show took a wild swing and tripped over a chair, which caused him to crash onto the floor with Khali on top of him. The boys waded in at that point to pry them apart and the fight was over. The brawl was fairly even, but Show still insists he lost because Khali landed on top. Now, if we were judging by the rules of a hockey fight, then yes, Show lost, but from where I was standing, it was an impressive back-and-forth scrap. Show might not have lost the battle, but he definitely lost the war when Vince made him apologize to Khali for throwing the first punch, during a closed door meeting a few days later.

Show apparently told Khali that he was out of line and shouldn't have swung first (although in the George Lucas rerelease, it was Khali who swung first) and that it wouldn't happen again. Khali nodded his head and said, "No problem, bro."

Big Show and I were together for the better part of five months before we finally got to the pot of DX gold at the end of the tag-team rainbow. In that time, our partnership experienced a lot of twists and turns and we even battled against each other when we challenged The Undertaker for his world title in a three-way dance on PPV. Our plan was to gang up on the Deadman and beat him up so bad that he would be easy pickings for the pin. Problem was, we couldn't decide who would get the victory; we each wanted to be the champion.

The three-way was good, not great, but it's become legendary because of a two-second ad lib that became one of my most famous lines.

We were in Washington, DC, and I had just thrown Taker back into the ring, when a fan in the front row yelled out, "Go back to Toronto!" I was in the middle of an intense title match (any match with Taker was intense), but for some reason, this guy's comment really annoyed me. First off, I thought it was the worst insult ever. We were in the United States, next door to Canada, the friendliest country ever, and there wasn't any unrest between our two nations, so there was no reason to tell me to go back. It wasn't like I was in Saigon in 1968 and the Viet Cong were demanding that the Damn Yankees (and Ted Nugent) get out. Second, I'm not from Toronto, I've never been from Toronto, and it ticked me off that even though this dummy knew I was from Canada, he hadn't done enough research to know what city. So I decided to let him know exactly where I'd grown up.

"I'm from WINNIPEG, you idiot!" I snarled without a thought and slid back into the ring.

I'm not sure exactly why, but my retort spread like wildfire. Ever since that moment, there hasn't been a day that goes by that somebody hasn't texted, Tweeted, Facebooked, Instagrammed, Vibered, Snapchatted or Ear-Sayed it to me, and if I could put that quote on a T-shirt, I would. I can't explain its appeal, but like I said earlier, you just never know what's gonna catch on, so why hassle it?

It's ridiculous that after all the monumental things I've accomplished in my career, the two bits I'll be remembered for the most are "I'm from Winnipeg, you idiot" and "Armbar."

Taker beat both of us and retained his title, but we were still the tag-team champions. Now with all of the animoisity cleared away, Show and I were a stronger unit and ready to focus on the sole remaining team we hadn't beaten: DeGeneration X.

DX was one of the most popular acts in WWE history and Shawn and Hunter had recently reunited, much to the fans' glee. They were cocky, comical, charismatic, and had no problems annihilating their opponents with their promos. But Show and I were beyond that and wouldn't allow ourselves to be pushed around or intimidated by them. DX vs. Jericho/Show was a guaranteed moneymaker as it was, but Vince wanted to raise the stakes even higher and make our match a Tables, Ladders, and Chairs and have it headline the next PPV.

In the same way Shawn and I had at first balked at having a ladder match for the world title a year earlier, the four of us weren't too keen on this idea at first either. But the TLC brand name brought instant importance and prominence to the match and, along with the fact that the tag titles were also at stake, made this match must-see TV (shut up, Miz). So we agreed to do the match on the condition we could do it our way—less stunt show, more psychology.

We already expected the crowd to be really into it because the PPV was in San Antonio, the home of Shawn Michaels. It always amazed me that even though the WWE booked PPVs months in advance, they always seemed to take place in the headlining babyface's hometown. Like when Cena came back from an injury to beat me for the title at Survivor Series 2008, it was in his hometown of Boston, or when The Rock challenged Cena for the title at WrestleMania 28, it was in his hometown of Miami. And the last time *Raw* was in Winnipeg, I won the first WWE Musical Chairs championship (documented in my Kama Sutra manual, *Undisputed*, available at sex shops everywhere), so I had that going for me.

The TLC was quite the spectacle and since there's nothing like a hometown crowd, we had them on the edge of their seats with our rollercoaster ride from the start. It all culminated with a breathtaking finish, where we trapped the two of them between a giant ladder and slammed it down multiple times in unison. Then I grabbed a chair and hammered the DX sandwich another half dozen times. At this point, Show freaked out and ripped the ladder in half, throwing all of the debris, both human and inanimate, to the floor. We had the perfect chance to grab the titles suspended above the ring, but alas we had nothing to climb. So I clambered up to the third rope and stood on Show's shoulders while he held my hands for balance. Then he slowly walked forward until he was standing underneath the titles and I let go of one of his hands and reached up to to grab the belts.

We had rehearsed this earlier in the day and it wasn't an easy task; as a matter of fact, it was a lot scarier than it had seemed when I thought of the idea. Just to stand on top of a seven-foot man's shoulders and keep my balance was hard enough, but to keep that balance while he was walking was almost impossible. When I let go of his hand and reached up for the titles, my equilibrium was thrown completely off. Looking up into the lights while shifting my weight on one leg and trying to stay stable with the other was like trying to cut the Gordian knot.

We tried it a few different ways and found the best way to make it work was to not rush it. Once Show ambled far enough out to where I could brush the titles with one hand, Shawn was going to come back into the ring and superkick him and Show would take a step back toward the ropes on the sell. I would then jump off his shoulders and crash through a waiting table that had been set up on the floor earlier in the contest. It was the only big stunt spot in the match, but I knew it would blow the roof off if done right because it had never been seen before.

But once we got into the heat of the moment, fired up by the energy of the crowd and the surge of our adrenaline, we moved too fast and I wasn't properly balanced when I stood on his shoulders. We gingerly walked to the center of the ring, but I didn't have my bearings when I let go of Show's hand and tilted too far to one side, almost falling to the mat. I steadied myself by bending my knees, but then I wasn't even close to reaching the titles when I reached up to grab them. It was obvious there was no way I'd be able to take the titles off the hook, so we were kind of just standing there waiting for something to happen as the crowd got quiet.

They came back to life when Shawn entered and connected with a massive superkick to Show's chin over six feet in the air, which was impressive enough on its own. The big man turned around on the sell, but forgot to take the step toward the ropes that I needed to be on target for the table. Timing was everything and I only had a second to decide how I was going to take the bump off his shoulders. It was the last fall of the night for me and I figured, "Fuck it, I'm going for it," and launched myself as if the momentum from HBK's kick had thrown me off balance.

The moment my feet left the solid base of Show's traps, I knew I was in trouble. I was too far away to clear the top rope, but I found myself already starting my descent. The only chance I had was to try to stand on the top rope and, to my surprise, I landed directly on that bitch, perched perfectly like a Persian parrot.

"Polly want a fuckin' cracker?" I said to no one in particular, feeling prouder than Kelsey's nuts. Then gravity took over and I lost my balance for the second time, jumping in vain to try and hit my target. The rope wasn't stable enough to get a good push-off and I hung in the air like Wile E. Coyote for what seemed like forever before plunging straight down. I had planned on landing in the middle of the table, but since I was plummeting toward the ground headfirst, I could see that wasn't in the cards. It seemed like I was going to miss the table completely, so I stretched out my arms, hoping to collide with some part of it, any part of it, and I did.

With my face.

I landed mouth-first on the corner of the table and I know this because I actually tasted it. It had a vaguely dirty flavor, like I had just licked a leaf. My hands bounced off the flat top, and my knees collapsed the second I landed, which made things look much worse. I'm not sure how I didn't break my leg, tear a pec, or recapture the coveted Lloyd Christmas look I had after I broke my teeth in the HBK ladder match, but I came out of it intact. It's funny that the four of us agreed to do the TLC only if there weren't any "dangerous bumps," yet the fall I had just taken was easily one of the worst of my career.

With me out of the picture and barely alive, HBK superkicked Show for a second time, and Hunter knocked him over the top rope with the mangled ladder. Then HHH held up the one-sided piece of hardware so Shawn could climb to the top, unhook the titles, and make DX the tag-team champions for the first time ever.

Meanwhile, I was lying on the floor, trying to get the taste of Lemon Pledge out of my mouth.

CHAPTER 25

Mean Mr. Mustard

Shortly after the PPV, we left for a European tour, with DX vs. Jericho/ Show headlining most nights. The tour consisted of a grueling twelve shows in twelve nights airport-hotel-arena-airport grind, which made it quite easy to burn out. The best way to avoid that was to break out of the routine and do some different things, so I decided to go check out Abbey Road, the site of one of the most iconic album covers of all time.

Our first show was in London, so referee Marty Elias and I navigated the intricate tube system and met my old high school chum Wallass, who'd moved to the UK from Canada years earlier. Wallass and I had discovered the WWE together and formed our own wrestling league, the BTWF (Big Time Wrestling Federation) along with our own technometal band, the BTWF Orchestra. We were also huge Beatles freaks, so walking across Abbey Road was on both of our bucket lists.

Now, when you see the famous photo of The Beatles walking across the intersection, the street looks so big, but in reality it's really quite small and stretches maybe twenty feet across. I was surprised that the crosswalk was in the middle of a busy intersection, with cars flying by rapidly every few seconds. The regular commuters who had to drive through it every day were probably sick and tired of the goofy tourists trying to stroll across while having their pictures taken. I bet they would've had no problem playing a little Death Race 2000 if they knew they could've gotten away with it.

There were a ton of gawkers congregating on both sides of the street, waiting patiently for their precious few seconds, and it was funny to see how they marched across when they finally got their turn. The Beatles weren't posing when the cover was shot; they were merely walking across the road with their arms swinging naturally. But these people were trying to reenact exactly how it looked on the cover, arms jutting stiffly from their sides and knees locked out, like nerdy tin soliders wearing khaki shorts with fanny packs.

Wallass and I showed up dressed appropriately: he in an all-black *Sprockets* ensemble complete with black beret, me in an open-throated McCartney-esque suit. Marty stationed himself on a corner of the intersection and waited until the traffic cleared. When it was our turn, I took off my shoes and socks for the pièce de résistance and marched across the most famous road in rock 'n' roll history.

Those three seconds were some of the frootest of my life. *Abbey Road* was my favorite Beatles record and cover (I love it so much, I got it tattooed on my left arm; ask me next time we meet and I'll show it to you), and here I was experiencing something most superfans never would. I stood in the middle of the street and drank in the special moment until a Fiat come scorching toward me and I had to take my leave.

"Hey, Jericho!" I heard the driver yell as he drove by.

I was such a worldwide superstar, I'd been recognized on the Beatles' own street!

"I'm gonna be famous, a star on the screen," I hummed to myself as I hopped up on the curb and stepped into a pile of fresh dog shit with my bare feet.

Happiness is some warm dung. Bang bang poop poop.

Wallass and me crossing Abbey Road. Note that I'm wearing a suit and have bare feet just like Paul. All I needed was a cigarette between my fingers and a Volkswagen Beetle with the license plate LMW-28IF parked behind me.

I continued my magical mystery tour a few days later before our show at the Echo Arena in Liverpool, when Marty and I visited a tourist attraction called The Beatles Experience. It boasted such gems as the original Sgt. Pepper uniforms and the reassembled remnants of the actual Cavern Club. There was so much history there that I was shocked when Marty told me it was already six P.M. I was in the main event that night (there it is again), so I wasn't late, but the doors had already opened and I had to walk across to the arena in plain sight of the thousands of wrestling fans who were now roaming the grounds. With no security, this could have turned into a real mob scene (or even worse, Victoria, British Columbia, Part 2—Electric Boogaloo). I needed a plan.

I told Marty to beeline it to the arena and not slow down no matter what. I would follow behind him with my head down, staring at his feet to guide me the whole way. We left the safety of The Beatles Experience into the walking live like Rick and Glen but without the benefit of zombie entrails hanging around our necks to camouflage ourselves. I stared down at Marty's sneakers as he led the way and as a result saw all types of shoes out of my peripheral vision. Cowboy boots, Doc Martens, loafers, dress shoes, high heels, wooden clogs (WTF?). If the WWE ever needs to do a survey on what kind of footwear their fanbase wears, I'm bouty bouty and rowdy rowdy.

It was funny how many hundreds of people were walking past me with no idea that the guy they'd be booing the shit out of only a few hours later was right in their midst. With all the concerts I'd been to over the years, I wondered if I'd ever walked past Bruce Dickinson or Mick Jagger in the parking lot before a show. It reminded me of the time I cruised past a kid wearing a Y2J shirt outside of the arena in Memphis and yelled, "Nice shirt, dude!" The kid barely glanced up and missed his chance forever. Too bad, junior.

Our luck held as we weaved through the oblivious crowd and made it to the side door of the arena. Marty went inside as I lingered behind reveling in the fact that I'd hidden in plain sight and fooled everyone.

"Sorry, suckers," I mumbled, and strolled like a boss through the sanctuary of the backstage door, ready to—

"Can I see your pass?" the security guard asked with arms crossed.

Pass? I vaguely remembered getting some sort of laminate on the first day of the tour but hadn't seen it since. After assuring the guard (who looked old enough to have worked for the actual Beatles) that I didn't need a pass, I attempted to walk inside for a second time.

"No pass, no entrance into the backstage. You'll have to go around front," the guard said wearily, his face stonier than a beefeater palace guard.

I'd come so close to safe passage and didn't have time to argue with Rip Van Wanker, especially since there was a small crowd starting to congregate around the door.

"But I'm Chris Jericho and I'm in the main event tonight, so I need to get in."

"No pass, no entrance."

The small crowd had grown and their ears perked up at the mention of my name. I was running out of time.

"Listen, man, do you see that poster on the wall behind you?" I pointed at a large event placard with my face plastered on it. "That's my face, ya dig? Do I look like I shouldn't be back here? I don't even have an English accent!"

"Hey, is that Chris Jericho?" a fan said excitedly. Uh-oh.

"No pass, no entrance."

"That is Jericho!" another bloke shouted and the chase was on. I gave Mean Mr. Mustard the stink eye and power walked away with the group of fans now in tow.

The unwanted entourage (great song title) grew larger and it was time to bail, so I broke into an all-out sprint. The crowd quickened their pace and suddenly I was having my own Beatle Experience as I ran around the side of the arena with a gang of screaming chicks (aka giggling guys) following closely behind me. I had no idea where I was going or how I would escape, but when I saw another side door, I threw it open and barreled inside.

"Don't ask me for a pass!" I yelled at the pimple-faced security guard sitting in the hallway.

"You're Chris Jericho, mate!" he said excitedly. "You don't need a bloody pass!"

Another day in the life of Y2J.

CHAPTER 26

Humbled

After the show in Liverpool, we took a charter to Paris and I was drinking Crown Royal, which is pure firewater for me. It was the only thing I drank at the time although I have no idea why, as the wicked elixir turned me crazy and the nights never ended well.

That's why Drunkicho was in full force when we arrived at our hotel at six A.M. There was always food awaiting us when we checked into our overseas hotels, and everybody went to grab a bite before crashing out. Most of the crew was sitting at the various tables eating quietly, except me—I was swearing up a storm.

Everything was "Fuck this" and "Fuck that," until finally Hurricane Helms pointed out that HBK was sitting at the next table with his family. He'd brought them on the tour for a working vacation, and to his credit, he didn't expect us to act any differently around them. Shawn, of all people, knew that boys will be boys on the road and didn't expect any of us not to party. However, Drunkicho was an obnoxious buffoon and didn't care about shielding the children's young ears from profanity. Hurricane warned me I was swearing too much and that I should think about toning it down a little.

"I'm not swearing that much! Besides, he shouldn't have his kids out this late anyway," I bleated belligerently.

Hurricane told me to keep my voice down and I said defensively, "I wasn't talking loudly."

But I was wrong, for Shawn and his family got up and left their table. I hoped I hadn't insulted them and yelled out, "See you tomorrow, man!"

He walked out the door without saying anything, but ten seconds later, he stormed back into the room, his eyes ablaze. "You shut your damn mouth," he warned me. "Yeah, my family is up late and if you've got a problem with that, go to hell!"

He let his words hang in the air as he glared at me and left the room.

"Shawn, wait!" I yelled after him. "You're my hero!" I pleaded, as if that was going to make a difference. I turned back to a dozen silent faces, feeling like the motherfucker of the year, and wondered what I'd done to make Shawn so angry. Sure I had cursed in front of his kids, but what was the big deal?

"It wasn't that you swore," Hurricane explained. "He's mad because you said he shouldn't have his kids here."

"I didn't say it that loudly," I protested.

"Uh, yeah, you did. You're too drunk to notice."

I got up from the table totally ashamed of myself and staggered guiltily back up to my room. I wrote Shawn a long, detailed text explaining how awful I felt and how embarrassed I was about what I'd said, hoping he'd still be awake. He didn't return it, so I figured he'd fallen asleep and would get back to me in the morning.

I slept most of the day away and, when I woke up, had the worst feeling in the pit of my stomach. I vaguely remembered what had happened, so I grabbed my phone to see if Shawn had texted me back. When he hadn't, I knew we had a serious problem. I paced around my room trying to figure out how I was going to smooth things over.

Obviously I had to apologize, but how was he going to take it? I wanted to call his room, but I knew he was with his family and I thought it was smarter to speak to him in person. I spent the rest of the day worrying so badly that I thought I was going to give myself an ulcer.

Finally the moment of truth arrived; it was time to go to the venue.

Heels and babyfaces traveled on separate buses during overseas tours, so I had no contact with Shawn as I rode to the arena in silence. I was still too embarrassed and ashamed to talk to anybody else, and besides, this was between the two of us.

The heel bus arrived first and when I stepped off, it was darkly cold outside, which matched the way I felt inside. I stood at the entrance waiting for Shawn to arrive and when he walked in, I asked if I could have a word.

"In a few minutes," he said curtly and walked into catering. I was too wound up to eat, so I waited anxiously in the corridor for half an hour, waiting for him to finish. Finally he left the hall and went up the stairs to the dressing room. I waited a few seconds and followed his lead. After knocking on the door, I summoned up the last of my courage and walked in.

He was sitting by himself and told me to close the door.

"I don't really have much to say to you, but let me be clear about something. All I care about is my family and I don't give a damn about you or what you think about them being here with me."

I hung my head like a whipped dog and tried to stammer out a stilted apology, reiterating what I'd texted him earlier.

"I don't care about your apology," Shawn cut me off bluntly. "Now, you listen to me. I've stood up for you so many times when people said you were a pain in the ass, but never again. You think you're untouchable, but you're not. This Best in the World shit is going to your head and you need to get yourself straight."

Each word broke away another little piece of my heart as my

childhood hero, mentor, and all-time favorite opponent explained to me how much of a jerk-off I had been. It was hard to listen to him talking to me this way, even though I totally deserved it. And he was only getting started.

"You need to start acting like a top guy if you're ever gonna be one. Staying up all night drinking and being an asshole . . . you're losing everyone's respect."

I expected him to tell me next that fat, drunk, and stupid was no way to go through life, but this was no joke and I was humbled because I knew he was right. There's a certain level of responsibility in being a top-level performer and a certain line you can't cross if you want to be taken seriously as a locker room leader. You've got to be an inspiration, not an embarrassment. You would never see The Undertaker drunk as hell and swearing in front of children at six in the morning.

On top of that, Shawn was right. I had created a monster with this new character and it had spiraled out of control. Sometimes I dropped into it so deeply that it was hard to let it go. The theory that Heath Ledger overdosed on sleeping pills because he could no longer sleep due to the dark depths he'd traveled to in order to portray The Joker in *The Dark Knight* made perfect sense to me. My commitment to the craft had warped me, causing problems in my life all across the board, and even though I knew it was happening, to hear it from my most respected peer made it hit home even harder.

"You're totally right, Shawn. I need to change things up. Can you help me?"

I knew Shawn had experienced similar problems in the mid-'90s when he had the reputation as the hardest person in the business to deal with.

Shawn slowly shook his head.

"You're on your own with this one, Chris."

Wow, that hurt. But he was right and the irony was that Shawn and

I were very similar in a lot of ways. We both came into the business branded as "little guys," which gave us huge chips on our shoulders and caused us to have to work extra hard to get noticed. We were both opinionated and deemed hard to deal with as a result but made it to the top of our crafts for that very reason. We both had egos in the stratosphere at times, but this time, Shawn pulled me down to earth faster than a skydiver without a parachute.

He was done talking, so I apologized again and left him alone. I didn't feel that he'd forgiven me, but later when we went over our match, he was a little friendlier, and that gave me a small modicum of relief. Then I sought out his wife, Rebecca, and apologized, as I'm sure my behavior had insulted her as well.

She accepted my apology and said what pissed them off the most about my behavior was me obnoxiously saying good night to Shawn as they were leaving.

"We felt it was a real Eddie Haskell two-faced thing to do. Like you were mocking him and challenging him to do something about it if he didn't like it."

That hadn't been my intention at all, but I understood how what I said could have been taken that way. When I got back to my room, I thought about everything that had gone down over the past twenty-four hours and decided I'd make some changes.

No more all-night Crown Royal drinking sessions while on tour, because I had responsibilities to live up to as a locker room veteran. More importantly, whether I was drinking or not, I needed to tone down the attitude I'd developed as a person—essentially learn how to separate church and state and leave the Jericho heel character where it belonged . . . in the ring. I'd have to make these changes on my own (as HBK said), but I was up for the challenge.

Shawn's words gave me a real wake-up call, and I'm thankful he said them. Vince told me years earlier that he wanted to teach me life lessons along with wrestling lessons and he has. But that night, Shawn taught me a major life lesson of his own that humiliated and humbled me, and I'll always appreciate that.

After that we became closer than ever and I still consider HBK to be one of my best friends in the business. Thanks, Shawn.

CHAPTER 27

Effeminate Tough Guy

When Big Show and I lost the tag-team titles to DX in December 2009, I wasn't supposed to be allowed on *Raw* any longer. But then Mike Tyson was booked for the show in mid-January 2010, and since Vince wanted my final Monday night blow-off angle to be with him, we needed to think of a way to get me reinstated. What he came up with was one of the most bizarre angles of my career.

At the final *Raw* before Christmas 2009, guest host Johnny Damon was going to grant Show one wish from Santa Claus. He would then confront Santa in the ring and ask that his tag-team partner and best friend, Chris Jericho, be allowed back on the program. Santa would of course say yes, but then that dastardly Hornswoggle would run in the ring and rip off Santa's beard, revealing that Jolly Old St. Nick was actually me. To make things even more preposterous, after I was unmasked like Shandi, Show and I would be attacked by a gang of midgets. It's as ridiculous as it sounds, but as Loverboy once said, we better start from the start.

The big story line of the night was Hornswoggle taking DX to Little People's Court for their constant mistreatment. Shawn and Hunter would crawl under the ring where Swoggle "lived," end up in another dimension and embark on a wacky Alice in Wonderland–esque journey to find him. It was as rotten as it sounds and you would have to be on opium to find any of it entertaining. They would eventually find the Little People's Courtroom populated with a dozen dwarves who would put them on trial and find DX guilty. It was completely hokey, the kind of thing you would only see in the WWE. Then after all that horseshit, Show and I would treat all the munchkins to a massive beatdown.

When the ragtag collection of minikins showed up for rehersal, it was amazing to see how small they really were. Vince even told a couple of them to go home because he was afraid they might get hurt in the melee. The idea was they would surround us in a semicircle and attack, but Show and I would eliminate every last one of them, until DX came to chase us away. The thing had the potential to stink out the joint and when we were finished going over everything, Vince looked at me and said, "My dad will be rolling in his grave after this." I responded, "Who can blame him? Besides, it's your fault. . . . YOU booked this shit!"

I put on the Santa outfit complete with fat suit, granny glasses, bushy white eyebrows, and gaudy circles of rouge on my face that made my cheeks look like roses, my nose like a cherry.

But it was quite convincing and nobody recognized me. I got the final approval from Vince, who gave me the thumbs-up but told me, "Make sure to change that prissy walk of yours. Everyone will know it's you if you don't."

Vince always mocks my sliding gait at every opportunity and once told me, "You're the most effeminate tough guy I've ever met." He also hated when I went through my scarf phase (that's why Alberto Del Rio wears them to the ring as a heel) and abhors it when I sit with my legs crossed.

Macho macho McMahon.

So I practiced walking like I had candy cane up my ass and spoke with a weird accent that was half Mrs. Doubtfire, half Stewie from *Family Guy*. I had to come up something; I wasn't about to be outdone by Fresh Ground Pepper Santa, now was I?

The segment began with Show in the ring summoning Santa to hear his wish, and out he came, with a rockin' version of "Jingle Bells" as his entrance music and a Bella twin on each arm. It was ricockulous to see SANTA CLAUS written in huge letters on the TitanTron (with accompanying falling snowflakes), like he was coming out to challenge Stone Cold Steve Austin for the world title. I strolled down the aisle doing everything I could not to walk like an effeminate tough guy, waving to the crowd like I was the pope and bellowing Ho-Ho-Ho like a Mo-Fo-Fo.

Santa commented that Show was the biggest boy he'd ever seen and it was probably a smart idea for Santa to sit on his lap instead. He asked Show if he'd been a good boy in his Stewie/Doubtfire drawl and he replied with a resounding, "Yes, Santa," in an over-the-top innocent voice.

Then he told Santa that his only Christmas wish was for his best friend, Chris Jericho, to be reinistated on *Raw*. Santa pondered the request thoughtfully and finally granted his request, which of course the crowd hated. I couldn't believe they were actually buying this shit!

Show and Santa celebrated until Hornswoggle jumped into the ring and pulled off Santa's beard. Santa stared at Swoggle in a not-so-jolly way and chased him out of the ring. The crowd finally got it and gasped in recognition as I ripped off the rest of my disguise and revealed myself.

"That's Chris Jericho!" said announcer Michael Cole with shock.

Then it was our turn to be shocked as Hornswoggle and his dirty half dozen (get it?) emerged from under the ring and hopped into position. I can only imagine how uncomfortable Show felt, as he had a phobia of little people (like the elephant and the mouse), but he held his cool and the standoff began. I'd told the tiny terrors before the show to wait until I gave the cue before bum-rushing us, because as always I wanted the crowd at its peak before the fight began. But the fans weren't too sure what to make of the preposterous scenario and were almost silent, so I decided it was time to get it on and get it over with.

I gave the cue, they charged, and I threw them off one by one like I was Gulliver, until there was only one little guy hanging on to my leg for dear life as I dragged him along the mat. This was even more ridiculous, considering I was wearing only Santa trousers, suspenders, big black boots, rosy cheeks, and a rummy's nose.

Show pulled the little guy off my leg and gave him a crushing side slam that shook him up so badly he had to go to the hospital for real. Then adding insult to injury, the Giant Destroyer picked him up by the legs like a Thanksgiving turkey and tossed him nonchalantly over the top rope.

I thought we would get major heat for beating up a gang of little people, but we were getting more of the *what the hell are we watching?* reaction, until I trapped Hornswoggle and pushed him into Show's massive mitt for a chokeslam. The crowd finally woke up and screamed at us to please stop, until the DX saviors ran down and chased us away.

It was a ludicrous end to the show, and when I walked through Gorilla, I asked Vince if his dad was still rolling in his grave.

"Ugh. He's doing a full-on gymnastics routine at this point."

A few weeks after Tyson's DX betrayal finally got me kicked off *Raw*, Show and I broke up forever. It happened after I was staging a full-on demonstration outside the arena in Hartford, protesting my unfair treatment by the WWE by marching back and forth with a placard that read STOP THE JERICHO EMBARGO!! I'm not sure what that means, but it still makes me laugh. I set up a petition that I wanted the gathering crowd to sign, expressing their desire to see me back on *Raw*. I figured nobody would participate as they would be happy to see Jericho finally get his comeuppance, but the opposite happened and the fans were signing it as quickly as they could. After a few attempts to find legit Jericho haters in the crowd, we gave up and added a few plants to insult me instead.

Finally, Show came outside to tell me he wouldn't be helping me with my quest to get back on *Raw* because we were through.

We thought it would be funny to do the scene like we were breaking up for real in some sort of a clichéd romantic comedy starring Vince Vaughn and Jennifer Aniston, and play it totally straight.

"I'm doing this for us, Show," I pleaded. "We deserve a rematch against DX and I just can't let it go. I don't want this to end!"

"Let it go, Chris. It's over," Show replied tenderly.

"Don't say that, Show! I stay awake at night thinking about us. What we had was special and you can't deny that!"

"It was special, Chris. Nobody knows me like you did. But it's time to move on. I'm on *Raw*, you're on *SmackDown*. . . . Long-distance relationships don't work, Chris. It's over."

"Is there someone else?"

Show shook his head. "No. But I'm moving on. Just know I care about you."

"I'm always going to cherish the memories, Show!" I yelled in desperation as he walked away and out of my life forever.

I ate a carton of Häagen-Dazs and cried myself to sleep that night.

CHAPTER 28

The Little People of America

I was in the locker room in Nashville, reading an article in *Guitar World* about Lynyrd Skynyrd, whose guitarists Gary Rossington, Rickey Medlocke, and Mark Matejka were on the cover. R-Truth came in and we started talking about the different music we'd listened to in high school and the differences between growing up in Canada and in the Deep South. The conversation turned to how there were more midgets in my high school (two) than black kids (one). He'd read my überpopular how-to manual, *A Lion's Tale* (have YOU?), and asked whatever happened to my diminuitive pals. I mentioned that one of them, Tanya Davis, had become a stand-up comedian and a favorite of the Maury Povich show, but I hadn't seen her in almost twenty years.

We had our match and after the show, Doc Amann asked me if I wanted to meet him out for a drink, since his girlfriend lived in town and knew a good spot across the street from the arena. I was still in my ring gear (even though I'd finished my match hours earlier) and told him I'd catch up with him later. I'm really lazy when it comes to taking off my stuff, and I wish there was a pill I could take that would make the sweaty spandex slide off on its own, or that I had a young Japanese boy to take off my stuff and then wash my back in the shower.

That's my definition of making it, fearless readers, but alas, since we weren't in Japan, I had to take off my own gear and wash my own back (#wrestlerproblems). But just because I didn't have someone to soap me down and help me feel fresh, that didn't mean Zack Ryder had to go without.

He was wandering around the locker room, looking for someone to Nair his back, so I stepped in, spread the luxurious lather on his lats, and shaved away. A few minutes later, his unwanted hairs were history, so I put on my short shorts and disappeared into the night.

I decided to drop by to see Doc for one drink but no more, as I had a four-hour drive to Atlanta for *SmackDown* and wanted to have a quiet night. I saw the bar across the street and stopped at an intersection next to a guy who looked vaguely familiar. I was pretty sure I hadn't met him before but after a few seconds, it hit me: He was one of the guitar players from Lynyrd Skynyrd who was on the cover of the *Guitar World* magazine I'd been reading earlier.

"Excuse me, aren't you in Lynyrd Skynyrd?" I said, paraphrasing the question I'd been asked a thousand times.

Mark Matejka smiled and confirmed that he was. I told him I'd just been reading about him, and we started talking. Turned out Skynyrd had a few days off and he had nothing going on that evening, so I asked him if he wanted to hang with me.

The Skynyrd guys are longtime wrestling fans and I'm a longtime Skynryd fan, so we had a lot in common right off the bat. When we got inside the saloon, I was telling him one of my favorite memories, of me, Dean, Chavo Jr, Eddy, and Benoit going to see them in Sturgis the night before a WCW PPV many years earlier. Meanwhile, the singer from the saloon's band recognized Mark and invited him onstage to jam. He sat in on a few blues tunes and then did "Don't Stop Believin'" by Journey (more on this EVIL song later). Then Mark motioned me over like he was David St. Hubbins and I was Nigel Tufnel, and a few seconds later

I was singing Journey's biggest song with the guitar player from Skynyrd. The heads of classic rock DJs all over the country exploded.

When the tune ended, we got more "Freebird" chants than Michael Hayes, but my work was done and I left the stage. I ordered a drink and noticed another one of the signs on the wall that I'd been seeing around town all day: NASHVILLE WELCOMES THE NATIONAL CONVENTION OF THE LITTLE PEOPLE OF AMERICA. Quite the coincidence since I'd been talking to R-Truth earlier about the Little People of Canada.

As if on cue, I felt a tug on my leg and looked down into the face of Tanya Davis . . . who I hadn't seen since Westwood Collegiate in 1988 and who I'd just been talking about hours earlier. What the hell was up with this day?! I wished Paul McCartney had been on the cover of *Guitar World* and that I'd been talking about Roxanne Falk, the hottest girl in my high school, instead.

I gave Tanya a hug and after catching up on our families and successes, she said, "You have to come meet my friends!" She introduced me to another ragtag group of little people who, I hoped, weren't avid watchers of *Raw* and seeking revenge on Big Show and me. Thankfully, they didn't want vengeance, just alcohol, and ordered a tray of shots. At this point I gave up on my plans for a quiet night, got down on my knees, and downed a lemon drop.

These people might have been small, but their drinking abilities were BIG and it wasn't long before I was on my knees with my new friends (including Mark) linked arm in arm, singing a reprise of "Don't Stop Believin'" (there's that EVIL song again) until five A.M. as the janitors mopped the floor around us.

Quiet night indeed.

CHAPTER 29

Glorified Rental Car Shuttle

We were in the midst of another European tour and had just finished a show in Zurich in front of one of the worst crowds I'd ever experienced. They had been silent for the entire night, seemingly with zero interest in the matches they'd paid to see. In my mind, they were all members of the cast of *Sprockets*, wearing black bodysuits with berets on their heads (similar to Wallass's Abbey Road ensemble), commenting in an accented sardonic tone, "Vat is vit all ze slamming and ze jumping? Ve just vant to see ze DAHNCING!" It was so bad that in the middle of my three-way match with Edge and Jack Swagger, I grabbed the mic and asked, "Are you people even alive? Should we just start dancing?" There was still no reaction, so we did the finish and got the hell out.

At least my analogy got a big pop backstage, especially from Kane, who came back from his match still laughing while imagining five thousand Dieters in the crowd doing the salmon spawning dance.

When the show ended, we were told that there was a change in plans for the rest of the tour. Originally, we were scheduled to take the bus to Innsbruck, Austria, for a show and then fly to a sold-out event in Istanbul that was going to gross over a million dollars. But there had been a massive volcano eruption in Iceland that had blown so much ash into the air, flying was now impossible.

This was a potential disaster for the WWE as, with the *SmackDown* crew in Europe and the *Raw* crew in Ireland, there wasn't enough talent stateside to do Monday's show from New Jersey. Since the *Raw* guys were stuck on the island of Ireland, they couldn't drive to a different airspace and were virtually trapped until the planes could take off. The last airport in all of Europe where planes were still flying out was in Madrid and since we were in mainland Europe, it was decided that the *Smack-Down* crew would drive the 1,662 kilometers (1,033 miles for the metrically challenged) to Spain and fly to New Jersey from there to do *Raw*. Our last two shows were canceled because we had to leave immediately to make it to Madrid by ten forty-five P.M. the next evening, the absolute latest we could take off to beat the oncoming volcanic ash cloud.

I was choked that we had to leave because I had planned a snowboarding trip in Innsbruck for the day with John Morrison, but my hopes to ski the Alps were dashed. So I was already in a pissy mood when I boarded the bus at eleven P.M. and prepared for the eighteen-hour drive, but at least I was traveling on a luxury liner with plenty to eat and movies to watch. There were far worse ways to travel, I thought to myself as I reclined my overstuffed comfy chair and drifted off to sleep.

I felt the bus grind to a halt and opened my eyes to find that we'd only been driving for three hours and were barely in Geneva. Due to the abrupt change in plans, our current bus couldn't leave Switzerland, so we had to switch to a new bus that would take us the rest of the way to Madrid.

Standing on the street, I noticed our new bus was a fair bit smaller than the old one and realized there was no way everyone was going to fit. I called John Laurinaitis to tell him this wasn't going to work, especially considering we were going to be on the road for another fifteen hours.

"It was our only option, Chris. Because of the volcano, everything else was booked up. We tried to get a helicopter, limousines, even rental cars, but everything was taken and all we could get was that bus in Geneva."

I reiterated that the new bus was simply too small and there was no way everybody was going to fit. Johnny said to squeeze in as many as we could and mentioned we had hotel rooms waiting for us to relax in once we arrived in Madrid.

"Sounds great. But we have to make it to Madrid first," I said, and hung up the phone.

Kane overheard me talking to Johnny and asked what was going on.

"I told John there's no way we can fit on this bus," I said, nodding at the medium-size coach. Kane looked at me quizzically and said, "That's not our new bus . . . THAT's our new bus."

He was pointing at what was essentially a glorified rental car shuttle that would've been hard-pressed to be classified as small if the other two buses were medium and large. We'd gone from a luxury bus to a passenger bus to a fuckin' clown car. From king status to geek status to no status.

There was definitely NO way that everybody could fit into this thing and it was decided that only those who were deemed essential to *Raw* were allowed to board. It was like a WWE version of the *Titanic* lifeboats, only instead of women and children, it was top guys and midcarders first. We were split up between the Glorified Rental Car Shuttle and another tiny van that had been drummed up to fit some of the overflow passengers. But all of the roadies and backstage crew members were left behind, along with a tag team called The Dudebusters, who as far as I know were never seen again. Last I heard, they had started their own cult in the mountains of Switzerland and had become gods.

The Glorified Rental Car Shuttle (GRCS) looked even worse on the inside than it did on the outside. There was no bathroom, no food or drinks, and the seats were like those on a school bus—cramped and thinly padded with a straight-up seat back that didn't recline. There was no way I was going to be able to handle this for the next fifteen hours, so I texted Vince to tell him that the GRCS wasn't good enough for the WWE crew. There wasn't even anything to eat!

"Guess you're gonna be hungry, then, pal. Deal with it, ha-ha!" was his reply. I flipped out and texted him the seven words that can never be printed in a book and let's just leave it at that.

We were on our own now, so we jammed all of our bags in the back of the bus and squeezed into our seats. I sat in the first row with my shins jabbed into the steel railing in front of me. The seat was so uncomfortable that I felt I was trapped in an iron maiden (bogus) and I'm only five feet eleven. I couldn't even imagine how bad it was for the really tall guys like Kane, Harry Smith, or Edge, who was already on the phone with Johnny asking for his release.

"I've had enough, this bus is terrible. I quit."

I wasn't ready to go that far, but I was close. If I was going to have to endure this for fifteen hours, it was time to Enter Sandman, so I put my feet up on the case of dark beer I'd grabbed from our beautiful first bus (I hate dark beer, but that's all there was), took half an Ambien, and drifted off.

I woke up with the new day's dawn breaking through the clouds as we approached the majestic mountains. The clock on my phone said seven A.M. and an oncoming road sign said MADRID – 1045 KM. Hmmm, that wasn't good. We'd been driving for four hours and had only gone about 350 kilometers, which meant we still had 1,000 kilometers to go. Turns out the GRCS wasn't much of a speed demon and was going a steady forty klicks an hour as we crawled up the inclined highway into the mountains.

I looked around the bus and saw different stages of uncomfortability: Edge was pretzeled in his chair a few rows behind me with his knees to his chin, Harry Smith was rocking back and forth in a fetal position and squishing Nattie Neidhart into the side wall, while Kane was stretched out on the floor of the bus, and Matt Hardy was dozing with his mouth pressed against the window next to R-Truth, who was the only other person awake besides me.

As the GRCS navigated its way through the windy roads of the Alps, cutting through France on its way to Spain, I noticed it was steadily slowing down. The engine was straining to get up the mountain, its transmission shuddering and hiccuping with every shift of the clutch, causing the entire chassis of the vehicle to shake. The two bus drivers began chattering incessantly in French as faint plumes of smoke emanated from under the hood.

The spare driver looked concerned as he opened the glove box and took out what I assumed was an owner's manual. He spoke in panicked French with the driver as the two of them tried to figure out what was causing the engine to overheat. I leaned forward and asked what the problem was, but the spare driver turned to me with wild eyes and said, "NO EENGLEESH!" I wished I had paid more attention to my high school French teacher, Mr. Tonnellier, and less to Roxanne Falk's ass.

The two of them continued babbling to each other and then got on the phone with the AAA (or I suppose the FAA in this case), as the temperature inside the GRCS creeped up to uncomfortable levels. The spare driver hung up the cell and closed the book in a huff, obviously flustered at the lack of answers he'd recieved. Then he looked at the sky, mumbling, and somberly CROSSED himself like a Catholic priest.

Truth and I looked at each other with wide eyes.

"Did you see that?!"

"Yeah, the brother just crossed hisself!!"

We turned back just as the guy reached into the glove box and took out a clear plastic bottle filled with brown liquid. He took a long pull, then passed it to the other driver, who took an even longer one. By the grimace on both of their faces, I can tell you that the brown liquid wasn't Lipton Iced Tea, kids. We hit each other with another double take, wondering how bad things could be that the drivers were crossing themselves and pounding straight whiskey while at the wheel!?!

Was the GRCS going to break down in the middle of the French Alps, leaving us stranded and forcing us to become cannibals like the Donner Party? Would I have to munch on Mysterio's calf like a drumstick, only to have Kane cane me over the head and eat my rump roast?!

In the midst of the uncertainty, Truth and I did the only thing we could do—cracked open the lukewarm dark beer and took a drink of our own.

It went down pretty harshly at first but about an hour later, that beer was tasting pretty fucking good and we were feeling a lot better about our fate even if the GRCS didn't agree. The good news was it hadn't slowed down any, but it was still only going somewhere between thirty and forty kilometers an hour. Angry drivers were zipping past us like we were Lloyd and Harry headed to Aspen, except at least Lloyd and Harry got to pee. We'd been driving for almost twelve hours and the dark beer was swishing around in our stomachs like water in a pail. It was a welcome sight when we finally saw a rest stop on the side of the road, for two reasons: (1) We were out of the Alps and (2) we could go for a leakski and grab something to eat. But we didn't have much time, as we were way behind schedule. It was almost one o'clock in the afternoon and we still had 550 kilometers (345 miles) to go to make the ten forty-five P.M. deadline. I called Johnny and told him we were still so far away from Madrid that we might not make our flight on time.

"What do you mean? We have day rooms for you!"

I told him he might want to think about changing the day rooms to night rooms, and he said the rooms weren't available at night. As a matter of fact, ALL the rooms in the city had been booked by stranded travelers (it was Cape Girardeau all over again), meaning if we didn't make it out of Madrid by ten forty-five P.M., we'd be stranded as well.

I ran into the rest stop to drain the main vein (the all-time worst slang ever for going pee) and get something quick to eat. I settled on a little apple pie in a box, some blue gum to get rid of the horrible after-taste of the dark beer, and a BAGUETTE. I bit into it and found out the hard way that it was more fun to say BAGUETTE than it was to actu-ally eat a BAGUETTE. It was like chowing down on an overcooked rock. The little apple pie in a box wasn't much better; it tasted like a little apple box in a box and left a worse aftertaste than the dark beer.

We scrambled back on the GRCS and flew down the highway at the lightspeed of seventy kilometers (forty-five miles) an hour, trying desperately to make up some of the time we'd lost in the Alps. It turned out that one of the drivers spoke Spanish, so Rey Rey could communi-cate with him. The driver told him we were lucky to still be moving, for the engine had almost overheated in the mountains and broken down. At that point my back was so sore from hours of being confined on the iron maiden bench, I was starting to wish we HAD broken down and cannibalized each other.

I kept Johnny in the loop about the progress we were making and he kept me in the loop about how the *Raw* crew was still stuck in Belfast, "stranded" in a five-star hotel surrounded by bars and restaurants. I belched up an acidic cocktail of dark beer and box pie and told him to tell the *Raw* crew to go fuck themselves.

He was relieved I'd been giving him constant updates, as he'd been trying in vain for hours to get ahold of Ricky Steamboat, our producer, and the guy who was supposed to be in charge of this band of gypsies. I told Ricky that the office had been trying to contact him but couldn't get through to his phone and he said nonchalantly, "Well, that's because I turned off my phone to save the battery in case of emergency."

"WHAT? Well, THIS is an emergency!!!"

Steamboat took action at that point, doling out gems of advice, like telling Rey to "Speak that language the drivers understand [uh, Span-ish?] and find out how much farther we have to go!" or warning us,

"Guys, there will be no more stops and we probably won't be able to check into the day rooms," at eight thirty P.M. with seventy-five kilometers to go.

Finally, after almost twenty-four hours of travel, we saw the signs for the Madrid airport and there was no time to waste since it was already a few minutes before ten P.M. We'd have to grab our bags and run straight onto the plane or we'd be stuck in Madrid with no hotel for who knows how long. (Maybe I could sleep under another conference room table?)

The lights of the airport shone bright as we all gave a cheer of delight . . . and then drove right past it. The driver had assumed he was going to the departure terminal but took a wrong turn, and you know how the old saying goes: "To assume is to make an ASS out of U and ME . . . and I'm gonna fuckin' rip the heads off of these jack-off drivers if I miss this flight." Or something like that.

By the time the driver wove his way back to the main road, we'd lost another fifteen minutes and it was 10:20 P.M. when we finally pulled into the departure area of the airport. Steamboat was yelling for us to get off the bus, file into a line, and pass our luggage from person to person like they were sandbags and we were trying to save the village from a flood. To his credit, it was a pretty efficient idea and we got our bags off in minutes. Then we made a mad dash across the airport, sprinting down the concourse like a gang of jacked-up O. J. Simpsons in a '70s Hertz commercial (dated reference). But instead of jumping over luggage carts, we were jumping over sleeping people. The floor of the airport was covered with so many bodies, it looked like the Black Death plague in 1665 London (*really* dated reference). Security knew we were coming and, since it was a charter flight, pretty much breezed us through customs at 10:32 P.M. They probably figured the risk of one of us blowing up the plane was worth it, as long as it cleared up space in the airport.

We darted to our gate and piled onto the plane like soldiers jumping onto a helicopter to escape Hamburger Hill in 1969. The pilot told us we didn't have much time and to find a seat immediately, so I ran to the back of the plane and strapped myself in. Some of the crew were still stowing their bags as the door closed and we taxied over to the runway faster than any other boy has ever gone.

We booked down the tarmac screaming into flight and I felt like Indiana Jones taking off in the biplane as the Incas threw their spears. As the wheels lifted off, I looked at my phone and saw the time . . . 10:44 P.M. We'd made it by the skin of our collective chinny chin chins. I reached down between my legs, eased the seat back, and breathed a sigh of relief.

Minutes later I was wolfing down an airplane chicken breast and an airplane chunk of beef (I'd asked for both) and it was one of the best meals of my life. I asked the stewardess for a Miller Lite to wash it down, and she replied, "I'm sorry, sir, we only have DARK beer."

I threw up in my mouth and asked for a straight vodka.

CHAPTER 30

Play More Songs

In the fall of 2008, I called Rich Ward and asked him if the time was right to fire up Fozzy again. After the All That Remains tour in the winter of '06, we'd gone our separate ways and hadn't done anything together since. In the spring of '08 there'd been a reissue of *ATR* called *All That Remains, Reloaded*, which included a bonus DVD of our 2005 Download Festival performance. When I watched, it reminded me how powerful a live band we were and I wondered why we'd been inactive for so long.

Fozzy had gained a lot of momentum from *All That Remains*, and the song "Enemy" had been our biggest hit ever, getting plays on over sixty stations across North America. But Rich and I got busy with other projects, and Fozzy ended up on hiatus.

The two of us missed playing together and decided it was time to get back to where we once belonged and write some new music. But it had been four years and our momentum had pretty much ground to a halt. All we had going for us at that point were a few good records under our belt and our fans' loyalty, but other than that, we were starting pretty much from scratch.

Rich and I believed we had the chemistry and the X factor (I ain't talking about Blaze Bayley) to be something special. After a long talk, we decided we were up for the challenge of taking Fozzy to the next level, but there would have to be a few changes made to the way we approached the band. If we were going to do it, we were going to do it all the way.

We decided there would be no more part-time efforts, no more half-assing, no more taking the band lightly. It was time to go hard or go home, so we made a new set of Fozzy fundamentals.

First off, Fozzy would now be our number one priority. That wasn't too hard a commitment for me to make as I was approaching forty and contemplating life after wrestling. I'd been playing in bands since I was twelve years old, and my two goals as a kid were to be a wrestler and to be in a band, and I was lucky enough to be doing both. My drive to get to the next level with Fozzy was immeasurable, and after climbing to the top of the wrestling world, I knew I could do it again in rock 'n' roll—but only if I approached it with total dedication.

Second, we needed a serious image makeover. Just take a look at our video for "Enemy" if you want evidence of our previous fashion faux pas. I was wearing gray cords (seriously, cords?) and a frumpy black long-sleeve shirt; Rich wore a cowboy hat; drummer Frank Fontsere wore camo pants with an orange shirt and a toque ("I've got an amazing outfit for the video," he had boasted proudly a few days before); and bassist Sean Delson wore a stitched Western long-sleeve and baggy Levi's with a wristwatch.

We looked bush-league terrible, which really surprises me in retrospect. I'd always been very conscious of my image in wrestling and in the early days of Fozzy, so I don't know why I allowed us to go grunge with *All That Remains*. Maybe we had focused so much on the "gimmick" of Fozzy in the early days of the band that we felt we needed to binge and purge ourselves of any type of style or fashion for a while? Whatever the reason, it was a bad decision, as people listen to music with their eyes as well as their ears, and if we were sounding like Black

Sabbath and looking like *Revenge of the Nerds*, we weren't going to get far. But those days were done and we were ready for an extreme rock 'n' roll makeover.

Third, we needed to solidify our lineup and stick to it. Because of our sporadic tours and lengthy bouts of inactivity in the past, the band was basically just a revolving door of musicians, with Rich and me being the only constants. But with our new attitude, we intended to be working a fuller schedule and wanted to put together the best lineup in Fozzy history.

The first order of business was to bring back Frank, the best drummer we'd ever played with and the perfect complement for Rich's heavy groove riffs. He'd been asked to leave the band in 2005 but we were ready for him to come back. However, when he showed up, he looked less like a rock star and more like Bubba Ray Dudley circa 1999. He'd gained a lot of weight, shaved his head, and grown a scruffy beard, but when we read him the new-image riot act he promised to update his look and get in better shape (which he did), so we gave him the benefit of the doubt and signed him up.

Sean Delson seemed like he was into the new way of doing things, but our second guitar player, Mike Martin, didn't really show much enthusiasm for our plans and we parted ways. We needed to find a replacement for Mike, but that could wait because the most important part of the new and improved Fozzy had to be the songs.

I'd been compiling ideas for a few years already and Rich was pleasantly surprised when I sent him fourteen full songs of lyrics a few days after we reunited. I write my lyrics starting with song titles and work backward from there, so when I come across an interesting phrase or sentence in a book, I write it down. Then when my muse visits, I scan through the list and find one that inspires me.

There was "Martyr No More" (I love the title); "Paraskavedekatriaphobia," (the fear of Friday the 13th and the best song title Steve Harris never wrote); "Pray for Blood" (my old friend Dr. Luther's catchphrase when he worked in Japan, which I turned into a tale about tenth-century Vikings); "God Pounds His Nails" (lifted from Stephen King's *The Talisman*); and "Broken Soul" (I envisioned it as a thrash song, but Rich had a different idea and it became our first ballad).

The standard way songs are written is to write the music first and lyrics second, but in typical Fozzy fashion, we did things our own way. Rich used my words to inspire him to create new songs or reworked them into the riffs and melodies he'd already written. After a few months of shaping and reshaping, we decided on the twelve songs that would make up our new record *Chasing the Grail*.

We began recording the album while our manager, Mark Willis, searched for a new record deal. *All That Remains* had been independently released on my own label, Ash Records, and even though it had sold fairly well, we still lost money when our distribution company went bankrupt (leaving me personally in the hole for about seventy-five grand), so we needed a new home. Unfortunately, our name value was pretty much nonexistent after lying dormant for four years, so our options were fairly limited. It was good news when our old friend John Howarth (of *Boots* fame) came aboard and signed us to his Australian-based label RIOT Records, making us their first worldwide release.

A few months later we wrapped up the recording and prepared for the release date. We knew the record was amazing but were a little worried. . . . Would anybody care about a new Fozzy album?

Turns out people did. *Chasing the Grail* debuted at number six on the *Billboard* Heatseekers chart, which was the first time we'd ever been on a *Billboard* chart of any kind. We just missed being on the actual *Billboard* 200 by only a few hundred units, which pissed me off because if I'd known, I would've bought the damn extra 253 copies myself.

With the record out, it was time to bring in a new guitar player and we had a private audition with only two candidates. Both guys were great guitar players, but as soon as I saw Billy Grey, I knew we had our man. Billy had played in Fozzy years earlier and I'd always liked him. And when he walked into the studio with his multicolored faux hawk, chain wallet, and Chucks, I saw he had the perfect look for the new-image Fozzy.

Our new lineup complete, it was time to get back on the road and we booked our first gig in almost three years at B. B. King's in New York City. Our return gig was the place to be in NYC that night as we played in front of an all-star cast, including my wife, Jessica, Bumblefoot from Guns N' Roses, Steve Brown from Trixter, Eddie Trunk and Don Jamieson from *That Metal Show*, Ripper Owens from Judas Priest, and Richard Christy from *The Howard Stern Show*. Vinnie Paul came on-stage halfway through the concert to present us with a tray of Jack Daniel's shots to celebrate our new album's release, and our old friend Mike Portnoy jammed on Judas Priest's "Freewheel Burning" with us. He was in town with his new bandmates from Avenged Sevenfold, and all five of them showed up together. I'd been an Avenged fan for years and it was froot to see them at our gig and I was impressed with their bond of brotherhood. It seemed that they went everywhere together like an actual gang, which was something I wanted Fozzy to be.

Charlie Benante and Frank Bello from Anthrax were also there and they brought their former singer, Joey Belladonna, to the show. They'd been considering bringing him back into the band and wanted to see how they got along and what the vibes were like in a social situation. They stayed for the whole gig, and a few days later Charlie told me Joey had rejoined Anthrax.

So Fozzy is taking credit for being the heavy metal Cupid that brought Anthrax back together with their long-estranged singer, due to our soothing sounds. Now if we can only get Slash and Axl to check out one of our shows. . . .

The gig wasn't our best as we were knocking off three years of rust, but it was a blast to be back onstage with the boys again and felt like home. Plus, the all-star cast and the packed crowd in attendance proved to us what we needed to know—people cared about The Fozz and were stoked to see us back.

As rock star as it gets backstage in NYC. I think I'm even drinking champagne for extra pretentiousness.

The next step was to return to our second home, the UK, where we'd always had an amazing fanbase. Our return shows in Nottingham, London, and Glasgow were sold out, which blew my mind, considering there had been such a long absence since our last tour. Then we headed back to Australia, where we also had a great following, and soon after were contacted by TKO, one of the biggest booking agents in the world (they repped The Cult, Buckcherry, and Anthrax among others) to see if we'd be interested in working with them. I called Benante for his advice and he said TKO was the way to go, so we said yes later that day.

One of the first shows our new agent, Dan DeVita, booked us on was the massive English festival, Sonisphere, which attracted up to 80,000 fans annually and this year boasted one of my all-time favorite bands as the headliner. After ten years of being in Fozzy and twenty-six years of being a fan, I was finally going to be on the same bill with the mighty METALLICA. I had to sit down when I got the news, because I felt like I'd been whacked over the head with the hammer from the *Kill 'Em All* album cover.

We'd taken a lot of flak through the years, partly because of the band's humorus roots, partly because I was a wrestler, and partly because we refused to give up. It pissed a lot of people off that we continued to get bigger, but we didn't care. The one thing the haters could never question about Fozzy was our passion and love for the music we were playing. And as a result, we'd made it to the point where we were deemed worthy to play on the same bill as METALLICA! Just looking at both of our names on the poster (ours was a half dozen lines underneath theirs, but that's nitpicking, isn't it?) made everything we'd gone through worthwhile. Seeing the Fozzy logo on the same placard as Metallica's gave me all the mental ammunition I needed, to know we could make it to the next level and to tell the haters to eff off. I felt like I did when I got my first magazine cover in Mexico, which verified that I wasn't "too small" to make it in wrestling.

As big as Sonisphere was, it was only one show and we were far from the headliners, so we weren't making a lot of money to play the festival. It's expensive to tour overseas, so to subsidize the tour, Dan booked a grab bag of other shows for us: smaller festivals, headlining club gigs, and a handful of shows opening for Anthrax. This was different from being one of the many bands playing on the same day as Metallica at Sonisphere; this was actually directly supporting them on their headlining shows. It was surreal to be playing with Anthrax, considering in 1988 I waited outside in the freezing Winnipeg winter to buy tickets to see them open for Kiss on the Crazy Nights tour. Now here I was over twenty years later about to play with them with my own band. Life is pretty rad sometimes!

Billbo Shaggins and I tear it up in front of a crazy crowd in Sydney in 2010. Later that night, GnR guitarist Bumblefoot jammed with us on "Stand Up and Shout" by Dio.

The first show we had with Anthrax was in Lucerne, Switzerland, and we had driven in from Germany the night before. When I woke up on the tour bus in mid-morning, the rest of the band had disappeared. Rich (The Duke of Metal) was a sightseeing freak and would convince whoever he could to go along with him to check out a statue or castle with him somewhere. He would also try to convince whoever was around to eat Indian food with him, but I'm not a fan and never went along. On many occasions I sat outside an Indian restaurant eating a peanut butter sandwich watching the guys chow down on tandoori through the window like a vagrant. Then a few hours later, I'd watch them run to the toilet in the dressing room with a case of the drizzling shits.

Duke texted me that he and the guys had left to take a cable car ride up a Swiss mountain and didn't bother asking me because he knew I wouldn't want to go. He was right, as it was a beautiful day and I wanted to find a place to go swimming, which would be a hell of a lot more fun than sitting in a tin box watching trees go by for two hours. Since we were in Switzerland, I figured there had to be a lake somewhere, so I put on a pair of shorts and wandered off into the parking lot. Using the Boy Scout powers I'd learned as a kid, I noticed that one part of the sky was lighter than the other, so that meant there was obviously water underneath it, right? I headed toward the fairer sky (it was a sunny day, so the whole sky was fair) but saw nothing more than brick buildings. Then a guy walked past me, wearing swim trunks and flip-flops, and holding a towel in his hand, and it was obvious where he was going. Accepting that my Boy Scout powers were the shits, I turned around, and followed him. I was literally two steps behind him and I'm sure he thought I was going to kidnap him to use as part of my very own Human Centipede. That actually was my plan, but it was foiled when his pace quickened and he speed walked like Santino over a slight hill and out of sight. I followed him in vain, but when I reached the crest of the hill, I looked down at one the most breathtaking landscapes I'd ever seen.

In the small valley below lay a beautiful park, lush with green grass and sturdy trees blowing slightly in the breeze. A crystal clear lake flowed freely through the middle of the valley, framed by the majestic silhouettes of the purple mountains surrounding it.

But it wasn't just the area that was beautiful; the people roaming all around it were as well. Tall muscular dudes and curvaceous tanned hotties in various stages of undress were everywhere. Some were playing volleyball, others were swimming. Some were catching rays on the beach, others were having a drink beside a big van that resembled an ice-cream truck but served alcohol instead.

I wandered around in a daze, hardly believing my good fortune, and laughing at the dumbness of my bandmates. While they'd chosen to see the sights of Switzerland zipping up a cable in a tin can, I was seeing all the sights of Switzerland I wanted to see right here. I found an open square of grass and inhaled the fresh air, listening to all the different languages being spoken around me, a mix of Italian, German, French, and English. The warm sugary scent emanating from the pastry truck that had pulled up beside the bar wafted through the air and I decided that this was the frootest place on earth.

I had a drink, took a swim in the freezing lake (it was exhilarating), watched a volleyball game (sadly, I wasn't invited to play . . . #nerd), and sat back enjoying the moment. It's something I rarely do in a life filled with planes, trains, automobiles, buses, hotels, venues, shows, buses, cars, hotels, and more planes. That's a mistake.

Not to get too preachy, but don't let life pass you by, guys. Sometimes it seems to me we have a tendency to constantly think about the next thing, the next challenge, the possibilities of what might happen the next day, both good and bad. I know because I'm guilty as charged (but damn, it ain't right) but sometimes I force myself to take a breath and bask in the moment, whether you're looking at a gorgeous lake in Switzerland or having a sandwich at Subway. Promise me you'll do the same sometime soon, ya dig?

I'm glad I did, because I'm going to remember that day and that place for the rest of my life.

The brightness of the sun began to fade, telling me it was time to leave the oasis and head back to the venue. It was our first night with Anthrax and I wanted to impress them and their fans, many of whom would be seeing us for the first time.

We played a decent set, but I went over the top in trying to get the crowd on our side by leading chants, telling stories, and basically begging for reactions. It worked to a degree, but much like being in the opening match on a wrestling show, there's only so much you can do to get people involved when you aren't who they paid to see. We walked off the stage to a nice "Fozzy" chant, which is always the goal, but due to my grand-standing we'd gone five minutes over our allocated thirty-minute set time. Again like in wrestling, going overtime is a serious no-no and a real show of disrespect. Since it was the first night, I knew we'd get some lee-way, but I wanted to let our bosses (and make no bones about it, the head-lining band are the bosses of their show) know that we'd made a mistake. I had a great relationship with the Anthrax guys, but I still felt the need to make amends. I knocked on their dressing room door and said sorry for our mistake, guaranteeing it wouldn't happen again. They looked at me quizzically, not knowing (or caring) that we'd gone over and wondering why the hell I was apologizing. I breathed a sigh of relief and with the first half of my atonement accomplished, I went into the production office to take care of the second half . . . talking to their tour manager.

The TM is the caretaker of the entire tour, making sure the shows are properly advanced, the dressing rooms are exactly right, the local promot-ers pay what they owe, and the opening bands get on and off the stage at the proper times. Anthrax's tour manager wasn't mad, but he was very clear that we weren't to go long again. He also gave me some great advice:

"Play more songs."

What he was trying to get across was the onstage equivalent of a rock station's commercial-free slogan, "Less talk, more rock." I'd spent so much time talking to the fans that it had disrupted the flow of our set, which left us less time to play our tunes.

"When you only have thirty minutes, try to get the crowd into it with your music, not your stage rap."

He was completely right and I still think of him when I'm putting together a set list to this day.

The poster of our first show with Anthrax in Switzerland. If you look closely, you can see my reflection in the window as I took the picture.

I learned another lesson by watching Anthrax play later that night. I'd seen them many times as a fan but got a whole new perspective on how good they were by watching them from the side of the stage as a peer. It was much the same concept as when young Japanese boys learn how to wrestle while watching the main-event matches from the apron side.

Anthrax were so tight and they looked like a team of assassins on-stage. Everything from their background vocals to the way they moved had so much power. Joey Belladonna was a great frontman and I don't mind saying I made a mental note of a few of his tricks and nicked them for myself. These were true pros, and even though Fozzy had come a long way as a band, I knew we still had a long way to go.

The next show was in Aarhaus, Denmark, a ten-hour drive from Lucerne, and Charlie invited me to ride with them on the Anthrax bus. There was no need to grab my bags, as Fozzy's bus was headed to the same place, so I grabbed my toothbrush and passport, slipped on my flip-flops, and jumped onboard. I was looking forward to hanging with

Charlie on the ride and discuss the detailed minutiae of all things Beatles.

He and I (and Mike Portnoy) had long agreed that the Fab Four were the best band of all time and nobody could even come close to touching them. If ever the eternal Beatles vs. Rolling Stones debate was brought up to us by an outside party, we would bring down the silver hammer upon their heads like Maxwell and that would be The End of the discussion. Unlike the infamous *Eddie Trunk Show* Judas Priest vs. Iron Maiden debate, where you could at least make a case for either band, to us there were no comparisons between John and Mick's boys and nobody could convince us otherwise. Until Andreas Kisser came along.

Andreas was the guitar player for the Brazilian band Sepultura, who was filling in for Scott Ian (who was in the U.S. with his newborn baby) on the tour and he totally disagreed with our Beatle bias. I'd never met Andreas but was quickly impressed with his intelligence and philosophical views, and as soon as he decreed his allegiance to the Stones, I knew Charlie and I were in for a challenge.

"How can you say the Beatles are the best band of all time?" he said as he took an apple and hollowed it out with a paring knife. "They couldn't play all of their songs live and The Stones can." It was an interesting angle to the age-old debate and it caught our attention.

"The Stones have almost fifty years of longevity," he continued, packing a large pinch of weed onto the top of the apple. "No other band in history can say that. The Beatles didn't even last for ten years. That's pretty unimpressive." With that he ignited his lighter in the middle of the apple and inhaled deeply. I, however, was quite impressed, both with his pro-Stones arguments and his use of an apple as a bong. I'd never seen that one before.

When he was finished, Charlie and I looked at each other, our Beatle bubbles burst. For the first time ever, somebody had put the shadow of doubt in our minds that the Stones might be better than The Beatles or, at the very least, could give them a run for their (you never give me your) money. That made us mad.

Still does. To this day whenever I see Charlie, if I want to make him laugh, all I have to say is "Fuckin' Andreas Kisser."

As the ride continued, the conversation turned to the night Cliff Burton died in a bus accident in Sweden in 1986. Anthrax was on that tour with Metallica and it was mesmerizing to hear their stories about Cliff (one of my all-time heroes), since they came through the ranks together and were very close.

Charlie's favorite Burton story came from when he was watching Metallica's set from the side of the stage (like I had watched Anthrax's in Lucerne). Every night before the guitar solo in "Master of Puppets," Hetfield always yelled something into the mic, but Charlie could never figure out what it was. (It's "FIX ME!") When he asked Cliff what it was, he responded, "It's PANCAKES."

I guarantee the next time you listen to "Master of Puppets," you'll think James says "PANCAKES!" too. It's all I ever hear at this point.

Cliff's death in the bus crash was traumatic for all that survived and the Anthrax guys still thought about it every tour. Joey even checked with the driver every night to make sure the guy was awake and feeling OK before he went to sleep. How could he not? Think about it: Part of being in a traveling rock band involves putting your life in the hands of the bus driver, who basically is a total stranger.

He (or she) drives through the night while the band is fast asleep and we don't know what he's been doing or what his personal habits are. He could be a drunken junkie, or maybe he hasn't slept in five days, who the fuck knows? But we have no choice but to trust him if we want to get any sleep and that's a scary concept.

It was almost five A.M. and we wanted to get some sleep, so we wound down the conversation, and I crashed in one of the empty bunks.

When the bus stopped a few hours later, I checked my phone and saw that even though it was only ten A.M., I already had a text from Fozzy's manager, Mark Willis.

"Fozzy bus in a crash. Bus is totaled, gig in Denmark is canceled. Everybody is OK."

WTF???

I called Willis and found out that at four forty-five A.M. Fozzy's spare secondary driver fell asleep at the wheel and drove up a raised median, turning it into a makeshift ramp. The bus went up on two wheels and skidded at an angle for fifty feet like something out of *Speed* before slamming back down on all four wheels. The impact shattered the panoramic front windshield, ripped off the side bus door (almost beheading our primary driver, who was sleeping in his bunk next to the door), and smashed the big-screen TV in the back lounge when it fell off the wall. It was amazing that in the midst of all the wreckage, even though the guys were shaken up, nobody was hurt and none of our gear was ruined. Even more amazing was that the Fozzy crash happened at almost the exact same time we were discussing the crash that killed Cliff Burton on the Anthrax bus.

Fozzy's bus was totaled after the crash in Germany. The door was completely ripped off its hinges and ended up in a ditch forty yards from the bus.

I was relieved that my brothers were OK, but they were still stuck on the side of the road somewhere in Germany, waiting for a replacement bus to come collect them. Since the gig in Aarhaus was off, I was going to have to take a train to Hamburg to meet them, and the only direct one left in twenty minutes. I had to haul ass to the station and I was still wiping the sleep out of my eyes when I sat down in my seat eighteen minutes later with only a bag of McDonald's, a toothbrush, and a pair of flip-flops to my name.

The train was crowded. I sat with one person beside me and two more facing me, all of them smoking and reeking of sweat. I had nothing to read and after three hours I was bored out of my skull, stomach-growlingly hungry, and my back was killing me when the conductor came down the aisle checking tickets. He gave mine a glance and told me I was sitting in the wrong seat. Where was I going to move? The only seat worse than mine was the toilet in the bathroom and that one was probably more comfortable with a better smell.

"No, sir, you have a first-class ticket. You should be sitting up in front."

I'd traveled all over the world, but I was a European train virgin and had no idea what the little 3 meant in the corner of my ticket. I mean, great Caesar's ghost, couldn't it have at least said FIRST CLASS on it somewhere??

I took my proper seat and my complaining back gave me a short reprieve for the next ninety minutes, until we finally reached the Hamburg station. As I was walking off the train, a businessman in dress shoes stepped on my toe, tearing the plastic strap off the flip-flop and leaving me half-barefoot. I found some tape and tried to MacGruber it together, but it didn't work and I had to just tape the whole thing to my foot.

I walked onto the street past a homeless man holding a tin cup, begging for change. His clothes were filthy and torn, his hair matted into natty dreads that half covered his dirty face. He was a complete shipwreck, except for the fact that he was wearing a pair of new tennis shoes that were nicer than the footwear I was sporting. He held up his cup and motioned for me to drop in a few coins. Then he glanced down at my shoes and said in a heavy German accent, "Never mind."

We played the show in Hamburg the next night in a dumpy little club, but it didn't matter because I was excited to be back in the city I'd spent six weeks in back in '93. After the gig, I went to check how much things had changed in the last eighteen years since I'd lived there. I headed over to my old stomping grounds, the Triangle of Decadance on the Reeperbahn, which consisted of a concert hall called Docks (which was still there), a strip club called the Cat Meow (which was not), and a Burger King (which also was not). It was a surreal experience to see how different everything was, like going back to your childhood home and seeing it painted a different color.

I was surprised how small and dead the Reeperbahn seemed, for I remembered it being much bigger and livelier as a twenty-two-year-old. It reminded me of when I returned with the WWE to the Knoxville Coliseum in 2010 after last wrestling there with Smoky Mountain sixteen years earlier. The night I worked the match with a broken arm (the full story can be found in my renowned medical thriller, *A Lion's Tale*, available at a doctor's office near you), the sold-out building had seemed like a stadium, but when I returned, it was like somebody had put the entire arena into the Death Star trash compactor and shrunk it.

I got the same feeling about Hamburg with the exception of the red light district. It was bigger than I remembered and populated with twice the girls lining the streets, waiting to be chosen like they were at an

X-rated sock hop. I wandered down the avenue as ladies of the night in all shapes and sizes propositioned me in German. When I told them I only spoke English, they yelled down the street, "American! American!" (I'm from Winnipeg, you idiot.)

That was the cue for all of the English-speaking women to reposition themselves strategically in my path and ask, "Won't you come into my room? I wanna show you all my wares."

Some of the girls were gorgeous and some weren't, but since I was only browsing, like Monty Capuletti, I continued walking until one persistent lass (who resembled a chubbier Janeane Garofalo) blocked my way.

"Hello, would you like a date?" she said with a smirk. "We can go upstairs. I'll take you in front of the fire and drain your balls."

I'd never heard it described like that before.

"I will drain your balls. No need to waste time, right? If you meet a girl and take her out to dinner, you could spend one hundred euros and still not have sex. Give me fifty euros and I'll drain your balls, guaranteed."

Can I get that in writing?

Now, I've never been into prostitutes, but if I was, I would've put her first in line due to her amazing sales pitch. With lines like those, she could've sold rehab to Rob Ford.

CHAPTER 31

Three Derelicts

Things were really coming together for Fozzy in every way. We were getting booked on bigger shows, our fanbase was growing, our reviews were improving, and our future was so bright we needed to wear shades (I do onstage), but there was one remaining problem. Whenever I watched our live performances on YouTube or saw pictures of us on-stage, I realized something ain't quite right. Like on *Sesame Street*, one of these guys was not like the others and that guy was Sean Delson.

He'd never fully adapted to our new-image philosophy and stood out like a sore thumb with his average Joe look, baggy T-shirts, and unortho-dox stage moves that made him look like a stalking praying mantis. I tried to act as his stylist, banning him from wearing watches or Levi's onstage and Googling rock 'n' roll clothing stores to help him find proper-fitting clothes. But I could tell his patience with my fashion requirements was growing thin. The other issue was he was a very good technical player in the Geddy Lee/Tony Levin mold, but that wasn't the type of bassist we needed. We wanted a dude who could groove like a mofo in the pocket of the musical pants of Rich Ward and Frank Fontsere, but we hadn't come across anybody who could quite do that. Then Paulie D came along.

Mike Portnoy told me that when he was putting together his new band Adrenaline Mob, he'd scouted a bass player in the New Jersey area named Paul Di Leo. Paul was one of those high-in-demand players that had gigged with such legendary artists as Joe Lynn Turner, Ace Frehley, Paul Simon, and BILLY JOEL! Adrenaline Mob was looking for another guitar player as well and since Fozzy was between tour cycles, I suggested Rich.

From the moment of their first rehearsal, Rich kept telling me about this amazing bass player who'd be perfect for Fozzy. I Googled Paulie, and the first thing I noticed was his image, which blew me away. He had his own thing going on and with his shoulder-length black hair, black skinny jeans, black vest, black T-shirt, black Chuck Taylors, and black strips of gaffing tape under his eyes, he looked like a cross between Johnny Ramone and Nikki Sixx. I told Rich if Paulie's playing was half as good as his look, he was in. Rich assured me his playing was even better than his gimmick and he was right.

So we made the decision to replace Sean. Switching band members is never an easy thing and Sean was a great guy and a good friend who had been with us for the better part of seven years, which made things even harder. But I think it was almost a relief for him when Rich let him go, because it was obvious his heart just wasn't into being in Fozzy anymore. This was evident by the last thing he said to Rich.

"Let's be honest. You and I both know Fozzy will never get any bigger than you are."

Those words lit some major fires inside me and I've worked my ass off ever since to prove him wrong. We all have and we've gained mountains of ground since Sean's departure, but (oh I say, Mama) a li'l aint enough for me. We were only getting started.

A few months later, Rich decided to leave Adrenaline Mob, took Paulie with him, and finally the lineup we'd been waiting eleven years for was complete: Chris Jericho, Rich Ward, Frank Fontsere, Billy Grey, and Paul Di Leo.

Rich was right about Paulie's playing. From the first time we gigged with him, I couldn't believe the difference he made to our sound. His tone, dynamics, stage presence, energy, everything. He was the missing piece of the Fozzy puzzle that we hadn't even realized we were lacking until he joined our band. With Paulie now in our ranks, we had gone from a good band to a dangerous band and we were ready to take over the world.

Our first gigs with Paulie were on the 2011 Uproar Festival tour in Canada, filling in for Sevendust for a week, with our debut being in Calgary's massive Saddledome.

It was the first arena show Fozzy had ever played and it just so happened to be an arena I'd also wrestled in with the WWE. I should call the Guinness people because I think that's some sort of world record— the only guy to ever wrestle AND play rock 'n' roll in the Saddledome.

To celebrate our first arena gig, Rich and I took a picture outside the Dome. The irony was that Jonny Zazula, who had signed us as a cover band to Megaforce Records eleven years earlier, always said we'd play arenas someday and now his prediction had finally come true.

Even though we were in the major leagues headlining the second stage of Uproar, we still weren't big enough to warrant our own dressing room and had to change in the Saddledome break room. The staff was milling around us, when a guy with a tray of popcorn around his neck recognized me and said, "Aren't you Chris Jericho? Wow, I figured you'd have your own private dressing room!" Not in this world, pal. At least not yet.

But I was so excited I would've changed in the stands. I knew this wasn't the WWE, where I was at the top of the food chain; and was ready, willing, and able to work my way to the top, the same way I had in wrestling.

Rich and me in front of the Calgary Saddledome, the first arena Fozzy ever played. In true rock 'n' roll fashion, we were standing outside because our gear was lost and we were waiting for the truck to show up.

Thankfully, Avenged Sevenfold was headlining Uproar and singer M. Shadows let me hang out in in HIS private dressing room. M. (Matt) and I had become friends after he saw Fozzy at B. B. King's, and we got even closer after A7X came over to my house in Tampa for a BBQ earlier in the tour.

Their new album, *Nightmare*, had recently hit number one on the *Billboard* charts and their touring schedule was crazy, so a day off of fun in the sun and a home-cooked meal at Irvine World (Toho TM) was a welcome change. Portnoy had joined Avenged temporarily after their drummer and best friend Jimmy "The Rev" Sullivan passed away a few months earlier, and when he called and asked if they could come over, The Irvine 5 were happy to oblige.

Once again I was impressed by their closeness as all five band members (and three of their crew) came over together to swim, Jet Ski, and chow down on some scrumptious steak. Ash, Cheyenne, and Sierra were excited to have "The Band" (as they called them) at our house, and "The Band" was really great with them. Shadows went swimming with my daughters and played Call of Duty with fellow gamer Ash. They even sat together with the exact same zoned-out look on their faces as they played. Ash later told me, "Out of all of my friends, Matt is the best at Call of Duty."

Jess put together an amazing spread and I was cooking up some rad "Steaks à la Jericho," while talking to Synyster Gates about Mr. Bungle, as Johnny Christ and Portnoy zipped across the lake on our Jet Skis. After a few spins, Johnny pulled into shore so Shads could take a turn. Matt stood in the shallow water of the shoreline, pushing the ski out onto the lake horizontally in front of him. I noticed Mike speeding toward shore as if he planned to do a drive-by and spray Shads with water, but it seemed like he was coming in a little too close and a tad too fast. I figured he knew what he was doing, so I turned back to the BBQ, but a few seconds later I heard a loud *CRASH*. My heart dropped because I was convinced of what had happened: Mike Portnoy had just killed his bandmate.

Time stood still and I could see the headlines on Blabbermouth .com already:

M. SHADOWS DEAD IN BIZARRE JET SKIING ACCIDENT AT CHRIS JERICHO'S HOUSE

MIKE PORTNOY REPLACES DRUMMER, KILLS SINGER

The way Matt had been pushing the ski out in front of himself, I was certain Portnoy had lost control and rammed into him, crushing him between the Jet Ski and the stone wall that separated the lake from my lawn. I was expecting to see him torn in two halves with his torso on the lawn, and his legs sticking up like bloody pipe cleaners between the barricade and the boat.

But when I turned around, Matt's legs were, thankfully, still attached to his torso and he was standing on them. He was laughing nervously with Dan the Body, one of their crew members who had caught the whole incident on video. Mike had indeed been coming into shore too quickly and, when he cranked the ski at the last second, lost control and broadsided Matt's Jet Ski. But instead of slamming the ski into Matt (and then into the wall behind him), it got caught in the wake and was sucked downward instead of forward, essentially causing it to just bob up and down in the water.

Shadows had gotten very lucky and when I asked Portnoy why he had come into shore so fast, he said, "I couldn't find the brake." That's because there ARE no brakes on a Jet Ski, ya big dummy!

Mike felt awful and kept apologizing profusely for damaging my ski, but all I cared about was that nobody got hurt. Sure, the side of the ski was smashed in and there were some holes in the fiberglass, but considering the alternative, I was pretty happy about everything. It was only a few days later, when I pushed the ski into the water and it sank instantly, that I realized how messed up it really was. I called our watercraft guru, Jet Bret, to come over and examine the ski. I thought maybe a seal had been broken or a spark plug had cracked, causing some water to seep in.

"Nope," Jet Bret said, "the ski sank because there's a hole in the bottom of it the size of a human head." Turns out Mike had raked the ski over a gaggle of rocks and I was now the proud owner of a totally worthless watercraft. But like my dad used to say whenever he had a fender bender, "It's only a piece of metal." I felt the same way. Besides, we still had an awesome day, and even though I lost a Jet Ski, I gained the right to bust Portnoy's balls about it forever.

And I'm never eeevvveeerrr gonna let you live this down, Mikey baby . . . NEVER!

———

Because we were only filling in for Sevendust for a few shows, we didn't have a tour bus as usual, so the plan was to fly after the show in Edmonton to our next show in Seattle. The budget for the mini tour was tight, so to save some money (and because I thought it would be fun), I asked Matt if I could ride to Seattle with Avenged.

He agreed, so after the Edmonton show I got on the bus, bearing gifts of Grey Goose vodka and Glenfiddich Scotch, our poisons of choice. A few minutes later Matt Tuck, the singer of Bullet for My Valentine, came on to see what was up. I had just met Tuck the day before and found out that he and his bandmates were huge Rich Ward fans. Matt was too nervous to speak to him at first, so he sent his guitar tech over to break the ice, and Bullet's bass player, Jay James, had THE WARD IS MY SHEPHERD tattooed on his wrist. (He had also broken his nose moshing at a Fozzy show in Cardiff six years earlier.)

Tuckie and I had hit it off right off the bat much the same way Shads and I had. The two Matts were good friends already, so we suggested Tuck ride with us to Seattle as well. A man of few words, Matt nodded his head and sat down. He'd come onboard with nothing more than the clothes on his back and a bottle of NyQuil . . . not exactly the fancy Scotch I'd contributed, but it would do.

The bus pulled out at midnight and a dozen of us sat in the front lounge having a few cocktails, telling tall tales, listening to tunes, and just talking about life on the road in general. As the night wore on, the rest of the guys went to bed one by one until it was just me, Gates, and the two Matts. We were all were pretty loaded at this point and the conversation moved in a more serious direction when the subject of Rev's passing came up. I'd been a fan of Avenged for years before I actually met them and was shocked and saddened when he'd passed away. I sent a message of condolence to them through Portnoy, partly out of respect and partly because I knew what it was like to lose one of your best friends unexpectedly.

I still found it hard to talk to random people about the Chris Benoit tragedy, but now that this mutual connection had been discovered, I found it easy to open up to them about Chris's death. I suspect that's the same reason why Shads and Gates were able to confide in me about Rev's passing.

Most of the time when someone asks about Chris, a wall goes up and I become very guarded, because while it's easy to vilify him for the atrocities he committed during the final days of his life, most people didn't KNOW him the way I did.

Chris was one of my best friends and there was so much more to him than the horrible murders he commited, just as there was so much more to Jimmy than the drug addictions that caused him to overdose. It was such a cathartic conversation for me (and I assume for them as well) because there were no judgments, no false sympathies. I told the entire story of Chris's death from my point of view and answered all of their questions, and they did the same about Jimmy's. It took a long time to get all of the emotions out of our systems—the sadness, shock, betrayal, uncertainity, love. The anger we felt toward them for leaving us behind, the anger we felt toward other people for their callous reactions, and the helpless guilt we felt in ourselves for not preventing the tragedies. It was a total cleansing, a bonding moment that I'll never forget, because sharing these feelings with two guys who'd been through a similar soul-crushing situation helped me to let go.

After our melancholy reflections ended, there were two options left: go to bed or stay up and keep drinking. Gates chose the former, while me and the two Matts (Tuck listened to our conversation in complete silence but heard every word) decided on the latter. The cocktails continued flowing until we had the bright idea to listen to some Helloween (one of Shads's and my favorite bands, so much so that we got matching tattoos of the Helloween pumpkin on the Sunset Strip a few years later) and sing along to the incredible vocals of Michael Kiske, which is never a good idea when you're fucked-up drunk.

After a little time, the combination of the long hours of talking, the hard alcohol, and the high-pitched screaming took its toll on all our voices, leaving us with nothing more than squeaky rasps. We had the next day off, thankfully because in one fell swoop of a drunken night, all three singers from Avenged Sevenfold, Bullet for My Valentine, and Fozzy had blown out their voices.

Maybe some of Tuckie's NyQuil could've helped?

The sun was up when we arrived at the U.S. border and filed off the bus to go through customs. I was dead tired, my throat was killing me, and my eyes were burning as the three of us sat on a bench in the corner of the customs area, waiting for our passports to clear. I looked around the room and noticed the rest of the band had subtly distanced themselves from us, and I don't blame them. With the way we looked and smelled, I wouldn't have been surprised if we were denied entry forever.

Then I saw three guys on the other side of the room who were in even worse shape than us. They looked like three derelicts and I knew there was no way customs was going to let THEM through. I looked at one guy in particular, who looked about a thousand years old, with hair matted to the side of his head, and deep dark bags supporting his cherry-red bloodshot eyes.

Wow, is that guy ever a mess, I thought to myself. Then I noticed the guy looked vaguely familiar, as did the tattooed dude to his left, and the long-haired bloke to his right.

I realized I was looking in a mirror. The three derelicts were us.

CHAPTER 32

Bonus Track

There's an Iron Maiden song called "Total Eclipse" that was recorded in 1982 during the *Number of the Beast* sessions. It's a great track that contains all the classic elements and techniques that make up a killer (pun intended) Maiden tune, but for some reason it wasn't included on the original version of the album. It became a "lost song," until it finally resurfaced on a *Number of the Beast* rerelease years later as a bonus track.

There are a few of these "lost songs" from my previous books, good stories that for whatever reason didn't make the final cut of *ALT* or *UD*. Most of them weren't included because they were only mildly entertaining or just plain irrelevant, but there's one story in particular that I could never figure out why it didn't make it. After all these years, I'm now going to rectify that situation and include the story . . . as a bonus track if you will.

Back in the spring of 1996, I weaseled my way onto the lineup of the World Peace Festival, a multipromotional wrestling show promoted in Los Angeles by Antonio Inoki, the president of New Japan Pro

Wrestling. I wasn't getting paid much and had to provide my own way there, but it was worth the gamble as I was a free agent hoping to get a job with New Japan or even WCW, who were also involved at the show. My plan worked. It was at that Peace Festival that Benoit first introduced me to Eric Bischoff, and the rest is history.

Konnan, a friend from my time working in Mexico, was running an AAA show the next day in Tijuana and asked if I would do him a favor and wrestle it. I'd never worked for any company in Mexico besides CMLL for Paco Alonso, the promoter who brought me to Mexico City in '93. I considered Konnan's offer for a few days, wondering if doing the single show would betray Paco and hurt my chances of going back to CMLL if I ever needed to. I decided it wouldn't, plus I could use the five hundred bucks Konnan was offering to pay some of my Peace Festival travel expenses. I agreed to the gig but made Konnan promise to throw in a hotel room and a plane ticket from San Diego back to LAX so I could catch the flight home to Calgary that I'd already booked.

I wrestled the show and was surprised by the reaction I received, or maybe I should say the lack of reaction. Even though I'd only been off Mexican television for a year, I'd never worked for AAA or in Tijuana and you could tell. I was expecting a returning hero's welcome, but just like when I returned to FMW in '92, nobody knew who I was. Plus, I was booed out of the building whenever I tried to work the crowd, which wasn't a good sign since I was supposed to be a babyface.

After the match, I grabbed my five hundred bucks, packed up the pieces of my broken ego, and headed back to the hotel. I briefly considered going to see the infamous Tijuana donkey show but decided to catch some sleep instead, as I had an early morning lobby call to take me to the airport. I didn't have my actual plane ticket yet, but Konnan told me my ride would be there at eight A.M. and I assumed I'd get it then.

The hotel Konnan had booked was quite seedy, but since I was only going to be there for a few hours, I was fine with it. Fine, that is, until I went into the room and found La Parka sprawled out on my bed. Well, I guess it wasn't officially MY bed . . . as there was only one, along with a ratty old couch. Parka was obviously more into the "first come, first served" way of doing things, instead of the "he's a guest in our country" way of thinking, and had no intention of giving up the room's only bed. So I settled down on the lumpy onion-smelling couch, which had probably soaked up the DNA of many a thrifty lothario, and tried to relax.

Then Parka went into the bathroom for over forty minutes, doing who knows what, and when he emerged, there was no water left. And by that I don't mean no hot water, I mean NO water of any kind.

Did I mention La Parka is an ugly duck? Imagine Donkey from *Shrek* (or Donkey from the donkey show) with bad acne and you'll get an idea of what he kind of looks like. That has nothing to do with my narrative, by the way; I just had to throw that out there.

Anyway, I slept horribly due to a combination of the lumpy onion couch and La Donka's bleating snores, so I couldn't wait to get the hell out of there when the morning finally came. I went to the lobby ready to go at seven forty-five A.M., a full fifteen minutes early, and was quite annoyed when the driver didn't pick me up until eight thirty A.M.

"What time is my flight?" I said and he assured me we were headed "straight there" with plenty of time. His tone worried me as I had a seven P.M. flight out of LAX to Calgary and had used my frequent flyer points to book it. If I missed it, I was screwed.

We drove in silence through the city (passing the infamous donkey show bar) until we pulled up at the border, the one you see in every movie that takes place in Tijuana. While it was a famous landmark and the gateway into the United States, it wasn't an airport.

"Here you go. The bus station is right over there," the *vato* said, pointing to a brown brick terminal across the road.

"Bus station? I thought we were headed to the airport?"

"Don't know anything about that, mano," he said, handing me a ticket and pulling away, tires screeching.

I couldn't believe that Konnan would screw me like this after all the years I'd known him! But considering that I was standing in a parking lot in TJ with no way to L.A. other than the bus ticket in my hand, I'd say I'd been stiffed harder than Sasha Grey.

Bottom line was I had a flight to catch out of LAX, so I had no time to mess about. I walked into the bus station and was directed over to my transportation, which wasn't a bus at all but a white Suburban. The driver was wearing a twelve-gallon hat with a twelve-gallon mustache to match and motioned me to get in. I warily climbed into the back, with my head ducked down so I wouldn't hit the ceiling, and took a seat in the last row. I hardly had any room in the cramped backseat and that got even worse when someone else got on and then someone else and so on. Pretty soon all of the space in the sixteen-seat van was gone and I felt like a cow in the back of a cattle car. Everybody was sitting with their bags on their laps and my fifty-dollar Target special looked like a Louis Vuitton compared to the cardboard boxes and garbage bags the other passengers were holding.

They were all speaking Spanish at one hundred miles per *hora* and then, for no apparent reason, they started singing.

I felt like the hitman sitting between Lloyd, Harry, and the Mexican hitchhikers in *Dumb and Dumber*, except I had no rat poison to put myself out of my misery.

"Mock!"

"*Si!*"

"Bird!"

"*Si!*"

Then the driver put on some mariachi music and the passengers went loco clapping along and doing those "Aiaiaiaiai!" noises that only true Mexicanos can make. The fiesta was in full swing . . . until we pulled over into a U.S. Immigration checkpoint.

We got off and lined up outside the van so the *federales* could check our credentials. The officer had probably seen nothing but Mexican passports all day, so his head was down as he gave a cursory glance to each person and mumbled a few words in Spanish. When he got to me, he looked at my passport and did a double take.

"Canadian? What are you doing here?" he asked with total surprise.

"Just trying to get to L.A.," I said dejectedly.

"Why didn't you take a bus? These transport vans can be dangerous!"

I explained my predicament and asked if he could give me a ride to LAX. He shook his head no and told me to be careful the rest of the way, as I cursed Konnan under my breath with every English, Spanish, and Klingon curse word (*baktag*!) I knew.

A few hours later, after making sixteen different stops for each passenger in sixteen different parts of SoCal, I finally got to LAX and made my flight back to Calgary. I was furious at Konnan, but the van ride wasn't a complete waste as I'd had two epiphanies along the way.

One: I'd never work for him again.

Two: I still wanted to see that damn donkey show.

CHAPTER 33

Deadman to Burning Man

In January 2010, after six months of rehab and recovery, Edge was ready to come back to the WWE. He was going to return as a surprise entrant in the Royal Rumble and eliminate me quickly. I'd been keeping our angle alive by dropping his name and burying him on a semiweekly basis for being injury prone and telling him to stay away from me if he ever came back, because he would get hurt worse.

Since it was only January, we still had enough time to salvage our angle and make the match a headlining attraction at Mania, but we'd have to act fast. So I had an idea that would make our bout a headliner instantly; we would wrestle for the world title.

If Edge came back and won the Royal Rumble, he'd be guaranteed a match at Mania for the World Championship currently held by The Undertaker. But Taker was scheduled for a rematch with HBK of their classic from the year before and didn't need the title to make their story line stand out. Therefore, if I won the belt at the Elimination Chamber, I could face Edge for it on the grandest stage of them all. Good plan, right? But it was easier said than done.

Vince hadn't made up his mind if he wanted to go with Edge or have Batista win the Rumble and challenge Cena for his world title (there were two world titles at the time . . . like in boxing). I thought it was a better story if Edge came back from a serious injury and won the Rumble. It would make his return that much more of an inspirational tale and was the perfect way for Adam to come back as a babyface, since Vince still wanted him to be the new face of *SmackDown*.

I wanted to speak to Vince to give him my thoughts before he made his final decision, feeling I'd be remiss if I didn't at least try. So I phoned him from the lobby of the Disney Animal Adventure Resort while on vacation with The Irvine 5, but I kept losing reception and it was pissing him off. He didn't like losing control of any situation (he doesn't even like sneezing) and the more my signal cut out, the angrier he got and the less chance I had of selling him on my idea.

The reception got better, and after my pitch, he said, "Well, that's certainly an option." This was Vince-ese for "I'm thinking about it, so don't bother me with this again." So I went back to watching giraffes with my kids and awaited his decision.

A few days later I got a call from Michael Hayes saying that Vince had made up his mind to go my way: Edge would win the Rumble, I'd beat Taker at the Elimination Chamber, and Edge and I would wrestle for the world title at WrestleMania 26.

Edge made his surprise return in Atlanta to a monstrous reaction and tossed me out of the Rumble immediately. Even though I'd only lasted a few minutes, Fozzy's "Martyr No More" was the theme song for the PPV, so I had that going for me.

The next month in St. Louis, the plan was I'd pin The Undertaker in the Elimination Chamber to become the World Champion, after an interfering Shawn Michaels nailed him with a superkick. I was honored, for it was a big deal to beat The Undertaker in any situation as he was still THE locker room leader and had the respect of every single employee in the WWE.

The froot thing was, Taker never abused his position or his pull, but he also had no problem reminding people of it when the situation warranted.

This was evident during our rehearsal for the Chamber match with me, Taker, Punk, Morrison, Mysterio, and Truth. When Truth and Rey showed up a half hour late, Taker gave them both a tongue-lashing, specifically laying into Truth, who was getting the biggest push of his career.

"Is this how you're gonna prove to me that you want to be a top guy? Show up late? If I can be here on time, you sure as hell can too. This won't happen again, WILL it?"

Truth stared at his boots and mumbled that it most certainly would not.

Nobody ever wanted to get on Taker's bad side, but Truth wasn't the only one to end up there that day. While he got on Taker's shitlist for being late, the other guy ended up on it by setting Taker on fire. Literally.

I was the third of the six performers to enter the 2010 Elimination Chamber and was standing in my pod of thunder awaiting Undertaker's entrance. I was stationed directly in front of the stage, so I had a bird's-eye view of the rampway as The Phenom entered the arena. It never ceased to amaze me how ominous his entrance was, and I was still in awe as he came down the ramp staring straight ahead unwaveringly, his arms slowly swinging by his side like an undead Terminator.

Suddenly, a pillar of fire shot up directly in front of him and he dropped character immediately and dodged to his left like a bug in a zapper . . . straight into the path of another flame. The second column engulfed him briefly and he hopped forward, right into yet another burst. This time his long leather trench coat caught on fire and he batted it out quickly, as he took off into a dead sprint.

When he finally got to the Chamber, it was obvious he'd gone from Deadman to Burning Man. The skin on his chest was a bright pink and his coat had melted, the ends shriveling up like a burnt black plastic Solo cup, and was still smoking as he peeled it off. Doc Amann hurried over to see how badly he'd been burned, but after a few minutes of conversation, Taker convinced him he could still do the match.

As any of you who have burned even the end of your fingertip can attest, it hurts like hell. Now imagine how much pain Taker was in with his entire upper body turning as red as a little Corvette, his skin stretched taut and shiny like it was going to split wide-open. He was the last man scheduled to enter the Chamber, so he had to wait in his pod for twenty minutes with nothing to do but pour bottles of water over his head and think about how much agony he was in.

We went through the match until finally it was his turn to enter the ring. I'd been watching him the entire time pacing the tiny pod like a caged beast waiting to be set free. Finally his door opened and we fed his comeback, but I could tell he was hurting big-time and I was concerned about even touching him. At one point I bumped him down, and when I went for the cover, I noticed the exposed skin on his chest had now blistered and was bubbling up in the more severe areas.

"Are you OK, man? Do we need to change anything?" I whispered pointedly in his ear.

"No, kid, let's stay with what we've got."

I could feel the heat radiating off his body and could smell his burnt hair. This dude was a tough motherfucker.

We continued on for another few minutes, until I eventually put him in the Walls of Jericho. The fans were going crazy in support of their hero, but all I could think of was how bad it must hurt Take to have his burnt flesh pressed down onto the canvas. Finally he made it to the ropes, then chokeslammed me and signaled for his Last Ride powerbomb finisher. At this point HBK came out from under the ring and superkicked him in the face. I warily covered him, knowing that Michaels would have no problem kicking me in the face as well. But he didn't, and I got the three-count to become the World Champion for the sixth time.

I rushed to the back in a hail of boos and headed straight to the trainer's room, where Taker and Vince were already sitting solemnly in silence, although I could tell they were in the middle of a deep conversation.

Finally, Undertaker spoke up calmly, "I don't want him to apologize, Vince. I don't want any excuses. I just never want to see him again. Because if I do, I'll kill him."

I could tell by the tone of his voice that he was completely serious and Vince felt the same way, because that was the last time we ever saw the Pyro Guy. He was fired (pun intended) on the spot and escorted out of the building immediately.

I never found out why the pyro had been set off three times in a row directly in front of The Undertaker, but it was definitely a major fuckup and he was lucky to still be alive. But he paid a steep price with second-degree burns all over his upper body and spent a few days in the St. Louis burn unit and a few more months off the road to heal. He later told me that the only things that saved him from serious permanent injuries, or even death, were:

1) the big-brimmed hat he wore to the ring, which covered his hair and half his face;
2) the fact that he'd wet his hair before he went through the curtain;
3) the long leather overcoat.

Seeing that coat up close, I realized how much it had shielded him from the flames. It was in tatters and looked like it had shrunk three sizes. The leather was bubbled up and split from the lining in places, as if it had been put in an industrial paper shredder.

I called him later and told him he was so tough he should've been born in Winnipeg instead of Texas, and he laughed . . . painfully.

I already had nothing but respect for Mark Calaway, but my esteem for the man went to a whole new level that day. He'd almost been burned alive and still put me over for the world title. We also had a killer match due to our excellent chemistry, something we found out months earlier during our first singles match.

It had been in Sheffield, England, the day after my thirty-ninth birthday and I'd tied one on badly the night before, spending most of the day on a couch in a dark room in the bowels of the arena. I set my iPhone alarm to not sleep through the show and felt like I was going to puke at any moment.

A few hours later, Taker and I tore the house down in a match I consider to be one of the best of my career, and I even included it on my first WWE DVD. The fact that it took us over a decade to get a singles match together was like working in a coal mine for years and finding a rare diamond that you'd always heard about but never seen. He was so easy and fluid to work with—and knew exactly what his character was—that it was the proverbial night off to be in the ring with him.

It was fun to reverse out of each other's trademark moves, like me spin kicking him in the face as he hit the ropes to deliver his patented corner clothesline or reversing his Hell's Gate (The Gogoplata, which morphed into the PooPoo Platter) submission into the Walls, which he then reversed into the PooPoo Platter and got the win when I tapped out. When I came back into Gorilla, Taker was sitting in a chair with a towel around his neck and a big goofy grin on his face.

"That was awesome, man! Really fuckin' great. Vince knows he has something with us."

I was ecstatic that he'd enjoyed it so much and even more so when he gave me the biggest compliment possible.

"I would work with you anytime, Chris."

That was all I needed to hear from one of the greatest performers of all time, even though we never wrestled with each other again.

CHAPTER 34

Superior DNA

After beating Taker for the world title, it was time to focus on the much-awaited Jericho vs. Edge match we'd been planning for years. We didn't have much of an angle at the start except the built-in story of the two former tag champions at war, but Vince fixed that quickly by adding a different dimension.

He called me into his office to discuss a promo I'd written about Edge, our successes and triumphs and Edge's biggest failure, the injury that destroyed what could have been the greatest tag team of all time. I could tell by the look of repulsion and disbelief on Vince's face that he wasn't buying it.

"Come on, Chris, you can do better than this. This is generic bull-shit! I want something with some meat on it. I want you to talk about DNA!"

Uhhhh, OK? I wasn't sure what he meant by DNA. Did he want a definition? A biology lesson?

"I want you to talk about Edge and his faulty DNA. How he always gets hurt because of his weak DNA and you never get hurt because of your superior DNA!"

Vince is a big believer in the law of the jungle and how only the strong survive. He often made the analogy that even the mightiest of lions when injured would be hunted and killed by the rest of the pack, so I went back to the drawing board to try and give him what he wanted.

I looked up the definition of *DNA* (deoxyribonucleic acid) and built it from there. I wrote a pretty unique promo about how DNA was the building blocks of a man's constitution and, much like height, looks, or intelligence, you were either blessed with good DNA or you weren't. Edge had been cursed and was injury-prone, while I never had to take one day off for an injury throughout my entire WWE career due to my superior DNA. I finished the promo with one of my all-time favorite lines.

"I don't know what it's like to make a triumphant return, Edge, because I've never been injured. I'm too busy winning titles."

Awwwww, snap! I love that quote because it was the perfect summary of our entire angle and, once again, Vince's seemingly ridiculous idea ended up being a great way to promote our match.

WrestleMania was going to be held on March 28, 2010, in the University of Phoenix Stadium in Glendale, Arizona, with a quadruple main event of Vince vs. Bret Hart, Cena vs. Batista, Michaels vs. Undertaker II, and Jericho vs. Edge. It was slated to be one of the biggest Manias ever and a few weeks before the show, I was asked to fly on Vince's private jet from *Raw* in Nashville to Phoenix for a press conference.

It was about a four-hour flight and Vince, Cena, Kofi Kingston, Laurinaitis, and I passed the time by playing cards, listening to AC/DC and The Rolling Stones (of course) and drinking straight Jack Daniel's. After the confrontation with HBK in France, I no longer drank brown alcohol, as Jack and Jericho still didn't get along. But I was hanging with the boss and there wasn't anything else on the plane, so I indulged. Bad idea because after four hours of being on the same aircraft, Jack kicked Jericho's ass. I was completely shitfaced (all of us were) when the plane landed, and I was in a nasty mood. Drunkicho was back and he was pissed . . . literally.

The plane pulled up on the tarmac and we stayed aboard for a few extra minutes to finish up our drinks. Kofi got up to leave, and Vince made some sort of a jokey comment along the lines of "Maybe you'll get over one of these days." I thought it was an unfair remark and caught up to Kofi on the runway.

"You have to go back on the plane and challenge him to a fight right now. If you don't, he'll know he can walk all over you whenever he wants. If you go challenge him, he'll love it and respect you for it."

I wasn't ribbing Kofi. I legitimately meant what I said and wanted to see him stand up for himself. To his credit, he only thought about it for a few seconds before marching back up the steps of the jet. I followed closely behind.

"How's your dad?" Vince asked me as I got to the top of the stairs. "Tell him to give me a call! I really like that guy and would love to chat with him again!" They'd met once.

Kofi piped up and said with some big-boy bass in his voice, "Vince, do you have a problem with me?"

Vince looked him in surprise as Kofi repeated the question.

"Maybe I do," Vince replied. "Do you wanna do something about it?"

Kofi swallowed hard, knowing he'd gone too far to turn back now. "Do you want me to do something about it?"

"Do you want to do something about it?" Vince repeated as he looked seriously into Kofi's eyes from his chair.

"Do YOU want me to do something about it?"

"Do YOU want to do something—" Vince double-legged Kofi

mid-sentence. They scuffled and rolled around in the aisle for a few seconds, until Vince got up laughing.

"That's the way to do it!" he belly laughed and got off the plane.

Kofi looked at me for justification and I gave him a big thumbs-up. I'm not sure if he gained Vince's respect that night, but he sure gained mine.

We got taken to a beautiful hotel in Glendale. When I checked into my room, it was almost five A.M. We had to be downstairs in the lobby by eight thirty A.M., so there wasn't much time to sleep. However, I had no intention of going to bed because I was staring at a lamp on the desk and it was bugging me.

The lamp stared back at me pompously and I decided I didn't like its attitude.

I karate-chopped it to the floor along with its goofy twin brother and smiled as they broke into pieces. Then I glanced at the large painting of a mixed bouquet hanging on the wall beside the bed and decided I didn't like the way it was mean-mugging me either. I grabbed it underneath its frame and ripped it off the wall, losing my grip in the process. It smashed onto the floor, and shards of glass splintered across the entire room. Satisfied with my handiwork, I lay down and promptly passed out. I woke up a few hours later, wondering when an evil invader had trashed my room.

The place was a mess, with broken glass and garbage all over the floor, bath towels flung askew amidst the twisted remains of the dearly departed Lamp Twins. I only had a few minutes to get ready for the press conference and even though my head was pounding and I felt bad about breaking the promise I'd made to myself after the HBK situation, I had to clean up my room first. I tried in vain to MacGruber the lamps back together, cleaned the glass up off the floor, and piled the big shards on top of the flat picture frame. I picked it up like a giant junkyard pizza and slowly walked to the door, figuring if I hid the picture in the staircase, nobody would notice it was missing (the giant rectangular outline on the wall wouldn't make it too obvious). I nudged the door open with my foot and barged into the hallway, running right into a maintenance man, who asked what happened.

"Uhhh . . . the uhhh . . . picture must've been put up on the wall wrong, 'cause it fell off in the middle of the night. Scared the shit out of me too!"

The guy took the painting out of my hands, saying, "Don't worry, Mr. Jericho, I'll take care of it for you. Not a big deal." He gave me a knowing wink and disappeared into the stairwell. The guy had a long braided beard and looked like a rocker, the type of guy I could see myself having a few cocktails with whilst we talked about metal. The type of guy that would have my back and help me get away with smashing a giant picture. If there's one thing I've learned, it's that you can always trust a bearded rocker and I knew we were gonna stick it to the man together in the name of rock 'n' roll! I went back into my room, put on my suit, and got ready to razzle dazzle the fine people of Arizona.

A week later I was called into Johnny's office and he was sitting in front of a stack of papers.

"What happened to your room in Phoenix?" he asked, and showed me photocopies of my trashed room. The lamps, the broken glass, the disengaged towel rack, and the smashed picture were all represented. That rat bastard bearded rocker had double-crossed me.

I admitted to Johnny that I'd drunk too much on the plane and took it out on my room. He said he understood and then presented me with a bill for seventeen hundred dollars, the cost of the damage I'd caused.

Destroying a hotel room was fun, but really expensive. Next time I'll leave the room trashing to the Keith Moons of the world and stick with stealing a couple extra bars of soap.

Now that all the promotion was finished, WrestleMania 26 had arrived and it was time to make the donuts.

Edge and I were the seventh match on the show and I think it turned out pretty good, but not great. We put together an exciting match filled with a multitude of flashy reversals and counters, to take the fans on a real roller-coaster ride, and it worked to an extent. My problem with the match is the same one I have with a lot of my stadium matches: It's hard to gauge the reactions of the audience when you're in a venue of that size. The crowd noise tends to travel up and out of the open roof instead of hitting you full force in the center of the ring, so I couldn't tell for sure if the spots were working.

But the finish, where I hit Edge with the title belt and followed up with a Codebreaker for the win, was damn good. I was a little surprised when Vince told me I was going over as I thought the idea was to build Edge into the face of *SmackDown*. That was still the overall plan, but Vince felt the fans would get behind him more if he had to chase the title longer. The match finish worked like a charm but paled in comparison to the real finish, where Edge got his revenge (and his Wrestle-Mania moment) by spearing me off the announce table through the guardrail on the floor.

This was a Michael Hayes idea and it sounded better in theory than it did in reality. Hayes had a habit of suggesting highspots that sounded completely insane, things he never would've done during his "slammin' and jammin'" Free Bird career. But if I could figure out a way to take the bump without cracking my head open, I was all for it. We met up the night before Mania to discuss the stunt with our prop guys. They decided the best way to do it would be to construct a breakaway guardrail wall with a three-inch rubber pad on the floor behind it to cushion my fall. The only thing I had to worry about was making it to that pad from the desk, which was easier said than done since I couldn't see where I was landing.

After I pinned Edge, I dragged him over to the announce desk, but before I could finish him off (I'm not sure exactly what I was planning to do), he turned the tide and slammed me on the table. Then he hurried to the other side of the Spanish announce mesa, which was next to the one I was on, and led the jam-packed stadium in a "SPEAR" chant as I slowly got to my feet.

I stood up fully as he galloped across the first desk, leapt over to the second, and drove his shoulder into my stomach. We flew through the air and I put my hand behind my head at the last second to protect myself as we crashed through the guardrail.

Any reservations I had about the crowd not being into our match dissipated when we hit the barrier, because they lost their shit at that point. It was over before it even started and I didn't feel a thing. As a matter of fact, my first thought when I landed was *That was fun! I wanna do that again!* Edge stood tall and unleashed a war cry as 65,000 fans joined him. I think I was one of them.

Two days later at *SmackDown* in Las Vegas, Vince called me into his office with Jack Swagger. Swagger was a hot new prospect who'd come up the amateur wrestling ranks and was enjoying his first big push in the WWE. In a dramatic turn of events, Vince had decided once again to not give Edge the title, but put it on Swagger instead. I'm not sure exactly why, but it didn't matter because Vince had made up his mind. Since Swagger had won the Money in the Bank match at Mania, he was going to cash the briefcase in against me that night after Edge speared me.

Swagger was nervous as Vince told him the plan and asked him if he was ready for the challenge. Jack said all the right things and Vince nodded with approval, then wanted to know if I had anything else to add. I thought of my Japanese upbringing, the way respect was taught to me, and decided to give Swags a little tough love.

"Are you ready for this, Swagger? Because this is a big deal and if you fuck this up, it's going to make me look bad and that is unacceptable. If I feel you are getting a big head or demeaning this title in any way, I'm going to come after you, do you understand?"

Swagger nodded, wide-eyed, and promised he wouldn't let me down. He left the office and Vince asked, "That was a little stiff, wasn't it?"

I didn't think so. Swagger was having a lot thrown on his shoulders that day and I didn't want to sugarcoat it for him. Being the champion was a huge responsibility and I wanted to strike a little fear into his heart to help prepare him for what was about to come.

Later that night, Edge speared me into oblivion, which was Swagger's cue to cash in the briefcase (which allowed him a title shot whenever he chose) and challenge me for the title. He gave the case to the ref, who quickly rang the bell, and Swagger dragged me up for his finish. When he stuck my head between his legs to give me his gut-wrench powerbomb, it reminded me of an idea I'd had years earlier in WCW but never got to do. I'd wanted Goldberg to literally spear me out of my shoes at the end of a PPV match, but since we never had the match, I thought it would be fun to do the same thing with Swags. I had a few seconds, as he played to the crowd, so I loosened my heel inside my dress shoe. Then as he pulled me up onto his shoulders, I kicked it off and shot it straight into the fans.

If you were in Las Vegas that night and caught my size eleven Hugo Boss, you possess the rarest of all Jericho merchandise. And now that the secret is out, I predict it will be more sought after than the Y2J bowling ball.

CHAPTER 35

That's Why I Listen

I got a call from Johnny that Lorne Michaels was producing a movie for the *Saturday Night Live* character MacGruber and wanted a group of WWE superstars to appear in the film. Mark Henry, MVP, Big Show, Kane, and Great Khali had already agreed to do it and they wanted me as well. Any time I've done projects outside the WWE, I've always tried to stay away from clichéd wrestling parts, so I was wary of agreeing right away. If all they wanted me to do was to have a wrestling match in the background of a scene or whatever, I wasn't interested. So in typical Jericho fashion, before agreeing to be in a major motion picture, I asked to see the script first.

They sent it to me and not only was it really funny, but I was the only WWE guy who had any lines in the film. I was happy to see that my character also had a name (I had no interest in being Lunkhead #2) and a one-on-one scene with MacGruber himself, played by Will Forte. I was Frank Korver, the leader of a group of mercenaries that MacGruber assembles to eliminate the evil Dieter Von Cunth and then accidentally blows up.

The MacGruber character is a parody of MacGyver, and is a bumbling doofus who constantly tries to disarm weapons but in the end just blows himself and his friends up. This was the first movie based on an *SNL* skit in years, so Lorne and his crew had high hopes for it. So did I, as it was my first big-budget movie and I wanted to make a good impression.

I flew into Albuquerque, New Mexico, a day early to hang around the set and meet all of my coworkers (like Speewee had for *Boots*), including director Jorma Taccone, who told me to shave the mustache I'd grown for the part because it was "too gay"; producer Seth Meyers, who was wearing a Coneheads baseball cap and told me if I had any funny ideas to give them a try; and stars Will Forte and Kristen Wiig, former Groundlings who were impressed that I'd also spent a year with the legendary improv troupe. As is usually the case when fellow improv-ers meet for the first time, we engaged in a bunch of unfunny comedy bits and laughed like we were Robin Williams in 1978. But lucky for me, my second attempt at engaging Forte in improv the next day was much more successful.

We were filming my big one-on-one scene with MacGruber in a sweaty little boxing gym on the outskirts of town, and it was stifling hot inside. The scene started with Grubes interrupting Korver's workout after finally tracking me down. We would banter for a few seconds until he asked me to rejoin his team and that would be the end of it. Pretty simple really, but once again in typical Jericho fashion, I decided my two lines weren't enough and wanted more. With Will's Groundlings training, I figured if I shot an extra line over to him, there was a good chance he'd pick it up. Plus, Seth had already encouraged me to be creative, so I figured nobody would get mad if I threw something extra against the sweaty gym wall. The worst thing that could happen was they would cut and tell me to stick to the script, right?

We ran through the scene a few times as it was written, while the lighting and sound guys set everything up, and waited until everyone was ready to go. If I was gonna take the chance to throw out some extra lines, I wanted to wait until the cameras were rolling and everybody was listening to what I was saying.

Jorma yelled "Action!" and I started bench-pressing until MacGruber called my name. I racked the weights in surprise, shocked that he was still alive.

"MacGruber?! The last time I saw you, you had just ripped a dude's throat out with your bare hands!"

"Classic MacGruber. Looks like you're keeping your bod pretty tight."

"You're looking pretty good yourself."

"Well, every day is a workout when you have to carry around a twenty-pound python in your jeans."

Now I was supposed to tell him we'd had some good times together, and that would be the end of my dialogue. While I felt fortunate to have been asked to be in the movie, my two lines were merely setups for MacGruber's jokes and I didn't want to be the only guy in a comedy who didn't get any laughs. So I thought I'd take a chance and instead of reciting my scripted line, I said, "You and your dick comments."

I didn't know if Will would take the bait and run with it or have a tantrum and kick me off the set. To my pleasant surprise, he ran with it.

"It's fun to say them."

OK, not bad, kind of funny. Now, like in a tennis match, it was my turn to volley something back at him quickly.

"It's fun to hear them."

Will was into it and with perfect timing replied, "That's why I say them."

The sign of a good improv scene is when it takes on a life of its own and this one just had. But I needed a tagline and a millisecond later I found it.

"And that's why I listen."

There was a brief pause after Jorma yelled "Cut!" and everyone on set burst out laughing, including Forte, Wiig (the funniest woman in America), and more important, Lorne Michaels, who'd snuck in when I wasn't watching. I'm glad I didn't see him, because I don't know if I would've had the balls to go off script if I knew he was watching.

But my ad libs were a hit and Jorma wanted to shoot the scene a few more times with my additional dialogue included. After a couple additional takes, we wrapped and I walked outside to get some fresh air. I was surprised to see Lorne, who was sitting in a canvas folding chair in middle of Video Village.

"Chris, I want to tell you that you were very funny. Thank you for your input."

While it was awesome to get a compliment like that from one of the greatest comedy minds of all time, there was something more distracting that was diverting my attention.

I couldn't get over how much Lorne sounded like Dr. Evil.

I'd always heard the rumor that Mike Myers had based his *Austin Powers* Dr. Evil character on Lorne Michaels, and after hearing him talk in person, there was no doubt in my mind that he had. His voice and mannerisms were exactly the same; all he needed was a bald cap and Verne Troyer by his side.

It was hard not to laugh as I chatted with Lorne about comedy and Canada, then I started noticing the similarities between him and another visionary I knew: Vince McMahon.

Think about it. Both created worldwide empires by taking a chance and doing something revolutionary. Both were told their respective brainchilds would never work and that they were crazy to even try. And both had created iconic entertainment juggernauts whose success rode on the shoulders of the individual performers who starred on the shows throughout the years.

Both men had to constantly regroup and create new stars when flagship names left their companies, whether it was Chevy Chase, Eddie Murphy, Adam Sandler, and Will Ferrell on *SNL* or Hulk Hogan, Bret Hart, Steve Austin, and The Rock in the WWE. They could make or break careers on a whim, as both decided who got the most airtime on their respective shows and determined who would get the chance to be the breakout stars or who would fade away, no matter how talented. Don't believe me? Check out Julia Louis-Dreyfus or Chris Rock's success on *SNL* or Bobby Roode and Barry Windham's in the WWE.

Plus, Vince and Lorne were both quirky, powerful, intimidating bosses whose distinct voices were often imitated by their employees.

I finished my conversation with Lorne, went back inside the gym, and beelined it over to Will.

"Dude, I just spoke to Lorne and I can't believe how much he sounds like Dr. Evil! It was so exact that I was expecting him to raise his pinky to his mouth and—"

Forte waved his hand in front of his throat in a slashing motion. My smile disappeared and I turned around slowly, certain that Lorne was standing behind me. He wasn't, but now Will was pointing desperately at my lav, the little mic clipped to the neckline of my tank top.

TURN THAT OFF, Will was mouthing to me frantically. I reached around to the pack on my belt and pulled the cord out.

"Take the batteries out!"

Concerned now, I took the back off the pack and shook them out into the palm of my hand.

"You can't say that!!"

"Say what?" I replied like Richard Pryor.

"You can never say that Lorne sounds like Dr. Evil! He hates it!"

"But he does sound like Dr. Evil."

"Of course he does! But he doesn't think he does and hates it when people say so. If he hears you saying anything about it, he'll probably fire you on the spot! So don't ever mention it again."

I thanked him for the heads-up; but what if Lorne HAD been listening to me in Video Village and was now waiting to fire me on the spot?

"Chris!"

I turned to see Lorne walking toward me.

This was it. I was going to be embarrassed in front of the entire cast and kicked off the set. I was never going to work in comedy again.

"Just wanted to say great work again today, Chris. See you tomorrow," Lorne said with a tight-lipped smile.

He shook my hand and I stifled a giggle, thinking about The Alan Parsons Project.

I was on set the next morning at five thirty A.M., shivering in an unheated trailer as the predawn drizzle danced off the cold tin roof. Even though we were in New Mexico in May, it was freezing outside and I couldn't wait to start filming to get some movement going. The day's scene consisted of MacGruber's mercenaries getting blown up after he inadvertently sets off a bomb in their van. It was an intricate shot that was going to take some time to get right, hence the early call time.

Kane, MVP, Mark Henry, and I were all on time and accounted for, but nobody could find the The Great Khali. After trying to track him down for hours, he finally answered his phone at nine A.M. While the rest of us had been up and ready at five A.M., Khali thought the pickup was for five P.M. and had spent the night ninety miles away in Santa Fe with some of his minions.

Khali was such a massive star in his native India that he would be chauffered around and wined and dined by his fellow Punjabis in almost every city in America. But while he was in Santa Fe acting like a big shot, the rest of the cast and crew were on set in Albuquerque waiting for him. Nobody seemed too upset about the delay, but I was. I felt he was giving the WWE a bad rap and fucking me over personally, because if anybody found out the delay was due to the "wrestlers" not being ready, that would make us all look like shit.

By the time he finally arrived on set a little after eleven A.M. and loped into his trailer without a word of apology to anybody, I was furious. I was cold, tired, and pissed off at his nonchalant attitude, so I threw open the door of his trailer and got right in his face.

"What the hell, man?" I said, looking him straight in the eye (which was only possible because he was sitting down). "You made us late for this scene because you were too lazy to get up on time. And everybody has been waiting on you! You made us ALL look bad, and if you ever do anything like this again, I will punch you right in your stupid giant face. Do you understand?!"

Khali glanced at me, the smirk never leaving his face, and said, "No problem, bro."

I stormed out of the trailer and bumped right into Val Kilmer . . . literally.

He was wearing black Crocs and a full set of green medical scrubs, even though he wasn't playing a doctor in the movie. Those were just his regular clothes. He glared at me and made a noise like the governor in *Blazing Saddles*.

"Harumph!" he growled as he brushed past me.

With all the adrenaline running through me after stupidly challenging Khali to a fistfight, he's lucky I didn't make him my huckleberry and knock him the fuck out.

Team MacGruber fired up and ready to go only minutes before we are blown to pieces. Lorne Michaels himself gave me this picture in a pure silver frame after we wrapped the movie.

Even though *MacGruber* bombed at the box office, it became a cult classic due to constant cable repeats and a great word of mouth. It's a favorite bus movie of Avenged Sevenfold and Bumpershine, and John Mayer loves it so much, he can recite the whole script verbatim. Seriously.

I was at an *SNL* after-party when he approached me, wearing a full storm trooper outfit (it was Halloween) and talking a bunch of gibberish. I'd never met him before and thought he was just really drunk, but after a few seconds, I realized he was perfectly reciting my lines from MacGruber.

"It's fun to hear them."

"That's why I say them."

"That's why I listen."

Mayer finished up the scene, then gave me his critique of my performance (his favorite scene of the film), his review of the movie ("an all-time modern comedic classic"), and his theory of how MacGruber was actually social commentary on the state of the world today.

Maybe it would've made more sense if he was just really drunk.

———

MacGruber was enough of a hit that Will, Kristen, and Ryan Phillippe were asked to guest host *Raw* at the Izod center in New Jersey (this was the show we flew in from Madrid for). I filmed a brilliant backstage bit with Will and Kristen, where I claimed to be starring in the sequel, sang a new version of the MacGruber theme using my name instead (Ja-REEKO!), and gave him advice for his "match" with Great Khali (I should've told him to punch him in his "stupid giant face"). Then I flirted with Kristen's character, Vicki, until she walked away singing my new theme song (Ja-REEKO!). It was a real test to have to hold my own with two of the funniest people in America, and I was proud of how funny it turned out to be.

After the show, Brian Gewirtz and I hung out with Kristen and her parents (who were big Y2J fans) and then went to meet with Forte and the rest of the *SNL* cast for dinner in Manhattan. It was like sitting in a WWE production meeting watching them discuss plans for that week's show, hosted by *Inception*'s Joseph Gordon-Levitt. They debated what skits would work, which ones wouldn't, and which ones might get cut last-minute by Lorne.

The conversation was delicious and my dinner even more so, especially when I noticed they had "Fresh Baked Apple Crisp" on the menu. Apple crisp was one of my mom's specialties, and even though nobody has ever made it as good as she did, it was rare to find it on a menu anywhere and I was dying to try it. Brian and Will agreed that the dessert choices were amazing and were excited to try something as well. We waited an unusually long time for the waitress to come back and I was practically drooling when she finally did.

"Hi," I said cheerily. "I'd like to get the 'Fresh Baked Apple Crisp' for dessert, please. It sounds amazing!"

"I'm sorry, sir, but your tab has been closed. Joseph Gordon-Levitt paid for everybody," she said with a smile.

What? That son of a bitch Levitt paid the whole tab without first asking if anybody wanted anything else? Who does that? I mean the nerve of that solipsistic blowhard! He had committed the most heinous of all culinary crimes. . . . Joseph Gordon-Levitt was a Dessert Denier!

To make up for the horrible reality that we wouldn't be having any dessert, we started drinking heavily and were pretty loaded when we left to meet Phillippe at a club. Forte and Jason Sudeikis were quite impressed that I was one-half of the double tag-team champions (along with Show), and insisted on walking through Times Square while wearing the titles. Thankfully, we didn't get mugged, as I would've had a hard time explaining the missing belts to Vince (he probably would've made an angle out of it).

We turned into a dark alleyway that was supposed to lead to the club, but only found a cluster of small Chinese shops instead. Then Will knocked on one of the unmarked doors and I wasn't sure if I was about to buy a drink or a Gremlin.

A blob of a man opened the door and, after exchanging a few words with Forte, led us through a kitchen and up a flight of stairs into one of the most happening clubs I've ever been in. Scantily clad knockouts were gyrating on the packed dance floor bathed in laser lights as house music pounded through the massive speakers at full volume. The walls must've been lined with titanium to keep the place soundproof, for I hadn't heard a single note in the alleyway below.

We went over to the VIP section where Ryan was hanging with his posse. He'd just been divorced from Reese Witherspoon, and the small sectioned-off area was boob to boob with girls of all shapes and sizes. In the few interactions we had, Ryan was really froot to me and greeted me with open arms. After some small talk, of which I only heard every two words he said due to the pounding beat, he introduced me to a couple of guys standing beside us.

"This is Nee-Yo and Tee-Yo!"

I shook hands and gave the fake Hollywood hug to both, but while Nee-Yo seemed nice enough, Tee-Yo just there stood stone-faced. There wasn't a lot of room to move, so I thought I'd try to alleviate the awkwardness by striking up a conversation.

"So do you guys have any shows coming up?" I yelled in Tee-Yo's face over the music.

"Huh?" he yelled back with a confused look.

Wow, this music was loud.

"DO YOU GUYS HAVE ANY SHOWS COMING UP?" I screamed into his ear.

"Nah, man, not really."

"OH, ARE YOU WORKING ON A NEW ALBUM, THEN?"

Tee-Yo looked at me like I was speaking Bocci and shouldered his way to the other side of the VIP area.

Brian came over and I told him how I'd just been blown off. "That Tee-Yo guy is a real jerk."

Brian asked me why and I told him, "Because when I asked him if he was going on tour or doing a new record, he just ignored me and walked away."

"Why would he be doing a new record?" Brian asked quizzically.

"Duh, because he's a rapper."

"He's not a rapper, he's a football player! That's T.O."

The guy was Terrell Owens, the three-time NFL Pro Bowl wide receiver, not Tee-Yo or, more specifically, T.I., the three-time Grammy winner I'd mistaken him for.

It's official. I am the #WorstFootballAndRapFanEver.

CHAPTER 36

Buddy Peacock

Vince decided he wanted to put some of the younger talent languishing down in the developmental territory in Tampa on TV, quick, so he devised the idea of pairing some of the new guys with established veterans in a pseudo reality show called *NXT*. If he was playing *Wheel of Fortune* he would've needed to buy a vowel for *NXT*, but he liked the cutting-edge froot factor of spelling it wrong. He also liked the idea of having me involved as one of the vets.

I balked at the idea as I didn't think the Chris Jericho character would care enough about anybody else to be their mentor. I also had no desire to increase my schedule, since I was already working four shows a week. Now with the *NXT* taping, I'd have to do five shows a week, not something that I saw in the cards. I talked it over with CM Punk, who'd also been asked to do the show and hated the whole idea as well. We decided we'd go to Vince separately so he wouldn't feel like we were ganging up on him (you never got what you wanted that way) and try to talk him out of selecting us.

When I told Vince my concerns, he smiled and told me he wanted the show to be a hit and needed my "star power." He also promised me I wouldn't have to work every Tuesday (I pretty much did anyway) and wouldn't have to do much on the show (which he was right about). Bottom line was he pulled his Jedi mind trick once again and I left the office feeling happy about doing *NXT* instead of hating the whole concept. Not sure how he always did that, but he did.

The following Tuesday, the seven *NXT* rookies were at ringside all bright-eyed and bushy-tailed, shaking hands and minding their manners. I'd been told my protégé was one Wade Barrett, a name I didn't recognize. I kept waiting to hear the name as the guys introduced themselves to me one by one: Justin Gabriel, Darren Young, Heath Slater, most of whom I'd never met before. I had met Bryan Danielson, who'd already made a name for himself worldwide with his amazing skills, but he had been told to think of another name for his WWE debut. His original idea was Buddy Peacock, but he went with Daniel Bryan instead and I'd say that was the better choice.

A tall, tough-looking Englishman named Stu introduced himself and shook my hand, but I was too preoccupied with finding Wade Barrett and kind of blew him off. I couldn't find him anywhere and was starting to get pissed off at the audacity of this guy making himself scarce on his first day of work. I asked Christian if he'd seen this Barrett character anywhere and he pointed at Stu, which was Wade's real name.

After being properly introduced, the two of us made a pretty good team for *NXT*. There were a few other interesting duos, including Punk and Darren Young, Matt Hardy and Justin Gabriel, Christian and Heath Slater, and Miz and Daniel Bryan (a hilarious concept that drove the "smart fans" crazy, as Bryan was already a highly respected veteran on the indy scene), but it was obvious to me Barrett was the ringer. We did a great job of feeding off each other onscreen and developed a good chemistry fairly quickly.

My role on the show was a mix of mentoring Wade and critiquing the other rookies with the pros. We'd sit on the stage, watching them perform their various tasks, grading them on score sheets. The sheets were then collected and the scores tallied to see who won. But we soon found out that our opinions pretty much meant nothing, so after that, if anyone ever read our score sheets, they would've found tic-tac-toe games, lewd remarks, and drawings of my old friend Mr. Cock 'n' Ballz.

I also had to wrestle on *NXT* once in a while, which I never wanted to do as I was in a bad mood from having to be there in the first place. Call time for TV days was usually two P.M., but I was getting there at five P.M. (or later) and didn't care. I couldn't be bothered getting there on time just to sit around all day doing nothing. On the days I did have to wrestle, it was a piece of piss to put together a short match against a guy with very little experience. I'd lay out the whole match and nobody had any better ideas anyway, except maybe Daniel Bryan, who I thought was excellent from the moment he walked into the WWE.

We wrestled each other on the very first *NXT* show, and even though we only had six minutes, it turned out pretty damn good, highlighted by Bryan overshooting me on a dive outside of the ring and slamming into the announce table at full speed. The wipeout looked vicious but because we were under a time constraint, I threw him right back inside and continued on like it didn't happen instead of teasing a count-out or changing the finish all together. It still bugs me that I made the rookie mistake of following along with the script instead of capitalizing on the moment. But I chalked it up as a lesson learned.

Bryan was explosive in the ring and had such an ingratiating quality that the fans dug, I knew he would get over big as he'd done it many times before in Ring of Honor and New Japan. It was the same principle that explained how guys like Eddy, Benoit, Rey, and I got to World Champion status: Once you learned how to get over, you could do it anywhere, be it a Dome in Tokyo, Japan, or a community center in Beckley, West Virginia.

Daniel had already toured the world on his own and been successful at every level. But he went through the same trial by fire as I did and found out quickly that when you first come into the WWE, it doesn't matter what you've accomplished elsewhere, you have to prove yourself from scratch. And at first it seemed that Vince didn't care for Daniel Bryan.

Because he was a vegan.

"Ugh, what kind of a person doesn't eat steak?" he once said to me in disgust.

So if you don't eat meat, you're obviously a jerk, right? That's why Bryan's first gimmick in the WWE was being a heel vegan. Also at first glance Daniel didn't look like the typical WWE superstar. He wasn't very tall, had an average look, and dressed like a hippie librarian. But he could wrestle like a motherfucker and knew how to connect with the crowd, which is why he's a top star in the business today, with one of the most popular catchphrases in history. (Who would've guessed ten years ago that the two most used words by the WWE Universe in 2014 would be *Yes* and *What?*)

If Daniel Bryan was the best member of the *NXT* "rookie" squad, then Heath Slater was . . . ummm, not the best. . . . And I was shocked when I heard Vince wanted me to put him over in a nothing match.

I furiously paced the empty arena floor, wondering why the hell I was supposed to lose to this rookie? I didn't want to be a part of this stupid *NXT* as it was, and now I was supposed to put over a young boy in his first match in the company? I was mad as hell and wasn't going to take it anymore and when I saw Vince I was going to tell him so. But fate stepped in and, thankfully, I ran into Pat Patterson first.

"Pat, you gotta help me. I'm so fucking pissed off right now. . . . Vince wants me to put over Heath Slater!"

Pat looked at me calmly.

"So whats?"

"What do you mean 'So what'?" I snapped back.

"So whats? Who care? It's not like anybody is going to remember this match anyway. If you were a babyface, it mights make a difference, but you're a heel, so go have funs with it!"

As much as I didn't want to admit it, Pat was right. Stu Hart once told me that the biggest marks in the business were the boys themselves, and I was proving him right. I knew better than to care about wins and losses and they usually didn't mean that much to me. Sure, if you're losing every night, you're not going to be around long, but if you have the ability to make the audience care about you and still win the big one from time to time, you'll always have a great spot in the WWE and stay over with the audience. Even though I knew that, my pride still got in the way sometimes. But as Marsellus Wallace once said, "Fuck pride."

It was my pride that caused me to flip out about losing to Slater, but the bottom line was it was my job to do what the boss wanted me to do and to make it great. That's the nature of show business, not just in the WWE. I mean if Steven Spielberg cast me in *Indiana Jones 5: The Search for Abner Ravenwood* and my character was scripted to get shot in the ball bag in the first ten minutes, I couldn't very well go complain and try to get it changed, now could I? If I did, he'd tell me to make like a tree and get out of there and cast my look-alike Jonah Hill in the part instead.

I've always compared being in the WWE to being on a good hockey team. Some nights you get thirty minutes of ice time and are expected to score the big goals, other nights you kill penalties or work the power play, and other nights you only play a few shifts a game. But if you don't play your designated role properly and to the best of your abilities, your team will lose. If you kick ass at your position, no matter how big or small of a role it may be, your team will win.

I always wanted my WWE team to win, so that night I wrestled Heath Slater and put that dude over to the best of my abilities. He pinned me with a small package, much to the crowd's delight, and left the ring with a huge win, while I left with more heat than I had before the match. Mission accomplished all across the board. Afterward I spoke to Vince about it and he reiterated Pat's theory.

"I wanted this finish because it helps you. When he won, it put the spotlight on you, not him. They might not even remember his name after this, but they'll remember the fact that you lost to a rookie and laugh at you for it. You'll get more heat as a result. Do you get that?"

I did and it was refreshing to know that even after twenty years on the job, there were still lessons to be learned. That's the way it should always be.

CHAPTER 37

Nexus Knuckleheads

I got a call from Barry Bloom in May 2010 that ABC was looking for a host for their new prime-time game show *Downfall*. I was swamped working five days a week with the WWE, but I thought it would be a smart move to at least audition. I flew to L.A. and had a face-to-face meeting with the producers, who explained the rules of the game and what was expected of me.

Downfall was basically a quiz show with a unique twist, in that all of the prizes were on a giant conveyor belt on the rooftop of a downtown L.A. skyscraper. If you could answer the questions within a certain time, the belt would stop and you would keep the goods. But the longer you took to give an answer, the faster the belt moved, until the prizes tumbled over the edge of the building and crashed to the street hundreds of feet below. A little more complicated than, say, *Deal or No Deal* but an interesting idea all the same.

The producers seemed to like me and asked if I was interested in doing the show. I told them I was but didn't really think it could happen due to my WWE schedule and never thought about it again. I didn't bother telling Vince anything about the audition, as I didn't want him getting involved and complicating matters like he had in the past when it came to his talent working outside projects. Besides, he'd never had a problem with me doing other things before and I figured if I actually got the job, I'd tell him then.

A few days later, on a Friday, I got a call from the producers, who asked if I could come in to audition again, this time for the ABC top brass. I'd made it to the final three and they wanted to see me in person in Los Angeles before the following Tuesday when they would make their decision. Problem was, I had *NXT* in Dallas that Tuesday and couldn't miss it because it was the season finale, and the winner was going to be announced.

I was convinced Barrett was going to win, so there was no way I could get out of *NXT*, but I didn't want to miss the opportunity to host a prime-time network TV game show. My chances of making it to Dallas for the show were slim, as there were no commercial flights that could get me in and out of L.A. on time. So I bit the bullet and arranged for a private jet to fly me Monday night after *Raw* in San Antonio to Los Angeles and then back to Dallas the following Tuesday afternoon. It was going to cost me fifteen grand, but that was a small price to pay if I got the job.

So after *Raw* I flew into L.A., grabbed a few hours of sleep, and headed over to ABC in the early morning for my audition. I got a quick debriefing from the producers explaining what they wanted from me (I saw the names Ian Ziering and Mario Lopez written on a manifest on the wall and assumed they were my competition), and was taken to a vacant rooftop. Then, in front of some of the most powerful people in television, I mimed and improv'd an imaginary episode of *Downfall*.

My Groundlings training was in full force that morning, as I described the expensive prizes that only I could see plunging off the imaginary conveyor belt. When I was done, I got a smattering of applause and everyone told me how great I was (typical Hollywood reaction). I thanked them and zipped back to the airport, where my jet took off at twelve thirty P.M. sharp. I landed in Dallas at five and weaved through rush-hour traffic to the American Airlines Arena, arriving just in time to get ready for *NXT*, which went live at seven P.M. One of the writers asked where I'd been all day and I said, "What do you mean? I've been here for hours hanging around in the stands."

It was a good thing everything panned out travelwise, because Barrett was announced as the winner, and the show ended with the two of us in the ring celebrating.

I celebrated again a few days later when Barry told me I got the job as the host of *Downfall*, even though I still hadn't told Vince that I was even up for it. When ABC placed a press release in *Variety* and *The Hollywood Reporter*, trumpeting the show and its new host, I thought it was awesome . . . until Barry called me in a panic.

"Stephanie just contacted me and said you're not allowed to host *Downfall*. When Vince saw the press release, he flipped out and said under no circumstances are you to do the show."

I was shocked. Obviously I had dropped the ball by not telling Vince about the gig, but this was a perfect chance for the WWE to get the mainstream coverage they craved, by having one of its top guys host a prime-time major network program. Not to mention I'd delivered it to him on a silver platter with no expense or effort on his part. Why would he forbid me to do it? It made no sense so I called him myself.

"Chris, I can't allow you do this show. It sets a bad precedent if I let talent go find opportunities on their own. Also we have an agreement with NBC and if you do an ABC show, our investors will be asking why you're not doing an NBC show."

This was total bullshit, even though I knew I'd insulted him by not telling him I'd gotten the job in the first place. But it was always easier to ask for forgiveness than permission, right?

"Look, Vince, I'm sorry for not telling you about this, but if you look at the big picture, this is good for all of us. I got picked for this job over fifty other people with celebrity value. If this show hits, it could be a big thing for the WWE and for me."

Vince refused to budge and reiterated that there was no chance in hell he was going to let me do the show.

That pissed me off.

"Vince, this is bullshit. You're fucking with my future and you're fucking with my family. I'm doing this show whether you like it or not."

"If you do it, I'll fire you on the spot."

"I'll quit first; my contract is almost up anyway."

"You are really stupid if you do this."

Now I really lost it.

"Stupid? All right, I'm going straight to the airport and chartering a plane to Connecticut so I can come over to your house and punch you in the face!" I screamed into the phone.

"I'll give you my address!" he yelled back.

I hung up on him. I couldn't believe things had come down to this, but I really felt he was screwing up a big chance for me. I went through my contract to try to figure out if he could sue me for quitting the company. I was poring through the various sections and subsections, when I heard the beep of an incoming e-mail from Vince.

"I hope you understand the reasons I can't let you do this. However, we're taping a film next month and I want you to star in it."

Who the hell "tapes a film" in this day and age?

I didn't understand Vince's logic in offering me the starring role in a straight-to-DVD movie that would take me six weeks to film and be seen by a few hundred thousand people, yet refuse to allow me to host a prime-time TV show that would take me a week to film and be seen by millions.

I told him I wasn't interesting in "taping a film" and asked him to rethink his decision. A few hours later he called me again, and this time it was a different Vince on the line.

"If you want something from me, then I'm going to want something from you," he said in a gruff Clint Eastwood voice. "I'll let you do the show, but I want you to commit to a new contract."

We'd been going back and forth over the last few months about what I felt were some low payoffs and I wanted some sort of restitution. I suggested stock options or a signing bonus for my next contract and he was hesitant because he'd never done anything like that before. I refused to negotiate a new deal or come back to the WWE until he made things financially right.

I reminded him I still wanted updated compensation for the past year. To his credit, Vince promised to go back through my payoffs to see what he could do (a few weeks later, I got a hefty six-figure check in the mail), plus he gave me his blessing to do *Downfall*. In return I agreed to come back to the WWE for another run.

Downfall only lasted six episodes and was panned by the critics, but they all agreed the one positive was my performance as host, and doing the show opened a lot of doors. It also opened another door between Vince and me, as I believe he respected the fact I didn't back down from him, even though he didn't agree with me at first. Conversely, I realized not keeping him in the loop and not telling him I was up for the job was the wrong thing to do. It was very disrespectful to him and I'm sorry for that. But the whole situation brought us closer as business associates and friends.

I've said many times that I believe Vince is a genius, and a perfect example is when he orchestrated the *NXT* invasion of *Raw*. He felt that since the *NXT* show had ended, the "rookies" would flounder without a specific role, so he decided to have all seven of them unite and annihilate John Cena on *Raw*. It was an incredible scene watching this pack of no-names become big stars in ten minutes by completely destroying Cena, the ring announcer, the timekeeper, and tearing apart and dismantling the ring for the first time ever on live TV. People had never seen anything like it before and the crowd in Miami was furious when Barrett stood center ring and announced that The Nexus were taking over the WWE.

It was mass chaos as they swarmed the superstars like a school of piranhas, using their vulgar displays of power to leave them laying time after time. The WWE fell on black days as The Nexus knuckleheads marched through the company with their vicious onslaught.

But who could stop them? Who could end their radical reign of terror? Chris Jericho, that's who.

To combat the evil invaders, Cena put together a group of freedom fighters that included R-Truth, Khali, John Morrison, and the returning Bret Hart. He approached Edge and me to help him even though we were bad guys, as Vince had pulled the plug on Edge's babyface run a few months earlier and turned him back heel. Cena approached us multiple times to join his Team WWE and help him defend the honor of his beloved company, but we kept refusing. After all, why would the two most dastardly villians on the planet want to help John Cena?

The stalemate came to a head on the last *Raw* before SummerSlam 2010 in Sacramento during a match between Cena and Bret Hart vs. Edge and me, with the Nexus members stationed ringside as lumberjacks. Eventually, they jumped in the ring to beat down the good guys as Edge and I powdered out to avoid the mugging. Truth and Morrison hit the ring to even the odds but were quickly overtaken by the numbers game. We continued watching Team Good Guy getting the shit kicked out of them as the crowd begged and pleaded for us to help. After teasing them by turning our backs, we eventually reconsidered and charged the ring, to a massive roar.

The two factions lined up like the Greasers vs. the Socs, staring each other down, waiting for the other to make the first move. The crowd was losing their shit to the point that the hard camera filming the action was literally shaking. If you were watching *Raw* at home that night and saw the picture on your TV moving wildly back and forth, it's because the Sacramento fans were stomping their feet so hard, it threw the tripod off balance.

We decided that the Nexus guys would wait to take action until I gave the cue, as some of them were green and I didn't want anybody jumping the gun. I stalled as long as I could, until the crowd reached their zenith, and then threw the sign. We charged at each other, converging in a sports entertainment wall of death, throwing hands and feet like ninjas until eventually the baddies bailed to fight another day. Team WWE stood tall in the aftermath, working the crowd like the white-meat babyfaces that we were.

I have to admit it was fun to be on the other side of the fence for the first time in years, and having the crowd chant "Y2J" again. It was amazing how much goodwill I'd built up with the audience over the last decade, in that I could be the biggest piece of shit for so long and yet with one act of valor be instantly back in their good graces. I think that's because you guys feel that no matter what, I always do my best to give you your money's worth. And I do!

The angle culminated at SummerSlam in Los Angeles with a seven-on-seven elimination match between Team WWE and Team Nexus. But I wasn't sure if I'd even be able to participate because on the day of the show, I could barely walk. If I put pressure on my left foot in any way, it felt like I was getting stabbed in the bottom of my arches. I wondered if I had a fracture or a bone spur and texted Doc Amann to tell him I wasn't sure if I was going to be able to work the show. He told me it could be a bone spur or a torn tendon and he'd check it out when I got to the Staples Center.

I have a reputation for never being hurt and for me to even consider not working the main event of the PPV, I knew something was seriously wrong. I was scared as I limped into Doc's office in great pain, using my luggage as a crutch and gingerly climbing onto his table. I took off my shoes and socks and explained the agony I was in.

"I'm pretty sure it's a bone spur, Doc. Maybe a torn muscle. It's the worst pain I've ever—"

"OK," Doc said. "I found the problem."

How could he diagnose the problem that quickly? Was it so serious that he was able to figure it out instantly? That was not a good sign! This was awful. I was going to need surgery and I was going to be out for . . .

Doc held up the tiny splinter he'd removed from the bottom of my foot with a pair of tweezers in about two seconds.

Never mind.

My mortal injury healed, I went into Vince's office, where the guys were putting together the match and where a returning Daniel Bryan had been hidden. He'd been fired after the initial Nexus invasion for choking ring announcer Justin Roberts (nice white teeth) with his own tie but had been forgiven and rehired and was now the secret seventh member of Team WWE.

The match was going to come down to Justin Gabriel and Barrett vs. a solitary Cena. John was insistent that Barrett pull back the mats and give him a DDT on the concrete floor as a false finish. After kicking out, he was going to pin Gabriel, then make Barrett tap out with his STF submission. Edge and I disagreed with John's logic and thought the DDT on the cement floor was unnecessary, especially since he was going to be winning by submission a short time later which we also disagreed with. (The Nexus was white-hot at the time and we thought it was way better to have Barrett win, but Vince wanted Cena going over and that was that.) But at the very least we knew it would be better to save the cement floor DDT for another day and have John barely squeak out the victory after being beaten down the whole match. John disagreed and felt the DDT was the way to go. So we reluctantly agreed to do his finish.

The angle had been built up so well that the crowd was primed and into it from the start. Each elimination was met with the desired reaction, including mine, where I was pinned by Heath Slater for the second time (this time at my request), who then went on to pin Edge shortly after. To remind people that we weren't officially good guys, Edge and I then attacked Cena and put the boots to him after our ousting.

Soon after, Barrett threw John to the floor, removed the padding, and DDT'd him on the concrete. The fans ooohhhed accordingly, then popped when he kicked out, but not as big as they should have. It was almost as if they knew that kicking out after being dropped on your head on cement wasn't believable. They had been taken out of the fantasy world we'd created, the same way they would've if they'd seen a boom mic in the middle of the Battle of Helm's Deep in *The Lord of the Rings*. John eventually won the match, but the reaction wasn't as good as it could've been after all the time we'd spent developing the story line.

Later in the dressing room, Cena approached me and admitted he'd made the wrong decision by doing the match his way.

"Don't forget, John, as good as you are, Edge and I have been in this business for forty years combined, so if we have an opinion about a finish, you should considering listening to us."

John nodded his head in agreement and then we shook hands, congratulating each other on a job well done. And I believe it was a job well done as I really enjoyed the Nexus angle. As a matter of fact, when I combined it with the recent HBK and Mysterio angles, I felt I'd produced a pretty damn good body of work over the last three years.

I used to tell people when I left the WWE in 2005 that if I didn't go back to wrestling, I'd have no regrets. But looking back, I realize that wasn't true. There was a lot more I wanted to prove and accomplish in my wrestling career at the time and I felt I'd improved by leaps and bounds since then. Now between the classic storylines and matches I'd been involved in during the last three years, and the additional three world title reigns, I finally felt I'd accomplished everything I wanted to do in pro wrestling.

Now that my contract was nearing its end, I was planning on taking a few months off to tour with Fozzy and then come back to the WWE a few months later. But something came up that changed those plans.

It was time for me to dance.

CHAPTER 38

The Dancing Beast

The first time I was asked to do *Dancing with the Stars* was right before my WrestleMania 26 match against Edge. I was kind of surprised that they'd asked me, then found out that my old party buddy Stacy Keibler had mentioned my name to the producers and was pushing for me to get on the show. I wasn't too sure if I wanted to do it, but upon Stacy's insistence that it was one of the best experiences of her life, I figured it would be worth at least taking the meeting. (In Hollywood you don't "have" meetings, you "take" them.)

The producers insisted that I'd be great on the show and that they would do whatever it took to get me prepared, including flying my dance partner in to practice in whatever cities my shows were in. But I'd never danced before in my life, and knowing how much work I already had each week with the WWE (as well as how crazy WrestleMania time was), there was no way I could handle the responsibility of learning a whole new craft. I respectfully declined and the producers told me I was welcome on *DWTS* anytime.

I passed a second time after they asked me again while I was in Ireland on tour with Fozzy at the beginning of September 2010. It kind of pissed me off that they'd waited until the last minute to ask as their season started in just a few weeks. It was like they thought I was just sitting around on the couch eating bon-bons with nothing else going on. But I still wasn't convinced I wanted to be on the show because if I was going to take on something as massive as *DWTS*, it would have to be my one and only priority. They'd have to give me more than two weeks' notice for me to get ready.

They took my words to heart and called me back ten days later to ask if I'd join the cast of the February 2011 season. They'd loved my personality in *Downfall* (*DWTS* was on ABC as well) and thought I'd be perfect for the show, and wouldn't take no for an answer this time.

I had to decide if I wanted to do this, for there were no more excuses why I couldn't make it work. I also felt that if I didn't accept their offer this time, they might never ask again, so I decided it was now or never. I had been reluctant before because I didn't know anything about the art of dancing, but after a quick chat with Stacy, she assured me I would do great and love the experience, so I made up my mind.

It was time for Dancing Is Jericho.

I called Vince out of courtesy to tell him I wouldn't be back in the WWE in January as planned, because I didn't want another *Downfall* situation messing up our relationship. Plus, if I was going to do this, I wanted his blessing. He gave it to me and felt it was a great opportunity for both me and the WWE, a complete 180 from his *Downfall* mind-set.

Now that I had a clear schedule and a clear head, it was time to do what I'd always done when I set my mind on something . . . kick ass and own it.

The first thing I decided to do was take private dance lessons of my own in Tampa. There was no way I was going to go onto one of the biggest shows on television with zero knowledge of what I was supposed to be doing. It wasn't easy, but after forty hours of training, I had a basic understanding of the dances I was about to be performing.

I was required to sign a confidentiality agreement and warned not to tell a soul I was going to be on the show. Then after a few weeks of radio silence, I flew to L.A. for the big cast reveal that was taking place after an episode of *The Bachelor*. When I arrived at the ABC studios I was whisked away in secrecy like the Manchurian Candidate. I got out of the town car to walk inside and two beefy bruisers in black suits and sunglasses held up a red curtain to shield me from the paparazzi hiding in the bushes, desperately trying to get an early shot of the highly anticipated new cast.

Once safely inside the fortress, I was led into the green room to meet the rest of the cast, some of whom I recognized (Kirstie Alley, Sugar Ray Leonard, Ralph Macchio), some I didn't (Mike Catherwood, Lil Romeo, Hines Ward), and went through the awkward process of trying to get to know all of them in five minutes. We were given a quick briefing on how the reveal would go and minutes later, I was onstage in front of a live studio audience being introduced as a cast member on the twelfth season of *Dancing with the Stars*.

Just being announced as a contestant on the show elevated me to a different level of notoriety instantly. As huge and loyal as the American WWE fanbase was, with about five million people watching *Raw* weekly, *DWTS* had close to twenty-five million viewers each episode and their fans were just as insatiable. They wanted to know every detail about the new cast, who our partners were going to be, what our personalities were like, and how we'd ended up on the show. I was besieged by reporters from every Hollywood gossip show and magazine, from *Inside Edition*, *Entertainment Tonight*, and *Access Hollywood* to *People*, *Star*, and *US Weekly*. *DWTS* was the crown jewel of network television, and the Hollywood cognoscenti lapped up every drop of its glitz and glamour accordingly.

Even though I had name value from the WWE and Fozzy, in the eyes of the Hollywood entertainment press, I was still a niche celebrity. Kirstie, Ralph, and ditzy playmate Kendra Wilkinson were the A-listers in their minds and were focused on the most. Initially, I believe they considered me the muscle-head wrestler who would probably trip over his own feet and be eliminated in the first week. But I knew differently and made it my goal to change their perceptions of what WWE superstars and rock 'n' roll singers were, for good.

I was ecstatic when I found out I had been partnered with Cheryl Burke, the professional dancer on the show I was most familiar with. I remembered watching her during Stacy's season and thinking she was the best, so being paired with her gave me a feeling that I could do well.

She came to Tampa for three weeks before the season premiere to train with me, and I liked her from the start. She was a great teacher in that she didn't tell me what I wanted to hear, she told me the truth, and the truth hurt a lot of the time. The first day we met, she put on some music and asked me to "just dance," to feel the rhythm of the music and do whatever felt natural. I lurched back and forth like Elaine Benes, grooving to the beat with my eyes closed. When I opened them, Cheryl looked repulsed.

"Ugh . . . we've got a lot of work to do."

She was right and work we did, for six hours a day, seven days a week, until I slowly started to get better. But dancing was one of the hardest things I'd ever done in my life. Learning how to hold my lines (a dancing term for keeping my arms and angles straight) and to move my feet in time with the beat was hard as shit and frustrating. With the constant repetition and difficult physical exertion, it reminded me of when I first started training to wrestle.

But I did have a few advantages from my other careers that helped me pick things up quicker. I was used to remembering choreography and distributing my weight gracefully from wrestling. I knew how to stay on top of the beat and how to follow the syncopation of the music from singing. Plus, my most potent weapon was knowing how to entertain a live audience and how to work the camera for those watching at home. When it came to that, I was a trained professional and wasn't going to freeze up while performing in front of a thousand people in a studio audience cheering (or booing) me.

But as the show came closer, I started to feel something I hadn't in a long time: raw nerves. I'd main-evented WrestleMania as the World Champion and played with Fozzy in front of 25,000 people, but now I was about to do something I'd never done before in front of millions of people while getting critiqued by a panel of experts. What if they said I was awful? That I could take, but what if I was voted off in the first round like I'd been on *Celebrity Duets*? (Read about that train wreck in my vocal instructional manual, *Undisputed*, available in music stores everywhere.) That would be unbearable and I vowed that no matter what, I would NOT get voted off first again. My ego couldn't handle it.

For the next three weeks, Cheryl literally put me through my paces as we worked on our first week's dance, the cha-cha, set to "Should I Stay or Should I Go" by The Clash (Joe Strummer was rolling in his grave knowing that his song was being used on *Dancing with the Frickin' Stars*) as a camera crew filmed our every move. We broke down the ninety-second dance into sections, meticulously practicing each one over and over again until it began to take shape. There were certain parts I did well (the quick footwork and spins) and other parts I didn't (shaking my hips and landing a jump at the beginning), but with Cheryl's guidance and tough-love style of coaching, I started to believe that I could actually pull it off.

We moved from Tampa back to L.A. for our last week of training and that's when it hit me how massive a spectacle *DWTS* really was. Every day, camera crews from the entertainment shows came into the studio to interview us and document our progress, while our own camera crew filmed them filming us. There were costume design sessions and fittings orchestrated by Cheryl, who not only designed all of our choreography but our outfits as well.

We had to film our routine (or our "wides") every Friday so that the producers could gauge what kind of progress we were making. On Sundays, there was a full dress rehearsal with the forty-piece band. Cheryl warned me that no matter how good or bad the rehearsal went, under no circumstances should we ever stop midway through. There were photo sessions, press interviews, appearances, and of course the nonstop rehearsing that went up to seven hours a day, every day, with no break for lunch. There was no reason to eat anyway since we didn't have the time or the desire to; dancing was hard enough as is without trying to do it on a full stomach. The training was so strenuous that I began to lose a lot of weight, although it was nothing compared to Kirstie Alley, who dropped over fifty pounds during her tenure on the show.

After a few days, I noticed that (like in wrestling) the producers wanted us all to have a gimmick. Kirstie was the wacky comedic actress, Kendra the ditzy no-filter playmate, Ralph the baby-faced ageless wonder, Hines the quiet yet charming athlete, and I was the wild cartoony wrassler. I think the last time the producers watched the WWE, Hulk Hogan was the champion, because they wanted me to act just like him. But to paraphrase Rob Halford, they had another thing coming.

"OK, we want you to rip your shirt off and growl at the camera," the director said while we were filming the opening show credits. Rip my shirt off? I'd never ripped my shirt off once during my twenty-year career and I wasn't about to start now. Besides, if I was going to go anywhere on this show, I was going to have to appeal to dancing fans, not wrestling fans. I doubted many of the WWE Universe were going to be watching me anyway, as *DWTS* aired on Mondays against *Raw*, plus I'd been the most hated heel in the company the last time they saw me. So I was going to have to rely on my charm and personality to get over, not my muscles and Y2J character.

"I'm not going to rip my shirt off. It's not really my thing," I told the director with a smile. "But just roll the camera. I'll give you what you want."

I shuffle-stepped my way toward the camera with an intense look and grabbed it with both hands, shaking it around like a psycho circus clown. The director loved it and had me do a few different takes, gathering the execs around to watch me mug for the camera. They realized right then that I wasn't their mama's stereotypical wrestler, I was a totally different animal. I was Chris Jericho.

The day of the season premiere arrived and as I put on my costume and got my hair and makeup done, I was clutched in the terrifying grip of my nerves. I practiced the steps over and over in my trailer and listened to Metallica's "Battery" to get into the zone (that had to be a first in *DWTS* history), until I was given the ten-minute warning. I stood backstage shaking and looking for the exit door, in case I needed an escape hatch. But as soon as our names were announced, I calmed down completely because it was now time to do the damn thang.

We hit the lights and the routine began as I leapt off the stage with bursting energy and landed in a perfect powerslide that would have made Jables proud. My nerves disappeared as I spun Cheryl around like a fiery top, both pairs of our feet moving in perfect spiritus mundi synchronicity. Ninety seconds of tight turns and hot moves later, I dipped her into our final pose, and a blast of pyro exploded into the air as the crowd sprang to their feet in applause. I looked around the packed studio with a shark's grin. Not everything had gone perfectly. One of the removable arms on my costume hadn't actually removed, and I'd messed up a few of the steps, but overall I was damn glad it was finished and was happy with my performance.

Thankfully, the judges agreed and even though they gave me a few harsh critiques (Len Goodman said my hips looked like they were cemented into place), they praised me overall and awarded us a solid 19 out of 30 score. Not bad for my first try, good enough to put me in the middle of the pack and to give me the confidence I needed to know that I could survive this contest and maybe even thrive in it.

My confidence was boosted even further the next night during the results show, when it was announced halfway through that I'd made it into the second round. Mission accomplished, baby! Funnyman Mike Catherwood was the first one eliminated, and I deemed my *Duets* denunciation disintegrated.

Kirstie Alley holds up a poster of her lemurs that my kids drew for her. During the *DWTS* season, she invited us over to her house in L.A. to play with her exotic animals, of which she has so many she has to employ a full-time game warden!

Our dance for week two was the quickstep set to "I Got Rhythm." It was a total 180 to move from The Clash to Judy Garland, and hearing her song on constant repeat during that week's rehearsals drove me nuts (who can ask for anything moooore), but after a while it was like working at a bell factory and I just stopped noticing. While the cha-cha was Latin based and revolved around the moving of the hips (which I had trouble with), the quickstep was all about fancy footwork and presentation, and I took to it instantly. Before too long, Cheryl and I were gliding around the rehearsal hall in an intricate syncopated routine that I loved. She had designed a 1940s-style baby-blue outfit to match the vibe of the song, and I slicked my hair back for that suave and debonair look. (It also made me look uncannily like my *NXT* protégé Wade Barrett.)

We absolutely killed it on show day, and the judges heaped praise upon us, congratulating me on my vast improvement. Bruno Tonioli jumped on his desk, waving his arms excitedly, calling me a dancing beast in his over-the-top Italian accent (which was apparently a high-level compliment), while Carrie Ann Inaba said I was a true contender. As we awaited our scores, I told a few on-camera jokes to show off my personality, which was my goal every week. I figured if I could make people laugh, it might get the people who didn't already know me from the WWE on my side faster. I felt if I could charm the granny panties off of the Middle American housewives, I'd have a better chance of hanging around longer.

A few minutes later we got our scores, but after all the amazing praise, I was a little disappointed when I only got 23 out of 30. The judges' scores didn't match their gushing comments and I didn't understand why. However, Team Chericho still did well enough to advance to the next round, and we went back to the dancing board.

The third week had a personal story theme and I decided to do a tribute to my mom (Sweet Loretta Modern) with a rhumba to "Let It Be" by The Beatles. The dance was preceded by a video package where I told the story of my mom's tragic accident and how it still affected me to this day. It was an emotional experience to put together that special dance for her (Cheryl's choreography was incredible), and the stage designers upped the ante by designing a set featuring a large framed photograph of Loretta on top of an old-time phonograph. The camera zoomed in on the picture as I put the needle on the record and the performance began.

I thought the combination of her story and the raw emotion of the dance would grab the audience by the heartstrings and pull me through to the next round easily, but the judges felt differently. Even though my transitions weren't as smooth as the week before and the dance didn't click like the quickstep had, I still felt they were a little harsh. My tango was mildly panned by the judges and given a score of 21 (I feel I was underscored), which led me to the final elimination position with daytime talk show host Wendy Williams.

The two of us stood under the hot spotlights like death row inmates waiting to ride the lightning. Time moving slow, the minutes seemed like hours and my heart raced like Jeff Gordon as I contemplated my fate. Would I stay or would I go? It was the worst mindfuck ever, and when they announced Wendy was eliminated, I felt no sense of triumph, no feeling of a job well done. I felt like I had advanced by default, like winning a silver medal. I'm assuming they put me in the kill zone to encourage anybody who liked me, but hadn't voted to get off their asses and pick up the phone next week.

I also noticed that the scores in general were higher this week, almost as if they didn't want to give out the bigger scores too early in the competition. In my opinion, if I would've done the exact same quickstep in week three that I'd done in week two, I might've scored a 25 or 26. Had I peaked too early?

My performance the next week proved that wasn't the case.

If there was anybody watching at home still sitting on the fence about me, I'm sure I convinced them of my prowess after my week 4 Paso Doble. It was orchestra week and Team Chericho performed the famous Latin bullfighting dance to the tune of Grieg's "In the Hall of the Mountain King" (I'd been a fan of Savatage's version for years) and it was my favorite performance of the seven weeks I was on the show. It was highlighted by me marching across the dance floor on my knees, completely in time with the music, an amazing Cheryl idea that had never been done on *DWTS* before. I put my wrestling knee pads under my tight satin pants to protect my knees, and the move tore the house down. We got a standing ovation from the live audience, and I had forty-two texts congratulating me when I got back to my trailer, and even a voice mail from my bro Sebastian Bach saying, "Dude, your Paso Robales was fuckin' great!"

However, once again the judges felt differently, and I was legitimately pissed off at their comments this time, especially Len Goodman's jab that I "had no idea how to follow the beat." That was total bullshit, but their disdain for my dance worried me because I HAD to make it through to the next round. If I did, I was going to get the chance to appear on the program I'd been dreaming about being on since I was a kid.

The Tonight Show.

Jay Leno's producers had agreed to book me as a guest that week as long as I was still an active participant on *DWTS*. So that had been my motivation for the last seven days: I had to kill the Paso Doble so I could advance to the next round and be on *The Tonight Show*. Thankfully, I didn't have to wait until the last elimination again this week, as my score of 23 was good enough to advance me to week 5. It was official . . . I was going to be on Leno!

I was a huge Johnny Carson fan as a kid and had been watching *The Tonight Show* my whole life. Some of my earliest childhood memories are of going on vacation with my parents and drifting off to sleep while listening to Johnny's voice in the hotel room while my mom and dad watched him from the next bed. For me, after everything I'd done, to be on *The Tonight Show* was THE true sign of making it. If you hadn't been on Carson (or Leno), then you weren't shit . . . and now that I'd been invited on, I was THE shit.

But I needed some fancy new duds to wear on my big night, so on the recommendation of wise cousin Chad, I went to the John Varvatos store on Melrose Avenue and bought a brand-new suit.

"Can you have this for me by Thursday?" I asked the salesman. "I'm going to be on *The Tonight Show*, so I need to have it ready."

Nothing made me feel frooter than saying that, even though the guy barely batted an eye and couldn't have cared less. It was Hollywood, so I'm sure he heard that line every day.

I did the pre-interview with one of the segment producers and gave her a myriad (amazing word) of ideas for Jay and me to talk about, not wanting to leave anything out. I was the second guest on the show, which meant if I could get five minutes of airtime, I'd be lucky. So I wanted to give them an overabundance of material to make sure I got the absolute most out of the little time I had.

Finally the night arrived, and I was relaxing in my personal *Tonight Show* dressing room (#bigshot), when Jay Leno himself walked in. He was wearing a denim shirt and blue jeans (The Canadian Tuxedo) and chatted with me for a few moments about our previous meeting at Road Wild 1998, the WCW PPV where he wrestled Hulk Hogan (if you don't know the story, Google it 'cause you ain't gonna read it here) and wished me luck. After he left, I took a second to drink in the moment of being in my private room in beautiful downtown Burbank, about to appear on the most famous talk show of all time. I'm ready for my close-up, Mr. Leno.

The first guest that night was the crimson-haired Diane Lane, who I had a huge crush on when she played Cherry Valance in *The Outsiders* in 1983. She was still hot, but kind of boring, and her segment dragged on and on and on and on. . . .

"I went to sleep the other night blah blah blah with my windows open and ever so softly blah blah the crickets were chirping . . ."

The crickets were chirping all right and tumbleweeds were blowing through the studio, as both the audience and Jay were practically falling asleep. Finally she ended her funeral dirge of an interview and it was time for me to pump up the volume in that mug and steal the show.

I bounded onto the stage with a burst of much-needed energy and the vibe in the studio changed instantly. My game plan was to talk as much as possible to not give Jay any openings to end the interview and my segment.

I began by saying how excited I was to be on *The Tonight Show* and told a joke about Sammy Davis and Lola Falana that died a death (I also wanted to walk onstage holding a martini like Dean Martin in the '60s, but that was nixed down by the producers). But I recovered quickly and continued on about how I was used to wearing spandex and rhinestones, so I had no problem with the costumes on *DWTS*. Then I talked about my penchant for chewing only blue gum (none of that stinkin' cinnamon) before all of my performances, how my uncle Russ was a dead ringer for Jay (they flashed his picture on-screen and he called me the next day to express how excited he was that he'd finally made it onto *The Tonight Show*) and how my son, Ash, had told everyone he knew to vote for me on *DWTS*.

"He knows like ten people!" I said flippantly.

My quip got a laugh, but I felt terrible afterward when Jessica told me I'd hurt Ash's feelings deeply because he really HAD told all his friends at school to vote for me. He was my biggest fan, and I had insulted him. Ugh, I'm such an idiot and I'm really sorry, Ashman!!

Frankly, all three of my kids enjoyed watching me on the show, and since none of them were big WWE fans, my being on *DWTS* finally made me froot in their eyes. Cheyenne and Sierra liked the fancy costumes and thought Cheryl was a princess. Ash liked the whole spectacle and had a blast when he came to watch me perform live.

My interview was going great, but I kept gulping water out of the mug on Jay's desk and buttoning and unbuttoning my suit jacket constantly, subtly showing how nervous I was. But I channeled my inner Robin Williams (my all-time favorite talk show guest) as I got up from my chair, used silly voices, and generally made fun of myself. I kept waiting for Jay to cut me off, but he never did, so I just kept on talking, until finally after nine and a half minutes he thanked me and went to commercial.

Wait . . . nine and a half minutes?

That was the same amount of time Diane Lane got and was unheard of for a second guest. I had just KILLED IT on the *THE TONIGHT SHOW* and mentally Barry Horowitzed myself as the crowd applauded.

Jay was ecstatic about the interview, thanking me more than once and asking me to come back anytime (I haven't been invited back since). I thanked him in return and took another sip of fine H_2O from the mug on his desk. Then I saw another mug of water on the coffee table in front of me.

I looked back at the mug on Jay's desk. If that mug was on HIS desk, then that meant it belonged to . . .

"Jay, have I been drinking your water the whole time?"

"It's OK, I've got plenty of mugs," he said in his famous squeaky voice.

I smiled sheepishly as an assistant hurriedly brought him a fresh water and whisked my cootie-infested mug away.

The next week our dance was the Viennese Waltz, a ballroom routine that entailed nonstop spinning and twirling—a big problem for me. These days if I do even one spin it makes me feel a little nauseous, which I'm pretty sure is some sort of side effect from over twenty years of taking bumps. I was feeling sick after the first rehearsal and wondered if I'd be able to pull this one off. But behind every good man, there is an amazing woman and mine pirouetted in and saved the day. Jess suggested I try wearing Sea-Bands, which are cheap woven bracelets with a small white marble in the center that presses against a pressure point and alleviates all motion sickness and nausea. So I gave them a try and, thankfully, they worked like a charm, allowing me to give my best performance of the competition. (Thanks for saving the day yet again, sweetie. You're the best wife ever!)

It was America week, and while we weren't dancing to "Sister Golden Hair" (much to my chagrin), our music was Whitney Houston's version of "America the Beautiful." We once again stole the show. Our costumes, choreography, and charisma all came together and led to our tightest and best performance of the competition. In weeks prior even during my good dances I'd felt a moment or two of trepidation on a few of the steps, but in week 5, everything was second nature. We were rewarded with a 26, our highest score to date, and even cranky curmudgeon Len Goodman gave us an 8 and a standing ovation.

However, my victory was short-lived and tainted by another final two elimination moment. It pissed me off to have to stand on the hot spot again after such a great performance, knowing there was no way I could be going home but still feeling that little worm of doubt that I might be wrong. Supermodel Petra Nemcova ended up getting axed, but after another mentally taxing torture session, I was angry again (I ain't talking about Dave Mustaine). I felt like the producers were messing with me, even though in retrospect, I think they were just giving the fans one last warning to vote for me.

Once again there was a reward for making it through the round, and even though it wasn't quite as prestigious as being on *The Tonight Show*, it was pretty damn close. By surviving week 5, I earned the right to be a guest on *Ellen*.

Ellen's producers had the same policy as Leno's: I had to still be in the running for *DWTS* champion if they were going to have Cheryl and me on as guests. Since we had advanced, we were booked. Ellen's vibe was a lot different from Jay's, and I was told straight off that if she didn't like me she would end the segment when she felt like it, no matter how short it was.

I arrived at the studio and got on the elevator, when a voice shouted, "Hold the door!" I hit the open button and on walked Tom Cruise and his bodyguard (who looked, as my dad would say, "like a cigarette machine with a head on it"). Cruise's hair was immaculate, his features perfect, and he was shorter than I expected, but his presence was overwhelming. It's awkward enough to stand next to a stranger within the close confines of an elevator car, but try doing it with one of the most famous people in the world. Tom stared straight ahead and I wondered what would happen if I struck up a conversation.

"Hi," I said. It was all I could think of.

Tom glanced my way for a nanosecond and slightly nodded, but I could tell by his reaction and his body language that he had no interest in talking to me. We arrived at our floor and Tom glided off with his sycophants, as I coughed from the secondhand Scientology that filled the air.

Thirty minutes later, I was announced as Ellen's next guest and I could tell from her lackadaisical intro that she didn't really know who I was and couldn't care less about me. I was proven right when her first few comments were so cold they would've made Mick Jagger's hand freeze. I knew I had to warm her up and soon, or she would cut off my segment like John Wayne Bobbitt's cock, and that would be that. I felt strangely comfortable with her, though, as I'd watched *Finding Nemo* with my kids so many times, I knew her character Dory's lines by heart.

"You know, Ellen, I feel like I know you already because I've seen *Finding Nemo* so many times with my kids. As a matter of fact it's nice to finally hear you say something other than 'P Sherman, 42 Wallaby Way, Sydney, Australia.'"

That got a nice laugh and broke the ice between us. From that moment on, Ellen was friendly, charming, and funny. We had a great interview and after a good seven minutes, she asked me if I would stay until the next segment and play a game. I agreed and she led me over to play Twister Hoopla, which was basically standing Twister, except you played with a partner and had to use each other's body parts to hold up various hoops. I was excited about playing but not about being put against my old *Downfall* rival Mario Lopez.

I'd seen Mario around over the years and we'd done a few shows together, but for whatever reason, he always rubbed me the wrong way.

"Hello, Lopez," I said with a sneer.

"Hello, Jericho," he said with false sincerity.

I didn't care what I had to do; there was NO WAY I was letting AC Slater beat me in anything. I could tell by the look in his eye that he felt the same way, but we maintained our fake smiles as Ellen picked two housewives from the audience to be our partners.

Twister Hoopla started out easy enough as Ellen spun two wheels with different body parts drawn on them, one for me and one for my partner, Jane. It landed on ELBOW and SHOULDER, so I had to pick up a ring off the ground and hold it to her shoulder with my elbow. Lopez and his partner had to hold up their ring with his knee on her hip. Ellen continued spinning the wheel for a few minutes until all four of us were straining our bodies desperately, trying not to let any of the rings fall.

While most of your garden-variety Ellen guests like Hugh Jackman or Dr. Oz would've given up with a good-natured laugh at this point, Lopez and I were locked in a duel to the death and we were taking the real housewives of studio county along with us. Not that they minded, as the prospect of a sixty-inch HD color TV (are there any black-and-white ones?) was much too enticing to give up on.

For ten minutes, the four of us contorted our bodies into positions that would've made the cast of Cirque du Soleil puke, our muscles straining and tendons stretching to the limits as Ellen called out directions. I had just stuck the point of my chin against Jane's thigh, the red ring dangling precariously between us, when my eyes locked with Lopez.

"*You know you can't win,*" I mouthed.

"*You'll never beat me,*" Lopez whispered.

"Shut up and concentrate! I want my color TV," Jane threatened.

Realizing that the game could go on for the duration of the show if she let it, Ellen called it off and ruled it a tie. I was a little annoyed because I knew I could've beaten Lopez with a few more minutes, but thanked her for ending it early the next day when I was so sore I could barely get out of bed. I've fallen off fifteen-foot-high steel cages, lost my front teeth to a stainless steel ladder, and done five hundred hack squats with Chris Benoit, but I've never felt my muscles in as much pain as they were that next day.

Twister Hoopla is hard-core! Twister Hoopla is hard-core! Twister Hoopla is hard-core!

I was having a great run on *DWTS* and felt I was getting better with every performance. But as Cheryl and I were rehearsing our tango to Journey's "Don't Stop Believin'" (the evil song I'd picked for Guilty Pleasures week) I couldn't quite grasp the choreography for some reason. I kept forgetting the moves and was the proverbial two steps behind the whole time. I was doing more rehearsal that week than I had for any other, but I just wasn't getting it. Neither was Hines Ward, apparently, as I found him sitting morosely by himself in the corner one afternoon. His dance was the same Viennese Waltz I'd done the week before, and he was having similar issues with dizziness. So I reached into my bag of tricks and pulled out the Sea-Bands.

"You've got to try these, man. They'll take care of everything," I said. He put them on warily, thanking me for my help.

Team Chericho continued practicing diligently throughout the week, but when we had to do our wides on Friday, I kept screwing up and it took a few tries to get something semi-decent. I was sure the producers formulated their initial opinions of our dances from the wides, but since we still had three days of practice left, I thought I'd be OK come showtime.

Then, two days later, disaster struck during the full-band dress rehearsal when I screwed up some steps and stopped halfway through. Cheryl looked like she'd just seen Fred Astaire's ghost as the air seemed to get sucked out of the studio.

"You can't stop!" she said with dismay.

Well, I just did . . . and I didn't see the big deal. If I was rehearsing a song with Fozzy and messed it up, I'd stop and we'd do it again. That's why it's called REHEARSAL, right? But seeing everyone's reaction when I stopped, combined with the lack of info about the next week's dance, suggested that we might be the ones going home that week. Even though I had surprised the producers with my performances and personality, I felt like my time was up with the judges, and no matter how well I danced, they'd already made up their minds.

My thoughts were validated when I watched my predance video package and it had the classic *DWTS* foreboding *these guys are in trouble* tone to it. It was funny because, out of the nonstop fifty hours we had rehearsed that week (I took a half-day break to see Metallica at The Big Four festival in nearby Indio, California), there was only one three-minute stretch early on where I'd gotten mad at my progress, yelling, "I can't do this!" in frustration. Of course the video package was based entirely on that one outburst (they even ran it in slow motion), giving people the impression that I didn't know what I was doing that week.

I'm a big show player and as soon as the red light went on and we went live, I delivered my best tango performance of the week. But I wasn't completely happy with it, nor was I completely happy with the finishing move of the routine. I spun Cheryl around by her arms and pitched her across the floor like a curling rock, but I felt a small pop and a flash of pain in my back as I did it.

The pain of a bruised ego soon followed when in a low-blow statement, Bruno told me in his Santino Marella accent that I looked like a "lump of granite" during my dance. Len disagreed and gave me another 8, but it was obvious that I'd gone from last week's Golden Child to this week's Shit Baby. When our final score of 21 ended up being that week's lowest, I knew our fate was sealed, especially when I was once again one of the final two in the elimination circle. However, this time there was no reprieve and I was given the axe.

I was sad to be eliminated but it was almost a relief, as I'd been away from home for seven weeks and was looking forward to being a daddy again. The amount of press coverage I'd gotten over the previous two months was incredible and I ended up as one of the media darlings of the season. I got a ton of "you got robbed" comments from journalists, fans and friends, which is always better than hearing "you were dog shit and it's about time you got kicked off." In reality I think I was good enough to last another week or two at the most, but there was no way I was as good a dancer as Ralph, Kirstie, or the eventual winner, Hines . . . who might not have even made it past week 6 if it hadn't been for my Sea-Bands (I should get an endorsement for this). You owe me one, Ward!

I still walked away a winner as I got to learn a little about the incredible art form of dancing, and took a chance and succeeded at something completely out of my wheelhouse (Bret Hart even said I had "big brass balls" for doing the show).

I used to think dancing was stupid and just for effeminate tough guys, but I came out of that experience thinking just the opposite: Dancing is one of the hardest but most rewarding things I've ever done. Plus, working with Cheryl Burke was simply amazing, and she made things easier and fun. We spent so much time together over those ten weeks and became close friends and I miss hanging out with her. For the record, I still think she's the best dancer on the show to this day.

Overall, Stacy was right; doing *DWTS* was one of the best experiences of my career and I'm proud of myself and very thankful that I did it.

PS: Here's some trivia for you: "Don't Stop Believin'" is the evil song that eliminated me from *Dancing with the Stars*, my bro James Durbin from *American Idol*, and Tony Soprano from *The Sopranos*. Piss off, Neal Schon!

CHAPTER 39

Yeah Boy!

Right after my elimination (even though my back was in some serious pain), I did the Jimmy Kimmel show to discuss my ousting, then hit the town to drown my sorrows with The Miz (who witnessed my elimination live in the studio) and my old friend Paul Gargano. We got totally loadski and stayed up all night getting our ya-yas out, which was the perfect way to blow off steam and wind up my *DWTS* experience. But when I went back to my apartment at five A.M., there was a car waiting to take me to my appearance on *Good Morning America*, a mandatory chore for eliminated contestants that I had totally forgotten about.

This was not good, for I was a complete mess . . . as in the slurred-speech-can't-talk-might-puke-at-any-minute type of mess. I showed up at the studio wearing the exact same clothes I'd worn on Kimmel the night before and slumped down next to Cheryl. She was getting mic'd up for our live interview via satellite with George Stephanopoulos in New York City. We'd spent enough time together over the past two and a half months (we'd even done a few joint book signings when our books came out at the same time and *Undisputed* made it all the way to number nine on the *New York Times* bestseller list) that she knew exactly what state I was in. Even though she was sitting right beside me, I took out my phone and clumsily texted her.

"I'm loaded. Not sure I can talk right now, so you might have to handle this for me."

She nodded and we went live. But once again, I'm a big show player and as soon as the red light came on, I snapped into charming Jericho mode and took over the segment. It was like when I used to come home drunk as a teenager and had to trick my mom into thinking I was sober. If I could fool Sweet Loretta Modern into thinking I wasn't hammered, tricking ten million viewers was going to be a piece of cake. I made jokes, graciously talked about my elimination, and said that I bowed out of the competition on purpose because I'd been invited to the royal wedding in England that weekend. I left 'em laughing, and the ABC publicist said I was the best eliminated guest yet. Even Gargano said he couldn't tell I was bombed—and he'd been right beside me drinking all night.

I went back to my apartment to crash and when I woke up, I checked my e-mails for the day's *DWTS* schedule. I was surprised that I hadn't gotten anything. Then I remembered I'd been eliminated, and it was a weird feeling having to adjust to life after *DWTS*. I had serious dance withdrawal and paced around my apartment like a junkie, looking for things to do. I'd been training seven hours a day, seven days a week for ten weeks, and now that that had been taken away, there was a huge void for me both mentally and physically.

Not that I could do a lot physically, as my back was really bad. It was getting hard to pick something up off the floor, get into my car, go to the gym, sleep, or even sneeze without feeling sharp pains, and I was starting to get worried.

A few weeks later, Cheryl and I got back together to run through our routine for the season finale, but things had changed. We both wanted to do well, but the intensity was gone now that there was nothing at stake. We practiced for hours instead of days and put together a loose routine of my "greatest hits" from previous dances. The knee walk, the big jump off the stage, and pitching Cheryl down the floor like a curling rock all made the cut.

We'd been paired with Sugar Ray Leonard in a mock boxing vs. wrestling dance-off, complete with ring intros from Michael Buffer. I'd met Buffer a few times when Eric Bischoff had paid him big money to introduce the main events at WCW PPVs in the '90s, but he'd never announced any of my matches. After all this time to finally hear his famous voice booming out my name was pretty damn froot, even if it was just for a dance recital and not a match.

Our routine went well (even though my back screamed when I pitched Cheryl down the floor) and it was a change to just have fun with a dance and not worry about getting judged. Plus, all I really cared about was getting a chance to do the Bruno imitation I'd been practicing ever since he'd low-blowed me with his final comments. I had it all planned out and asked host Tom Bergeron on the downlow to inquire during the post-dance interview what I'd been up to.

After our performance Tom asked me the question and I said I'd been working on a Bruno imitation and wondered if the audience wanted to see it. Of course they did, so I went into a wild and wacky frantic tirade in perfect over-the-top Bruno-ese, jumping up on the table and kicking my legs flamboyantly.

"Bruuuuuno the daaaaancing judge. Flailingggg his armsssss aboutttt and holding his worrrrrrrrrrds for no apparent reasonnnnnnnnn!!"

My imitation tore the house down and Carrie-Ann Inaba gave me my first and only 10 of the competition. Afterward, a producer pulled me aside and sternly said that even though my imitation was hilarious, he was a little annoyed that I hadn't gotten it approved beforehand and that it had gone on too long. Oh well, it's always easier to ask for forgiveness than for permission, right?

Cheryl and I pose on the first day of rehearsal, thinking of all the 10s we are going to get over the upcoming weeks. While we didn't get any 10s for dancing, I did eventually get one for my Bruno (who's photo bumbing us) imitation.

The second Cheryl spin had aggravated my back injury even further, and after the *DWTS* finale, it got progressively worse. I felt a constant slicing in my calf as if there were a tiny imp sawing on me with a hacksaw 24/7. I'd wake up every few hours in terrible pain, unable to get out of bed. I was in a bad way and couldn't take it any longer, so I went for an MRI, which discovered a herniated disc. The doctor said there were a few things I could try to alleviate the agony, but most likely I needed surgery to fuse my spine, and that my wrestling career was now in jeopardy.

It was ricockulous to think that I'd wrestled for over twenty years with hardly any injuries, but a couple months of dancing was enough to bring the hammer down on my career for good. I'm sure the two decades of constant punishment had loosened the lid of my peanut butter jar and dancing was just the final twist, but either way, I had to make some decisions. My first decision was there was no way I was getting back surgery. HBK had a similar procedure and had eventually returned to wrestling, but it had taken him five years to do so. I didn't want to wait five years, plus I felt that at almost forty if I had surgery, I might not be able to come back. I was going to have to find another way to cure my problem. There had to be something I could do that, combined with my iron will (aka stubbornness), would make the pain go away.

I weighed my options and a few weeks later went for the first of three epidurals (the same painkilling shots Jess got while giving birth), which worked for a few days, until the agony was unwelcomed back like Kotter. I started going for acupuncture a few times a week, which helped a little, but I was losing the war as the pain was affecting me both physically and emotionally now.

I was cranky and easily irritated and snapping at Jess and the kids constantly because I never knew when the sawing would start. I was about to resign myself to surgery, when Diamond Dallas Page stepped in.

One day after an acupuncture session, I posted a picture on Twitter (@iamjericho) of my back pierced with a dozen needles, and got a call twenty minutes later from an unknown number. I had just sat down for lunch at Burger 21 in Tampa (best in the world at what they do) and when I checked the voice mail afterward, it was Page.

"Bro, I saw your picture and you need to call me now."

I hadn't spoken to DDP in years, but I had been following his new career as a yoga guru. I figured he was going to try and get me to start doing his program, but I had no interest. *Yoga is for hippies, women, and effeminate tough guys,* I thought to myself. Then a sharp razor blade of pain sliced through my leg, making me wince, and I reconsidered my mindset.

I called DDP a few minutes later.

I explained the problems I was having and he knew exactly what I was going through. He'd herniated not just one but two discs in the mid-'90s and was told by doctors he would never wrestle again. He too decided he wasn't going to accept that diagnosis and designed his own yoga program to help with the pain. A few months later he was totally cured and went on to win the WCW world title three times. He sold me on his program hard, and at the end of the conversation, I reluctantly agreed to give it a try. He promised to send me his DVDs with the caveat that I would actually follow through and do the program. That wasn't a problem; I had no other choice.

The first couple of sessions were awful, as I could barely bend over without yelping in pain. I'd prided myself during my career on never warming up before a match and my horrible current flexibility reflected that. I couldn't touch my toes and had zero balance, and trying to execute the various poses was causing me excruciating agony.

Since Page had created his own style of yoga, he'd renamed the classic poses to fit his wrestling background (the Showstopper, the Road Warrior, the Cobra) and created some poses of his own, including the Hulk Up and the patented Diamond Cutter. I felt like a total mark when I first did the Diamond Cutter pose while yelling "BANG!" in an empty room since Page used to incessantly push his catchphrase back in WCW ad nauseam. If Benoit and Eddy could see me now, they'd be laughing their asses off and calling me an FOP (Friend of Page), the dreaded nickname for Page's disciples back in the day.

Over the next few weeks, the poses got easier as my flexibility improved, and I started to see a difference. The pain was still there, but the volume had been turned down. It got increasingly better, and after three months of daily (sometimes twice daily) sessions, I was pain free. It was a miracle and I ain't talking about Smokey Robinson (or his lemons).

The curious thing was, not only was I free of pain from the herniation, I was pain free period. Before my back injury, I used to climb out of bed feeling a hundred years old, knees tight, back sore, and neck stiff, but now I bounded out of bed like a kid at six o'clock on a Christmas morning. The only time I felt any pain was when I got lazy and didn't do any yoga for a few days.

Nowadays I don't lift weights or go to the gym very often, it's all DDP Yoga, push-ups, and boxing training. The best thing about DDP Yoga is I can do it anywhere—outside the tour bus, in the dressing room, or in my hotel. Gone are the days of having to schlep around town looking for a gym; now I carry the gym on my computer.

Page's program not only saved my career but my quality of life as well, and for that I am eternally grateful. I highly recommend it to anybody experiencing any kind of pain, no matter how big or small. If you are having issues, go to www.ddpyoga.com now for more info and tell him CJ sent ya.

So thank you, DDP. I'm proud to be an FOP and am happy to have FELT . . . THE . . . BANG!

Doing DDP yoga in my Miami hotel room a few days before Mania 28.

After *DWTS* and DDP yoga, I'd lost a lot of weight, which was something I'd been concentrating on doing ever since I stepped on a scale after Ash's seventh birthday party on September 24, 2010. I'd spent the day eating chicken fingers and drinking beer and that evening I weighed 230 pounds.

I was about to turn (lordy lordy, look who's) forty and was getting middle-age chunky, so I decided right then and there that Homey don't play that. I haven't drunk a beer since, and that (along with dancing and the yoga) helped me drop almost eighteen pounds. But with no more beer and no more brown alcohol allowed for Fat Jericho, I had to find something else to drink when it was time to rock the party.

That's when I invented the Yeah Boy!

For my fortieth birthday, I chartered a plane and flew my all-time favorite party pals and their wives to Turks and Caicos for a week of drunk in the sun. In order to be invited, you had to be obsessed with music and love to drink, which eliminated some of my closest friends but left me with just the cream of the party crop.

I assembled quite the rogue's gallery of rockers, including wise Chad, his brother, my cousin and nicest guy in the world, Todd (what's the good word!), Crazy Eyes Speewee, Rybo, Ajax, and Lenny Olson aka Dr. Luther (and the best man at my wedding). It was in the midst of the nonstop party that I discovered I liked the taste of straight vodka with ice and no pollutants. I was sick of drinking cocktails where the sugar in the mix made you bloated and got you hungover, so I had the genius idea of drinking the vodka with ice only.

That's when the official cocktail of Chris Jericho was born: Grey Goose and ice aka the Yeah Boy! (as coined by Fozzy's Paulie D). While it might sound harsh at first (my father-in-law, Ronnie Lockhart, calls it a true alcoholic's drink and he may be right), the good news is, you will never get a hangover from drinking one.

Ever.

Now, while you might end up tired the next day, you can say goodbye to the pounding head and puking. Think about it: The remedy for avoiding a hangover is to drink water to hydrate yourself throughout the night, right? So by using only ice as my mix, I'm already a step ahead.

So, fearless readers, if you follow Dr. Jericho's prescription, you will never get another hangover again! (Or at least that's what I tell myself.)

Yeah Boy!

After quite a few Yeah Boy!s, I was stoked to pick up this hot chick on the beach in Turks & Caicos. Yes, that is a hot chick and not Rybo.

CHAPTER 40

The Billy Crystal of Heavy Metal

I was at *Raw* in Columbus when I got a call from Josh Bernstein from *Revolver* magazine, the biggest heavy metal publication in America and the creators of the Golden Gods, the first-ever heavy metal awards show.

He wanted to know if I'd like to be a presenter of one of the awards at the ceremony, but in typical Jericho fashion, I told him I'd rather host it instead. After a few back-and-forth calls, I was hired to be the cohost along with Andrew W.K.

I flew to L.A. for the press conference at the Rainbow on the Sunset Strip in Hollywood, along with Lemmy, Dave Mustaine, my bro Zakk Wylde, Chuck Billy, Rob Halford, and Vinnie Paul. It was quite the array of legends and a good indication of the star power that was going to be in attendance at the show.

The second annual Golden Gods Awards was a huge success, kicking off with an opening vignette of W.K. and me riding down the Sunset Strip on Rob Halford's Harley and pulling upright onto the stage of the Nokia Theater. None more metal.

The crowd who filled the Nokia were there to have a good time but were also wild and unruly. I had no problems shutting up the hecklers as I'd had plenty of practice dealing with loudmouths on a microphone.

But poor Andrew W.K. wasn't as verbally equipped and looked like he wanted to disappear when they started chanting, "Camel Toe! Camel Toe!" at him and his dirty off-white jeans. I was the opposite. When they booed Lars Ulrich during a video he sent in congratulating the show, I told them all to shut the hell up and reminded them if he was actually there they'd be lining up to blow him in adulation.

Lars did show up the following year, and I did too after being named the sole host of the show. Josh and the *Revolver* head honchos said I was welcome to host the show for as long as he was in charge.

I was now the Billy Crystal of heavy metal.

I looked forward to doing the show since it was like hard rock summer camp, a place where, once a year, everybody saw all of their friends and some familiar faces (Bumpershine).

Ozzy walked past me backstage giggling, "Who the fuck are you, man?" and then literally had no idea who the fuck I was an hour later when I introduced him to present an award. He walked out onstage, and when I opened my arms to give him a big hug, he shambled right past me without a glance. It was the ultimate burn.

I brushed it off and went backstage, where I saw Gene Simmons. I'd never met him before, so I went and introduced myself.

"Hey, Gene. I'm Chris Jericho, the host of the show."

"Ahh, aren't you a handsome man," he said, smiling lasciviously. "I would fuck you if I saw you in prison."

"Not if I saw you first," I replied, not missing a beat.

Gene nodded his head with a silent *touché*.

I introduced Ronnie James Dio (I didn't spill red wine on him this time) in what turned out to be his last-ever public appearance before he died. Then, a year later, I brought out his widow, Wendy, for a touching tribute to her husband. She was accompanied by Ronnie's best friend, Geezer Butler, which left me a little gobsmacked. I'd been a Geezer fan for years but had never met him.

"I know you," he said in his lazy Birmingham accent. "I've been watching you on *Dancing with the Stars*. . . . I even voted for you." Yes! Anyone who thought my appearance on *DWTS* wasn't metal could now suck it forever because THE Geezer Butler voted for me!

My time on *DWTS* was more metallically validated when Alice Cooper walked onstage and told everyone to vote for me.

"Chris is doing more to bring metal to the mainstream than anybody here right now. A vote for him is a vote for heavy metal!"

Alice was right and the fact that I was on *DWTS* the same week Zakk Wylde appeared on *American Idol* (playing with my buddy James Durbin, a gig I helped set up) was one of the signs of the metalocalypse.

Zakk is my brother and we always have a blast together, and he saved the day one year, when Alice pulled out of the opening segment just minutes before the start of the show. Josh and I had written a skit where I would come onstage and thank myself for doing such a great job as host every year. I'd slowly build my speech and get the crowd sick of my bravado, then at the right moment Alice would come out, whip me with his riding crop, and chase me away.

For some reason, Alice decided he didn't want to do the skit and pulled out thirty minutes before showtime. Josh was freaking out, but I calmed him down and sent him to find Zakk.

Wylde and I are a couple of idiots with the same sense of humor and I knew we could figure out something quickly. After a few minutes of brainstorming, I walked onstage and delivered the same speech I'd planned with Alice, except it was Zakk who came out and interrupted me. Obviously, Zakk doesn't have a riding crop (maybe he could've used his beard?), so I had him cut me off by calling me a douche.

"Hi, Zakk, what are you—"

"Douche."

"Wait you can't—"

"Douche!"

"Hold on, Zakk, you—"

"Douche! Douche! Douche!"

It was an interesting idea to have the host be the butt of the joke, as I was the guy who had to gain the audience's trust and control the ebb and flow of the show, but it worked. It showed the crowd that I had no problem taking the piss out of myself, and that gave me a better connection with those who didn't know me and thought I was just a wrestler guy.

Zakk waits behind me to call me a douche at the Golden Gods Awards. I love the look on his face: It's obvious he can hardly wait to give me a verbal Black Label beatdown and a sloppy kiss.

I also had the experience to improv and go with the flow when things unexpectedly changed, no matter what was thrown at me. Case in point, I had just come off stage after introducing Deftones, when Josh ran over in a flurry.

"Joe Perry is coming and wants to be on the show."

Wow, OK. If the legendary guitar player from Aerosmith wants to be on the show, then we better find something for him to do. I had an idea.

We had twenty minutes to figure out what we were going to do before Deftones were done and I was due back onstage. So Josh and I hustled down to the underground parking garage, and by the time Joe

Perry showed up, we had only had about seven minutes to put something together.

Joe got out of his limo and stared off into space like he could give two shits about the whole thing. I'd never met him before, so I figured that was just his personality. Either that or he was stoned. Maybe both.

Josh was being diplomatic and cordial, as he should've been, considering he was in charge. But I had a show to run and only a few minutes to get things figured out, so I had no time for formalities.

"Hey, Joe," I said to one of the most famous guitar players in rock history, "here's what I'd like you to do, as it's kind of been a running joke on the show. I'm going to go onstage and talk about myself and when you're ready, walk out to the mic and call me a douche. Can you do that?"

Joe stared at me calmly and took a drag from his cigarette.

"Yeah, I can call you a douche."

Not exactly the first thing you want a member of the Rock and Roll Hall of Fame to say to you, but I didn't have time to think of anything else. I hit the stage, just as Deftones singer Chino Moreno (and a dead ringer for Batista) walked off, and started into the same spiel I used earlier about how great I was. The crowd grew restless until finally Joe Perry glided onstage. They erupted as he sauntered over to the podium, reached into his pocket . . . and lit up a joint. He leaned into the mic and I got a lungful of secondhand THC as I waited for him to call me a douche.

He surveyed the crowd and glanced over at me, preparing to deliver his line.

"Jericho," he said, and I smiled in anticipation of how the audience was going to erupt when he put me in my place. "You . . . need to save the Australian Aborigines! Go to worldpeace.org to find out how you can help."

What the hell was he talking about? That wasn't in the script.

"Oh, and by the way, Jericho . . . you're a motherfucking DOUCHE."

The crowd loved it and so did Joe as he took another drag of his spliff and wandered off the stage with a smirk. I haven't seen or spoken to him since.

It wasn't an easy task to be the master of ceremonies of the GGs, but the job got even harder when I pulled double duty and played the show one year when Fozzy was invited to kick off the festivities. We decided to open with a medley of songs by the greatest metal bands of all time (Sabbath, Priest, Ozzy, Metallica, Maiden, Pantera, and Dio), and then segue into our own tune "God Pounds His Nails" from *Chasing the Grail*.

To start things off with a bang, we were going to pull our old "smash the boom box with a baseball bat" routine that we'd done at the Astoria in London years earlier. The show would start with a spotlight shining on a stool with a boom box on it. A roadie would walk onstage and press PLAY, and Justin Bieber's "Baby" would blast through the speakers. The crowd would of course boo the shit out of it, until I came out onstage with a bat over my shoulder and smashed the hell out of the tape player as the band hit an open chord in time with my blows.

We were ready to go as the lights went out and the crowd buzzed, except we'd forgotten to find a roadie to press PLAY on the boom box. Dave Grohl had just showed up backstage to hang out, so I grabbed him by the arm and asked him to do the honors.

He was totally froot with it and wandered onstage to a massive cheer. When he hit the button and assaulted the room full of metalheads with the soothing sounds of "Baby, Baby," they revolted and practically started throwing rotten tomatoes at him. He waved his arms in protest, laughing, "I didn't know! I didn't know!"

Afterward he chased me around the dressing room, throwing

grapes at me and yelling, "You bastard, you set me up!" He calmed down and worked the room (which included Alice and Slash), telling us how he had recently gone to the hospital convinced he was having a heart attack, only to find out he had just drunk too much coffee. Ahhh, the life of a rock 'n' roll madman.

Dave Grohl and I do our best heavy metal faces at the Golden Gods after discussing the merits and mad sex appeal of Justin Bieber.

It was good to see Slash again, after first meeting him during a cover shoot for *Revolver* a year earlier. It had been an awkward first meeting, as it was difficult to have a conversation in between the rock poses and faces we were making for the camera.

A few months later, I went backstage after his gig in Toronto to say hi to him and his drummer Brent Fitz, who I went to high school with in Winnipeg. Fitz wasn't my favorite person back in those days because his band, Seventh Heaven, was always better than my band, Scimitar. They got the better gigs and the better girls and I'd been jealous of him for that. Then in the early '90s he'd left Winnipeg to follow his dreams the same way I had and he'd achieved his goals by getting gigs with Vince Neil, Alice Cooper, and now Slash.

We became great friends, and a few years earlier we'd even put together our own all-Canadian tribute band called Coverboy. The idea was we played only songs by Canadian bands like Streetheart, Aldo Nova, Tragically Hip, Kick Axe, and of course Loverboy. It was a great concept and had so much buzz that our first gig was on top of the CN Tower in Toronto at a party for the 2007 Grey Cup. We had a great show and we were in the hotel lobby afterward when Paul Dean, the original guitar player from Loverboy, got on the elevator with us. Brent knew him vaguely and told him about our band.

"That's great," Paul said. "Did you know our original name was Coverboy?"

"No! Why did you change it?"

"Because we wanted something more manly," he said, straight-faced.

Yeah, I could see that. Forget Slayer or Five Finger Death Punch. When I picture a name dripping with testosterone, I think Loverboy.

I hadn't seen Fitz much since the Coverboy gig, so it was great to catch up with him in Slash's dressing room. After a few minutes, Slash was told by his tour manager that he had to leave to go to an official after-show party that had been booked by the venue.

"I don't really want to do it. I'll only go if Jericho comes with me."

I was flattered by Slash's odd request and of course agreed to go. We headed over to the Tattoo Rock Club in downtown Toronto, a venue Fozzy had played before (and where I got my Fozzy *F* hand tattoo), and we sat side by side in a back booth in the VIP area as the clock struck midnight.

There was a huge tub on the table in front of us, filled with all types of booze provided by the club, who obviously didn't know that Slash had been clean and sober for years.

"Do you drink?" he asked, and when I told him I did he replied, "Good, I don't drink anymore, but I like hanging out with people who do."

I poured myself a Yeah Boy! and we talked about his career (his favorite guest appearance he'd done was playing with Ray Charles), his wardrobe (his top hat is the original one he bought in the '80s and never leaves his side), and dinosaurs (he was an amateur paleontologist like me). I found him to be extremely intelligent, soft-spoken, humble, and just an all-around great guy. We had an amazing conversation amidst all the beggars and hangers-on, but as soon as the clock hit one thirty A.M. (he must have had a contract to stay for exactly ninety minutes), we were out the door. In the car on the way back to his hotel, he extended the ultimate new millennium show of friendship by following me on Twitter (you can too at @iamjericho). I asked Fitz later why Slash was insistent on having me accompany him to his appearance.

"Slash likes interesting people and he wanted to hang out with you. Besides, he really likes you."

"How do you know that?"

"Because he talked to you without his sunglasses on."

I was in Slash's dressing room again after another successful edition of the Golden Gods headlined by Marilyn Manson. I'd never been a huge Manson fan, but to see him up close from the side of the stage, I finally got his magnetic personality. He was an amazing performer. I was mesmerized by his movements and ominous vibe . . . until he rolled on the floor and exposed his fishbelly white gut. It kind of spoiled the moment to find out that the Antichrist Superstar was actually a skinny fat guy, but overall it was a good gig.

It got better when Johnny Depp walked onstage and joined Manson on guitar for "Beautiful People." He was a pretty good player too; he had originally moved to Hollywood to be a musician. When that didn't work out, he decided to give the acting thing a try and I'd say it worked out pretty damn good for him.

After Depp and Manson tore the house down, I closed the show with my final words to the crowd and walked offstage. I ran into Slash and he asked if I wanted to go up to Manson's dressing room to say hello to Depp. I had a few post-show duties to take care of and told him I'd meet him there. Ten minutes later, I walked up to Marilyn's private dressing room, but before I could open the door, I was stopped by a mountain with eyes.

"Can I help you?"

"Yeah, Slash invited me up here to hang."

"I understand," he said, not budging.

"But I'm Chris Jericho! I hosted the show tonight and want to say hi to the guys."

"I understand," he said, staring straight ahead like a statue.

"But Slash is waiting for me in there."

"I understand."

"You're saying I can't go in?"

"You understand."

I most certainly did and skulked away to support the Australian Aborigines like the douche I was.

CHAPTER 41

The End of the World as You Know It

During my time away from the WWE, I noticed a lot of the character traits I'd created during my last run had been . . . shall we say . . . borrowed by other superstars. A lot of the heels were now talking slowly and wearing fancy suits, none more blatantly than The Miz. He'd gotten a huge push as the World Champion and had even headlined Wrestle-Mania 2011, but it was funny hearing him talking in almost the same cadence and style as me while wearing the expensive clothes. Soon afterward was the rise of CM Punk, who had completely morphed his character into a rogue loose cannon, who said what he wanted when he wanted.

He was getting over huge and calling himself The Best in the World, which was a direct rip-off of my "The Best in the World at What I Do" catchphrase. I didn't really care and I wasn't around to dispute him anyway, but I started thinking . . . What if I was?

Ever since I told Vince I was doing *DWTS*, I'd been waiting for the right time to call him to come back. I didn't want to return to the WWE to just be there; I wanted to have a specific story line. And I'd just found it.

Best in the World vs. Best in the World.

It was a major angle that I could really sink my teeth into, and I suspected Vince would like it as well. He was a pushover for something that was being done for the first time and boasted a catchy tagline.

It wouldn't be the first time Punk vs. Jericho locked up. We'd wrestled dozens of times before, and we always worked well together, so I thought a heel Jericho vs. a babyface "Voice of the Voiceless" CM Punk screamed money.

Now that I'd thought of the right angle, I needed to think of the right way to be reintroduced. I was known for my grandiose intros into the company from the classic Millennium Clock countdown to the cryptic Save Us vignettes, so the challenge was to come up with something new that was more *Return of the Jedi* than *The Exorcist: Part III.*

I was listening to Art Bell, on the radio, talking about how the Mayans had predicted that the end of the world was coming in December of 2012. I started toying with the idea that when I came back to the WWE, it would be "the end of the world as you know it."

It would be the end of the world because everything that had been going on within the company would change. It would be the end of the Jericho imitators, the end of the raping of my creativity, and the end of CM Punk as the World Champion. I thought it was a perfect topical tie-in for all the hoopla surrounding the supposed Mayan disaster coming in 2012, the same way my millennium countdown had coincided with the Y2K scare in 1999.

My plan was to return during the first *Raw* of 2012 and start my vignettes a month beforehand. Since it was already August of 2011, I had to move fast, so I contacted Vince's office to set up a meeting with him at WWE headquarters in Stamford, Connecticut. I could've just called him with my plan, but I wanted to pitch it to him in person so he could feel the passion I had for the story and gauge his reaction face-to-face.

When I walked into Vince's office (I'd only been there once before, in 1999), I think he was genuinely touched when he found out I'd flown up to Conneticut just to see him. After we exchanged a few pleasantries and told a few bad jokes, it was time to get down to business.

"So I hear you want Punk at WrestleMania, huh?"

I went into my pitch, running down the ideas and the timeline of what I'd come up with. I explained the whole Best in the World vs. Best in the World story line and how I wanted to make the angle personal. Much like when I had punched Shawn's wife in the face or removed Rey's mask, I wanted to do something so underhanded it would take our feud to a completely different level.

I wanted to tattoo him with my initials.

I could think of nothing more humiliating than being branded by another person. Getting a tattoo was such a personal choice that having to wake up for the rest of your life with your enemy's name carved into your skin seemed like the ultimate violation.

I thought Punk would dig the tattooing idea, and Vince seemed to like it as well. I filled him in on the vignettes I wanted to produce to herald my arrival and he nodded his head and took a few random notes. He mentioned that the Mania plan at the moment was for Punk to defend his title against Alberto Del Rio, but he was interested in my idea. However, he had a problem when I told him I only wanted to sign a six-month contract.

"Six months? Our fans will just be getting used to having you back and then you're going to leave again?"

I explained that the new Fozzy record was coming out in the summer and we were going on tour to promote it, so there was no way I could stay any longer.

"Hmmmm. Well, the only other guy I would consider signing for a short-term deal is Shawn Michaels, but you guys are special cases. So let me think about it and get back to you."

A few days later Vince called me and agreed to bring me back for a six-month contract and do Jericho vs. Punk at WrestleMania. It didn't take long to figure out the terms of my deal after that, although I didn't get everything I wanted.

He still wouldn't budge on paying for my cars or hotels, and he didn't want me to change my ring music. Punk had recently adopted "Cult of Personality" by Living Colour as his new theme and I wanted to follow his lead and use "Nightmare" by Avenged Sevenfold for my character's rebirth. But Vince felt it was the wrong move.

"You're only coming back for a short time and I don't want to confuse people. 'Break the Walls Down' will be Chris Jericho's music until the day you stop wrestling."

We discussed my vignettes further, and much like he had with the Save Us videos, Vince decided to leave the creative decisions up to me, Kevin Dunn, and video production whiz Adam Penucci. I'd worked with Adam on both of my previous intros and considered him to be the best in the world at what he does.

We spent some time on the phone and I explained to him I wanted something creepy and bleak, something that would get across the apocalyptic tone of "the end of the world as you know it." We threw some ideas back and forth until we figured out exactly what we wanted to do, and got to work.

The vignettes featured faded-out shots of empty fields and playgrounds and focused on an eerie little boy sitting at a desk in the middle of an empty classroom, quoting scriptures in a weird, nasally voice. Then the camera zoomed in and the kid ominously said, "It will be the end of the world as you know it." Then *IT BEGINS* flashed on the black screen in white letters.

It was sinister, grim, and totally vague, with a dark tone that was the exact opposite of the bombastic, "showbiz"-style vignettes I'd done the previous times. Kevin Dunn had also decided, instead of airing the piece before a commercial break, to have a YouTube address subtly pop up at the bottom of the screen. He wanted the vignettes to go viral and take off via word of mouth, instead of bashing the fans over the head with them like we'd done in the past.

The first link was posted exactly six weeks before I was going to make my debut on January 2, 2012, and created an instant buzz. Over half a million people clicked on the link during the week, and speculation started immediately about who was returning. Due to the dark nature of the videos, some thought they were for The Undertaker or Kane, characters who had an evil history in the WWE. Others thought they were for me but then dismissed their own claims, saying they were too dark to represent Jericho. In reality they were meant to be that way because they were supposed to represent the end of the world, not a new character for me.

As the weeks went on, we added more elements to the videos, including a teenage girl who joined Nasal Boy in reciting the scriptures. This caused a whole new wave of controversy as the fans tried to figure out who the girl represented. Was the boy representing The Undertaker and the girl Michelle McCool? Were Chris Jericho and Stephanie McMahon returning to the WWE together? Or was the girl supposed to be Karma? Why I'd be returning with her, I had no idea. Maybe I was the father of her baby?

The bottom line ('cause Stone Chris said so) was that the girl never represented anything, she was just an additional element that Penucci added to increase the weirdness of the videos. Sorry for all the confusion, guys.

No matter the theories, people were talking and they were primed to see who was going to reveal themselves on the first *Raw* of 2012. The vignettes had done exactly what we needed them to do: create a buzz and prepare the crowd for my arrival.

Now it was time for me to prepare for my arrival as well.

My first order of business was to call Lance Storm and have him put aside a few days in December for us to train. Lance had been my go-to guy when I was ready to return in '07 and he was the only one I trusted to help me get ready for this return as well. Vince had suggested I go to the FCW training Center in Tampa, and I loved the idea of working out in my own backyard, but I wanted to stick with the best. If I'm re-forming Van Halen, I call David Lee Roth, not Gary Cherone, ya dig?

Twenty-two years later, Lance and I pose outside the venue of our very first match, the Moose Hall in Ponoka, Alberta. I went there first, then Lance took a pic of himself a few days later and Photoshopped our shots together. Looks totally real, doesn't it!

Second, I wanted a whole new look for my return. Since everyone was wearing suits in the WWE now, I wanted to ditch that look and go for something completely different (The Larch), but what could that be?

I saw a picture of James Hetfield wearing a pair of distressed leather pants at Metallica's MTV Icon tribute and I thought they looked really froot. I couldn't find any online, so I Googled "distressed leather" and found a designer in L.A. named Jonathan Logan who made those types of clothes. I shot him an e-mail and I gave him my idea of a distressed leather jacket with studded rhinestoned sleeves (I'd nicked that from Alice Cooper). Jonathan said he could do it but had a lot of work on his plate, so we decided it would be best for me to come to his shop to brainstorm.

I went to his studio in the fashion district in downtown L.A. and showed him what I had in mind. He came up with a few sketches and said he'd get started as soon as he was finished with his current projects.

"What are you working on now?" I inquired.

"I'm doing all of Justin Bieber's outfits for his next tour. Then I have to make a few jackets for David Lee Roth for the upcoming Van Halen tour."

Well, if that wasn't happenstance, I don't know what was. When I first started in the business, I wanted to be the David Lee Roth of wrestling, and now by total coincidence we had the same costume designer!

Jonathan also did all of Brad Pitt's leather wardrobe and had just done an outfit for Alicia Keys for a DJ set she had done. He showed me a quick clip of her spinning at the club, wearing a jacket with a half dozen flashing lights sewn on the front. A flashing light went off in my head.

"How do those lights work?"

They were controlled by a switch in the pocket that turned them on and off like Christmas lights.

"If you were able to stitch in a half dozen lights, could you stitch in a couple hundred?"

"Of course I could," he replied with real swagger.

And that's how the idea for the famous Jericho lighted jacket was born. Over the next few months, the amalgamation of Hetfield distressed leather, Cooper studded sleeves, and Keys lights came together perfectly.

It makes me laugh when people ask me why the WWE doesn't sell lighted jackets at the merch stand. . . . They don't because the damn thing cost me almost ten grand, that's why! Expensive, I know, but I'm sure Paul Stanley said the same thing about Kiss's costumes in 1977. The Starchild knew just as well as I did that in showbiz you have to spend money to make money.

Nothing like this had ever been done before, so my original blue-and-white lighted jacket was a prototype and it acted as one. Like Clark Griswold's Christmas lights, if one of the hundreds of thin wires in the lining of the jacket broke or malfunctioned, the whole string of bulbs shorted out. The broken wire could be easily fixed with a soldering gun, but the problem was trying to find where the damn thing had snapped off in the first place. But technical difficulties aside, the jacket was the perfect addition to the Y2J legacy and became a late career trademark. As a matter of fact, at this point I think they could stick the jacket on a mannequin in the middle of the ring and turn it on and the fans would be happy. Some legacy, huh?

The first cut of the famous jacket. This was so early in the process it didn't even have lights yet. I'm gonna use that same stand on my retirement tour—set the thing in the ring, turn the jacket on, and collect my paycheck.

My new look complete, it was time to head up to Calgary to train with Lance and see what I could or couldn't do. While my back problems had pretty much cleared up, I was nervous about how it might feel after taking a few bumps. DDP yoga had been good enough to Band-Aid me together during everyday living, but taking bumps in the ring was a whole different world. What if the jarring falls and uncontrolled motions of having a match caused the buzz saw blades to begin biting again? The only way to find out would be to get back on the horse and ride.

I met Lance outside his school on a snowy day in December in suburban Calgary. I'd asked him to keep his students out of the building for the day because I didn't want a group of rookies witnessing me getting carried out of the ring if the pain came back; so it was just the two of us.

I'd been told by my amazing Tampa physician, Dr. Chris MacLaren, that the worst thing I could do for my back was a Lionsault (my patented backflip off the second rope) and suggested I retire the move for good. So of course I decided that was the first thing I was going to try. Go hard or go home, right?

I stood in the middle of the ring looking at the middle rope like it was my white whale, scared to try the move but more scared not to. If I didn't get this out of the way right now, it was going to screw with my entire psyche and affect my training. I had to get rid of the doubt inside my head quickly because if I didn't, I was going to get hurt, and the only way to conquer the fear was to move full speed ahead and get this funky monkey off my back. It was like passing a car on a one-lane highway with another vehicle approaching; you have to speed by as fast as you can with no hesitation, or risk a head-on collision.

I didn't have "head-on collision" planned on my schedule today, so I said a quick prayer and thought of Joel Goodsen's motto.

"What the fuck," I whispered and took off running.

I jumped onto the second rope and let my weight force it downward until it reached its nadir. I pushed off with my legs, threw my arms in the air, and tilted my head. I flipped backward, rotated, and landed picture-perfect on my stomach. I lay on the mat for a few seconds, waiting for that burning buzz saw blade to tear up my insides, but praise God, it didn't happen and I felt great.

Since the spell had been broken and the curse had been lifted, we spent the next few hours having mock matches and running through some of my patented moves to see how they felt. To my pleasant surprise, I pulled them all off pain free: Codebreakers, crossbody blocks from the top rope, enziguris, bulldogs, Walls of Jericho. They all felt better than ever, especially the Codebreaker, which had always seemed to hurt me more than my opponent.

Since I came back in 2007 with my new finish of the Codebreaker, I wanted to come back in 2012 with a new move as well. I had the idea of doing a sliding forearm to the face and calling it Apocalypse Now. I practiced the move a dozen times with Lance, making tweaks along the way. It looked badass and I was excited to start using it as soon as I returned. I texted Vince to tell him that I had a new finishing move and his reply was typical McBad comedy.

"You already have a finish . . . looking at the lights!"

Hardee frickin' har.

I actually only used the move once, during a match with Kofi Kingston in Dubai. But I decided I didn't have the time or the patience to get it over and I gave up on it after a few weeks. So if you want to use Apocalypse Now as your new finish, fearless readers, be my guest.

Once I could do my patented Lionsault without any pain, I knew I was ready to return to the WWE.

Now that I was warmed up and ready to return to the grueling full-time WWE schedule, my free time was about to be cut down significantly. So before I went back, I wanted to do one last thing for myself and check out one of the Metallica XXX anniversary shows in San Francisco.

I'd been contacted a few months before by Lars's assistant to see if I would do a short video congratulating them on their thirty-year career and was blown away. To be asked by the mighty Metallica to give my thoughts on their legendary career for these monumental shows was a huge honor. I whipped up a ninety-second soliloquy praising them for all they'd accomplished and thanked them for all they'd done for me.

"No matter what I've been through in my life, Metallica has always been there for me. Thanks to James, Lars, Kirk, Cliff, Jason, and Robert for always having my back," I concluded.

Then Lars invited me to come to as many of the four shows as I could. My schedule was pretty packed as I had a lot to prepare for with my return only weeks away, so I was only able to go to the first show. But it was one of the best nights of my life as a musician and a fan, because it was something that had never been done by a band and might never happen again. Over the course of the four shows, Metallica played a whopping EIGHTY songs encompassing their entire career—rare tracks, instrumentals, songs they'd never played live before, some of their famous covers joined by the original guys who played them, and all in front of a small number of lucky hard-core fans who'd won tickets from their fan club.

I walked into the 1,200-capacity Fillmore in downtown San Francisco with Speewee and good friend Brian Slagel, the founder of Metal Blade Records (and huge hockey nut), and saw it had been transformed into a veritable Metallica museum. They had assembled an amazing collection of rare Metallicartifacts including Lars's infamous early '90s white leather jacket, the Gibson Explorer that James was playing when he was horribly burned by a pyro blast (just like The Undertaker), rare posters from their early days, and a jean jacket once worn by my hero Cliff Burton.

We waited for the show to start in the VIP balcony as a New Orleans brass band played instrumental versions of Metallica tunes, and various dignitaries milled about, including Jason Newsted, who was rejoining the band for the first time in a decade to play a few songs. Then I was introduced to Biff Byford, the lead singer of Saxon (one of my favorite bands), who was there to sing his band's classic "Motorcycle Man" with Tallica.

"When I was fourteen, I only asked for one present for Christmas, the *Crusader* album by Saxon," I gushed to Biff like a teenager.

Then I was taken to meet Cliff Burton's eighty-year-old father, Ray, and was kind of starstruck. I couldn't believe I was standing next to my hero's dad and he was so froot to talk to, standing there wearing his Cliff Burton T-shirt and Metallica button. One of the highlights of my fanboy career for sure.

Meanwhile the various tribute videos were playing on a big screen to the crowd, some getting massive responses (Lemmy), others getting booed out of the building (Avril Lavigne). My video aired in a great slot between Michael Schenker and U2 and I'm proud to say I got a bigger cheer than Bono (who's still awesome, #alionstalecallback).

I was laughing to Slagel about the response to my video, when I saw a skinny tall dude with a faux hawk standing in the corner trying so hard to look like Hetfield it was pathetic. The guy walked toward me and I realized it WAS Hetfield. I couldn't believe how great he looked and how much weight he'd lost since I'd last seen him eight months ago at The Big Four show in Indio, where he'd been getting quite beefy.

He told me how much he appreciated my video and how much it meant to them. After some small talk (I was still a little tongue-tied to be talking to Jaymz), I asked him how he got into such good shape.

"I've been doing the caveman diet," he said simply.

Caveman diet? I hadn't heard of that before. James explained that it consisted of eating only meat, chicken, fish, berries, nuts, eggs, and vegetables; basically no breads or carbs, processed foods or sugars. You only ate what a caveman could hunt or forage from the land.

"But didn't cavemen only live until they were like thirty years old?"

"Yeah, but that's because they all got eaten by dinosaurs," James said with a smirk.

All jokes aside, the concept sounded interesting and DDP had been urging me to start a gluten-free diet anyway, so if the Caveman Diet was good enough for Papa Het, it was good enough for me. I started it the next day, lost ten pounds in the first three weeks, and have stuck with it ever since. I've changed its name to The Hetfield Diet (much to Zakk Wylde's chagrin) and don't even consider it a diet anymore. It's just the way I eat. So if you're looking to drop a couple pounds, I strongly suggest it.

I spent the rest of the night drinking Yeah Boy!s (cavemen had vodka, didn't they?) and going nuts with one of my favorite bands as they celebrated their career with their closest fans. I ended up in the photo pit thrashing all around, acting like a maniac, but I was interfering with the cameramen who were filming the show and was asked to move by their head of security, Big Mike.

"But James said I could stand here," I lied.

Big Mike shook his head and dragged me out of the pit by my ear like I was seven years old.

A few minutes later, back in the safety of the balcony, I texted HHH (who'd also done a video) to tell him mine had gotten a much bigger pop (it had), and he asked why wasn't I home watching *Raw*. I laughed, but it would only be a few more weeks before I was watching *Raw* . . . this time live and in person.

Hanging with the amazing Ray Burton, father of Cliff. He was the star of the show in the VIP room of the Fillmore and told me that after twenty-eight years, he was still Metallica's biggest fan.

CHAPTER 42

CM Drunk

The first *Raw* of 2012 was in Memphis, Tennessee, but to keep the hellhounds off my trail, I flew into Nashville (over two hundred miles away) instead. Even though most of the fans suspected by that point that I was the one behind the End of the World videos, I wanted to keep my return as much of a secret as possible. The best way to do that was to avoid the fans who waited at the airport for autographs and would instantly post the news of my arrival online if they saw me.

Alas, my careful efforts to go incognito were in vain; I was somehow spotted at the Nashville airport. A picture of me standing stoically in the baggage claim, holding my black leather computer bag by my side, was posted within minutes. As soon as I saw it I counterattacked by tweeting a recent picture of me, Speewee, and the very wise Chad snowboarding in Banff, and claimed it was from that day, which started an online debate as to my whereabouts. A few minutes later, fans began posting Photoshopped pictures of me standing stoically with my leather bag at famous landmarks around the world like a bizarre *Where's Waldicho?* There I was standing next to the pyramids in Egypt, on the grassy knoll during the Kennedy assassination, and my personal favorite, crossing Abbey Road with The Beatles.

Crossing Abbey Road with The Beatles, courtesy of a mysterious Photoshopper who made this and a dozen others, including one of me and my briefcase standing next to Princess Diana's destroyed car in the Pont d'Alma tunnel in Paris.

I drove to Memphis and parked my car on a dark side street close to the arena, then was picked up by a black sedan and escorted under the cover of night by Bruno Lauer to a backstage bus to await my cue.

Toward the end of the show, the last of my vignettes played to the live crowd and ended with Nasal Boy saying ominously, "The end of the world as you know it begins NOW."

The lights went down and the fans were humming like a bird waiting for something big to happen. I hadn't been gone long enough for them to forget who I was like they had for my 2007 return, so this time when my patented "Break the Walls Down" war cry resounded through the arena, they went ballistic.

I hurried out onstage in total darkness and hit the switch inside the pocket of my new accoutrement (fun word), powering on the hundreds of blue lights crisscrossing the jacket and turning me into a new millennium version of the Electric Horseman . . . sans swank '70s Robert Redford mustache.

When the lights illuminated and I appeared onstage, the crowd went wild, which was all fine and El Dandy, except I was supposed to be the bad guy, remember? Even though I'd ended my last run as a heel, I'd now reached the status where people were excited to see me no matter what side of the fence I was on.

Penucci had anticipated this reaction when we were working on the videos and suggested, to remedy it, I take away the thing that my fans loved about me the most.

My mouth.

"What if after all this buildup and hoopla, you came to the ring and said absolutely nothing?"

I loved it. By staying silent, I'd be verbally blueballing all the Jerichoholics who were excited to see me again. Everyone would be expecting some witty repartee or my famous catchphrases, but by not giving them what they wanted I'd leave them feeling ripped off, confused, and less apt to cheer for me the next week.

I strutted down to the ring, but as soon as I stepped through the ropes, the jacket's entire right arm of lights went dead. I must've snapped a wire with my movements as the fragile electronics weren't designed to withstand that sort of expansive motion. But it didn't matter. The crowd was hot, hot, hotter than hell, and I stood there for five minutes with a shit-eating grin on my face, basking in their glory and holding the mic in front of my mouth. Then I dropped it on the mat and retreated out of the ring, still grinning.

Vince's first comment when I came through the curtain was "Your jacket broke already? Well, that was rotten!" But besides my wardrobe malfunction he loved the segment, so much so that he decided he didn't want me saying anything at all until my first match three weeks later at the Royal Rumble. I thought it was a great idea and spent the following weeks thinking of creative ways not to say anything during a promo.

I came out the next Monday and pulled the Silent Bob gimmick again, this time welling up with fake tears at the reaction I was getting and mouthing the word *Why?* (a trick I stole from Hulk Hogan, who had done the same thing during a huge crowd reaction in Montreal a decade earlier) as the fans wondered what the hell I was doing. The next week, I came to the ring with a T-shirt gun and shot merch into the crowd while screaming "Yeah, Yeah!" for no reason in particular. The crowd was onto me at this point and knew I was trolling them, but instead of booing, they just got apathetic.

The reactions got better during the Rumble match when I made it to the final two with Sheamus, but it confused the crowd when he eliminated me and won. I thought it would've been better for the Best in the World feud for me to win the Rumble, but the decision was made to go with my favorite Irishman instead.

Finally, the night after the Rumble, I broke the silence and did a long promo about how the talent in the WWE had robbed me of all my ideas and inventions. The suits, slow-talking promos, high-flying moves, sparkly tights, anything I could think of, I took credit for. (The "Chris Jericho invented everything" gag is still as popular as ever. I even read a tweet today saying, "Chris Jericho invented Chuck Norris.") Finally I zeroed in on the catchphrases and called out Punk for stealing mine, which drew the ire of the crowd and Punk himself.

He was the most over babyface in the company, and his reaction was off the charts when the opening riff of "Cult of Personality" played. The fans were looking forward to seeing the two of us butting heads in a verbal dual and we gave them what they wanted.

"So you invented everything, huh? Did you invent Canada too?" he smirked.

Then he got serious. "While you were off dancing with the stars, I was here swimming with the sharks" (such a great line), alluding to how he'd conquered the WWE machine with his new character. At the end of the fifteen-minute segment, the battle lines had been drawn and the WWE Universe was ready to see who really was The Best in the World.

The thing I admired most about Punk was, like me, when he said he was The Best in the World, he truly believed it. We were a lot alike and had come through the ranks of the WWE the same way (as did Shawn Michaels), both of us accused of being egomaniacal, arrogant, and hard to deal with because we had confidence in our abilities. Neither one of us had been groomed to be World Champions from the start. We'd gotten to the top by being all-around performers who could make anybody look good and stood firm in our beliefs to take no shit from anybody, including each other.

A few years earlier, in 2010, we had a live event in a little barn of a building in Amarillo, Texas, on the same day Canada was playing for the Olympic gold medal in hockey against the United States. It was a monumental battle between the two biggest rivals in hockey history, and as a Canadian, I was excited to watch it. The afternoon's match was Punk and me vs. Morrison and Edge, and since we were all familiar with each other's styles, we agreed to call the match in the ring and not get together beforehand so that Edge and I could watch the game. We sat on the crew bus and watched Canada beat the U.S. in overtime, with the final goal scored just as my ring music began.

Punk started the match and did a few spots with Morrison and then Edge. I stood on the apron waiting for the tag, but he kept ignoring me. He stopped Edge and started getting heat on him but still didn't tag me in. I started getting hip to the fact that he planned on working the whole match himself.

I stood on the apron watching him do all the work and munched some popcorn from a ringside fan, until Morrison finally got the hot tag and pinned him. I wasn't selling it outwardly, but inside I was fucking pissed, especially when a fan hit me in the back of the head with an empty Pepsi can as I walked to the back.

I called the four of us into the trainer's room after the match and asked Punk what his problem was. He opened up instantly and admitted he felt Edge and I had been unprofessional in watching the hockey game instead of putting together the match beforehand.

I wasn't having any of it and exploded right back, "You can't call a match in the ring? I don't need to explain myself to anybody in this arena, never mind you. And you wanna talk about unprofessional? If ONE person out there bought a ticket to see me, you just took that away from them. If you had a problem with me watching the game, you should've said something back here, not in the ring. What you did out there was fucking unprofessional!"

We agreed to disagree but to this day I still feel he was out of line, although I have to admit the guy has balls. It's one of the reasons why I requested to work with him, and one of the reasons why I knew he would be into the idea of me tattooing my initials on him.

I ran the idea past him and he agreed it was a great way to take our feud to a completely different place from any of the others on the show. He even offered to fly his regular tattoo artist in from Chicago to teach me how to do the simple procedure, but we still needed final approval from Vince, who had strangely been avoiding the subject whenever I asked him about it.

When I got to the arena in Boston before *Raw*, I found out from Michael Hayes why Vince was ducking me.

"He doesn't want to do the tattoo angle. He found out that people bleed when they get inked and is totally against it now."

I still wanted to hear Vince's reasoning for myself, so I went and asked him why he'd canceled the angle. He admitted he was concerned about seeing even a few drops of blood, but he also felt that tattooing Punk wasn't all that big a deal.

"He's got so many already. What would one more even matter? Plus, it would be so small that nobody would even care," Vince (who had no tattoos) explained.

I pointed out that it didn't matter how big the tattoo was or how many Punk had, I was violating him and he would have to live with that every day.

I could tell by his expression that Vince was rethinking his decision, but then he went back to his fear that tattooing Punk might make him bleed, and I knew I'd lost the battle. But in typical McMahon fashion, even though he'd nixed my idea, he had an alternative.

"I know Punk's dad had some drinking issues. Why don't we use that? You can accuse Punk of being one drink away from ending up an alcoholic just like his father."

It was a heavy subject, but if going there took the fans to that different emotional level and legitimately made them angry, I was all for it. But was Punk? He was and immediately waved off any concerns and felt we should go for it all the way.

That night, I went on *Raw* and told millions of people worldwide that CM Punk's father was an alcoholic and Punk himself was such a failure that it was just a matter of time before he ended up the same way. I got a serious "oooooohhhhh" reaction when I dropped that bomb, and the few remaining Y2J fans soured on me pretty quickly.

It was an uncomfortable subject for a lot of people as it hit them pretty close to home. Every day, I read on my social media pages how much of an asshole I was for using something as serious as alcoholism in a wrestling angle, but that's precisely why I was doing it. Now people legitimately wanted to see Punk kick my ass.

But the angle was so strong that Vince began to have second thoughts about what kind of match he wanted us to have at Wrestle-Mania. The following week on the last *Raw* before the PPV, Michael Hayes once again delivered some bad news.

"Vince doesn't want you guys to have an actual match at Mania. He feels you've gone too far with the alcoholic thing to go out there and do highspots. He wants you to have a ten-minute brawl and end with Punk getting DQ'd for not breaking the count when he has you in the ropes."

Talk about a shitty finish for one of the main events of WrestleMania! I originally wanted the match with Punk because I thought we could have a modern-day Steamboat-Savage classic, but things had changed and Vince DID have an interesting point. I'd taken things way too far by bringing Punk's family into the fray and had almost peaked the angle too soon. In retrospect, we should've started the alcoholic father storyline after our Mania match, the same way Shawn and I used Rebecca to ramp up our feud after already working each other for a few months. But now it was too late and we had painted ourselves into a corner.

Neither Punk nor I wanted to give up on having some semblance of an actual match, but Vince's mind was set. I think the only thing that saved us from the quick DQ finish was that Sheamus was winning the world title from Daniel Bryan in eighteen seconds on the same show, and after some serious discussion, Vince decided he didn't want two short world-title matches. So he compromised by adding a stipulation that if Punk got disqualified in any manner, he would be stripped of the title. That way he wouldn't be able to go completely ballistic on me because he'd have no choice but to follow the rules. I thought that was a pretty clever solution, and now that we had our marching orders, all we had to worry about was the match itself. And I was going to do everything I could to make it a classic.

Since I was in one of the three main events at the biggest show of the year, I wanted to do something special for my entrance into the Sun Life Stadium in Miami. I was the heel, so I wouldn't be getting ziplines or elaborate spaceships lowering into the ring like Edge had a few years ago (nor did I want Stay Puft marshmallow inflatable letters spelling out my name like Miz had), so it was up to me to think of something original.

I called Jonathan Logan again and asked him to make me a new jacket with five times as many lights as the first one. He created a masterpiece that boasted more bulbs than a greenhouse, with a remote control that both turned the lights on and changed the speed at which they blinked. He'd also included a zipper in the lining to make it easier to get to the broken wires (which happened on a weekly basis); and when opened, the electronics pattern looked like a damn NATO circuit board.

The jacket was heavy and Jonathan said if he made the same one for Justin Bieber, his slight frame wouldn't be able to support it (I'm sure David Lee Roth could've worn two of them and done a spinning roundhouse kick at the same time because he was DAVID LEE ROTH). I wasn't sure my financial frame could support it either because this one was even more expensive than the first one. How much? Let's just say I paid four hundred bucks for my first car (a '76 Volare) and this jacket was 37.5 times that. But it was WrestleMania, dammit, and using the Paul Stanley theorem, I was once again going to spare no expense. Plus, the jacket looked like it was worth every penny and was going to be one of the visual highlights of the PPV.

I spent the day of the show in the bowels of the Sun Life Stadium doing yoga, talking to Punk about the match, and doing a press conference with new WWE Hall of Famer Mike Tyson, where I forgave him for betraying me and knocking me out the last time we saw each other.

Afterward, I walked out onto the massive stadium stage and took in the thousands of empty seats, thinking about how amazing a phenomenon WrestleMania was. Vince was coming up the rampway, and I asked him, "Do you ever just take a minute to reflect on all this? You should, man. . . . What you've accomplished is incredible."

He looked at me strangely for a moment, then turned and surveyed the stadium for a good ten seconds. Then he looked back at me and said, "Thanks for that, Chris. Now let's get to work."

When I got back to the dressing room, everyone was giving me weird looks and giggling. I asked what was up and they finally gave in and showed me pictures of Christian and Brodus Clay parading around the dressing room in my jacket, one looking like a broom covered in a bedsheet and the other the epitome of Fat Guy in Little (Light-Up) Coat.

Finally it was showtime and I was taken around the stadium to the Gorilla position in a golf cart, switching my jacket on and off to make sure there were no issues. I didn't want a reprise of the night I debuted my blue jacket and have it conk out, but now satisfied that this new one worked perfectly, I was ready to rock.

I paced around Gorilla as the prematch hype video played, waiting to hit the stage and make history. The package ended and I turned my jacket on one last time to make sure it worked properly before my music hit and it did.

On one side.

The lights on the left part of the jacket flashed brighter than a thousand suns, but the lights on the right were darker than Darth Vader. I couldn't believe I'd paid fifteen fuckin' grand for this thing and it was already broken!

The stupid jacket threw me completely off my game. I was so ticked off, I totally forgot about my match because I was too busy thinking of how I was going to keep 75,000 people (and VINCE) from noticing that only fifty percent of my amazing Technicolor dreamcoat was working.

I came out onto the stage leading with my left side, so the cameras could only see the lighted part of my jacket. Then I lurched down the 150-foot rampway sideways like Bela Lugosi holding his cape in front of his face (pull the strings), doing my best to make sure the camera could only shoot the flashing side. I didn't know if I was fooling anybody, but I was never so relieved to hear Punk's music in my life, so I could finally take the jacket off.

My wardrobe malfunction behind me, Punk and I had an excellent match. I started by trying to goad Punk into getting disqualified by taunting him about his father and begging him to hit me with a chair.

He came close to losing it, but held on to his emotions and decided to take out his frustrations on me by kicking my ass the old-fashioned way.

We jam-packed the bout with killer spots, including me suplexing Punk over the top rope all the way to the floor, me catching him in the Walls as he was going for a top rope frankensteiner, and him diving on me halfway across the floor from the top turnbuckle. It climaxed with an intricate series of reversals and rollouts that ended up with me tapping out to his Anaconda Vice submission.

Overall, I was very happy with the match and while it wasn't the Steamboat/Savage classic I'd originally envisoned, I think it's underrated. In my view, it was better than the Rock vs. Cena contest that closed the show and ended up as the second best on the card behind Taker-HHH, which tore the house down. I think some fans had such high expectations for our match that it fell short in their eyes, but it didn't to me. I dug it and was excited to continue working with Punk, as we were only getting started.

This is the original finish I came up with for the Mania match with Punk, in my hotel room a few days before the show. Some of it we used, some of it we didn't, but you gotta start somewhere.

The next night on *Raw* in Miami, I claimed that not only did Punk's dad have a drinking problem, his sister was a junkie as well. Then after he got crushed by Mark Henry, I came down to insult him even further by pouring whiskey over his head. I was hell-bent to make sure he fulfilled his drunken destiny one way or another.

When I pushed my way through the crowd to approach the fallen Punk, I had a Jack Daniel's bottle made of the dreaded sugar glass, and filled with iced tea, in my hand. Originally, Vince had insisted that actual Jack be used to fill up the bottle, but I balked at the idea, considering that Punk really was straight-edge and I didn't want him swallowing a mouthful of the real stuff. Besides, who was going to know?

"People in the front row will know it's not real alcohol if they can't smell it," Vince claimed (which reminded me of Ed Langley's thoughts about ether from twenty-two years earlier). So we were going to pour actual alcohol over a teetotalor's head just to impress twenty people sitting at ringside? Finally, Vince acquiesced and switched it to tea, but then we had a lengthy discussion about whether I should smash the bottle over Punk's head or not. Vince was concerned that Punk might get cut and I thought of how much things had changed since 2002, when Kane had thrown me through a sugar-glass picture window and I spent the rest of the night picking dozens of sugar slivers out of my back.

Punk was insisting I smash it over his head, but Vince was reluctant and wanted me to hit the ring post just above his noggin instead. Either way was fine with me as I knew the angle was going to be a standout no matter what. We went through it a few times and the props guy warned me not to swing the bottle too fast so it didn't break apart in the air before making contact.

I hopped over the barricade and slowly stalked my prey, wearing a swank pair of Jonathan Logan distressed leather pants, pointed dress boots, and no shirt. If I was going to trample on a man's dignity, I was going to do it with style.

"Here's to ya, Punk," I taunted, raising the bottle in the air and slowly pouring the sweet amber over his head. It streamed through his hair, down his face, and into his mouth as he vainly attempted to spit it out, as the crowd's hostility toward me hung in the air like the southern Florida humidity. I scoped the audience, secretly impressed with their reactions, and decided to stomp Punk in the face for the final coup de grâce. As I lifted my left foot in the air to deliver the fatal crushing blow, my right foot slipped in the pool of iced tea and I fell on my ass.

It was the worst thing that could've happened at the worst time. There was no getting out of it, no way to cover it up. It was like Jason Voorhees raising his machete over his head to kill a helpless coed and slipping on a banana peel.

I had killed the intensity, and the impact of the attack disappeared like a thief in the night (I ain't talking about Bruce Kulick) once I'd busted my tail. All I could think to do was completely ignore the fall, pop right back up on my feet, and smash the bottle over his head (it exploded a millisecond before it made contact for the blown spot daily double).

I had botched the angle big-time. Can you imagine what would've happened if I had slipped and fallen as I was about to punch Rebecca Michaels?

Stupid pointed dress boots.

We got back on track the next week when I accused Punk's mother of illicit behavior and claimed Punk was a "bastard," which to Vince was the ultimate insult.

Not sure if being called a bastard would win any best insult awards, but it was better than the worst insult I've EVER heard, delivered by The

Miz. We were in Montreal and he was berating the crowd in French about all of the things he hated about the city—their language, their hockey team, their specialty foods.

"*J'deteste* Montreal! *J'deteste les Canadiens! J'deteste* poutine!" he screamed.

"What? He hates poutine? That tasty concoction of French fries drowned in gravy and covered with cheese curds? I'M GONNA KILL HIM!"

Poutine insults aside, referring to Punk as a bastard seemed like a pretty lame putdown to me, so I decided to add an additional insult of my own. During my previous attack, some of the Jack Daniel's (tea) had gotten down his throat, so in my mind I'd done what I had promised and gotten him to take his first taste of alcohol. So I deemed him CM Drunk. Then I attacked him again and this time poured an entire six-pack of beer over his head. But this time I didn't slip, and the attack worked like a drunken charm.

At the next *Raw* in Detroit, I cheekily had a liquor basket delivered to him during his in-ring promo. That seemed to be the last straw for poor old Punk, as later in the show I went spying on him in his dressing room and saw him sodomizing a cat.

I'm just making sure you're still paying attention, fearless readers.

What I really saw when I peeked into the dressing room was CM sitting in the corner, surrounded by empty bottles from the liquor basket. Now that I had actually gotten him drunk with my evil trickery, my conspiracy plan was ready to take the next step. I found a little-known codicil in the WWE talent contract that said if a performer was drunk during a show, he would be fired. In Punk's current state of intoxication, he would be stripped of the title, and since I was the number one contender, the title would go straight to me. At least that's the way I saw it.

The next step of my plan was bringing out a pair of Detroit cops to administer a roadside DWI test on him. If they determined he was over the limit, he'd be terminated and relieved of his championship duties immediately. I called him out and a few seconds later, he wobbled down to the ring, slurring his speech slightly and doing an overall great job of acting drunk. Even though he never partied for real, Punk always hung out with the boys until the wee hours of the morning, so he'd been around plenty of drunks in his life (myself at the top of the list) and knew how to play it perfectly.

The cops made him balance on one leg and count to ten, walk a straight line, and then asked him to say the alphabet backward. When I pitched the idea to the writers that Punk should actually recite the letters backward, I was shot down and told that nobody could do that even if they were sober. So I wrote down the alphabet backward, memorized it for twenty minutes, and enumerated all twenty-six letters to the writers in reverse order, without error.

Punk now did the same (although he got the *R* and the *T* mixed up), slowly picking up the speed of his delivery, before dropping his drunk act and revealing that he'd been faking it the whole time to trick me. When he finished with the letter *A,* he punched me in the face. It was an entertaining segment that set the stage for our blow-off match, an extreme street fight in Punk's birthplace, Sweet Home Chicago.

The Windy City crowd was as raucous as always (my favorite wrestling crowd in the U.S.) and we had a perfect match, even better than Mania, in my opinion. We wore the old-school '80s street fight uniform, a pair of jeans with knee pads and boots pulled over the top, and taped fists. Then we beat the holy hell out of each other with kendo sticks (which left me with some wicked welts on my back), garbage cans, ring bells, and all sorts of other assorted plunder. Punk's sister, Chaleen, was in the front row and got revenge on behalf of her family by slapping me in the face hard when I taunted her. Punk used that momentum to put me through the announce table with an elbow from the top rope and then sprayed me in the face with a fire extinguisher while I had him in the Walls of Jericho. I was so worried about closing my eyes to protect them from the spray that I forgot to close my mouth and swallowed some of the weird white frozen foam. Not the healthiest of snacks, but for the next few days, I didn't have to blow on hot food before I ate it.

He eventually finished me off with the GTS, and the Punk-Jericho feud was officially in the books . . . at least on TV. But the angle was so hot, we continued working together in different countries all over the world, wowing the crowds with our magic tricks.

There was one country in particular, though, that wasn't too happy with me or my tricks.

CHAPTER 43

Professional Flag Kicker

The WWE tours all over the world, but when we were invited to perform in China for the first time ever, it was a major coup. We'd been on TV over there for years, but it was hard to make any headway due to all the other entertainment options in the country and the fact that the Chinese government didn't really understand what we did. But they wanted to book us as one of the few American acts to perform at the 2010 World Expo in Shanghai, along with a symphony orchestra and a Right Said Fred concert. (I keed, but what a mental image!)

We were in the middle of an Asian tour and flew to Shanghai from the Tokyo Haneda airport, which was jam-packed with chain-smoking Japanese businessmen. We were told to wear suits on the plane to make a good first impression in China, which was a good idea in theory, but Haneda was so smoky and stuffy that I wanted to barf all over my sweet Hugo Boss ensemble. Thankfully, I made it to Shanghai without hurling, and when we landed we headed straight to the venue.

As we drove through the city, I marveled at the brilliant architecture of the immaculately constructed buildings, each one seeming more beautiful than the last, as if the designers were playing a game of one-upmanship with each other. We arrived at a gorgeous multitiered arena that looked like a fortress and was about as hard to get inside as one. Armed guards checked our passports and looked through our bags multiple times before allowing us entry.

Backstage workers and security guards buzzed around, doing a whole lot of nothing and wearing very concerned looks on their faces as they did it. I was whisked away to a press conference and placed in front of a gang of suit-clad reporters, with nary a smile among them. They asked me generic questions and I responded with sarcastic and comical answers that would've brought the house down in any other country. But not with this lot. Either the translator wasn't properly relaying my words, or these guys had no sense of humor.

"Is it illegal to laugh in China?" I deadpanned. Nobody laughed . . . in fear of incarceration, apparently.

As strange as the press conference was, the show itself was even stranger. We were briefed beforehand that the show was sold out, but we weren't allowed to punch or choke our opponents and under no circumstances could we do anything on the floor. If we did, the government officials would shut down the show, as they were skittish about having us there in the first place.

But when I walked out for my match, I was surprised to see a largely empty arena with nobody on the floor and only a few pockets of fans scattered around in the stands. Directly in front of the ring was a long table decorated with bunting and flowers, and sitting behind it was a group of diplomats in tuxedos like something out of a James Bond movie. I guess they wanted the best seats in the house to witness this barbaric display of Western entertainment.

But the strangest part was that the upper deck was jam-packed with rabid fans screaming and cheering our every move like teenage girls at a One Direction concert. Besides the upper-deckers, though, the rest of the meager audience sat on their chopsticks and did nothing. A sold-out show usually meant a lively, standing-room-only crowd in a packed house. What kind of sellout was this?

Later I found out that all the tickets had been bought by the government, which then distributed a small portion to the fans and threw away the rest because they were afraid a riot was going to break out. Guess nobody had filled them in that we were entertainers and not actual bloodsport fighters.

Punk and I share a smile for some ringside fan after some match in some arena.

What the Chinese government didn't understand about the WWE, the government in Dubai did, and we were treated like royalty during our three-night stand in Abu Dhabi. I noticed the audience was wearing an interesting mix of fashions, some in Western-style street clothes, others in traditional Muslim garb. I was teaming with R-Truth, and during his rap sing-along entrance, it was hilarious to see people in burkas and keffiyehs hopping up out of their chairs, raising the roof, and chanting "What's up!" like something out of *The Naked Gun*.

Much like Shanghai, Abu Dhabi was immaculate and boasted spotless streets lined with perfectly groomed shrubbery, and every car on the street seemed to have been built within the last few years. We were staying thirty minutes outside the city in a brand-new entertainment complex complete with five-star hotels, a waterslide park, a Ferrari theme park, and bars and restaurants everywhere. (There was even a Tim Hortons!)

After the show, we went to have a few drinks at a posh nightclub on the top floor of one of the hotels. I was enjoying a fine Yeah Boy! and minding my own business when a mean-looking balding dude with dark skin, a unibrow, and a bad attitude started barking orders at us in Arabic. He was obviously drunk and not very happy that the American (I'm from Winnipeg, you idiot) pigs were invading his territory. He finished his tirade, and his friends started laughing at Unibrow's witty repartee. He went back to the bar, but he had rubbed me the wrong way and I thought I'd give him a little what-for. So I followed him and, without a second glance, threw my shoulder into his back with a solid twist. Uni was off balance, so my little nudge caused him to lose his footing and he stumbled into the wall as I disappeared through the crowd. Apparently, he didn't appreciate my love tap and was waiting for me outside when we left the bar about an hour later.

Uni and his crew where lined up on the curb and looked pretty intimidating in their black sport coats. I hoped I hadn't gotten in over my head, but just in case the situation got out of control and I had to take a swing at someone, I stuck my old-school hotel room key (didn't know they still made these) in between my first and middle fingers.

"Hey, motherfucker, I've been waiting for you," Uni said, looking like Samuel Jackson but sounding like Michael Jackson.

"I see that," I replied, fingers clenched around my weapon.

"You just made a big mistake, pig. My father owns twenty-seven percent of this city and I have all the power here."

Wow, that was a random number.

"You messed with the wrong guy and you're going to pay for it with YOUR LIFE. . . ."

My life? I expected him to finish his sentence with "Dr. Jones!" and laugh diabolically. What was with this guy?!

"I am placing a bounty on your head for twelve million dollars. You have twenty-four hours to live!"

I'd never had a bounty placed on my head before and I actually felt kind of froot, like I was The Outlaw Josey Wales (sans Tarantino commentary, of course). But there was something I had to know.

"Is twelve million dollars a good bounty?" I asked, feeling like Larry David. "Like in the grand scheme of things, is that a lot of money to pay for someone's head? If I were say, Mel Gibson, would it cost more to have me executed?"

"Careful, man!" Jack Swagger warned me in a panic. "This is the Wild West over here. You can't talk back to these guys!"

He was probably right, but I didn't know how things worked in Abu Dhabi and was curious. Maybe placing bounties on people's heads was an average thing over here, like playing Parcheesi or going to Applebee's was in the States.

But if I only had twenty-four hours to live, then I needed to know the answer to one more question.

"OK, I understand you're going to pay somebody twelve million for my head, but if your dad owns twenty-seven percent of this city, then why are you driving yourself around in a Dodge Charger?"

Uni fumed and Swagger cringed, worried that I was poking a bear. My eyes drifted to the top of the buildings across the lot and wondered if there was a rifle scope trained on my head at that very moment.

"You have one day to live!" he reiterated as he got in the Charger, followed by all five of his cronies. They kept filing in as if it was an ugly clown car, until they were all stuffed in like a pack of teenage girls driving to the mall. They were practically sitting on each other's laps and their intimidation factor pretty much flew out the open window of the Charger at that point.

"Twenty-four hours!" Uni said one last time as one of his minions squished up against his shoulder from the backseat. . . .

He gunned down the road and squealed the tires around the corner as Swagger and I started laughing and waved bye-bye. (By the way, in case you're wondering, I did not die within the twenty-four-hour time limit.)

I was excited to tour Brazil as I'd never been, and the WWE was now headed there for the first time to try to open up the possibly lucrative market. But the tour got off to a rocky start when our first flight out of the States got canceled and we didn't arrive in São Paulo until a few hours before the show.

It was a hot steamy evening and I was already sweating as I prepared to face off against Punk in the main event (there it is again . . . I'm such a worker). The crowd was a decent size but hardly a sellout and they'd been fairly quiet throughout the show, as if they were still trying to figure out what it was they were watching (maybe they just wanted to see dancing). The arena security made up of members of the Brazilian Army lounged around the arena with their guns displayed on their hips to remind everyone who was in charge.

Punk came down to the ring and got a good reaction when he hopped on the apron, waving a Brazilian flag that a ringside fan had given him. As he marched past me, brandishing the banner, I thought about snatching it out of his hand, but he didn't come close enough. He draped it on the turnbuckle and ref Mike Chioda took it to hand back to the fan.

"No, give me that flag, Mikey," I hissed.

I wanted to do something to wake the crowd up, so I took the flag from Chioda, dropped it to the mat, stomped on it twice, and kicked it to the floor in a hail of boos. It was a standard heel tactic that I had used many times before, but even that didn't get the response I was expecting. People were mad, but not "jumping out of their seats wanting to kill me" mad, which was what I was hoping for.

We began the match and I had just started getting heat on Punk about five minutes later, when I noticed out of the corner of my eye a second ref in the ring. Did Chioda get hurt?

"Stop the match now," Charles Robinson whispered in my ear, but I ignored him and continued my beatdown.

"Seriously, Chris! You have to stop the match NOW and apologize for kicking the flag or you're going to get arrested!"

I stopped kicking Punk and took a step back. The entranceway was now swarming with Brazilian soldiers, all of them glaring at me. Then John Laurinaitis ran down the aisle, waving his arms and yelling, "You need to apologize now, Chris! This is real, so don't joke around!"

I could tell by Johnny's demeanor that there was some serious shit going on, so I grabbed the mic in the center of the ring and addressed the crowd as Punk sold his beatdown in the corner.

"I just want to say that I would never purposely disrespect the country of Brazil or your beautiful flag. I did what I did to entertain you and I would like to sincerely apologize to everybody here in the arena and to the entire country of Brazil. I'm sorry."

The crowd applauded respectfully but seemed a bit confused, as if they were wondering why I was apologizing in the first place. I turned my attention back to Punk (who'd been waiting in the corner patiently), and like a kid yelling "game on" after a car zooms by in the middle of a street hockey game, I continued the match.

Punk won the bout and then wore the flag like a cape as he made his ringside victory lap, slapping the fans' hands all the way. His lionizing of the banner was the payoff to me kicking it earlier and was what we had planned the entire time. Bad guy assaults flag, good guy assaults bad guy, then beats him, and gets revenge on behalf of the entire country.

I felt that having to give the apology in the middle of the match was a little overdramatic, but if that's what the authorities needed in order to calm down, then so be it. But when I walked through the curtain, everybody was staring at me with a threatening glare, like I was Flounder walking into the roadhouse to see Otis Day and the Knights. I went past a group of soldiers and their eyes bored a hole straight throught me, with one older guy in particular (who looked like the Nazi that Indiana Jones throws through the windshield of the truck in *Raiders of the Lost Ark*) giving me the real stink eye.

Dean Malenko, the road agent on the tour (along with Johnny), rushed over and pulled me into his office.

"When you kicked the flag, that old guy went crazy. He's some sort of colonel and wanted to rush the ring and arrest you right then and there. We had to beg the guy not to do it and he settled for an apology, but he's still furious. He thinks all of this is real and wants to take you right to jail."

I could only imagine having to spend the night in a Brazilian prison, wearing nothing but my sparkly short little wrestling trunks. I'd be targeted as a lady boy instantly. That was a dash of cold-water reality and I realized just how much trouble I was in.

I hurried back to the dressing room and changed my clothes just in case the colonel changed his mind and decided to take me away. I also thought I'd better text Vince and head this off at the pass before he found out from somebody else and things got out of hand like the

London glow stick incident. I shot him a message explaining that I had upset the Brazillian Army by kicking a flag and I wouldn't do it again on future tours.

Vince replied immediately, "There will be no more Brazilian tours for you or any of us. The WWE will no longer be allowed to perform in Brazil in the future! WTF, Chris!"

I don't know who told him we wouldn't be able to go back to Brazil, but I tracked down our marketing rep and asked if that was the case. He said he hadn't heard anything along those lines, but it didn't matter because Vince was already seething.

I texted him back and told him I'd kicked flags a dozen times before in the States, Canada, Mexico, Japan, and nobody had ever been this upset before. But Vince wasn't having it.

"It was F'N stupid! When was the last time I allowed this kind of shit? 1985? Go home, you're suspended. We will talk when you get back to the U.S. Thanks for ruining what would have been a great market for us. Who knows how this is going to hurt us elsewhere?"

Suspended? Now I was pissed off. After all I'd done for the WWE over the years, he was going to punish me for doing my job as a heel? I called him immediately and he barked that he was too mad to talk and not to call him again. So I texted him and told him he should have my back in a situation like this instead of turning on me.

Then I started getting messages from random people saying they read on wwe.com that I'd been suspended. I went online and read the headline: CHRIS JERICHO HAS BEEN SUSPENDED INDEFINITELY DUE TO AN IRRESPONSIBLE ACT OF DENIGRATING THE BRAZILIAN FLAG.

The word *denigrating* had Vince's fingerprints all over it, so I knew he had written the statement himself. It bugged me that he had posted the info so quickly, as he really could've just ignored the whole thing. But he felt the WWE had to officially acknowledge the incident and deal with it before videos of the incident popped up on YouTube.

I asked him if he'd even seen what happened (he hadn't) because if so, he would know that I didn't do much more than lightly stomp on the flag and slide it out of the ring with my foot. Vince didn't care and created a self-fulfilling prophecy, because once wwe.com posted the info, it spread quickly.

"Great. The story just broke on *TMZ*," Vince texted me.

"That's because you posted the info thirty minutes earlier," I fired back.

In Vince's mind, he had to suspend me to cover his ass with the Brazilian government as well as other countries around the world that he hoped to do business with in the future. I couldn't blame him for it. He had to show that if any of his employees insulted a country or broke the rules, they would be dealt with immediately. And I had broken the rules, since kicking a flag was a felony in Brazil . . . although that was something I wish they would've told me BEFORE the show.

Now that I'd been kicked off the tour, there was a mad scramble to find me a flight out of Brazil. Rather than leave me there by myself and take the chance I'd get carted away by the authorities in the middle of the night, Vince decided it would be best for me to take the overnight charter to Ecuador with the rest of the crew and fly home from there the next day.

He eventually called me to make sure I was safe, and to say he wanted me out of the country ASAP. He made it clear that under no circumstances was I to allow myself to be separated from the rest of the company, and then explained why he was so angry at me.

"These people have nothing but pride for their country. All they have is the flag and what it represents. What if the fans had rioted and somebody got hurt? That would've been on your hands."

The irony was, I had kicked the flag to TRY and get the fans to riot. In retrospect, it was a bad idea. Vince then said we'd talk in the morning about about how long my suspension would last, and hung up. It was time to board the plane, but as I was walking down the jetway, I was stopped by a soldier. After Vince's warning not to get separated, I envisioned myself being dragged away in a ball and chain in front of my coworkers. The guard looked at me menacingly, reached into his pocket . . . and pulled out a camera.

We took a picture together with his crew and I boarded the plane. Just as we were taking off, I shot Vince one last text and told him I had made it out of the country and thanked him for checking up on me.

"I love you, you idiot. AC/DC still the best band."

I told him I loved him too as the wheels left the tarmac and flew me out of harm's way.

A shot from my impromptu photo session with the Brazilian airport police, taken after I'd been kicked out of the country. I clutch my passport in my hand and promise myself never to give it to anybody—until I was forced to hand it over to a cop in Ecuador the next night.

———

I woke up in Quito, Ecuador, to another handful of texts asking me what I thought about being suspended for a month. A MONTH? I hadn't heard anything from Vince since the night before, so once again I surfed over to wwe.com to find out private information about my own life (the same way I found out I'd been drafted to *SmackDown* a decade earlier).

I was livid at Vince. How dare he inform his social media minions about my punishment before telling me first? Ironically, a few minutes later I got a text from Vince asking if I was having any any fun yet and to call him. But there was no way I was going to call him, as the battle lines had been drawn. I felt double-crossed and disrespected and had nothing to say to him.

I spent the whole day in the hotel room stewing, the disgraced pariah who wasn't even allowed to go to the arena with the rest of the crew. That night I was given a police escort to the airport (I have no idea why) and had to explain to every Tomas, Raphael, and Geraldo why I was flying home at the same time the WWE show was taking place.

Once again, as I was boarding the plane I was stopped by a security guard, but this one didn't want a picture. He wanted me to follow him and led me out the side door of the jetway (the one they use to deliver your gate-checked luggage) onto the tarmac. I was taken to an open hangar and asked to give up my passport. I reluctantly handed it over even though I'd always been told to never give up my passport. But what choice did I have?

Nobody knew I was down here on the runway, and without a passport, I was a nameless faceless persona non grata who could be taken away with no recourse. What if the Brazilians had called ahead and put an Abu Dhabi–style bounty on my head? Was I going to be taken to prison in the middle of the jungle and left to rot like Rambo?

After the longest ten minutes of my life, the soldiers came back with my checked luggage and rummaged through it for a few minutes. Satisfied that I didn't have automatic weapons or a brick of cocaine hidden in my bag (I did in a secret compartment), they returned my passport and escorted me back onto the plane.

I flew home and was fuming for the first few days of my suspension, until I realized that having some unexpected time off wasn't such a bad thing after all. I had an amazing family with a gorgeous wife and three beautiful children, the weather was great, and I had some money in my pocket. Life wasn't so bad after all.

I didn't respond to Vince's next two calls and it was only after he apologized via voice mail that I finally decided to call him back.

"Listen, I'm sorry that the news of your suspension was posted online before I could call you myself. There was a miscommunication with wwe.com and they released the info without my permission."

I didn't know if I bought his explanation, but it was the closest thing to an apology I was going to get from him, so I dialed his number.

I explained that I felt he'd posted the info online as an eff-you and then asked if the suspension itself was my only punishment or if I was going to get fined as well. He told me he'd have to think about it and would get back to me. A few days later, I got a call from HHH, who told me Vince was fining me half of my guarantee for the month that I was suspended. I hung up on him the second the words left his mouth and dialed Vince's number immediately, wanting to hear the verdict from him and nobody else. But he didn't answer.

His decision made me even angrier because if you added up all the money I was going to lose from the suspension and now this fine, it could total over six figures. Batista had been fined one hundred grand for directly defying Vince, and here I was standing to lose more than that for something I'd done on the spur of the moment and had no idea was against the rules.

I explained this to Vince when he finally called me, and our conversation quickly escalated into an all-out argument. He insisted that he needed to announce to the media that he'd suspended AND fined me to send a message to Brazil and all other countries like it that behavior like mine wouldn't be tolerated.

After a thirty-minute debate, he dropped the fine to ten thousand dollars and said he never wanted to discuss the matter with me again. When it was all said and done, he never actually took the ten grand out of my check, so I don't think I got fined anything. Plus, I still got paid my full guarantee and earned it by spending the next month pulling Ash, Cheyenne, and Sierra on an inner tube around our lake; not bad work if you can get it!

Maybe I should become a professional flag kicker?

CHAPTER 44

Explode at Download

The ironic thing about my thirty-day suspension was I had already blocked off ten of those days for Fozzy to play the 2012 Download Festival with Metallica, Black Sabbath, and Soundgarden. The UK was our biggest market and with a hundred thousand people expected to attend, it had the potential to be our biggest gig ever.

When we arrived in England the day before the show, rain was coming down in sheets, drenching the festival grounds and causing complete chaos. We spent the evening watching the weather channel and hearing reports of the horrible lines of traffic that had caused a few bands to miss their sets (it was the final countdown for Europe, as they had to cancel). The whole site had been turned into a mud pit, and people had retreated into their tents to wait out the freezing rain.

We were scheduled to play Saturday at noon sharp and I was concerned that nobody would even be there to see us with such miserable conditions that early in the day. But there was nothing we could do except prepare for the worst, so we left the hotel at eight A.M. to give us plenty of time to make it to the festival grounds.

The rain had finally stopped and we were making good time, when we rounded a corner and saw a large body of water submerging the road in front of us. It was too big to be classified as a puddle, for it had settled under a bridge at the base of a hill and flowed over onto the sidewalk. The water level had risen higher than the wheel wells of the van and there was no way we were going to be able to drive through it without totally drenching the undercarriage. We were in some serious trouble . . . or so I thought.

Rich Ward had been on the road for years and part of his duties when touring with Stuck Mojo was driving the van in their early days. He'd been through situations like this before and had a plan as he jumped in the driver's seat and drove forward, slowly steering the ship through the angry seas. The Duke maneuvered over to the sidewalk and popped the front passenger-side wheel up on the curb, which took the left side of the van out of the water and gave us the traction we needed to drive through to the other side of the puddle. It was a genius move and even though the right side of the van was covered in mud, and water had dampened the entire floor of the vehicle, it didn't matter. We had crossed the River Charon without paying the Ferryman his penny and were free to continue on toward the biggest show of our career.

When we arrived at the massive field, the weather was overcast but still holding and we prayed that it would stay that way at least until our set was done. At eleven thirty A.M. we were taken over to the massive stage to set up and prepare for the show. I wondered how many people we'd be playing in front of, because even though it wasn't quite noon, I knew the Download crowd liked to arrive early. How many would there be? Five thousand? Fifteen thousand?

I wasn't even close.

There were only about five hundred fans scattered about the muddy lawn, watching the first band of the day. It was a total letdown, but I promised myself that no matter how many people showed, we were still going to have a great show, and retreated backstage to warm up.

Thirty minutes later I was called out of the dressing room as our intro music played. I walked up the lengthy flight of stairs leading to the stage, ready to rock this flock of five hundred people like they were five thousand. I ran out in front of the crowd and surveyed the massive field before me, but things had changed and there weren't five hundred people there anymore.

There were thirty-five thousand.

Considering how empty the field had been only minutes before, I was agog (still a great word) at how many people were now out there and how quickly they'd arrived. It was as if a Hollywood special effects team had added them via CGI. The crowd spanned as far as my eye could see and the fans in the front row were crushed up against the barricade, almost spilling over into the arms of the dozens of security guards that lined the steel railings. They were loud, they were intense, and they were there to see Fozzy. And now it was time to explode at Download!

We only had a twenty-five-minute set, but in that short time we gave Download the full-on Fozz experience. We didn't have dragons flying from the ceiling or pyro blasting out of the drum set, but what we did have was pure electric energy that commanded the crowd completely. When we hit that stage, We were the whole F'N show.

We opened with "Pray for Blood" and over the course of the next five songs, I climbed the scaffolding of the stage, led the crowd in sing-alongs, and filmed them after stealing the camera from an unsuspecting tech. The fans had a blast as Rich did the famed Duke Dance and played the chunkiest rhythms known to man; Paulie D kicked his leg up past his chin and threw down basslines that would make Geezer Butler blush; Billy stuck his out his tongue and threw shapes like the rock star he is; and Frank performed his patented sticks tricks and lipstick fix, all the while laying down the thunderous grooves like only he can.

At the end of the set, the crowd (including a blow-up love doll that was waved in the air the entire show) roared its approval and chanted "FOZZY, FOZZY, FOZZY" as we lined up in front of the appreciative thousands and snapped a picture for posterity. We had just played the show of our lives and our thirty-five thousand friends behind us knew it too.

The day got even better when I was summoned into Metallica world, the compound of dressing rooms that acted as their inner sanctum for the day. Lars was waiting and asked how our gig went, mentioning that he'd like to see us sometime (I'm still waiting). I saw James and we talked about the ups and downs of the Caveman Diet and how it was affecting our cholesterol levels. It wasn't exactly the conversation I imagined having with him when I was in high school, but I wasn't just a fanboy anymore. After all we'd been through, James was practically my best friend now, right? Right?

We got onto the subject of the hotel I'd stayed in the night before and how the guy at the front desk was a total jerk. James told me how he used to get his revenge on those types of people in the early days of Metallica.

"Whenever we had bad service or front-desk assholes, I'd take a dump in a plastic bag and leave it in the bottom dresser drawer of my room. The maids never looked in those things and a few days later they would have no idea where the horrible smell was coming from." Papa Het giggled.

Now THAT was the type of conversation I imagined having with him when I was in high school.

Lars gave me a couple side-stage passes for their show and I watched them play the *Black Album* in its entirety from only a few feet away. Michael Starr from Steel Panther was checking out the show with me and I had to tell him the title of each song they played, as he wasn't familiar with the biggest album in heavy metal history.

"You've never heard 'Sad But True'? 'Nothing Else Matters'? 'Enter Sandman'?"

"That's the only one I know. I was always more of a Van Halen guy."

That statement alone would've made us instant enemies in 1988 and I would've been obligated to fight him. But since it was 2012, I let it slide.

Part of being on the road is checking out the sights, and this statue of Phil Lynott outside of Bruxelles bar in Dublin was a must-see for Paulie, Billy, and me. Note my Solo cup, which contains a fine Yeah Boy!

My suspension was winding down and I was ready to return to work. I'd had a great time being a full-time daddy and husband, but it was time to get back on the road and finish off the last two months of my WWE contract. However, during the unscheduled month off, I felt I'd lost all my heel momentum and it was time to finally give up on my villainous character and turn babyface. I thought it was what the fans wanted, and after two and a half years of dirty deeds done dirt cheap, it's what I wanted too.

The WWE had been promoting my return for a week with an amazing video package they'd put together using footage from Download that made Fozzy look like the biggest band on the planet, and the crowd was pumped and ready to see me. I started the show doing a promo with Cena, and the fans responded to me like a babyface right off the bat. The promo went great, as did our main-event match (there it is again); it was always fun to work with him. It was also fun to share a few cocktails together, so we went out for few celebratory drinks after the show. The night ended up being pretty tame, but that wasn't always the case when the two of us were together.

I'm not exactly Bon Scott, and I don't drink all the time (despite what a lot of the stories in this book might suggest), but when I let loose it's not often someone bests me when the Yeah Boy!s are flowing. But much to my chagrin, whenever I've gone head to head with Cena on the drinking fields, I usually lose.

I suffered my worst defeat to Cena a few years earlier when we toured Alaska (despite it being forty degrees below zero, he wore jean shorts the whole time and never complained about the cold). After a show in Anchorage, we hit the bar to keep warm and went pretty hard for a few hours. There were plenty of fans hanging around and John started counseling a troubled young couple, giving them marital advice like a beefy Dr. Phil. They were listening intently and, after some deep soul-searching, agreed with Dr. John that they were made for each other and should call off their impending divorce. Their marriage saved, we staggered back to my room to have a few more drinks.

When we got upstairs I opened the door and that's the last thing I remembered until I woke up fully clothed under the covers of my bed a few hours later. I had no idea where I was and almost screamed when I saw a dark figure sitting in the corner of the room.

As my bloodshot eyes adjusted to the light, I realized the dark figure was Cena, still drinking and scrolling through my iPod. In the ultimate show of drinking dominance, John had taken off my shoes, tucked me into bed, and was drinking MY beer while listening to MY tunes.

Cena: 1

Y2Loser: 0

CHAPTER 45

The Queen at Live Aid Principle

I still had a few months left on my contract, but since I was leaving after SummerSlam to go on tour with Fozzy, I was the lame duck of the company. I had a decent feud with Dolph Ziggler that ended with him beating me on my last *Raw*, which caused me to get fired (again). It was a scenario that was decided on two hours before the show began, when Vince decreed that general manager AJ Lee was going to force me to put up my career against Dolph's Money in the Bank briefcase. So Vince, HHH, and I sat in his office going over different scenarios right up until the last minute.

"Can't anybody in this place think of a damn decent finish?" Vince snapped in frustration before deciding that, after Dolph beat me, I would drop him with a couple of Codebreakers and leave the ring with a smile. It was a froot feeling to walk out of the arena with "Y2J" chants ringing in my ears, knowing that I had passed the torch to Ziggler to help him get to a new level. Now it was time to hit the road and take Fozzy to a new level as well.

After all the momentum we'd gathered from *Chasing the Grail*, we wanted to keep it rolling by making a new record as soon as possible. All of the hard work we'd done over the past few years had paid off, for we'd been signed to Century Media Records (one of the biggest metal labels in the world) by our old friend Paul Gargano who was now an A&R man with the label. CMR was the biggest record company we'd ever signed with and was the perfect place for us to showcase who we were as a band.

Knowing that we were now under a huge microscope, Rich and I set out to make the best album of our career by writing the type of songs that we did best. It had taken us a few years to get it right, but the sound that The Duke had crafted for Fozzy (and started with Stuck Mojo) consisted of really heavy, groove-based riffs, combined with melodic vocals stacked with multiple harmonies. If Metallica and Journey had a bastard child, it would be Fozzy.

With so much at stake, we wanted this new record to be our *Black Album*. Just as Metallica had done on their breakthrough album, we were looking to write a cohesive unit of songs that had a similar vibe and feel but still had the diversity we were known for. If any song didn't fit that edict, it was dropped. Rich concentrated on writing the catchiest hooks of our career and if he couldn't imagine an a cappella doo-wop band gathered in a back alley snapping their fingers and singing our choruses, he knew it wasn't working.

Rich Ward is an underrated genius, and the amazing music he came up with for the record proved it yet again. His cohesive unit of songs came together over the next few months, from the dark melodies of "Spider in My Mouth" to the thrash metal blast beats of "Blood Happens" to the ballad (and the first song Billy ever helped write with us) "Inside My Head," every song seemed better than the last. I wrote lyrics inspired by Stephen King stories ("Spider"), TV shows *Dexter* and *The Walking Dead* ("Dark Passenger," "Walk Amongst the Dead"), history books ("Storm the Beaches," about the invasion of Normandy that was inspired by a letter I found written by a soldier to his mother right after the famous battle), and Rich's riffs (*Sandpaper*, the first word that popped into my mind when The Duke played me the slinky main melody).

We thought "Sandpaper" was catchy enough to be the first single off the record, but when I was tracking the vocals, I felt something was missing. I wondered what it would sound like if there was another voice on the chorus, like a duet? My kids insist on listening to the Hits 1 channel on XM whenever I drive them to school (Cheyenne and Sierra love One Direction, and Ash digs Imagination Dragons, although they all like Fozzy) and I noticed that while many Top 40 artists featured guest artists on their songs (Jay-Z featuring Alicia Keys, Lil Wayne featuring Nicki Minaj, Vanilla Ice featuring Gerardo), rock bands rarely did.

So I called Shadows and asked him to take a listen to the demo and consider doing the vocals for the prechorus, "a cat scratch, a whiplash, a witch hunt in black." A few days later he called me back and said he'd love to be involved but was going to do two different versions—the first one the way we wanted him to do it, and the second one the way he wanted to do it.

His version included additional harmonies he'd come up with and a different arrangement that made it a sleeker and more streamlined song. His input and ideas were invaluable, and it was a huge honor to have him involved on a professional, musical, and personal level. Thanks, M.!

Our hard work paid off, as "Sandpaper" by Fozzy (featuring M. Shadows) was a success, spending twelve weeks in the Top 10 on XM Octane (wassup, Jose!) and was the perfect representation of the sound of our new record. We'd entitled it *Sin and Bones*, which Rich came up with when he sent a text describing how he was turning into "skin and bones" on a European tour, and autocorrect stepped in.

When it came time to do a video, I was having a problem figuring out how we could do one without Shadows, whose vocals were featured so prominently in the track. I had the idea of using the moving-camera-in-the-woods gimmick from *Evil Dead* to mask the fact he wasn't there. Then Rich took things further by suggesting we do a full-on *Evil Dead* homage and found an old cabin in the middle of the woods outside of Atlanta with an adjacent creepy graveyard that we could use for the set. I called Sean McEwen, who had directed *Albino Farm*, and he wrote an excellent script treatment that perfectly fit the vibe we wanted.

Over the next two days, we shot a fittingly eerie short film featuring Sam Raimi's moving-camera gimmick, hellacious demons attacking the cabin, Fozzy being possessed (Rich couldn't get the white contacts we all were wearing into his eyes, so we just stuck his hair in his face), and satanic vines that molested us and caused our demise. It was an impressive piece of work (especially considering the budget we had) that got even better when Shadows called last-minute to say he wanted to be in the video.

Sean and Gargano went to his hood in Orange County to film him on a green screen so we could insert him into the video wherever we wanted. Shads only had a few hours to get everything done, so I got worried when Gargano called me to say there was a problem.

"Shadows refuses to film anything until he gets some red licorice."

I knew Shads liked to chew on Red Vines licorice whenever his throat was sore, but he was only lip-synching for the video and I thought he was being a little bit of a prima donna with his request. But he was doing us a huge favor and I wanted him happy.

"Well, if he wants red licorice, then get him some red licorice, Paul."

Gargano fired back that it wasn't his job to drive around looking for licorice and said Shads would have to get it himself. I flipped out and told him to stop effin' around, but he never replied. A few minutes later he sent me a picture of a pouting Shadows mid-tantrum with his face turned away from the camera and his arms crossed.

I couldn't believe he was acting that way, but I continued blowing up Gargano's phone, telling him to go get some damn Red Vines.

"Dammit, Gargano! Don't blow this for us! Get him some fucking licorice!!"

The next text I got was a picture of the three of them laughing and giving me the finger. It was *Boots* all over again.

Shadows pouts as he waits for his red licorice during the green screen shoot for the "Sandpaper" video. I was totally buying into this rib, until I saw this pic and the slight curve of a smile on the side of Sean McEwen's face.

Licorice or not, the "Sandpaper" video was also a success, amassing over a million views on YouTube and winning the Rebel Life Media award for Best Heavy Metal Video of 2012.

Now that we had a great video and were confident we'd made our best album ever, we were hoping that everyone else would agree. Our hard work was vindicated when *Sin and Bones* became the best-reviewed album of our career (esteemed English rock journalist Malcolm Dome called it a masterpiece), our biggest-selling record, and our highest-charting effort when it debuted at number one on the *Billboard* Heatseekers chart and cracked the *Billboard* 200 at number 143 (a first for us). It also opened the door to the biggest tour of our career, the 2012 Uproar Festival headlined by Shinedown and Godsmack.

While we'd played a few Uproar dates the year before, this time we were asked to headline the second stage for the entire six-week tour stretching from sea to shining sea, our first-ever full-length U.S. jaunt. We played thirty minutes a day and got a great reaction on most shows, especially in Indianapolis, where we had six circle pits and eight pairs of flashed tits. (That's a total of sixteen boobies, by the way.)

Since our set was so short, we decided to adapt what I call The Queen at Live Aid Principle. Inspired by Queen's legendary 1985 performance at Wembley Stadium in London (it's been voted the greatest gig of all time), they stole the show with only a scant twenty-minute set filled with pure energy and less talk, more rock. It was all the time they needed and I wanted Fozzy to have the same seek-and-destroy attitude.

The Shinedown guys respected our work ethic and dug our sound and I spent most of my nights after the show riding around in golf carts with guitarist Zach Myers. He had a skeleton key that started the carts in all of the venues across the U.S. and we'd cruise the woods surrounding the amphitheaters, scouting out the hidden graveyards and secret streams, and searching the parking lots for stragglers.

We found some in Dallas when we saw two girls drinking in their car at two in the morning. I grabbed my artist's laminate, walked up to their window, and tapped it with my finger.

The chick in the driver's seat slowly rolled the window with a worried look on her face.

I flashed my laminate in her face and said, "Dallas Police. Are those open containers?"

She mumbled that they were, but they were waiting for her boyfriend to come get them and weren't going to drive. I berated her for drinking in public and told her that she was in serious trouble with the law. While I was in mid-scold, a pickup truck pulled up and her lumberjack of a boyfriend unfolded out of the front seat, asking menacingly what was going on.

Paul Bunyan changed his tone when I flashed my laminate badge and said, "I think you should drop the attitude, son, and watch how you speak to the police. You don't want to end up jail with these two, do you?"

He backed off immediately and began apologizing for his girl's behavior. I confiscated the bottle of Jack they'd been sipping on and told the girls to get into the boyfriend's truck.

"If you return to this car within the next twelve hours, it will be impounded and you will go directly to jail, do you understand?"

All three of them nodded their heads and promised they'd stay away. There was a new sheriff in town and I had the laminate to prove it.

In full costume at our Uproar Cop 'Stache Bash in Salt Lake City. Paulie is so froot he didn't need a mustache, just a police hat. My mustache (if you can call it that) is real, BTW.

I had so much fun impersonating a cop (I think that's illegal, right? Oops!) that I encouraged the whole tour to join in when Fozzy hosted the inaugural Cop 'Stache Bash (Duke's idea), the best after-show party of the tour. Everyone was required to wear a mustache or grow one of their own (I did), and dress like a '70s cop. There were gallons of red and blue vodka punch, donut holes, and a DJ that played nothing but disco.

The Bash was a huge success and afterward we were celebrating on our bus, when I glanced out the window and saw Rich approaching the front door. There was a partition between the driver's area and the lounge, so I pulled down my pants and bent over to give him a surprise. I heard the sound of the sliding door opening, but Rich didn't react. That confused me and I couldn't figure out why there wasn't a giggle or at least a groan of disgust. Suddenly everybody in the lounge burst out laughing, and when I turned around, Rich was standing there with his pants down, eyes closed, and ball bag tucked between his legs, *Silence of the Lambs* style. We gasped in unison and hiked up our respective pants, realizing how close we'd come to my bare ass grinding into his naked nut sack. Ahhh, life on the road.

Uproar was another win for Fozzy and opened a lot of touring doors for us worldwide, especially in our biggest market, the UK. Dan DeVita booked us on a co-headlining tour with U.S. metallers Soil, who were fairly popular in England a few years earlier and were making their big return. As co-headliners, we had equal billing and equal set times, but insisted on going on before them even though we had a bigger name than they did in most of the markets. Our theory was that if we went on first, Soil's fans would have to watch us even if they didn't know who we were, which meant we would be playing to the maximum audience each night.

The Soil guys were great, which was lucky since we had the worst tour bus of all time. There had been a fuckup at the bus company and all that was available was a dark, depressing dirge of a coach that resembled a mortuary on wheels. It constantly reeked of cigarette smoke because the slovenly driver (who looked like the Rancor's keeper) wouldn't stop smoking no matter how many times we asked him not to. On top of that, the damn thing was FREEZING.

Many a night I shivered under the covers in my bunk, fully dressed with my hoodie up and a scarf around my neck as my breath plumed out of my mouth. I couldn't even read a book because my hands got too cold if I took them out from under the blankets.

As bad as the bus was, our shows were awesome and we played to packed houses all across the country in London, Birmingham, Manchester, and Brighton, where, much to my surprise, Rod Smallwood, the manager of Iron Maiden, came to see us. I'd known him for years and when he told me he was coming and asked what time we were on, I told him eight thirty P.M. even though we were on at eight forty-five. I figured a guy that busy would probably show up late and I didn't want him to miss anything.

We played a cracking show that night and I scoured the audience, looking for Rod's face the entire set. I didn't see him and thought maybe he had jammed out on us, but minutes after the show was done, there was a knock on our dressing room door.

"Rod! I wasn't sure you had made it."

"Of course I made it. I told you I would, right? Did you think I was some kind of creep? You made me wait, though, I was here at eight fifteen, you wankers!" he replied crankily.

I asked him what he thought of the show and he looked at the shirt I was wearing with The Rev's face, and Rich's that boasted a ghost's face, and said, "It was quite good, but you guys shouldn't wear shirts with big white faces on them. They're distracting."

Not exactly the offer to tour with Iron Maiden I'd been hoping for, but I told him we'd make better fashion decisions the next time he came to see us.

The tour was winding down and we had just pulled up to the venue in Frankfurt, when I caught a whiff of fresh cigarette smoke drifting through my bunk. There must've been a vent in the driver's area that connected to mine, because I could always smell it the minute he lit up. Cigarette smoke and cold temperatures are a singer's worst enemy on tour and this fat-ass slob was responsible for both of them, even though we'd told him dozens of times to turn up the heat and to NOT SMOKE ON THE BUS!

I'd had enough of his disrespect and was sick of being diplomatic, so I stormed into the venue and straight over to where he was stuffing his chubby face with junk food.

"Hey, asshole! We've told you a dozen times on this tour that there is no smoking on the bus, but you won't listen and I'm over it. If you light up one more time in there, I'm going to slap your fat face and shove that pack of cigarettes straight up your ass, you got it?"

It was quite gratifying to see *Sin and Bones* debut at number one on the *Billboard* Heatseekers chart . . . ahead of Volbeat no less. And I just noticed Florida Georgia Line is on there too!

HEATSEEKERS ALBUMS

			ARTIST LABEL & NUMBER/DISTRIBUTING LABEL (PRICE)	TITL
1	HOT SHOT DEBUT	#1 1 WK	FOZZY CENTURY MEDIA 8883 (15.98)	Sin And Bone
2	4	77	VOLBEAT VERTIGO 016814/UNIVERSAL REPUBLIC (13.98)	Beyond Hell/Above Heave
3		NEW	YOUNGBLOOD HAWKE UNIVERSAL REPUBLIC DIGITAL EX (2.98)	Youngblood Hawke (EP
4		NEW	TEXAS HIPPIE COALITION CARVED 30040 (12.98)	Peacemake
5		NEW	THE DIRTY GUV'NAHS DUALTONE 1614 (12.98)	Somewhere Beneath These Southern Sky
6		NEW	SUCH GOLD RAZOR & TIE 83329* (12.98)	Misadventure
7	5	72	THE HEAD AND THE HEART SUB POP 915* (10.98)	The Head And The Hear
8	12	4	GREATEST GAINER RODRIGUEZ HEY DAY/LIGHT IN THE ATTIC 41850/LEGACY (12.98)	Searching For Sugar Man (Soundtrack
9	8	44	NERO MTA/MERCURY/CHERRYTREE/INTERSCOPE 016371/IGA (9.98)	Welcome Reality
10		NEW	THE MODERN POST MARS HILL 007 EX (4.98)	Grace Alone (EP
11	10	14	FLORIDA GEORGIA LINE REPUBLIC NASHVILLE DIGITAL EX/UNIVERSAL REPUBLIC (5.98)	It'z Just What We Do
12	1	2	LIANNE LA HAVAS NONESUCH 531819/WARNER BROS. (12.98)	Is Your Love Big Enough
13		NEW	CORB LUND NEW WEST 6239* (14.98)	Cabin Fever

The driver yammered an apology in his German accent and fled out of the room. I looked over and the Soil guys were staring at me wide-eyed in fear, with their knees pulled up to their chins.

"I promise I won't smoke anymore either . . . and I don't even smoke," bassist Tim King whispered worriedly.

CHAPTER 46

Old Habits Die Hard

With the Soil tour finished, Fozzy was done touring for a few months and since I had an open spot in my schedule, I called Vince to see if he was interested in having me back in the WWE from the Royal Rumble to WrestleMania.

"Contact HHH," he answered. "He's your man."

"OK, but you'll always be my man, Vince."

There had been a gradual shift in hierarchy during the last few years as Vince was grooming HHH to take over the company after he was gone. I totally understood that, so I called Hunter and, to his credit, we made the deal for my return in about ten minutes. I would come back as a surprise entrant in the Rumble and continue on until WrestleMania.

Now that I was coming back to the WWE for a fourth run, I started thinking about what I could do to build up my return this time around. The vignettes heralding my previous entries had been so grandiose and classic, I wondered what I could do to top them. Not to mention I was famous for having the big buildups, so if any kind of mysterious vignettes aired, people would pretty much know they were for me.

So I started thinking it might be a good idea to go in the opposite direction and keep my return at the Rumble a complete surprise. But was that even possible in this day and age when everyone had a cell phone camera, a Twitter account, a Facebook page, and a big mouth? It seemed like a real long shot that my secret could remain under wraps for that long.

There was no reason to go train with Lance again as I'd only been away from the WWE for a couple months, but there were a few other projects to finish before I returned, the biggest being the web series I'd cowritten and cocreated called *But I'm Chris Jericho!*

BICJ was an idea that my collaborator Gary Rideout and I had come up with six years earlier when I did the play *Opening Night* in Toronto. The idea was to do a spoof of what I was really going through at the time, when I left wrestling and went to Hollywood to study acting. I started thinking what if Y2J was kicked out and blackballed from the wrestling business, forcing him to make a career change where he has to start at the bottom of an industry that couldn't care less about who he was or what he'd accomplished in the past?

Gary and I wrote a couple sizzler scripts and pitched it around Hollywood in a few different incarnations for a year or two with no success, and I moved on to other projects. But Gary never gave up and called me toward the end of 2012 to tell me he'd sold the show (it had been so long that I asked him "what show?") to Shaw Cable as a ten-episode web series. I was proud of his tenacity for sticking with the idea and was excited to show off my comedic skills.

We shot in Toronto and it wasn't easy getting the ten episodes finished in five days, but the shows were so well written that the scenes flew by. We assembled a great cast that included acclaimed actors Scott Thompson from the *Kids in the Hall* (a comedic genius), Colin Mochrie from *Whose Line Is It Anyway?* and Andy Kindler from *Everybody Loves Raymond*, who played my bumbling agent. I loved the idea of Jericho being the straight man surrounded by a cast of idiots in a world where nothing goes right for him. It ended up being a legitimately funny (in my opinion) body of work and I was VERY happy with how it turned out. The episodes have over one million views and if you haven't seen them, go check it out on YouTube or butimchrisjericho.com now. If you don't laugh, I'll refund the money you paid to watch it.

This is what I wore for the filming of *But I'm Chris Jericho* . . . during breaks.

After filming the final scene where I wore a French maid's outfit, I drove straight to the airport (sadly, without the French maid outfit) to fly to Anaheim for the 2013 NAMM convention. NAMM stands for North American Music Merchants and this was an annual affair where the most famous musicians in the world gathered to do signings and shill for their respective endorsers. It was also a giant party and a chance to see all your friends from other bands who were on the road the majority of the rest of the year.

My signing was on Saturday in Anaheim and since the Royal Rumble was the next day and just a short flight away in Phoenix, NAMM was the perfect smokescreen to fool the fans into thinking I wouldn't be there. Surprisingly, my return still hadn't leaked online, which I considered a huge coup since wrestling websites had been predicting the returns of John Morrison, Shelton Benjamin, and Carlito for weeks but hadn't mentioned my name once. Plus, I'd been tweeting about my signings at NAMM on Saturday (which were legit) and Sunday (which were not), so the hellhounds had been thrown off the trail so far.

The NAMM party was in full swing and Shadows was also there for a signing, so after my appearances were finished, we headed out to the wilds of the OC to hang out with the other Avenged guys and some of their friends, including a stoic dude named Chris, who I renamed Graham. Not sure why; I guess he just looked like a Graham, ya dig?

I spent a large part of the night trying to convince Shads and Graham to go see Stryper, as I was stoked to see them again after joining them onstage the prior year to sing their version of the Scorpions' "Blackout." I'd written in my 1988 high school yearbook that someday I was going to join Stryper, and there I was some twenty-odd years later onstage, filling in for Michael Sweet as their lead singer. It was another awesome dream come true and I praised God for letting me have that moment.

But now that I'd had a few Yeah Boy!s, it was time to be professional and split back to the hotel, for I had my big Rumble return the next day and wanted to be well rested.

But on the car ride back to the Marriott, I decided for some reason that I wanted to kiss Graham on the lips. Why he needed a kiss from me I have no idea, but it made perfect sense at the time. Graham kept refusing, which only made me angrier and, considering I was the guy who'd once spent three hours trying to convince The Undertaker to let me kiss him on the lips in Tokyo (he eventually let me give him a peck on the cheek), I wasn't about to give up that easily. We pulled into the parking lot of the hotel and I gave him one last chance to let me kiss him, but he refused again, so I got out of the car, pulled the driver's door open, and started chasing him. We ran around the car a half dozen times like something from a drunken Three Stooges routine, except there were only two of us and Graham wasn't drunk. Shadows was in the backseat laughing his ass off as Graham jumped back in the driver's seat and locked the door. I jumped on the hood of the car (like the idiot in Victoria, British Columbia), screaming, "You WILL kiss me, Graham! You WILL kiss me!" as a crowd gathered around and hotel security wandered over to see what the problem was.

"Sir, you're going to have to get off that car right now," one of them said forebodingly, "or I'm calling the police!"

I doubted that he was going to be ringing Stewart Copeland, so I put my pride aside and backed down because I knew if I didn't, I'd probably spend the night in jail, miss my flight to Phoenix and my chance to be the secret entrant in the Royal Rumble, and probably lose my job to boot(s). I slid off the hood, bashfully telling the rapidly multiplying security force, "I was only kidding," and got back into the car. Graham quickly pulled out of the lot wearing the exact same facial expression he'd sported all night.

My facial expression was one of panic, however, when I woke up late the next morning and had to rush to the airport to catch my flight, only to find to my relief that it had been delayed.

Finally the plane was ready and it was time to shock the world with the surprise return of the century (that still hadn't been leaked). I was starting to feel the adrenaline and a flock of seagulls flew around in my stomach when I thought about walking through that WWE curtain in just a few short hours. But I was paranoid that a fan was going to spot me and ruin the surprise by posting a picture of me online like they had the last time. I had a nervous feeling and hoped I wouldn't be sitting next to anybody who was going to recognize me . . . but it was just the opposite. I wiggled my way into my window seat and realized I was sitting next to Joe Walsh.

We shared a glance of recognition and exchanged greetings. He was wearing a blue nylon sweat suit and a big grin and as we were visiting (Auntie Bev TM), a lady walked down the aisle, holding a plastic pillbox in her hand, the kind that has a compartment for every day of the week. As she was maneuvering between the two aisles of seats, she bumped into an errant elbow and spilled the tablets all over the floor.

"My cranberry pills!" she yelped in dismay as they bounced off the carpet. I glanced beside me and saw an empty seat, so I looked down and saw Walsh crawling on his hands and knees, feverishly picking up the pills as fast as he could.

He looked up at me sheepishly and said, "Old habits die hard, brother."

CHAPTER 47

Favorite Moment of My Career

I landed in Phoenix and crept off the jetway, half expecting a group of fans to be waiting there yelling, "Gotcha!" and snapping pictures to send directly to wrestlingobserver.com. But there was nobody there, so my delayed flight from Anaheim had turned out to be a blessing. Since I'd landed almost two hours late, the fans were already at the arena for the five P.M. start time.

The plan was for me go to the building and head into an underground parking lot, where I would once again hide on a crew bus (like I had in 2012) until it was time for my appearance. The airport limo with the tinted windows maneuvered through the mobs of fans milling about the arena, none of them aware that Y2J was inside. We drove down the rampway, and one of the heads of talent relations, Mark Carrano, scurried me onto the bus and told me to sit tight. The show started and I kept checking online to see if I'd been spotted, but unbelievably, there still wasn't one mention of Y2J.

Dean Malenko came onto the bus and, after a quick reunion, told me I was going to be the number two entrant in the Rumble, which I thought was a stroke of genius. Having me appear right off the bat would blow the roof off the proverbial joint and create a buzz that would last for the entire sixty-minute match. The first entrant would be Dolph Ziggler, the man responsible for my firing, so it made perfect sense from an angle perspective to have me come out next.

I was feeling great until I was told I was needed in a meeting with the other twenty-nine Rumble participants to discuss the match. OK, the jig was up. There was no way that many wrestlers could keep their mouths shut about my return, but almost none of them knew I was in the building and were legitimately surprised to see me. I shook hands, busted Santino's balls, and shared a quick nod of respect with Cena as we hadn't seen each other for a while.

We went over the plan for the Rumble and it was decided I was going to be one of the final five, which meant I was going to be out there for a while and that's the way I liked it. I've always been a pressure player; the more responsibility I have in a match, the better.

With the order of the Rumble finalized, I went to get a tune-up for my blue light-up jacket from WWE's master prop guy, Mark Shilstone, whose repairs had saved my jacket from ruin dozens of times.

Finally the pre-Rumble package played and it was time for me to make my way to the ring. Right before I left the sanctity of the bus, I Googled "Chris Jericho Royal Rumble 2013" for the last time and once again saw nothing. We'd pulled off the impossible in these social media crazy times and kept a secret; not one fan in the world knew I was in that building.

I walked through Gorilla, shocking the superstars who hadn't yet heard the news, and gave Vince a big hug.

"Thanks for coming back," he said. "I'm really glad you're here."

I was glad to be there as well and happy to hear the solid reaction of boos Ziggler got when he was announced. He sauntered to the ring and grabbed the mic, challenging anybody from the back to come out as the second entrant. He didn't care who it was, as he was ready to beat up anybody.

The arena buzzed with anticipation over who was going to answer Dolph's challenge, and Kevin Dunn kept the audience waiting (and waiting) until they were ready to burst. Finally he hit the music and out boomed my familiar war cry at fifty thousand decibels.

"BREAK THE WALLS DOWN!"

I've always said that the biggest reaction of my career was for my 1999 debut against The Rock in Chicago. But as amazing as that one was, the reaction I received right then in Phoenix blew it away. While the fans might've suspected it was me in '99, they had absolutely no idea this time, and because it was a total surprise, they went absolutely WILD as a result.

It was such a thrill to see the fans, MY fans, jump up on their feet and lose their minds when JERICHO flashed across the Tron. It was the loudest ovation I ever received in my twenty-two years of wrestling and could be the favorite moment of my career . . . something I'll never *EEEVVVEEERRR* forget.

With the roar of the crowd ringing in my ears and my amazing fans awaiting, I adjusted my trunks, touched my toes with a yoga stretch, got a thumbs-up from Vince, and strutted through the curtain to do what I do best.

Entertain all of you.

August 2, 2013–February 28, 2014

ACKNOWLEDGMENTS

Thanks to God and Jesus Christ for allowing me to write book number three and for guiding and protecting me as I continue down this long and winding road. I don't always make the right decisions, but I know when I don't, you'll always be there to let me know and forgive me! JESUS ROCKS!!

Thanks to all of YOU who are reading this! The fact you have stuck with me for twenty four years and three books worth of experiences and continue to support me in everything I do means the WORLD to me! That ain't no cliché, that's the truth! It's no secret that I have the greatest fans *EEVVEERR*, because JERICHOHOLICS really are the BEST IN THE WORLD AT WHAT YOU DO!!

For those about to Jericho . . . I salute you!

To everybody mentioned in this book, thanks for your love and friendship and for allowing me to occupy a small space in your life. I have the most amazing friends, colleagues and family and I LOVE YOU ALL!

Thanks to my partner Pete Fornatale for dragging another excellent tome out of me and for getting all of my pop culture references, no matter how obscure or ridiculous they may be! Here's one more for ya: "Whatsamatter wit chu, boy?"

Pete would also like to thank Ron Epstein for transcribing and editing assistance along with general encouragement.

Big thanks to everyone at my new home at Gotham Books and the Penguin Group, including Charlie Conrad, Leslie Hansen, and Lindsay Gordon. Let's knock this bad boy out of the park!

I'd also like to thank the auteurs who took the photos included in this book: Jessica Irvine, Scott Superka, Dave Spivak, John Howarth, Eli Roth, Brian Gewertz, Lance Storm, Barry Bloom, Brian Beasley, Stephanie Cabral, Random Brazilian Airport Cop, Jack Slade, Paul Gargano, Angie Bubley, Oliver Gestin, Some Weirdo on the Sunset Strip, and the fine folks at WWE Entertainment.